LIVING FOLK RELIGIONS

Living Folk Religions presents cutting-edge contributions from a range of disciplines to examine religious folkways across cultures. This collection embraces the non-elite and non-sanctioned, the oral, fluid, accessible, evolving religions of people (*volk*) on the ground. Split into five sections, this book covers:

- What Is Folk Religion?
- Spirit Beings and Deities
- Performance and Ritual Praxis
- Possession and Exorcism
- Health, Healing, and Lifestyle

Topics include demons and ambivalent gods, tree and nature spirits, revolutionary renunciates, oral lore, possession and exorcism, divination, midwestern American spiritualism, festivals, queer sexuality among ritual specialists, the dead returned, vernacular religions, diaspora adaptations, esoteric influences underlying public cultures, unidentified flying objects (UFOs), music and sound experiences, death rituals, and body and wellness cultures.

Living Folk Religions is a must-read for those studying and teaching Comparative Religions, World Religions, and Religious Studies, and it will also interest specialists and general readers, particularly enthusiastic readers of Anthropology, Folklore and Folk Studies, Global Studies, and Sociology.

Sravana Borkataky-Varma is a scholar of Indian religions focusing on esoteric rituals and gender, particularly in Hindu Goddess Tantra. She is the Instructional Assistant Professor at the University of Houston. At present, she is a Center for the Study of World Religions fellow at Harvard Divinity School, Harvard University.

Aaron Michael Ullrey is a Historian of Religions focusing on magic and the religions of South Asia, especially tantras associated with Śaivism and Jainism. He teaches Religious Studies at the University of Houston and is a Sanskrit language instructor at Naropa University.

LIVING FOLK RELIGIONS

Edited by
Sravana Borkataky-Varma and
Aaron Michael Ullrey

Routledge
Taylor & Francis Group
LONDON AND NEW YORK

Designed cover image: Getty – photography by Maico Presente

First published 2023
by Routledge
4 Park Square, Milton Park, Abingdon, Oxon OX14 4RN

and by Routledge
605 Third Avenue, New York, NY 10158

Routledge is an imprint of the Taylor & Francis Group, an informa business

British Library Cataloguing-in-Publication Data
A catalogue record for this book is available from the British Library

ISBN: 978-1-032-19040-2 (hbk)
ISBN: 978-1-032-19041-9 (pbk)
ISBN: 978-1-003-25746-2 (ebk)

DOI: 10.4324/9781003257462

Typeset in Bembo
by codeMantra

CONTENTS

List of contributors ix

Introduction: Three Little Words 1
Aaron Michael Ullrey and Sravana Borkataky-Varma

PART I
What Is Folk Religion? 17

1 Interrogating the Folk-Classical Divide in the Study of Indic Religions through a Local Bengali Ritual Performance 19
Frank J. Korom

2 The *Sādhū* Who Came for Lunch: Revising Tropes of Disconnection in the Jain Diaspora 35
Tine Vekemans

3 What Makes Folk Buddhism? 49
Alyson Prude

4 Why a Folk Religion May Not Exist among Followers of an Abrahamic Faith: The Case of Sunni Egypt 64
Hasan El-Shamy

PART II
Spirit Beings and Deities **87**

5 Goddess Trees in the Forest of Bliss: Local Place and Translocal Space in a City of Pilgrims 89
David Gordon White

6 Bhairava, Hanumān, and the Deified Dead: A Material Study of Vernacular, Official, and Folk Registers of Living Hinduism in Vārāṇasī, North India 113
Seth Ligo

7 There Is Something in Me: Narratives of LGBTIQ+ *Sangomas* (Traditional Healers) in South Africa 126
Rachel C. Schneider

PART III
Performance and/or Ritual Praxis **143**

8 Sufi Festivals in Contemporary Morocco: Authorizing and Performing Folk Religiosities 145
John C. Thibdeau

9 Mantras for "Every God and Goddess": Vernacular Religious Ritual in the Literature of Sabhapati Swami 160
Keith Edward Cantú

10 Observing Buddhist Precepts by Divination: Practices According to *Zhanchajing* 178
Xingyi Wang

11 Spellbinding Skalds: Music as Ritual in Nordic Neopaganism 191
Padraic Fitzgerald and Mathias Nordvig

12 Cremating the Body Politic: Mapping the Materiality of the Indo-Caribbean Mortuary Ritual Corpus 204
Keith E. McNeal

PART IV
Possession and Exorcism 229

13 Talking to the Other Side: Spiritualism as "Vernacular Religion" in Central Ohio 231
Hugh B. Urban

14 Becoming a God: Spirit Possession Practices at a South Indian Temple 244
Julie Edelstein

15 Post-Christianity and Esotericism: A Study of a Satanic Exorcist 257
William Chavez

16 Controlling the Lore: A Survey of UFO Folklore in the United States 275
Diana Walsh Pasulka

PART V
Health, Healing, and Lifestyle 291

17 Indigenous Revitalization, Rock Music, and the Holy Spirit: The Religious Logic of Healing at Lake Junaluska 293
Jason E. Purvis

18 The Triple Goddess: Examining Maiden, Mother, Crone in Wiccan-Witchcraft Traditions 307
Jason Mankey

19 Lifestyle Brands That Rock Your Soul: Wellness Culture as Folk Religion in North America 325
Anya Foxen

Index *341*

CONTRIBUTORS

Keith Edward Cantú is a Research Fellow at FAU Erlangen-Nürnberg in the DFG-funded project "Alternative Rationalities and Esoteric Practices from a Global Perspective." His monograph on the yoga of Sabhapati Swami will be published in 2023 by Oxford University Press.

William Chavez, PhD, is a Religious Studies lecturer at the University of California, Santa Barbara. He studies the doom and gloom of religious imagination. His doctoral dissertation examines the practice and popular mediatization of exorcism in the United States.

Julie Edelstein was born in New Jersey. She earned her undergraduate degree in Religion from Temple University, her Master' degree in Religion from Syracuse University, and is currently studying for a PhD in South Asian Studies at Harvard University.

Hasan El-Shamy is a professor of Folklore (Emeritus), Indiana University: Departments of Folklore, Near Eastern Languages and Cultures, Islamic Studies, and African Studies. His published innovations include "Folkloric Behavior," "mental health in traditional cultures," "religion among the folk in Egypt," "The Brother-Sister Syndrome in Arab cultures," and typology of traditions.

Padraic Fitzgerald is a doctoral candidate at the University of Denver whose work focuses on material religion, religion and music, and Neopaganism. He is an adjunct instructor of religious studies at the College of Charleston and Arapaho Community College.

Anya Foxen is an assistant professor of Religious Studies at California Polytechnic State University, San Luis Obispo. She is the author of three books: *Is This Yoga?* (2021, with Christa Kuberry); *Inhaling Spirit* (2020); and *Biography of a Yogi* (2017).

Frank J. Korom is a professor of religion and anthropology at Boston University, where he teaches a wide range of courses pertaining to South Asia, his major geographical region of expertise. He is also a co-editor of the journal *Asian Ethnology.*

Seth Ligo specializes in the materiality of lived Hinduism. Focusing on marginalized deities and communities, he charts relationships between religious text, ritual prescription, and living traditions. Currently, at UNC-Asheville, his work appears in the *International Journal of Hindu Studies.*

Jason Mankey is a writer and researcher who currently calls Northern California home. He has published nine books and speaks at far too many events across North America. When not writing or traveling, he enjoys spending time with his wife Ari, his cats, and a nice dram of single malt Scotch.

Keith E. McNeal is an anthropologist with a specialization in Caribbean ethnology and Atlantic cultural history with a long-term focus on Trinidad and Tobago. He holds appointments at the University of Houston and the University of the West Indies.

Mathias Nordvig holds a PhD in Old Norse mythology and has a general background in Nordic literature and languages including Old Norse, Danish, Norwegian, and Icelandic. He teaches Nordic and Arctic cultural studies at the University of Colorado-Boulder.

Diana Walsh Pasulka is a professor at the University of North Carolina, Wilmington. Her research focuses on the intersections of technology, belief, and spirituality. Recent books include American Cosmic: UFOs, Religion, Technology, and Encounters: AI, UFOs, Religion.

Alyson Prude is an associate professor of Religious Studies at Georgia Southern University. Her research focuses on issues of power and authority, relationships between normative Buddhist and indigenous traditions, and contemporary *delogs* in Nepal and Tibet.

Jason E. Purvis is currently an independent scholar and researcher interested in religions throughout U.S. history, Indigenous traditions, religion informing processes of decolonization, and how theories of religion can help explain the construction of race and far-right extremism.

Rachel C. Schneider is a religion scholar and director of the Religion and Public Life Program at Rice University. Her research focuses on the intersections of religion and inequality in contemporary South Africa and the United States.

John C. Thibdeau is a Visiting Assistant Professor of Islamic Studies at the University of Rochester. He has a PhD from the University of California, Santa Barbara in Religious Studies with a specialization in Islamic Studies. His research focuses on contemporary Sufism and religion and politics in the Middle East and North Africa.

Hugh B. Urban is a professor in the Department of Comparative Studies at Ohio State University. He is the author of numerous books, including *The Path of Desire*; *Secrecy*; *The Power of Tantra*; *Magia Sexualis*, and others.

Tine Vekemans holds the Ācārya Mahāprajña Chair for Jain Studies at the department of Languages and Cultures at Ghent University, Belgium. Her research pertains to Jainism in the twentieth and twenty-first centuries, Jain migration, and Jainism in the digital realm.

Xingyi Wang is an assistant professor at Hong Kong Polytechnic University since 2022. She is specialized in East Asian Buddhist history and thought. Her research includes Buddhist monasticism, Vinaya studies, Pure Land Buddhism, ethics, Yogācāra thought, and Buddhist art.

David Gordon White is the author of six books on South Asian religions and cultural contacts and exchanges across Eurasia. He has received multiple awards from the John Simon Guggenheim and Fulbright Foundations, and the American Council of Learned Societies.

INTRODUCTION

Three Little Words

Aaron Michael Ullrey and Sravana Borkataky-Varma

Three words can do a lot of work, especially these little words: living, folk, religions.

The word "living" encompasses embodied cultures, religions-on-the-ground, evolving and innovative practices. Such practices reinterpret tradition in contemporary, even novel, contexts. Living religious formations have been contrasted with so-called historical religions, but living religions too are historically situated. Being alive now, living religions are situated in the current time period, though related to what has come before, and they aim to persist in the future. Such religions engage revered scriptures, but they do not locate complete authority in scripture; their canon, furthermore, is open to new sources and fresh interpretations. They are less about orthodox belief than practice, and they include traditions of innovation.

"Folk" refers to people, the German *volk*, capturing more a register than any actual or specific people. Folk religions—or the folk mode of religions—encompass religious engagments practiced by everyday people, not just the official lore and actions of elites, clerics, and authorities. Following Leonard Primiano on the relationship between the vernacular and the elite, folk religions are not limited to the non-elite but are practiced, as well, by religious authorities as an additional mode, even an alternate mode, to individual, sanctioned, clerical religious activities. Anytime an authority explains a scripture using vernacular language, they engage in the vernacular mode of religion, and throughout the history of religions elite authorites are observed engaging folk modes alongside orthopraxy (Primiano 2022, 1995). Folk religion may be documented in orthodox sources and among orthodox figures, but it is usually judged ancillary to orthodox practices and beliefs, if not outrightly prohibited. The persistence and prevalence of such practices and regulated prohibitions reveal the ongoing importance of folk modes.

DOI: 10.4324/9781003257462-1

Not "Religion", singular and capitalized, but "religions", plural and not capitalizaed. Religions are those multiple traditions that organize beliefs and practices about interactions with invisible or superhuman beings (Spiro 1966). Human cultures and human consciousness perpetually change and rearrange practices and thought matrices deemed religious. There is no "Religion" out there, but religions are ever-encountered and diverse: Buddhisms and Islams and Christianities, not Buddhism, Islam, and Christianity. This simple shift from proposing Religion to religions is at the heart of Religious Studies, the discipline from which this volume emerges.

Each word is instructive. And the project to engage living folk religions is aimed not to set out a new methodological or theoretical paradigm but to encourage scholars and students to think about religions in productive manners. Shifting into the folk register opens new archives, such as UFOlogical literature (Walsh Pasulka); opportunities for data collection and organization, such as Nordic Neo-pagan rituals in musical performances (Fitzgerald and Nordvig); and a shift in perspective by which unexpected sources might be theorized in ways that push received understandings of religions, such as a Satanist exorcist (Chavez). Our contributors have not only engaged in the classic methods of literary analysis and ethnography (White, Korom), but they also engage marketing and advertising (Foxen), a popular queer autobiography (Schneider), and contemporary musical performances (Purvis).

Our gaze is not merely upon the present, for in studying folklore and folkways, we must look at the historical past, the past as surviving in and influencing the present, including the ethnographic present (Yoder 1976: 6). Folk religion, folklore, and folklife are no longer limited to European cultural studies, such as those found in North American folklore studies, or religious practices that do not fit into established categories, such as those found in Chinese folk religion. It is not limited to the urban versus the rural, for, as will be demonstrated, folk religions often circulate in cosmopolitan contexts. Valuing folk religions destabilizes underpinning assumptions by exploring folk religions worldwide, encompassing both meanings of the German term *religose volkskunde*, "the folk-cultural dimension of religion" and also "the religious dimension of folk-culture" (Yoder 1990: 80). We do not delve into historic arguments on authenticity or the dangers of "fakelore", since we argue that any practice or source considered authentic by religious folk shall be considered genuine and authentic; nor do we reduce folk religions to political machinations or parody (Chidester 2003, Fox 1980). We also do not view folk religion to be eternally opposed to sanctioned religion.

The designation of folk and folk religions has been largely cast aside the last forty years, though the study of folk religions has carried on under other terms. Such study has often been called something else, for the term "folk" was considered *passe*, reductive, or even colonial (critiques which apply to certain cases of prior scholarship on the topic). But folk religion is not merely popular religion (a dissertation advisor once directed a colleague of ours to cut all mentions of folk and simply substitute the term popular); popular religion—for instance non-denominational, protestant megachurches—may reproduce all the schema of sanctioned, ecclesiastical religions, just on a large scale and with folksy informality. Folk religion is not just ascribed based the number of adherents but is a mode of religion based on practice and conceptions of authority.

Examining folk religions dislodges overemphasis on the usual clusters of well known religions and regions, and that turn resolves textual biases for its data are mostly non-textual; this shift disrupts *sui generis* theories of religion, the current, cutting-edge bugbear. Considering and reconsidering folk religions in all cultures embraces the non-elite and non-sanctioned, the oral, fluid, accessible, evolving religion of people (*volk*) on the ground. The tension between sanctioned and folk religions has not just animated emic religious conflicts but enlivened the academic study of religions since the foundation of the discipline. "Folk religion" must be embraced within the categories of the vernacular, popular, lived religion (Primiano 2022, 1995, Long 1987, Orsi 1987). Despite contemporary generations decrying the boredom and tedium of rituals (as can be attested by most undergraduate teachers and religious leaders working with youth), ritual remains the core vehicle for maintaining and transmitting folk religions.

The two editors of this book have their own interpretations of living folk religions, and their journeys exploring living folk religions is addressed below. The general project began by an impulse to reconsider folk religions and the idea of folk religion; a mere reconsideration was not enough. What exactly was reconsidered? We proceeded from uncertainty, with the certainty that this lack of focus would be productive. Like all good projects, we started before we were ready.

Folk religion, ambivalently related to the study of folklore (the study of the cultural products of specific people), takes up a different set of authoritative texts and authoritative persons than have been emphasized in the history of religions, and these different conceptions of authority are addressed by many of the chapters in this book. Voices are emphasized over texts, innovation over stasis, local instead of translocal, and particular versus universal. Such practices are more pragmatic than transcendent, more concerned with daily uncertainties and anxieties than attaining salvation or enlightenment (Mandelbaum 1966); they reveal vibrant folk religions all around us, near and far. We flip Redfield's great and little traditions (1965), for the little was greater all along. Conversations with contributors and evolving drafts complicated this thrilling inquiry. A term like folk religion can come to mean anything, so it requires some definition, but not so rigorous as to make that definition reductive. Folk religion is a term that does work.

Sravana's Story

The idea for this edited volume germinated while I was doing fieldwork in 2019 at the Bālājī temple, a healing center in Mehndipur, Rajasthan. In many South Asian ontologies of healing, health, and well-being, there is a deep orientation to the *relational* (Kakar 1991: 274). According to Sudhir Kakar, this relational orientation is so elemental in India that "a restoration of the lost harmony between the person and [their] group... was one of the primary aims of the healing endeavors in the local and folk traditions" (Kakar 1991: 274). South Asian conceptions of the person and their community include sacred, other-than-human relations such as ancestors, deities, and *bhūta* ('spirits') of many kinds. Deity and spirit possession phenomena and rituals – understood as relations with deities and spirits – are intimately intertwined with healing, health, and well-being. These relations are between folk, the human folk "seen" and the non-human folk "invisible." Traditional healing interventions, such as those at the Bālājī temple, generate, maintain, and repair harmonious relationships between humans and other humans and also between humans and other-than-human beings, i.e., between the seen and unseen. I began to wonder how different communities, people, and spaces, such as temples and shrines, provide and regulate paths of communication with the "other side", the other side of death's threshold, the side not necessarily seen with physical eyes: possession, exorcism, and so forth. While writing "The Dead Speak: A Case Study from the Tiwa Tribe Highlighting the Hybrid World of Śākta Tantra in Assam" (Borkataky-Varma 2017), I spoke with groups and individuals who tended that other side, and I came to appreciate and value these alternate spaces of healing. I decided to focus on possession, interviewing the living and the dead. Any serious study of the possession phenomenon interrogates conceptions of the person and the self, especially the self that experiences possession. What or who is possessed? Who is doing the possessing? (Smith 2006: 18). How do the living interact with the other side? What does it mean to relate to and have a relationship with the other side?

Christian theology largely regards "the self as an inner, unchanging, stable, and ultimately detachable core" (ibid. 2006: 19) understood to be the soul. The Hindu traditions conceive the self, the person, even the soul to be separate. This is elucidated by distinctions between the Sanskrit words *puruṣa/puruṣottama* and *ātman/brahman*. *Puruṣa* is a man/person, while *puruṣottama* refers to the highest person; some may refer to him as Kṛṣṇa or Śiva or a *devtā* (god) or a *devī* (goddess). The *ātman* is a localized microcosmic iteration of *brahman*, located in the human heart, while *brahman* is the supreme being or state of being described in Hindu sacred texts as "ineffable and beyond human comprehension," as "truth (*satya*), knowledge (*jñana*), and infinity (*ananta*)," and as "existence (*sat*), consciousness (*chit*), and bliss (*ananda*)" (Narayanan 2004: 25). Personhood is associated with *puruṣa* and *ātman*, a more local, microcosmic, divisible "self", while selfhood is associated with *puruṣottama* and *brahman*, a realized and indivisible macrocosmic "self".

The classical Indian view of the "self" portrayed in Sanskrit texts is actually "a self with permeable layerings and boundaries, both of which constantly shift and mutate" (Smith 2006: 10). This is contrary to conceptions of the self portrayed in Indological scholarship, a tradition of scholarship self-rooted in Classical Hinduism and conceived through the Sanskrit medium, primarily pre-dating the fifteenth century. The Indological conception of the self was shaped by academic agendas set by European notions of authentic, "respectable" scholarship (Smith 2006: 6). European colonial influences canonized particular areas of study, resulting in a Victorian, sanitized, Brahmanical presentation of "important objects" (Smith 2006: 6). Possession did not fall into these 'respectable' categories. Possession was largely seen to be only practiced by the "illiterate and un-cultured" (Borkataky-Varma 2017).

My research nuanced my teaching, and I began to create a Hinduism course focused on lived folk performances, rather than dominant scriptural, historical, and ritual paradigms. In the fall of 2019, I taught "Introduction to Hinduism" (RELS 234) at the University of Houston. I played it safe with the title, but the syllabus engaged a wide range of approaches to studying Hindu traditions. Forty-plus undergraduate students registered for the class. My initial pedagogical experiment aimed to present Hinduism in a different way than selecting a few Vedic readings, dwelling on the epics and the *Bhagavadgītā*, and then telling Puranic tales. At the end of the semester, I was convinced by the merits of integrating lived folk elements in my classes focusing on Hindu traditions. My students better grasped the outlooks and ritual schemas that shape my view of Hinduism as both a scholar and practitioner than when taught using the Indological model.

Hired as a Lecturer of Hindu Traditions at the Harvard Divinity School, I decided to further my pedagogical experiment, and I taught parallel courses to graduate and Ph.D. students in the fall of 2020: Introduction to Hinduism (HDS 3399) and Folk Hinduism (HDS 3425). The contrast proved instructive. The more traditional course, Introduction to Hinduism was described as follows:

> The religious tradition we now know as Hinduism originated on the South Asian peninsula and developed over the last 3500 years. This course examines the principal themes of traditional Hinduism. It gives special attention to the historical development of the tradition and its relation to social and cultural life in India. We will evaluate how Hinduism arose and how it developed over time in response to social, cultural, and historical variables. To the extent possible, the course will examine different forms of Hindu religious expression created within what we now call India. These forms include written texts that have been significant in the Hindu tradition but also rituals that have been central to religious life, patterns of social action that embody Hindu values, and images that display the form and powers of the world. They thus offer the student of religion a unique opportunity to study not only Hinduism but to reflect comparatively and globally on the diverse histories, functions, and roles of religion in human civilizations, not to mention contemporary geopolitics.

The description of the Folk Hinduism class took a different perspective:

> Courses on Hinduism have predominantly been approached via literary and textual avenues, through which its ancient, philosophical, abstract, and transcendent features are highlighted. Even ethnographic accounts of Hinduism have been dominated by attention to the Sanskritic and Brahmanic elements derived from such a scriptural, elitist grounding. Such foci are limited because of the neglect of oral traditions and attention to Hindu practices, particularly at the local, and regional levels, and the role of specific household and cult deities, rituals, and festivals in sustaining a religious worldview.

The sources and conceptions of authority and authoritative contrasted. Folklore is the body of culture shared by a people and preserved in tales, proverbs, jokes, and practices. Its study is generally distinguished from the field of Anthropology and Religious Studies because folklore limits itself to cultural products, though those products are widely defined. In class, the students explored the contribution that mythology makes to the larger field of folklore and folk Hinduism, examining how myth is transmitted and preserved in cultural artifacts; they did not just focus on contents of the myths. Epic texts in Hinduism are not only considered the greatest of Hindu mythologies as preserved in Sanskrit but are recognized to provide background and context for folk tales and folk practices. For example, students examined many *Rāmāyaṇa*s, instead of one great tale, and they explored Draupadi's characterization differed in the different *Mahābhārata*s. The course was not limited to Sanskrit sources but expanded the Epics to their form and context in many languages and contexts. We explored living rituals and performance traditions, such as *theyyam*, possession-centered folk performances of Kerala, and exorcism in the Mehandipur Bālājī Temple, where the living and the dead engage each other in complicated relationships mediated by possessed community members. Interacting with the dead could not be easily observed in Boston, so we examined digital documentation of spirit possession, mediumship, and we questioned how those online spaces allow access to otherwise "secretive" practices. Finally, we surveyed folk Hinduism in the diaspora, looking at communities in Trinidad and Tobago where Hindus adapt their Hinduism to set and maintain roots in the local community.

Vasudha Narayanan, in 2000, challenged teachers and scholars to explore Hinduism as practiced by people, especially those people oriented toward goddesses and who perform artistically. That challenge can be met by a turn to living folk religions. Hinduism is no longer an exotic religion in a book deriving from older "books", its interpretation mediated by clerical caretakers. Hinduism should be studied as it is lived, studied as folk, in particular non-elite folk, practice it.

My experiment was not without detractors. Several graduate students and colleagues questioned the merit of teaching Hinduism from the lens of folk Hinduism. One senior colleague stated, or rather implied, I was not really teaching Hinduism, because how can I speak about diversity unless the students have mastered the fundamentals? According to this colleague, fundamentals can only be learned from a traditional course syllabus that spends a whole semester reading Hindu scripture selections. For example, a teacher must not introduce the complexities of many *Rāmāyaṇa*s until the class has spent several weeks performing a close reading of Valmiki's *Rāmāyaṇa*. Yet, what *Rāmāyaṇa* should students examine, the Valmiki Sanskrit text that few Hindus read, the beloved Hindi *Rāmacaritamānas* whose refrains ring out across South Asia, or the regional *Rāmāyaṇas*, especially those performed at annual festivals, now stretching across the globe? Must authority be placed in scriptures, or might anything practiced by Hindus be considered authoritative? A few students were frustrated by my choice of texts and the guest speakers I invited; they sought a more traditional Hinduism class characterized by Sanskrit literature and philosophy. The loudest protest was over Devdutt Pattanaik, the popular Indian author who writes on Hindu mythology, sacred lore, legends, folklore, fables, and parables. But how could I not invite such a voice? More importantly, why would I not invite him? His books are extremely popular in India, where they are prominently displayed on bookstore shelves. By excluding him from the conversation was I silencing a mass of Hindu voices? Examining traditions in flux, even counter-traditions, seems the only way to conceive any tradition authentically, for traditions are always in conflict and strife regarding contradictions, and such contradictions are found in and around all religious traditions; arguably, the conflicts and contradicitions are the most exciting part of Religious Studies.

Scorn and reductivism seeped and spread. The more pushback I received, the more I was determined that my students think outside the box and consider what a range of Hindus—as opposed to gurus and pandits and elite educators—were reading. Where are Hindus getting information? How have folk dance and drama transmitted Hindu ways of being? How do people from lower castes access divinity? How do folk *devās* and *devīs* cohabitate with mainstream Vedic divinities? What is the role of music? What is televised? What is the impact of advertisements when Hinduism reachs new medias? How do video games use Hindu mythological stories? Hindu traditions are rooted in oral transmission, and a few hundred kilometers can completely change the so-called Hindu terrain, sometimes even a few kilometers. Hence, why must we encapsulate? Why is studying possession any less important than studying *Upaniṣad*? Why is studying magic any less important than studying temple architecture? Are there inherent biases in the poets we choose to teach and analyze in the classroom? And what about the role of higher education proffessors? How does the ivory tower enter the syllabus, and how does the ivory tower shape the delivery of a course? I can go on and on. But you get my point!

One night I was frustrated, and I decided to do something constructive. I pitched an idea to Routledge University Press for an edited volume teaching World Religions, i.e., religions in the world, from an alternate perspective focused living folk religions. Routledge loved the idea. This volume would contain mostly South Asian religions, a hopeful antidote to the World Religions projects framed by Western Religions, the so-deemed history-making, era-transforming World Religion. Given the scope of the project, I needed a trusted colleague who could help me. Aaron Michael Ullrey was the perfect scholar for this project: a seasoned professor who had taught not only Hinduism courses, but World Religions, Asian Religions, and Religion and Magic: he currently teaches courses in Sanskrit language at Naropa University and Religious Studies at the University of Houston. We re-examined the scope of our edited volume and decided to incorporate a multiplicity of religions and geographic regions while still challenging Western conceptions of religion and folk religions. Our volume aims to include more religions, religious content, and religious actors living in the world today than found even in World Religions textbooks. It will satisfy the specialist engaged in any of the content or theoretical perspectives, but, moreover, it provides an opportunity to teach Religious Studies, especially Introduction to Religious Studies or World Religions, in a fresh and exciting way.

Aaron's Story

Self-reflecting, the notion of a folk mode of religion outside established religions has always intrigued me, mostly due to its different conception of authority, so different from the fundamentalist, Calvinist Christianity that shaped me. A religion outside Church and scriptures suggests diverse viewpoints and suggests that religious viewpoints could change as a result of personal experience; new viewpoints could be adopted after productive encounters with other religious cultures. I even spent a few years practicing trance meditation with a USA-based neo-Shaman and SRF yogi (Self-Realization Fellowship) in Kalamazoo, Michigan, by name of Peter Richards (a social worker and former seminarian; he operated using anthropologist Michael Harner's *Way of the Shaman* system, and he traced his authority and spirit contacts to past lives and ancestral experiences in Finland). Sure, this is the syncretism of a dilettante and cultural consumer, but it is also the syncretism of youth, and I find many of my evolving scholarly views about religion result from thinking about times before I was a scholar, when I was more a practitioner, a seeker in the spiritual marketplace of the late twentieth century.

During my late teen years, I read a book about magic and psychic self-defense (not the classic book titled *Psychic Self-Defense*, by Dione Fortune), in which the author depicted himself to be an expert in eastern European folk magic. The title, the author's name, and the physical book are was teaching at Youngstown State University, at that time, and now offers lost to me. The book described a ritual in which a person bathes in water filled with carnation blooms, and the operator rubs these petals all over his or her body. This was supposed to remove all sorts of ills, from curses to negative self-image. I performed this ritual during angst-ridden times, and it worked; the truth of magic is that it relieves the pains of inertia, of being stuck, of having no hope. I encouraged several friends to do this practice, and they too reported feelings of lightness, cleanliness, and positivity. This lived folk religious ritual was pulled from a book published by a popular, occult press, performed by me in an earnest immediate manner, and it spread, also by me, to others. Folk religious practices can come from a wide range of sources and can circulate in surprising ways; tradition only needs to be passed once to be declared a tradition or categorized traditional.

While undertaking this project to explore living folk religions, I noticed for the first time two curious uses of the term folk: folk punk rock music and folk horror films. I wondered how these contemporary aesthetic trends related to the topic of this volume. They proved instructive.

Folk punk rock music is usually framed as a combination of folk music and punk music, but that does not capture the genre. It may be punk rock songs played on more traditional instruments (such as mandolin or acoustic guitar), or it may be traditional folk music played on punk instruments(electric guitar, bass, and drums). Folk punk often combines acoustic instruments and electric instruments. Song contents and lyrics are aligned with folktales and American gospel, often with an Appalachian spirit. Unlike the twentieth-century folk music revivals, there is no sense that an original or old-time musical tradition is being rediscovered, for folk punk revels in its newness, in its innovative deployment of ostensibly older forms of music. While working on this book, I attended a concert by folk punk standouts, The Goddamn Gallows, who inspired me to see folk cultures in new forms. The musicisans reworked refrains on gospel songs, "Ya'll M*****F*****s Need Jesus", and re-presented black metal standards in a folk manner, such as Venom's classic "In League with Satan". Similar musical curiosities are documented by Fitzgerald and Nordvig and Purvis below.

Folk horror films eschew conventions of modern horror by placing events in rural areas, in the ambivalent nature and the differently structured, harkening back to forgotten folkways and obscure cults; these areas emerge as sites of danger. Folk horror invokes the strange, uncanny, and ancient; the pre-Christian re-emerges to challenge not only Christianity but to challenge the Christian age that shapes modernity. These unofficial and dangerous religious practices and beliefs are the will of the people, the folk, and they challenge the orthodox, causing characters and audiences to wonder if the so-called old ways were the right ones and what that would mean to a modern person. Folklore is mined and deployed to bring a fresh experience of terror, often in a primordial or dangerous rural landscape. An excellent documentary on the genre *Woodlands Dark and Days Bewitched: A History of Folk Horror* tracks the genre from such horror classics as *Wickerman* and *Blood on Satan's Claw* to contemporary shockers like *Midsommar* and *Jug Face*. Perhaps such horror films are folklore in a new medium.

Such topics encouraged me to think more widely about folk religion. These pop-culture moments of folk punk and folk horror demonstrate a renewed interest in the folk mode to invigorate the arts. While the folk mode is conceived as a throwback to something old, it is also used to make something new, capturing the innovative nature observed in folk religions. Yet, this folk mode is imaginary. It does not call back to any actual history but creates an imagined history. In this way, the folk mode provides a place for innovation through imagination.

I am a specialist in South Asian religions, particularly pragmatic rituals, i.e., magic, in archives preserved in Sanskrit and Hindi languages. As a teacher, I offer courses on Sanskrit language and Religious Studies topics such as Hinduism, Yoga, Asian Religions, World Religions, and Religion and Magic. Teaching Introduction to Hinduism, I spend the first two-thirds of the course surveying literature, philosophy, and ritual, but the final third of my course presents subversive ethnography that challenges usual depictions of Hinduism and Hinduisms; the topics include malicious and benevolent possession, rituals of wonder, ceremonies, and more. In short, the last part of my course is about folk Hinduism, and the first part prepares the students for this intervention. The subversive ethnography is subversive because it challenges typical arguments about Hinduism; for the most part, it is not subversive for its practitioners. If all death rituals are about gaining heaven, then how should ideals of release (*mokṣa*) or even rebirth be explored? If god is abstract essence or temple presence, then how might a person possessed speak as a god? If god sets the fate of all humans at birth, then how do magic rituals compel god to do differently than her will? The folk component challenges master narratives and privileges the descriptive over prescriptive.

Magic ritual sources—namely the magic tantras, a genre of Sanskrit sources dedicated to pragmatic rituals, mostly of the aggressive sort, i.e., black magic—are my main research area, and these curious texts capture, reproduce, and interpret folk religion in intriguing ways. Though written in Sanskrit, albeit Sanskrit of a low register, such sources sometimes contain vernacular ritual lore and vernacular language commentaries and glosses. I particularly study the so-called six magic results (*ṣaṭkarman*) and the rituals that bring about these magical results: *śānti-puṣṭi* (tranquilizing-increase), *vaśīkaraṇa* (subjugating), *stambhana* (immobilizing), *mohana* (bewildering), *vidveṣana* (dissent), *uccāṭana* (eradicating), *ākarṣaṇa* (attracting), and *māraṇa* (murder). The rituals are undeniably fascinating. Spells, mystic diagrams, concoctions, and ritual actions are presented literally and figuratively to afflict and even kill one's proverbial neighbors. Aggressive results are meant to displace rivals so that a sorcerer might take up a victim's good life, their money, and their family. Whether edited and published or found in hand-written manuscripts, these magic tantras reproduce a widespread, pan-South Asian discourse about pragmatic rituals. Adding to reproduced records of ritual lore, these sources also preserve innovations by individual authors, who add to what they copy after studying many magic texts and perhaps documenting rites preformed by professional sorcerers, of whose ranks these authors editors may even belong. More important, here, is that they document rituals of local folk. One particular version of the *Uḍḍīśatantra*, edited by C. M. Srivastava, presents the typical six-result rituals from Sanskrit sources, but Srivasta attaches an appendix about other rituals (*anya prayog*) in each chapter: writing in Hindi, he presents rituals, variations, and ancillary lore that I have never found in Sanskrit sources. These appendices present lived folk rituals alongside time-honored, aggressive magic rites, appealing to non-Sanskrit sources and innovative techniques performed by folk (Ullrey 2023, Ullrey 2016).

Studying grimoires—books of magic spells be they from South Asia, Ancient Greece, Medieval Europe, or contemporary pulp—reveals lived folk religions, for the spell books create and reproduce non-sanctioned, non-elite, non-scriptural practices that may not be mainstream but are performed by folk from all walks of life. I push against the notion that living folk religions are not textual; there are many texts about folk religions, prescriptive and descriptive, but those texts are not considered scriptural and are not authoritative in an expected manner. A survey of contemporary titles on folk magic, kitchen witchcraft, hoodoo, and the like bears this out.

Returning to my opening statement, I frame living folk religions by considering subjectivity and authority. For a Calvinist, the folk interpretations are wrong, but as a person emerging from Calvinism, probably the most honest of my identities, the folk mode is freedom from the structures of authority. As a scholar—once described as an unyielding non-practitioner—looking to folk religions focuses my attention on religions as they are lived, historically and in the contemporary world, highlighting description rather than prescription. A Tibetan lama may look at the practices of lay folk all around him, deem those the activities of the ignorant not leading to liberation, and thereby not really Buddhist (Prude), ignoring the lived practices of Buddhists all around him. Modern people, in a similar manner, look at phenomenon not material or not materially explained, and they argue such rituals or practices are superstitions with no value, rather than understanding superstitions as a means to make sense of chaotic worlds. The cleric who draws authority from tradition will see anything contradicting or not consistent with orthodoxy and orthopraxy to be invalid, but that which is considered invalid is the very stuff of people's religious lives (and those clerics often informally participate in the folk modes they reject). Folk religions are immediate, present, and even transgressive because they resist and sometimes contradict traditional authority.

Contributors and Contributions

What follows is not a survey of a static thing called living folk religions; in fact, each contributor conceives folk religions as appropriate to their own project, to the data and archives each scholar draws upon. Contributors are diverse, including junior and senior scholars, also including doctoral candidates and independent researchers.

Each author was asked to define and shape their inquiry and research findings to explore living folk religions. There was no specific definition of folk religion to which they were beholden. Some bristled, initially, at the term folk, seeing the term to be dismissive and reductive, but upon further consideration, each found the term productive; one senior scholar, who did not bristle at the term folk, off-handedly stated that folk religion was exactly what he was researching these days. Contributors were directed by several fine essays authored by Dan Yoder in *Discovering American Folklife: Studies in Ethnic, Religious, and Regional Culture* (1990) and Leonard Primiano's masterful article "Vernacular Religion and the Search for Method in Religious Folklife" (2022, 1995), as well as entries on folk religions in *The Encyclopedia of Religion* (1987) . Chapters in this volume are organized by the following section titles: "What Is Folk Religion?", "Spirit Beings and Deities", "Performance and/or Ritual Praxis", "Possession and Exorcism", and "Health, Healing, and Contemporary Lifestyles".

The first section, titled "What Is Folk Religion?", sets the stakes of identifying something as folk religion. Frank Karom documents the vernacular, folk performance of a portion of a more elaborate, older text, and he demonstrates that this performance renders a Bengali epic tale accessible to a crowd, entertained and educated; all the while, the performer experiences himself the bliss of bringing the tale to life. Some religions have an ambivalent relationship with the folk mode. Jains generally locate authority in classical, scriptural sources and clerical, monastic leaders, but contemporary Jain charismatic leaders challenge traditional regulations—such as monastic prohibitions against traveling across the ocean or using technology. Such challenges posit new models for Jain authority and renunciation today. Tine Venkemans explores what happens when a *sādhu*, a good renunciate ascetic, comes to eat with laypeople in the United States, an occurence once unthinkable. Such a *sādhu* suggests new modalities of charismatic authority and modern renunciation innovations aimed toward layfolk, leading to a surprising lay and folk modes of Jainism. Taking up another tradition, Alyson Prude documents *delogs* ('das log), Himalayan people who die and return with a message for the living, namely teaching that audiences need to get their acts together and practice dharma. Prude explains that folk Buddhism has been cast aside by scholars and monastic authorities to be inauthentic Buddhism, but the *delogs* and their lore reveal that these folk religious practitioners challenge what it means to be authentically Buddhist. They are Buddhists, and they consider their practices authentic, so this must be authentic Buddhism. Hasan El-Shamy complicates the categories of folk and non-folk. He argues that what is called folk Islam in Egypt is not folk at all: it is not separate from nor does it challenge ecclesiastical authority. Egyptian practices of *zar* and *zhikr*—possession dances and the repetition of divine names, respectively—that might be considered folk Islam are thoroughly connected to the Quran, Hadith, and ecclesiastical traditions; in this way, folk Islam is not separate from formal Islam.

The next section, "Spirit Beings and Deities", describes two traditions that address supernatural entities in the city of Benares, India, and also an exploration of sexuality and gender among traditional South African healers; each chapter explores the relationship between humans and non-humans or no-longer-humans. David Gordon White turns his attention to shrines and temples dedicated to or associated with trees in Benares, India. Numerous authoritative sources describe pilgrimage sites and temples connected to the great Hindu gods around the sacred city, but such high temples bear little influence on the daily lives of residents who venerate trees and deities in trees to guide and protect their daily lives; tree veneration stretches back to the earliest days of religion in the subcontinent. Seth Ligo also examines folk religion in Benares, noting the intersection of the dog-riding, ambivalent god Bhairava and the muscled, monkey god Hanuman with folk cults to *bīr bābas* and *satīs,* who are specific, neighborhood deities. He argues that lived religions revering these gods and tending to their relationships are a dynamic process founded on both scriptural appeal and local innovations. Rachel C. Schneider focuses on biographies and narratives about LGBTQ+ *sangomas* (traditional healers) in twenty-first-century South Africa, who find justification for same-sex sexuality and even protections from homophobic violence in spirit-healing practices that creatively negotiate and engage indigenous African religions and Christianity in postcolonial Africa.

In the section titled "Performance and/or Ritual Praxis," contributors describe ritual and performance themes in living folk religions. John C. Thibdeau describes the "politics of festivity" in Morroco, in which festivals are sites in which folk gather to engage the sacred in a direct manner and how this engagement has political components. Sufi festivals are sponsored by the Moroccan state to transform such activities and gatherings so they might signify a Morrocan cultural identity and public piety in which the nation and moral order are connected to festival performance; all these elements challenge the creeping authoritarianism from radical Islam. Keith Cantú examines the ways mantra lore mantras, regarding spoken or meditated prayer spells, in Tamil-language vernacular writings embrace the works of the modern yogi Sabhapati Swami, resisting neo-Hindu tendencies against pragmatic mantras thought to be worthless or mere superstition. Xingyi Wang highlights divination in a sixth-century Chinese source. Divination may be the most common folk ritual, performed throughout the world and across cultures. This Buddhist, Chinese text incorporates and sanctions uses of non-Buddhist indigenous divinations practices; even a venerable, canonic master takes up the dice to consult the divine. Padraic Fitzgerald and Mathias Nordvig explore the contemporary world of Nordic neopaganism in which modern bands, such as Wardruna and Heilung, reconstruct pre-Christian, Nordic-German rituals to enliven their musical performances, drawing crowds to partake in an imagined ancient time made anew through music. Finally, Keith E. McNeal describes Indo-Trinidadian Hindus in the twentieth and twenty-first centuries adapting their Indic mortuary rituals to a new context, condensing ritual technology and combining it with Caribbean corpse internment practices, demonstrating a multi-dimensional folk praxis.

Religion may be the interaction with invisible beings, but sometimes those invisible beings enter humans to speak with the living. How might living folk religions reckon with possession and exorcism, especially considering how pervasive these practices have been in defining what is and is not real or authentic religion? This question is explored in "Possession and Exorcism". Hugh Urban examines spiritualism in contemporary America, documenting three practitioners in central Ohio, USA, who use novel forms of spiritualism with clients and in communities. Spiritualists, he argues, speak with and about the divine based on lived, vernacular experiences channeling invisible spirits and divinities. Julie Edelstein describes possession practices at the Pandi Koyil temple in South India, establishing that individuals who experience possession enter a relationship, sometimes a quite ambivalent one, with gods who possess. William Chavez critiques the contemporary mediatization of exorcism practices (depictions in print and on screen) as a fringe religion; in fact, he notes that adherents of modern Satanism, in attempts to define themselves contra Christianity, reproduce logics in the practice of evangelical Christianity. Post-Christianity and anti-Christianity reproduce the very schema of Christianity they oppose. Chaves interviews a contemporary, satanic exorcist to demonstrate this dynamic. Finally, Diana Walsh Pasulka considers the lore about non-terrestrial folk religions, showing that folk or people's UFO (Unidentified Flying Object) lore counters official government representations. Government agents have aimed to shape those UFO religions, using what Walsh Pasulka calls "stealth folklore" to spread disinformation and destabilize UFO movements.

The final section of the book, "Health, Healing, and Lifestyle," describes modes of health and healing in reference to contemporary lifestyles; contributors highlight indigenous Americans, contemporary wiccan-witches, and yoga enthusiasts. Jason E. Purvis documents the interplay of indigenous and evangelical Christian conceptions of healing and ritual performance. The indigenous evangelical band Broken Walls not only spreads the message of evangelical Christianity but also reforms Christian and indigenous ritual practices so they might fit together meaningfully. Jason Mankey tracks the concept of The Goddess as trifold—Maiden, Mother, Crone (MMC)—in contemporary wiccan-witchcraft practices. While the idea of this triple goddess became widespread in the late twentieth century, it cannot be found in pre-modern mythology and lore. Today, this very conception of The Goddess as MMC, which was itself constructed in the twentieth century, is challenged by wiccan-witches for being too connected to a narrow conception of womanhood and gender; such challenges demonstrate the evolving folk aspect of wiccan-witchcraft. Finally, Anya Foxen examines modern, physical cultures, especially yoga, exploring claims about the connection of the soul, wellness, and exercise. The connections are based on prior esoteric theories evolving through and in physical cultures. In this way, wellness culture is yet another site in which folk practices and folk ideologies work themselves out.

Pedagogy

While the two of us are scholars on Hinduism and tantra, albeit approaching the religions from different perspectives, we were both inspired to explore living folk religions by teaching World Religions. Teaching World Religions is difficult, especially deciding what is on and what is off the table to be highlighted and compared, as Jeffrey Kripal argues in his new-school textbook, *Comparing Religions: Coming To Terms* (2014), a text we both use in our World Religions courses. Students want a basic overview of the beliefs and practices for various religions, all presented in a tight, discrete manner, but this rarely provides real insight into religious people and religious practices in this world. We expand the usual World Religions format in our courses by including such religions as Jainism, Sikhism, Indigenous American religions, and African religions, but merely including more religions in a course does not increase religious literacy, save for students being able to quickly and briefly expound the beliefs of each religion covered but little about religions generally. The more important change is to introduce themes that encourage students to move across traditions and explore the varied ways human consciousness expresses itself.

The book at hand would be a perfect textbook for World Religions; it will provide case studies to explore themes, especially if used in addition to another World Religions textbook such as Kripal's *Comparing Religions* or Prothero's *Religion Matters: An Introduction to the World's Religions* (2020). Thinking about charisma among religious figures, the essays of Purvis and Chaves productively interrogate what counts as "Christian" and how unexpected agents may deploy Christianity. On religious actors, students might read the *sangomas* in Schnieder against the *delogs* in Prude, questioning what are the messages of the actors and how their message is influenced by gender and sexuality. Students often see religion as a thing of the past, from hoary antiquity, but Foxen and Mankey show evolving trends in religions that are happening right now, evolving in gyms and bookstores all around.

This book can augment any undergraduate religions course, but it will also advance graduate students to new methods of study and topics up-and-coming in the field. The models of lived religions endorsed by Robert Orsi (1987), Nancy Tatum Ammerman (2007), and David D. Hall (1997), or the four aspects of religion—namely, creeds, codes, cultuses, and communities—set out by Catherine Albanese (2007 [1999]), should not be studied on their own or only in reading the tradition that a graduate student specializes but should interpret across cultures, boundaries, and even topics. Furthermore, the wide range of data throughout the essays will stretch graduate students beyond their own evidence silos.

The academic study of religion has moved beyond only studying the religions that shape world history to study the worlds shaped by religious people.

Works Cited

Albanese, Catherine L. *America Religions and Religion*. Fourth ed. Wadsworth Cengage Learning 2007. [1999].

Ammerman, Nancy Tatom. *Everyday Religion: Observing Modern Religious Lives*. Oxford University Press, 2007.

Borkataky-Varma, Sravana. "The Dead Speak: A Case Study from the Tiwa Tribe Highlighting the Hybrid World of Śākta Tantra in Assam." *Religions*, vol. 8, 2017, p. 221; doi:10.3390/rel8100221

Chidester, David. "Fake Religion: Ordeals of Authenticity in the Study of Religion." *Journal for the Study of Religion*, vol. 16, no. 2, 2003, pp. 71–97.

Eliade, Mircea and Charles J Adams. *The Encyclopedia of Religion*. Macmillan Publishing Company, 1987.

Fox, William S. "Folklore and Fakelore: Some Sociological Considerations." *Journal of the Folklore Institute*, vol. 17, no. 2/3, 1980, pp. 244–261.

Fortune, Dion. *Psychic Self-Defense - the Classic Instruction Manual for Protectingyoursel.* Weiser Books 2011 [1930].

Hall, David D. *Lived Religion in America: Toward a History of Practice*. Princeton University Press, 1997.

Harner, Michael J. *The Way of the Shaman: The Definitive Handbook*. HarperOne 2009 [1990].

Janisse, Kier-La et al. directors. *Woodlands Dark and Days Bewitched : A History of Folk Horror.* Severin Films, 2021.

Kakar, Sudhir. *Shamans, Mystics, and Doctors: A Psychological Inquiry into India and Its Healing Traditions*. University of Chicago Press, 1991.

Kripal, Jeffrey J. *Comparing Religions: Coming to Terms*. Wiley, 2014.

Long, Charles H. "Popular Religion". *The Encyclopedia of Religion*. Ed. Mircea Eliade and Adams. Macmillan Publishing Company, 1987, pp. 443–452

Mandelbaum, David G. "Transcendental and Pragmatic Aspects of Religion." *American Anthropologist*, vol. 68, no. 5, 1966, pp. 1174–1191.

Narayanan, Vasudha. *Hinduism: Origins, Beliefs, Practices, Holy Texts, Sacred Place*. Oxford; New York: Oxford University Press, 2004.

Orsi Robert A. *The Madonna of 115th Street: Faith and Community in Italian Harlem 1880–1950*. 2nd ed. Yale University Press, 1987.

Primiano Leonard Norman et al. *Vernacular Religion : Collected Essays of Leonard Primiano.* New York University Press 2022.

Primiano, Leonard Norman. "Vernacular Religion and the Search for Method in Religious Folklife." *Western Folklore*, vol. 54, no. 1, 1995. 37–56.

Prothero, Stephen R. *Religion Matters: An Introduction to the World's Religions.* W.W. Norton & Company, 2020.

Redfield, Robert. *The Little Community And Peasant Society and Culture*. 4th impr ed. University of Chicago Press, 1965.

Smith, Frederick M. *The Self Possessed*. Columbia University Press, 2006.

Spiro, Melford."Religion: Problems of Definition and Explanation." *Anthropological Approaches to the Study of Religion*. Ed. Michael Banton. London: Tavistock, 1966, pp. 85–126.

Ullrey, Aaron Michael. "Magic Rituals". Brill Encyclopedia of Hinduism Online, forthcoming 2023.

———. *Grim Grimoires: Pragmatic Ritual in the Magic Tantras*. 2016. University of California Santa Barbara. Doctoral Dissertation.

Yoder, Don and Henry Glassie. *American Folklife*. University of Texas Press, 1976.

———. *Discovering American Folklife: Studies in Ethnic Religious and Regional Culture.* UMI Research Press, 1990.

PART I
What Is Folk Religion?

1

INTERROGATING THE FOLK-CLASSICAL DIVIDE IN THE STUDY OF INDIC RELIGIONS THROUGH A LOCAL BENGALI RITUAL PERFORMANCE

Frank J. Korom

Introduction

The debate over what terms label a small community's system of belief and worship has been going on for quite some time (e.g., Bell 1989; Davis 1974, 1982; O'Neil 1986; Primiano 1995; Yoder 1974) in the study of religion. That debate has resulted in several binaries, such as great/little, high/low, urban/rural, official/non-official, written/oral, transcendental/pragmatic, and—most notorious of them all—classical/folk, to name just few from the long list of what Barbara Kirshenblatt-Gimblett (1988) would call "mistaken dichotomies." In the field of South Asian Studies, more specifically, the debate over levels of religious orthodoxy and orthopraxy are well known, having hovered over center stage for decades, if not centuries. Milton Singer (1972) famously followed his mentor Robert Redfield (1951, 1956) in distinguishing between great and little traditions in his contextual study of Hindu cultural performances in the city of Madras, now renamed Chennai.

I do not wish to engage in grand dichotomies that separate folk from classical, etc. This path of reasoning has already been proven spurious by Ananda K. Coomaraswamy (1937) in the Indian context, where he argues the classical (*mārga*) and the regional (*deśī*) are simply two sides of the same coin that need not be separated for merely analytical purposes (Korom 2006: 13–15). Rather, I wish to focus on what Nancy Ammerman (2021) has termed "lived religion."[1] It is precisely at the intersection of seeming opposites that the practical, lived, and local dimensions of religion come to the fore, and it is this intersection that I want to suggest is what has been termed "folk" by Don Yoder (1974), the late doyen of folklife studies, or again, more recently, "vernacular" by his student Leonard Primiano (1995).

DOI: 10.4324/9781003257462-3

What binds these terms listed above is the concept of locality; that is, those factors that situate a given set of beliefs and practices in one specific place or cluster of closely associated and geographically contiguous places, coherent within a commonly shared ethnolinguistic worldview.[2] The term "local" religion, here, refers to the complex of practices and beliefs woven around the special quality of a particular place, which would include but not be limited to its sacred sites, indigenous conceptions of deity, and idiosyncratic rituals, all of which are grounded in a community's sacred history, whether oral, written, or both (Christian Jr. 1981: 3; Korom 2020b: 287).

It seems to me that a locative definition highlights the power of place without creating problematic dichotomies. It also allows for connecting the local to the regional, then to the transregional, which ultimately can be braided into the national and even the transnational (Blackburn and Flueckiger 1989; Korom 2006: 135–149, 164–181), given that the Indian diaspora is by now a global presence (Korom 2000). What we have, then, is not a series of dichotomies opposed to one another but a sliding scale of relationships that glide together in a dialogical fashion, allowing for local ingenuity to rework ideas and concepts into ever-new existential concerns that have immediate urgency to the group studied. This dialogical process unfolds over time and space for millennia and is, in my estimation, the innovative factor that allows for religious traditions to remain vital and dynamic, especially in modern times in the face of secularization and other intervening matters that threaten the very existence of any traditional religious system. Moreover, the dialectical relationship between binaries, to which we may now add sacred and secular, become road markers along a continuum that allows opposites to converge and diverge repeatedly over time and through space in an ongoing process of maintenance and change. The road markers are, of course, navigated by human ingenuity, as we shall see in the ethnography below.

A perfect example of how larger concerns that have been unfolding gradually through time and across space get indigenized and localized is the Bengali genre of *maṅgalkābya* (auspicious poetry), a vernacular tradition emerging in medieval Bengal (i.e., 1204–1757 CE) and continuing in both oral and written forms to the present. Medieval Bengali literature presents accurate historical glimpses into the so-called "folk" culture of the period, as several indigenous scholars have shown (e.g., Khalek 1982; Raychaudhury 1978; Sanyal 1982).[3] *Maṅgalkābyas* have been an area of interdisciplinary inquiry because they are the dominant genre of Middle Bengali poetic prose, presenting a unique view of Bengali religion and culture that often takes specific theological turns not found elsewhere in India (Dimock 1976). At the same time, they are a regional aspect of transregional and national concerns, since they share many Wittgensteinian "family resemblances" (*Familienähnlichten*) but remain locally unique.

One of the main functions of *maṅgalkābyas* is panegyric, since each text praises a specific deity in the Bengali pantheon. I turn my attention solely to Dharmaraj (King of Dharma), not only because of his significant role in the genre as the creator of the universe (Korom 2020a) but also due to significant ethnographic evidence (e.g., Bhaṭṭācārja 1975: 653; Sen 1975: 153) suggesting this corpus of texts about the deity, known collectively as *dharmamaṅgal*, were still being performed in his honor during annual ritual occasions as late as the 1960s.[4]

While numerous poetic versions of *dharmamaṅgal*s have come down to us in various stages of completion, the early eighteenth-century work written by Ghanaram Cakravarti (1669–?) is the one on which I wish to focus in this section because the singer I discuss below claims familiarity with it, and even shares the same surname.[5] According to his descendants who celebrate his birthday annually in his natal village, Ghanaram's text is normatively perceived to be the most popular version because it is considered to be more poetic and complete. But Sandra Robinson (1980: 4) has pointed out that certain versions are more closely associated with specific sites of worship usually located near an author's place of birth. This is the case with Ghanaram, who is mostly associated with the northern Rarh (roughly equivalent to modern-day Burdwan, Bankura, and Birbhum districts) area of Bengal, since we know from his signature verse that he was born in the village of Krishnapur, located in Burdwan District (Sen 1975: 188; Korom 2020a: 257–258). Further, because medieval authors were often writing under royal patronage and singing for the court, popular renditions performed by singers utilizing local versions must have flourished among broader audiences at ritual sites and elsewhere, for there are intertextual references in the written sources themselves that suggest this. It is therefore not very surprising to find Ghanaram's text being the basis of inspiration for the performance that I analyze below.[6]

The Context[7]

With the temperature slowly declining from an oppressive 43°C heat during the late afternoon—an incredibly hot day dripping with humidity even by local standards—just before the full moon of the lunar month of Baishak (April/May), the sun slowly begins to set while a band of musicians—playing *ḍhāk*s (large barrel drums), *ḍhol*s (small barrel drums), and *kartal*s (cymbals)—boards a rickety stage across from a small earthen temple with a thatched roof. The temple houses an aniconic stone representing the deity Dharma. As they position themselves and tune their instruments, the crowd milling about to partake in local attractions specially arranged for the occasion—like a hand-spun Ferris wheel—slowly start assembling around me and my cassette recorder, which is acting stubbornly due to the fiery heat that is melting my tapes on the ground in front of the stage. Suddenly, there is a "breakthrough into performance" (Hymes 1981: 79–141).

The musicians "frame" (Goffman 1974) the performance by beginning to play in a lively manner, signaling to everyone within hearing distance that the ritual is about to start. They play about fifteen minutes until the audience members are seated quietly on the ground in front of the stage, and then a bare-chested man in his early sixties wearing a crisply starched white *dhotī* and jingling ankle bells, with his sacred thread prominently hanging across his chest and a white fly whisk in his right hand, walks onto the stage.

His name is Bhujangabhushan Chakravarti, a Brahman bard who learned his singing craft from a hereditary line that includes his father and grandfather. Barely literate, he earned his title *bhujaṅgabhūṣaṇ* ("serpent ornament") due to the prominent size of his canines, which drew him both scorn and respect as a child. Some of his peers ridiculed him for his "fangs" while he was growing up here in Kamarpara, a village of approximately 3,000 residents located in the Illambazar administrative block of Birbhum District, where the performance was taking place on this day. Others saw his sharp teeth as an auspicious sign of a future calling to be a singer of *maṅgalkābyas*.[8]

Maṅgalkābya composition emerged after Bengal became Islamicized from the thirteenth century onward. Oftentimes, such texts competed to sway devotees away from one deity and ultimately pledge allegiance to another. Some songs are epic in form and content, since human agents in the texts engaged in violent battles with one another in the name of the specific deity for whom they were fighting. This is especially true of the *dharmamaṅgal* sub-genre, dedicated to the deity Dharma, also known as Dharma *ṭhākur* (lord). Dharmaraj is a generic title for a variety of classical figures associated with Indic religious history and mythology, ranging from the Buddha to Yama to Yudhishthira in the Sanskrit epic Mahabharata, but in the Bengali *maṅgal* literature, it refers to an otiose deity who rides an owl and is responsible for the creation of the universe (Korom 2020a).[9] Once having created the universe, he ascends to the heavens where he reigns supreme over the various worlds, or *loka*s, assigned to different deities of the Hindu pantheon. He is thus an absentee god, so to speak, who imposes his gaze upon human affairs from far above, except when called (*dāk*). The ritual performance in which Bhujangabhushan and his troupe are about to engage is thus an attempt at calling out to the absent deity, imploring him to appear and grace the assembly with blessings and good tidings of ānanda (joy).

*Pūjā*s (worship services) for Dharmaraj were widespread in eastern India during the middle period of Bengali history when the *maṅgalkābya* literature flourished. Such rites declined between the thirteenth and nineteenth centuries, however, as the deity became absorbed into the pan-Indian image of Shiva as a result of what Srinivas (1956) termed Sanskritization, which led to a blending of local, regional, and national phenomena that had been crisscrossing for much of history as Hinduism moved from the western part of the subcontinent toward the Bay of Bengal in the east, absorbing virtually everything it encountered. Singing Dharma's epic is rare nowadays. In fact, I only found one village in which any portion of the narrative was performed during my fieldwork in the late 1980s and early 1990s. Instead, what one mostly finds performed during the Dharma *pūjā* in the Rarh region today is the "thunder" (*garjan*) of the *ḍhāk* and *ḍhol* drums. The slang term *gājan* for thunder is thus often used to describe this worship ritual. Residents judge the success of the annual ritual in terms of the amount of *dhum-dhām* (revelry), the number of drummers in attendance, and the overall size of the event.

The reasons for the decline in sung performance are complex but are almost certainly economical, for singers of auspicious poems usually composed and performed in the royal courts that no longer exist. However, a parallel oral tradition was associated with local rituals in the past and continues in Kamarpara today. To what extent the local, oral tradition is connected to the regional, written one is tendentious, but it does allow for what Charles Briggs (1988) has called "scriptural allusions," where an oral tradition echoes a written text and/or vice versa (Korom 2004: 846). The fact that each village—or cluster of villages—has its own way of performing the rituals for Dharmaraj, even though they mostly occur around the three days following Baishak *purṇimā* (full moon), suggests that different aspects or events of his narrative have long been associated with distinct locations within Rarh (Korom 1999b).

Bhujangabhushan's Paścim Udaẏ Pālā[10]

According to the written tradition, Dharmaraj's worship declined on earth as more and more people began worshipping the goddess Candi. Dharma must thus compete with Candi for devotees, but like with humans, the deities often fight proxy battles, using earthlings to do their bidding. Dharma thus causes the dancing *apsaras* (semi-divine, celestial maiden) of Indra—the king of the divine pantheon—named Ranjavati to be reborn on earth. To make matters worse, Ranjavati is to be married off to an old king named Karnasen, who is not able to fulfill his sexual duties on their wedding night, nor any other night. Ranjavati must thus perform *tapasyā* (austerities) by throwing herself onto a spiked plank at a place called Campai *ghāṭ*. This is all prearranged so Dharmaraj can manifest himself as an old, wandering ascetic who gives her the boon of a son (Korom 2020b: 299–303). The event occurs in Ghanaram's text more than eight hundred pages before Lausen's dismemberment.

Between the two monumental events of severe austerity and self-sacrifice, we find varied archetypal hero's journeys with distinct Bengali twists, including a riddling contest with a prostitute and subduing an iron rhinoceros: tests and feats weave a marvelous adventure. Lausen's cowardly brother Karpur accompanies him on his quest in the textual versions, and along the way, they eventually encounter a fierce Dom (Dalit) warrior named Kalu Ray, who becomes Lausen's outcaste general in the ongoing battles with the hero's evil uncle Mahmud. The textual narrative provides the contextual and mythological background for the variegated rituals that occur annually throughout the region, all of which are tied to specific locations in villages scattered throughout the three districts constituting Rarh. At no one site are all the rituals performed, so there is no version of the *gājan* that includes all of the elements we find practiced here and there.

Now, to return to Kamarpara, the musical prelude soars to a climax, and a more somber mood is established by slowing the beat, almost to a crawl.

Bhujangabhushan, the *gāẏak* (singer), begins his *bandanā*, or salutation, to the deities. Having revered many of them, he finishes with Sarasvati, the Hindu goddess of learning and music, whom he invites to alight on his tongue, to assure the success and efficacy of his performance. He implores everyone in the audience to chant "*hari, hari, haribol*" (say Hari, Hari, Hari). Hari is the appellation for the supreme absolute that takes away all sorrows from his devotees in the Vedas, Hinduism's oldest texts. In more modern times, the name is almost synonymous with Vishnu, the lord of preservation, part of the *trimūrti*, the Hindu triad also consisting of Brahma, the creator, and Shiva, the destroyer.

The *bandanā*'s liturgical style imitates chanted Sanskrit mantras to captivate and mystify the audience. After the incantation, the singer shifts into narration, apocryphally stating that Dharma's worship used to be performed in the Himalayas, but nowadays it continues "with varied names almost in every village."[11] "But this Dharmaraj has no image," he states, for "it is worshipped in stone form (śilāmūrti)." He explains that what distinguishes this form from any old stone is the impression of a left foot on its surface. It was Ranjavati, he goes on to say, who first "introduced" Dharmaraj worship to "our country" (āmār deś). Introducing semi-divine celestial characters who get reborn on earth to carry out a deity's wishes is a common motif in vernacular Indic literature, responding to the classical pattern of Vishnu's *avatāra*s (reincarnations) in Sanskrit texts. He then contextualizes his performance as follows.

"Why did she bring it? How did it take place? A song on that matter will be performed here. And today the theme of the song is the 'western rising.' Many will be amazed to hear that because we are accustomed to see the sun rise in the east. But, yes, it happened! And who made it possible to happen? It will be discussed here, how it was performed. He was the king of Shashthigarh. His name was Karnasen. Lausen, son of Karnasen, performed austere, spiritual exercises and sacrificial oblations, propitiating Dharmaraj. And collecting a boon from Him made the sun rise in the west." After framing his narrative, Bhujangabhushan elaborates how Ranjavati ended up marrying Karnasen, stating, "now I am going to tell how that very marriage of Karnasen's woman came about." Throughout the forthcoming performance, the singer and his entourage will oscillate back and forth from song to speech, which is a distinctive feature of such devotional rituals, not just in West Bengal, but throughout India. As the instruments wail again, Bhujangabhushan sings, "come on, pray to hail (*jaẏa*) Ram!" He sings how the king prepares for his journey in a horse-drawn carriage after performing austerities and animal sacrifices while chanting Sanskrit *mantra*s to Gaudeshwar, the place where Ranjavati lives. Arriving at Gaudeshwar, his feet are washed, and he is seated on a jeweled throne. Here, the *gān* (song) style ends, and the singer again implores everyone to hail Ram. He explains how each of the bride's and groom's parties arrive and take their places in the wedding hall. Bhujangabhushan instructs the audience in the correct manner of seating guests by introducing formal speech (*sādhu bhāṣā*) vocabulary, such as *chădnatalā* ("wedding solemnization place"), *kanyāpakṣa* (bride's side), and *patrapakṣa* (groom's side).

Then he breaks back into performance, singing the wedding ritual culminating in the couple's eyes meeting for the first time. The following festivities are also sung in a merry mood of celebration, ending with a feast that consisted of fifty items, all of which are described in great detail, as is common in epic recitation throughout the world, where banquets are described in great depth (Bowra 1952: 179–214).

The bard uses spoken discourse to explain the rite known as "keeping the newly married couple awake all night." This playful event is a standard portion of Bengali marriage rituals in which the newlywed couple is forced to remain awake the first evening together alone; they are constantly interrupted by the jocular banter of the women at the event. In this case, Ranjavati's maidens occupy the newlywed chamber to disturb the couple by jesting about how ugly are their husbands. One opines, "Listen, my dear, my husband has a big hunch on his back. Do you know what he does when it is time to sleep? He needs a pile of pillows: five, six, seven pillows are needed to provide him with support. Otherwise, he falls [off of the bed]. And if he were made to lie with face up, you know what would happen?"

The bard and his chorus break into song again, singing "[he] becomes a boat if made to lie on his back. Again, if he were made to lie on his chest, he would look like a bridge! Jaya Ram." The oscillation between song and speech, between humor and seriousness, continues for some time; each maiden describes a funny incident to pass the time until the sun rises. The women in the audience pull the drape of their saris over their faces as they giggle at the humorous discussion, while the unmarried girls burst out in laughter as they learn what to expect at their own future nuptials. The goal is, of course, to keep the newly wedded couple from consummating the marriage, since Bengali lore suggests that sexual intercourse on the first evening will lead to disharmony in the future. But for the audience, it is also about entertainment and education.

In the morning, the maidens dress their new queen, and she sets off with her elderly husband to his home. Bhujangabhushan then explains how they try to conceive for days, but are unsuccessful. Ranjavati learns that if she successfully propitiates Dharmaraj through the performance of *tapasyā*, then her wish of having a child will be fulfilled. Eventually, her austerities lead to the birth of Lausen, after she consumes sweetmeats, fried fish, and soaked rice "on an auspicious day." Due to lack of colostrum, the child is fed goat's milk for the first three days, after which the queen eats garlic and begins breastfeeding him on the fourth day. The song mode again ends here, and the singer returns to the narration.

"It was in this manner that King Lausen was born," Bhujanga says. Soon thereafter his father dies. Becoming king, Lausen attacks and conquers all surrounding kingdoms and assumes the title *mahārāj* (great king). The subjugated rulers, often referred to by ethnohistorians as "little kings" (Dirks 1988), then conspire together to trick Lausen into undertaking an impossible task that will lead to his downfall. So they go to his court, where their spokesman says the following: "We find daily that the sun rises in the east and sets in the west. We want this daily motion to be reversed—rising in the west and setting in the east. No one else can do this except you." Lausen takes the challenge and asks for his mother's permission to go to the forest to perform his austerities, but she prefers him to become a householder instead of a renunciant.

Despite his mother's reluctance, he undertakes a journey to a deep, thick forest known as Hakanda, along with an entourage of followers, including his pet dog named Beto and his aunt whom Ranjavati insisted must go along. He performs a *yajña* (fire sacrifice) in the forest by pouring gallons upon gallons of *ghī* (clarified butter) onto the sacrificial fire. Lausen repeats his actions day after day, month after month, Bhujanga narrates, but nothing happens. Our forlorn king finally opines to his aunt, who, in response, recites a proverb in Hindi, a language not known to the audience, about the wheat grinding wheel and the stick that turns it, indicating that everyone can see the wheel, but few notice the stick that turns the wheel. "Devotion is like that," she says, urging him not to lose faith. She then supplicates him to worship "his deity" with a hundred-petal (śatdal) lotus.

At this juncture, Bhujanga again acts like epic singers all over the world by taking on the persona of the main character, and he speaks in the first person (Lord 1960: 164–165). Breaking back into song, singing as Lausen, he asks the following: "Aunt, where can I get hold of a hundred-petal lotus?" He intentionally repeats the line for dramatic effect: "Aunt, where can I get hold of a hundred-petal lotus?" She gives him several answers concluding with, "whatever there is in the entire universe exists within one's heart. If you are unable to find a hundred-petal lotus to worship Niranjan (= Dharmaraj, the "stainless one"), sacrifice your body parts as an offering of worship."

The singer returns to spoken narration to explain what this severe act means and why it must be done. He repeats the aunt's words about the body being a microcosm of the universe, and then screams, jolting the audience. "This pair of arms becomes the stem of your lotus. The fingers become leaves of your lotus. Those two feet of yours constitute the root of your lotus. I say, your face becomes your hundred-petal flower." The ritual performance approaches its climax. The singer-*cum*-narrator now announces he will explain how each piece of the hero's body is transformed into a flower that falls at the feet of the creator deity, as Lausen weeps.

"And what did he say to his mother," Bhujanga asks? He breaks dramatically into song: "Hey dear, Dharma is calling me, dear mother, Dharma is calling me." This line is repeated progressively, but ever more rapidly, as the drums resound louder and louder. In a list-like fashion, he sings how with each *daṇḍa*—a traditional measure of time—Lausen cuts off a different part of his body, shouting, "Dharma is calling me." Each piece is cast into the fire pit (*kuṇḍa*) as *argha*, an offering given to a respected guest at reception, after which it becomes a lotus that falls at the feet of Dharma, who has secretly manifested himself in human form at the site of the sacrifice. The singer now reverts back to speech, building to the climax. He says, "now when it became the seventh *daṇḍa*, the king turned into skin and bone. Only the head was left [loud shout]. Then the king slashed from his right side and the head fell off from his right side." The chopped-off head is weeping and chanting Govinda, a name of Krishna, and the aunt dies because she could not bear the loss of Lausen. Even *kāmadhenu*, the mythical cow of plenty whose flow of milk never ends, dies out of grief! Finally, the head becomes a hundred-petal lotus that falls at the feet of the lord in disguise. Bhujanga concludes by echoing a refrain that he uses throughout the dismemberment scene: "Then the wind arrived and blew a soft breeze."

Despite his self-sacrifice, there is still no sign of Dharma's benevolence, which results in all of the people accompanying Lausen to Hakanda dropping dead out of bereavement. Only Beto, his faithful dog, remains alive. He continues to stand guard over the great sacrifice that has occurred on that fateful day. Hearing the dog's whimpering, the goddess Sarasvati takes pity on him, petitioning Vishnu and Madana (= Kama, the deity of erotic desire) to do something, but they inform her that Lausen performed the sacrifice without taking *dīkṣa* (initiation) first, thus negating its effect.

A long debate then ensues between the deities, and Sarasvati tries to convince the male gods to whisper *dīkṣa* into the right ear of Lausen, but still, they refuse.[12] The goddess, therefore, wishes Narada, an ancient Vedic sage known to be an itinerant storyteller, to perform the initiation. According to the singer, however, Narada is a Brahman who cannot initiate anyone because he was never initiated himself. Arguing all night, Narada finally vows to attain initiation by the first person he sees in the morning. The first person he spies when the sun arises is Kalu *hăḍi* herding his pigs.[13] In the textual tradition, this is Kalu Dom, Lausen's untouchable general, referred to above. Narada hesitates because Kalu is ritually impure. He begs the goddess for another chance to fulfill his vow, so the next day it is again Kalu who appears before Narada. The sage gives in and confronts the mighty warrior, demanding that Kalu initiate him. Now Kalu becomes the reluctant one. He sends Narada into the forest to gather food, which Kalu then partially consumes. After his meal, he tells Narada to eat his leftovers, which in Hinduism is considered a ritually polluting act, especially since it is the leftover food of an outcaste. A series of trials and tribulations transpire before Vishnu and his consort finally acknowledge Narada, allowing him to take the form of a fly and whisper the necessary *mantra* into Lausen's severed head's right ear.

Dharmaraj is now satisfied and approaches the site of the sacrifice, but Beto will not allow him to enter the sacrificial arena because the deity is still in the form of a human being. The hound demands that he show his cosmic form before granting him access to the sacred grounds. Dharmaraj demonstrates his divine manifestation to please Beto, after which the dog bows down before him. Witnessing the canine's act of devotion, the deity offers him a boon for his faithfulness, though Beto only wants his master resuscitated. Dharmaraj then sends the dog into the forest and commands him to return with the first flower he encounters. Beto is destined to become whatever flower he finds. He spies an ākanda bush ("dogbane" = *calotropis* = milkweed) deep in the forest and brings its flower to the deity. The Lord changes the dog into that flower and enters the sacrificial grounds where the dead are lying. Chanting, "*jiẏo, jiẏo, jiẏo*" (live, live, live), he sprinkles *mritasanjivani,* life-restoring nectar, on the departed, and they all sit up, including Lausen in a reconstituted body. The hero asks his Lord, now morphed into the form of Narayana, another appellation for Vishnu, to make the sun rise in the west. At noon, Narayana calls out to the solar deity, Surya, three times, after which the sun arrives with folded hands to fulfill Lausen's request that he rise in the west and set in the east.

The singer concludes by singing, "Hence, in brief, I conclude the *pālā* here." He again implores everyone to chant "*hari, hari, haribol,*" concluding with the following blessing:

May the fields become full with crops.
May the clouds get filled with water.
May Dharmaraj shower welfare on this Kamarpara village.

Conclusion

What may we conclude from the sensational, multivocalic performance recounted above? The participants worship the village deity during the fallow time of the year when the hot season will eventually give way to the cooling monsoon rains that bring fecundity to the soil each year, as the final blessing suggests, but what more can we learn from the immediate performance context in the specific locality that I have described above? We could fruitfully look at what is being communicated and how. What are the aesthetic devices used by the bard to bring home his main points? How are conveyed words transformed into artistic communication as he breaks through into performance?[14] I conclude by reflecting on the power of performance in ritual to achieve efficacy, while at the same time returning to the terminological question concerning "folk" and "classical" raised at the outset, thereby linking these interconnected issues.

First of all, Bhujangabhushan does not recite the text from a written source, as do Ram devotees with Tulsidas' cherished Ramcharitmanas, for instance, nor does he recount the entire text from beginning to end.[15] Instead, he is more selective, focusing on one key *pālā* (episode) of a medieval, vernacular text known as the Dharmamangal. Bhujangabhushan's performance is not simply a shallow reduction of the more ornate written text but an independent work of art designed specifically for his unique, local audience, which muddies the water that flows between written and oral.

The orally performed text focuses only on a small portion of the written one, which is almost one thousand pages long in Ghanaram's version. The relationship between the written and oral versions of the core narrative can thus only be speculative since the singer does not recite directly from a written source. Instead, Bhujangabhushan's oral version is a creative rendering of an imagined *Ur*-text that only exists in the collective minds of scholars, even though the singer mentioned Ghanaram's composition by name to me in conversation. As Paul Ricoeur (1971: 146) argues, a text achieves its significance in interpretation by actualizing its semantic dimension. Bhujangabhushan's performance thus provides efficacy to the corresponding rituals performed annually for Dharmaraj in Kamarpara by eloquently combining the creative use of language with paralinguistic features that have an emotional effect on the audience.

By combining local flavor with vernacular texts that themselves draw on classical Indic materials, a dialog is continued that flows through India's indigenous religious traditions for millennia, from the Vedas, to the Sanskrit epics, and to regionally inspired vernacular texts, only to end up, finally, back in the oral stream that is passed on from one generation to the next in village contexts like the one described here. The literary chain to which all of these links belong is threaded together by the oral tradition—the backbone of so-called "folk" religion—that exists to locally reframe, rework, and make sense of the rich diversity that is Hinduism. It would be fruitless, however, to try and suggest in which direction the narrative flows, since it moves back and forth from written to oral endlessly in an "emergent" fashion (Georges 1969).[16]

The contours of song and speech above are a form of code shifting that allows different accomplishments: for the performer, it brings about a self-admitted sense of *ānanda* (bliss), and for the audience, it offers a sense of *jñān* (knowledge). For the audience, the latter is important because the medieval text is not readily available, nor do the largely non-literate participants understand its contents. What they do know is that Dharmaraj is the *grāmyadebatā* (village deity) who is worshipped by all castes during the annual *pūjā* to bring about the alleviation of suffering and guarantee a bountiful harvest.

Bhujangabhushan fulfills a dual role as an entertainer and a spiritual teacher, fusing these two roles through his use of easily comprehensible but aesthetically pleasing verse coupled with prose. Such ritual innovations based on some hypothetical scriptural source have been often called folk religion or apocrypha in the past. However, even though the term "folk" (*lok*) has become antiquated over time due to its colonial and ideological legacy, it is still part of a continuum of terminology in use today, even by the people we study. Still, I would prefer to opt for the term "local" and combine it with theology, since Bhujangabhushan's exegesis goes beyond mere orthopraxy to reflect upon orthodoxy in the doctrinal sense of the term, where a religious system's basic points of belief are worked out and debated through the medium of hermeneutics; in other words, the exegesis is the religious or theological counterpart of what Alan Dundes (1966) usefully terms "oral literary criticism," referring to verbal commentaries on items of folklore. Oral exegesis in Bhujangabhushan's rendering of the *paścim udaẏ pālā* is a creative work of art that situates his community's local practices and understandings of those practices within a larger regional sphere of activities and beliefs related to Dharmaraj, which are in dialog with yet other written and oral traditions that are transregional and even national, as evidenced by references to Vedic characters and texts that are incorporated into the local worldview to create coherence out of streams of thought and practice that have been flowing in multiple directions throughout the course of the development of Hinduism.[17]

Although it would not be prudent to attempt a reconstruction of precisely how the Bengali Dharmaraj relates or does not relate to other Dharmaraj figures who have appeared throughout Indic religious history (Korom 1997a), we can acknowledge there are continuities from past to present that connect Kamarpara to other practices and beliefs in West Bengal and beyond. We can also acknowledge innovations that are uniquely local, fulfilling Christian Jr.'s criteria for considering Bhujangabhushan's performance to be an integral aspect of a highly localized phenomenon with undeniable connections to ever-larger concentric spheres as one moves out from this village to the administrative block in which it is situated, to the district in which the block is situated, to the state in which the district is situated, and finally to the nation in which the state is situated. In other words, the performance and narrative communicate some essential ideas about what it means to be a Hindu resident and devotee of Dharmaraj in Kamarpara, Birbhum District, West Bengal within a much broader context that crisscrosses throughout time and space, which is the basis of India's richly variegated Hindu tapestry that is not seamless but loosely woven, allowing for an incredible amount of diversity as well as local innovation, even while recognizing the fabric from which the bolt is cut. It is this underlying logic that constitutes the amalgamated magic of religious folk practice.

Notes

1 I use Leach's (1968) term "practical religion" in a somewhat different sense than what he intended to mean something similar to Claude Lévi-Strauss' notion of *sauvage*. Leach feels that interpreting everyday religion according to canons and doctrine can be misleading. True enough, but his insistence that theological philosophy is preoccupied with the afterlife while practical religion is obsessed with the existential present is too simplistic. To rob the average worshipper of eschatological concerns is unacceptable, especially in the light of the fact that Hindus do, in fact, speculate a great deal about the afterlife on the folk level (Blackburn 1985). More acceptable in the South Asian context is Mandelbaum's distinction between transcendental and pragmatic complexes: "One is ultimate, supernal, derived from Sanskrit texts; the other is proximate, local, validated by vernacular tales" (Mandelbaum 1966: 10).

2 This is not to say that "coherent" means uniform or uncontested, since the very nature of any religious worldview suggests an ongoing and negotiated dialectic between one locality and another within larger and larger concentric spheres of contact and influence. I have argued elsewhere that this is the dynamic tension that exists between the local and the global (Korom 1999a), which Yoder (1974: 11) sees as the defining characteristic of "folk" religion; namely, that it exists in tension with "organized" religion in any given community or society.

3 For an overview of the rise of Bengali vernacular religious and literary movements, see Korom (2020b).

4 Out of all the *maṅgal* texts, the *dharmamaṅgal* corpus is somewhat distinct. Due to its massive length, martial imagery, royal patronage, and thematic content, it most resembles what we might call "epic" in English (Bandyopādhyāẏ 1980: 352).

5 There is a considerable amount of structural and narrative consistency, even though each author emphasizes or elaborates certain portions of the story (Bhaṭṭācārja

1975: 629). Mayur Bhatt's version, for example, is more ritually oriented by focusing on the story of Ramai Pandit, the person believed to be the author of the *Shunya Puran* (Empty Purana), one of the religious movement's liturgical texts. He is also credited with being the first performer of the *pūjā* (worship service) for the deity Dharmaraj. On the other hand, Ghanaram's narrative most fully develops the story of the hero Lausen, Dharmaraj's crusader on earth, which is why I chose it for my study.

6 One of the distinctive features of studying local religion is its context dependency, which means focusing methodologically on the context of performance instead of solely the resultant text itself. See Korom (2013).

7 The fieldwork and archival research for my work on the Dharma phenomenon was carried out between 1987 and 1989. It was funded by grants from Fulbright-Hays, the American Institute of Indian Studies, and the Ford Foundation.

8 This particular village is known for specific rituals that correspond directly to the narrative to be sung later in my description, which is what makes Kamarpara unique in relation to other Dharma rituals in the region. The fang symbolism discussed, of course, alludes to *nāgrāj*, the king cobra, both revered and feared in the region.

9 Because his identity is obscure and regularly confused with a host of other mythological and historical figures, he is often referred to as a "syncretistic" deity. However, I have found this characterization to be completely misleading, because it pejoratively suggests a lack of consistency devoid of human agency. See Korom (1997a, 1997b).

10 The feature most associated with Kamarpara is the *paścim udaẏ pālā* ("western sunrise section"), which is the penultimate chapter of the written epics—most prominently in Ghanaram's version of the text—in which the hero Lausen hacks his own body to pieces out of loyalty to Dharmaraj. Due to this act, the deity descends from the skies and revives everyone destroyed in the preceding battles (Korom 2020b: 307–309). Kamarpara is associated with this event in the sacred geography outlined in the written texts and also by austerities performed by a group of Dharma devotees (*bhaktyās*) who represent the various parts of the hero Lausen's dismembered body when they are paraded around the village while reposing on spiked palanquins.

11 All translations from the oral text are my own based on the word-for-word, handwritten 90-page transcription of the performance I recorded.

12 The same ritual act of whispering initiation into the ear of a sacrificial victim is performed in nearby Goalpara, a village close to Shantiniketan, also in West Bengal, where a communal goat sacrifice is performed on the last day of the three-day ritual by beheading each goat with a scimitar. After the beheading, the presiding Brahman priest whispers into the right ear of the severed heads one by one. This ritual action demonstrates a symbolic substitution of an animal for an actual human sacrifice, such as the self-sacrifice performed by Lausen. In other parts of the state, a specific white goat termed *lui* is sacrificed as a surrogate for Lausen (Robinson 1980: 170–173).

13 This term refers to a scheduled caste of West Bengal that also ranks low in the local hierarchy, like their Dom counterparts in the textual tradition. Both are known for herding pigs and performing an annual pig sacrifice at Dharma's *pūjā*. See Korom (1999b: 141–142).

14 "Breaking through" into performance is a phrase coined by Hymes (1981) to refer to the verbal parting from the existential world into the narrative one.

15 Scholars of Indian religion and performance traditions, such as Philip Lutgendorf (1989), have noted a similar oscillation between the spoken word and sung speech during acts of ritual recitation. He argues that the actual text of Tulsidas' beloved Ramcharitmanas is a chanted recitation (*pāṭh*), while the oral exegesis (*kathā*) of the narrative, which is to say the interpretation of the text being recited by the cantor, is spoken. The sung or chanted text is thus interspersed with the spoken word reserved for interpretation. This equally applies to the case study presented here, with some necessary and notable modifications.

16 Von Stietencron (1989), for example, even argues that the very term "Hinduism" is a "deceptive" one. Inspired by him and J. Z. Smith's 1990 usage of Christianity in the plural, I have argued that we must do the same with Hinduism. See Korom 2019.

17 Lausen's dog, for example, has a parallel in the Sanskrit Mahabharata, where Yudhishthira, the final Pandava brother to die at the end of their epic battle, is accompanied on his pilgrimage to heaven by a dog, who is actually Dharma in disguise! Such intricate connections must, however, be compared with a healthy dose of caution, since the dog is also an important and pervasive character in the tribal religious practices of the Santal people who live in close proximity to Hindu Bengalis and interact with them daily in cultural, economic, political, ritual, and linguistic ways. See, for example, Bompas (1909).

Works Cited

Ammerman, Nancy T. 2021. *Studying Lived Religion: Contexts and Practices*. New York: New York University Press.

Bandyopādhyāẏ, Asitkumār. 1980. *Bāṅglā Sāhityer Itibritta*, 3. Kalikāt: Maḍārṇ Buk Ejensī.

Bell, Catherine. 1989. "Religion and Chinese Culture: An Assessment of 'Popular Religion'." *History of Religions* 29/1: 35–57.

Bhaṭṭācārja, Āśutoṣ. 1975. *Bāṅglā Maṅgal Kābyer Itihās*. Kalikātā: Mukharji eṇḍ koṅ.

Blackburn, Stewart H. 1985. "Death and Deification: Folk Cults in Hinduism." *History of Religions* 24/3: 255–274.

Blackburn, Stuart H. and Joyce B. Flueckiger. 1989. "Introduction." In *Oral Epics in India*, ed. Stuart H. Blackburn, et al., pp. 1–11. Berkeley: University of California Press.

Bompas, Cecil. 1909. *Folklore of the Santal Parganas*. London: David Butt.

Bowra, Cecil M. 1952. *Heroic Poetry*. London: Macmillan & Co. Ltd.

Briggs, Charles L. 1988. *Competence in Performance: The Creativity of Tradition in Mexicano Verbal Art*. Philadelphia: University of Pennsylvania Press.

Christian Jr., William. 1981. *Local Religion in Sixteenth Century Spain*. Princeton, NJ: Princeton University Press.

Coomaraswamy, Ananda K. 1937. The Nature of "Folklore" and "Popular Art." *Indian Art and Letters* 11/2: 76–84.

Davis, Natalie Z. 1974. "Some Tasks and Themes in the Study of Popular Religion." In *The Pursuit of Holiness in Late Medieval and Renaissance Religion*, ed. Charles Trinkhaus with Heiko A. Oberman, pp. 307–336. Leiden: E.J. Brill.

———. 1982. "From 'Popular Religion' to Religious Cultures." In *Reformation Europe: A Guide to Research*, ed. Steven Ozment, pp. 321–343. St. Louis, MO: Center for Reformation Research.

Dimock, Edward C. 1976. "A Theology of the Repulsive: Some Reflections on the Sitala and other Mangals." In *Bengal: Studies in Literature, Society and History*, ed. Marvin Davis, pp. 69–73. East Lansing: Asian Studies Center, Michigan State University.

Dirks, Nicholas. 1988. *The Hollow Crown: Ethnohistory of an Indian Kingdom*. New York: Cambridge University Press.

Dundes, Alan. 1966. "Metafolklore and Oral Literary Criticism." *The Monist* 50/4: 505–516.

Georges, Robert. 1969. "Toward an Understanding of Storytelling Events." *Journal of American Folklore* 82: 313–328.

Goffman, Erving. 1974. *Frame Analysis: An Essay on the Organization of Experience*. Boston, MA: Northeastern University Press.

Hymes, Dell. 1981. *"In Vain I Tried to Tell You": Essays in Native American Ethnopoetics*. Philadelphia: University of Pennsylvania Press.

Khalek, Muhammad Abdul. 1982. "The Elements of Folk Literature in Mediaeval Bengali Poetry: Folktales." *Journal of the Folklore Research Institute, Bangladesh* 7: 85–97.

Kirshenblatt-Gimblett, Barbara. 1988. "Mistaken Dichotomies." *Journal of American Folklore* 101/400: 140–155.

Korom, Frank J. 1997a. "'Editing' Dharmaraj: Academic Genealogies of a Bengali Folk Deity." *Western Folklore* 56/1: 51–77.

———. 1997b. "Oral Exegesis: Local Interpretations of a Bengali Folk Deity." *Western Folklore* 56/2: 153–173.

———. 1999a. "Reconciling the Local and the Global: The Ritual Space of Shi'i Islam in Trinidad." *Journal of Ritual Studies* 13/1: 21–36.

———. 1999b "'To Be Happy': Ritual, Play, and Leisure in the Bengali Dharmaraj *pūjā*." *International Journal of Hindu Studies* 3/2: 113–164.

———. 2000. "South Asian Religions and Diaspora Studies." *Religious Studies Review* 26/1: 21–28.

———. 2004. "The Bengali Dharmaraj in Text and Context: Some Parallels." *Journal of Indian Philosophy* 32/5–6: 843–870.

———. 2006. *South Asian Folklore: A Handbook*. 2006. Westport, CT: Greenwood Press.

———. 2013. "Introducing the Anthropology of Performance." In *Anthropology of Performance: A Reader*, ed. F. J. Korom, pp. 1–7. Malden, MA: Wiley-Blackwell.

———. 2017. "Introduction: Locating the Study of Folklore in Modern South Asian Studies." *South Asian History and Culture* 8/4 (2017): 404–413.

———. 2019. "On the "ism" in Middle Bengali Religiosity." Unpublished paper presented at the *17th Annual Meeting of the European Association for the Study of Religion*, University of Tartu, Estonia.

———. 2020a. "The World According to Ghanaram: A Partial Translation of His *Gitarāmbha*." In *Wegen durchs Labyrinth: Festschrift zu Ehren von Rahul Peter Das*, ed. C. Brandt and H. Harder, pp. 255–275. Heidelberg, Germany: CrossAsia.

———. 2020b. "Vernacular Religious Movements." In *History of Bangladesh: Sultanate and Mughal Period*, 2, ed. A. M. Chowdhury, pp. 287–320. Dhaka: Asiatic Society of Bangladesh.

Leach, Edmund R (ed.). 1968. *Dialectic in Practical Religion*. Cambridge: Cambridge University Press.

Lord, Albert B. 1960. *The Singer of Tales*. Cambridge, MA: Harvard University Press.

Lutgendorf, Philip. 1989. "A View from the Ghats: Traditional Exegesis of a Hindu Epic." *Journal of Asian Studies* 48/2: 272–288.

Mandelbaum, David G. 1966. "Transcendental and Pragmatic Aspects of Religion." *American Anthropologist* 68/5: 1174–1191.

O'Neil, Mary R. 1986. "From 'Popular' to 'Local' Religion: Issues in Early Modern European Religious History." *Religious Studies Review* 12/3–4: 222–226.

Primiano, Leonard. 1995. "Vernacular Religion and the Search for Method in Religious Folklife." *Western Folklore* 54/1: 37–56.

Raychaudhury, Tapan. 1978. "Medieval Bengali Culture: The Nonelite Elements." In *Mass Culture, Language and Arts in India*, ed. Mahadev L. Apte, pp. 142–151. Bombay: Popular Prakashan.

Redfield, Robert. 1951. *Little Community: Viewpoints for the Study of a Human Whole*. Chicago, IL: University of Chicago Press.

———. 1956. *Peasant Society and Culture: An Anthropological Approach to Civilization*. Chicago: University of Chicago Press.

Ricoeur, Paul. 1971. "What is a Text? Explanation and Interpretation." In *Mythic-Symbolic Language and Philosophical Anthropology*, ed. David Rasmussen, pp. 135–152. The Hague: Martinus Nijhoff.
Robinson, Sandra P. 1980. *The Dharmapuja: A Study of Rites and Symbols Associated with the Bengali Deity Dharmaraj* . Ph. D. Dissertation. Department of South Asian Languages and Civilizations. University of Chicago.
Sanyal, Hitesranjan. 1982. "Literary Sources of Medieval Bengali History: A Study of a Few Mangalkavya Texts." *Occasional Paper No. 52*. Calcutta: Centre for Studies in Social Sciences.
Sen, Sukumār. 1975. *Bāṅglā Sāhityer Itihās*, 1. Barddhamān: Sāhitya Sabhā.
Singer, Milton. 1972. *When a Great Tradition Modernizes: An Anthropological Approach to Indian Civilizations*. New York: Praeger Publishers.
Smith, William L. 1982. "The Celestial Village. The Divine Order in Bengali Myth." *Temenos* 18: 69–81.
Smith, Jonathan Z. 1990. *Drudgery Divine: On the Comparison of Early Christianities and the Religions of Late Antiquity*. Chicago: University of Chicago Press.
Srinivas, M. N. 1956. "A Note on Sanskritization and Westernization." *Far Eastern Quarterly* 15/4: 481–496.
von Stietencron, Heinrich. 1989. "Hinduism: On the Proper Use of a Deceptive Term." In *Representing Hinduism: The Construction of Religious Traditions and National Identity*, ed. Günther Sontheimer and Hermann Kulke, pp. 11–28. Delhi: Manohar.
Wittgenstein, Ludwig. 1953. *Philosophical Investigations*. London: Blackwell Publishing.
Yoder, Don. 1974. "Toward a Definition of Folk Religion." *Western Folklore* 33/1: 2–15.

2

THE *SĀDHŪ* WHO CAME FOR LUNCH

Revising Tropes of Disconnection in the Jain Diaspora[1]

Tine Vekemans

Differences between Jain monastic and lay lifestyles, as established in doctrinal texts and perpetuated by traditional community structure, lead to marked differences in patterns of mobility. These differences in mobility suggest an absolute rift between the estimated 300,000 lay Jains[2] that have settled outside of South Asia and the Jain mendicant community confined to South Asia. Combining historical examples and observations from ethnographic fieldwork,[3] I argue that diaspora–mendicant interactions are more common and varied than often thought. Juxtaposing widely held expectations of mendicant absence with the observed lived reality of—albeit limited—mendicant presence, the contrast reflects a clash between two approaches to the study of religion, i.e. a 'top-down' approach starting from doctrine and a proposed ideal of orthodoxy, and a 'bottom-up' approach focussing on individual sentiment, belief, and practice. Case studies conducted through a lens of vernacular religion are a helpful tool to productively study diasporic lay–mendicant interactions; such interactions reveal Jainism as it is lived, interpreted, and performed by different individuals within a modern context.

Introduction: The Fourfold Jain Community and Two-Tiered Applied Ethics

Jainism is a religious tradition that came to prominence in the sixth century BCE in South Asia. *Mahāvīra*, Jainism's twenty-fourth enlightened teacher, is acknowledged to have been an older contemporary of the Buddha. The focus of the Jain tradition, generally, is the individual soul's journey through multiple rebirths towards ultimate enlightenment and liberation.[4] Sociologically, the Jain community consists of four groups, divided over two categories. In the lay category,

DOI: 10.4324/9781003257462-4

we find (1) male and (2) female 'householders.' In the mendicant category, we find (3) male and (4) female renouncers – referred to as 'mendicants,' 'monks/ *sādhūs*,' and 'nuns/*sādhvīs*.' The principles for which Jainism stands are identical for lay Jains and mendicants alike,[5] but the way these principles are translated into rules and vows that structure daily life differs significantly. Rules set forth for lay adherents are flexible to enable them to perform duties to family and society; the rules set forth for Jains who take initiation as monks or nuns are more stringent.[6] Traditionally, lay and mendicant communities are intertwined through mutual service. Lay people feed the mendicant community, provide services as needed, and supply mendicants with medication when necessary. Mendicants inspire devotion in their lay followers, for these religious figures are symbols of spiritual progress. Additionally, they provide the lay community with teachings on Jain principles, offering both worldly and spiritual advice (Babb 2016: 54, 62–63).

The two-tiered interpretation of Jainism's ethical imperative (i.e. somewhat flexible rules for lay adherents and more stringent injunctions for mendicants) has resulted in divergent modes of mobility. The mendicant lifestyle instructs monks and nuns to lead a wandering, peripatetic life for most of the year. They are not allowed to use mechanical means of transport—cars or planes—and must stay close to a sufficiently sized lay community, for they rely on that community for sustenance in the form of daily alms. These rules and injunctions lead to mendicants enacting high mobility within a limited radius but make it impossible for Jain mendicants to travel outside the subcontinent. When lay Jains move away from the South Asia, as they have done in increasing numbers starting in the early twentieth century, the intensity and modes of contact with the mendicant community inevitably change. The effects of the straining of lay–mendicant connections are an aspect of diaspora Jainism[7] that regularly arises in scholarly work on the Jain diaspora, as well as in accounts by diaspora Jains when they relate how the different strands of mutual interdependence dissolve or become severely strained when lay Jains settle outside of South Asia. Collective, social, and sensory aspects of traditional lay–mendicant interaction—such as giving food alms from the family kitchen to passing nuns, joining a crowd to listen to a monk's discourse, and touching a monk's feet—make way for a more individual, cerebral version of devotion, centring on practices such as including a picture of a monk or nun in the home shrine or collecting books, audio recordings, or video clips of mendicants. These mendicant figures and ascetic traditions thus become a part of the religious tradition which is addressed indirectly through inspirational stories and contemplations, but not directly engaged with, except by those devoted enough to travel to India and seek interactions they personally perceive as authentic.[8]

This radical reduction and transformation of lay–mendicant interactions gives rise to the common trope in which diaspora Jains are perceived to be cut off from the mendicant community. However, as my own experiences conducting fieldwork in different locations in the diaspora will illustrate below, this trope obscures a much more diverse reality of experience and praxis and, thereby, must be revised.

Mendicant Encounters in the Jain Diaspora

> *I'm afraid we will have to reschedule our interview today, but if you can make it, please do come to our house. This will be interesting for you. A* sādhū-jī[9] *is coming for lunch…*
>
> *Voicemail message, Nov. 2016, Atlanta (USA)*

My interest in the subject matter at hand can be traced back to this short voicemail message. I was in the USA for fieldwork on the Jain diaspora and digital media, and I remember being so puzzled by the contents of the message that I stood in my hotel room and listened to it two more times. My field notes during the lunch with the *sādhū-jī* resonate the same confusion:

> *I was seated on one end of the table, next to my respondent. There were about ten people present, all with their attention fixed upon the* sādhū-jī *(?), who was installed in what was clearly the place of honour, at the centre of the table. He was dressed in white monks' robes. The man of the house and a family friend were seated on either side, and these three men were engaged in lively conversation on the* sādhū's *work in Hong Kong (?!) while eating together, passing dishes to each other, etc. The lady of the house [my respondent] was less involved in the conversation, but was beaming, clearly honoured to have this* sādhū-jī *in her house.*
>
> *Field notes, Nov. 2016, Atlanta (USA)*

From what I thought I knew about Jainism, the stringent rules imposed on initiated monks and nuns made it impossible for them to be present in North America. For that matter, how could they sit down with lay followers for a festive meal? Hence, the '(?)' in my notes and the focus on eating arrangements. In a subsequent interview with the *sādhū-jī* who came to lunch, who was named Nirmalsagar (°unknown, $^{d.}$1978), I learnt that he has resided in Hong Kong since 2004. While he left his mendicant order in India, he felt compelled to share his wisdom with Jain adherents overseas. At the time of our interview, he gave regular religious classes in Hong Kong and occasional lectures and talks elsewhere.

Following my first confusing encounter in Atlanta, I came across other mendicants and mendicant-like figures in London and Antwerp. In an interview with a teacher at Shri Chandana Vidyapeeth (SCVP) in London—namely, a Jain *pāthśālā* (religious school) for children and adults run in collaboration with the India-based charity Veerayatan—I was enthusiastically informed about the impending visit of the ācārya (mendicant leader) of the *Amarmuni Sampradāy*, the mendicant lineage behind the charity. In London and Miami, I experienced the role Terapanth *samaṇīs*[10] take up in diaspora communities and institutions. In Antwerp, I observed the impact of occasional mendicant visits. Respondents devoted to lay gurus in the tradition of Śrimad Rājchandra[11] (Salter 2002) often indicated that they maintained close personal relationships with their respective gurus, and I was whisked away for a meet and greet with one such guru,

Rakeshbhai Zaveri, when we were both attending a play by his followers in St. Albans. I became aware, additionally, of diverse modes of computer-mediated communication and interaction between respondents in the diaspora and mendicants in India, representing an increasingly common avenue of digital religion.

Back home, reading field notes and interview transcripts, I concluded that while some respondents sincerely lamented the lack of lay–mendicant interaction available to them, other experiences and observations refuted the idea of an absolute rift and indicated the presence of different types of mendicants and mendicant-like figures in the diaspora. I set out to investigate further.

History and Typology of Mendicants in the Jain Diaspora

The presence of Jain mendicants outside South Asia has developed in tandem with the formation of the modern Jain diaspora, and it is therefore a relatively recent development. However, such departures from the stereotypical ideal of the wandering mendicant have emerged in Jainism at various times throughout its history. The *chaityavāsin* movement (domestication of mendicants) did not so much centre on the use of mechanical transport which is necessary to enable a mendicant presence outside of South Asia but rather introduced the idea that monks could have a fixed abode. This movement created Jain mendicant classes separate from the fully initiated wandering mendicants; in these groups, mendicants could own property and generally stay in one place (Jain 2010: 860–866). In the *digambara* tradition, clothed *bhaṭṭārakas* (sedentary clerics) were at times more numerous than the naked peripatetic monks (Detige 2020). The śvetāmbara tradition similarly brought forth the now all-but-defunct category of *yati* – sedentary renouncers (Babb 2016: 65; Cort 2001: 43–46; Villalobos 2021).

Since the 1970s, the growing Jain diaspora and the rise in international events pertaining to spirituality and interfaith affairs appealing to Jains have renewed the examination of Jain teachings and traditional rules of conduct. Within lay and mendicant institutional contexts as well as on an individual level, the desirability of adapting mendicant practice to the necessities of modern-day life and the potential benefits of reaching out to Jains overseas were considered.[12] Debates no longer centre around mendicants leading a sedentary life or managing property; rather, they concern possibilities for reaching out to global audiences, by facilitating forms of overseas travel or by enabling digital communication. The first mendicants to respond to invitations to travel overseas did so on an individual basis, and they explicitly or tacitly left their monastic orders. Some of these travelling mendicants choose to settle overseas, while others continue to live in India but travel overseas on a regular basis. After leaving their orders, these figures are denoted independent or former mendicants. Institutionalized mendicant travel existed to a small extent in the first half of the twentieth century in the guise of those aforementioned *bhaṭṭārakas* and *yatis*, but new iterations followed, especially in the decades after the first individual mendicants chose to travel.

In addition to the mendicants discussed above, some religious authority figures in Jainism are not part of a mendicant lineage and have not taken initiation. Such spiritual gurus develop teacher–devotee relationships with their followers that reflect significant aspects of the traditional lay–mendicant relationship and may resemble traditional mendicants in their dress and lifestyle. Although lay teachers have existed in Jainism for centuries, the tradition of the late nineteenth-century lay philosopher Śrimad Rājchandra led to several lineages of lay gurus with diverse claims to advanced spiritual progress or self-realization. As these gurus have not taken mendicant initiation, they are not bound by the rules that traditionally govern mendicant life. As such, they can travel abroad and make use of technology without much deliberation.

Individual Travelling Monks

Settlers and Visitors

One of the first and perhaps the most famous monk responding to the stream of invitations was the Śvetāmbara monk Chandraprabhasāgara (°1922, $^{\text{d.}}$1942, $^{\times}$2019), who became known as gurudev Chitrabhanu. Although his personal motivations to go against injunctions and travel the world were undoubtedly complex, engaging with the growing Jain diasporic community and teaching Jainism to European and American students and seekers was a strong factor (Dundas 2002: 273; Rosenfield 1981). Chitrabhanu travelled to Europe, East-Africa, Hong Kong, and the USA, where he eventually settled in New York City. While lay Jains had occasionally been invited to speak at interfaith events, the presence of this Jain monk at events such as the World Vegetarian Congress in the Netherlands and the Third Spiritual Summit Conference at Harvard Divinity School inspired awe and was instrumental in making Jainism and its philosophy known to the broader public. In the USA, Chitrabhanu established the Jain Meditation International Center, which was initially meant to accommodate his Western disciples but also attracted local Jains; the center grew into the first Jain temple in the USA.[13] Five years after Chitrabhanu, another Jain monk settled in the USA. Sushil Kumar (°1926, $^{\text{d.}}$1941, $^{\times}$1994), a śvētāmbar *sthānakvāsi* monk, left India to travel in 1975. In the USA, he established International Mahavir Jain Mission (IMJM) in 1981, which also manages Siddhachalam (established in 1983), the self-proclaimed first Jain *tīrth* (pilgrimage destination) outside India. He also established a new Jain lineage, the Arhat Sangh, of which he was named the main ācārya in 1980 (Federation of JAINA 1994: 35). Together with Chitrabhanu, Sushil Kumar was instrumental in organizing American Jain communities under the umbrella of the Federation for Jain Associations in North America (JAINA) and providing the non-sectarian and engaged ideology that underpins this organization's project today.

A more recent arrival on the North American scene is Acharya Shree Yogeesh (°1955, $^{\text{d.}}$1970), who runs ashrams (religious retreats) and related organizations in

India, North America, and Estonia. In the USA, Siddhayatan Hindu-Jain[14] *tīrth* (pilgrimage centre) is his main location. More broadly non-sectarian than the teachings of Chitrabhanu and Sushil Kumar, Yogeesh offers spiritual teachings that combine elements of Jain philosophy and yoga. Although his de-emphasis of religious boundaries appeals to American and Mexican followers and seekers with no South-Asian origins, it seems to have impeded large-scale support within the diasporic Jain community. That said, Yogeesh was the first to perform Jain initiation ceremonies in North America.[15] Outside North America, similar figures have settled in other places where there is a Jain diaspora community. Nirmalsagar (whom I met in Atlanta, cf. supra) is based in Hong Kong, and Satish Kumar (°1936, d.1945), who left his monk order at 18 to become a Gandhi-inspired peace activist, in the UK (Kumar 1992).

Whereas the monks above are based in the diaspora, others, like ācārya Dr. Lokesh Muni[16] and the brothers of the *Bhandu Triputi*,[17] are based in India, but travel abroad on invitation. Although he travelled only once (to visit the Jain community in Kenya), Kanji Swami (°1889, d.1913, ×1980), a śvētāmbar *sthānakvāsi* monk turned celibate *digambar* lay teacher, succeeded in gaining a sizeable following in Gujarat, and the Gujarati Jain diaspora (Dundas 2002: 265–267, 271).

Independent and Former Mendicants

The border between independent mendicant[18] (someone who has left their mendicant order) and a former mendicant (someone who has left their mendicant order and is no longer considered a mendicant) is often unclear. In the former category are placed Sushil Kumar, Dr. Lokesh Muni, and Yogeesh, who have left their original monastic order but continue to wield the title of ācārya within their own circle of followers and organizations and live according to their own interpretation of mendicant customs. In the latter category are placed former monks now considered lay teachers, such as Chitrabhanu and Satish Kumar, whose decision to marry and raise a family cemented the departure from monkhood, and Kanji Swami, who explicitly stated he was to be seen as a lay teacher. While not retaining monastic titles, all three retained elements of the mendicant lifestyle. Their previous experience as Jain monks adds to their charisma and knowledge as teachers, and they are commonly referred to with the honorific '*guru*' or '*gurudev*.'

Institutionalized Mendicant Travel and Western Orders

Individual monks who decided to travel had a major impact on Jainism's fame in the Western world and on the Jain communities in diaspora. In India, the evidence of their impact within the Jain diaspora and their contribution towards a global understanding of Jainism amplified discussions within lay and mendicant circles regarding the viability of institutionalized frameworks within which travel might be allowed for Jain mendicants. At the same time, initiatives emerged to organize Jain monastic lineages based outside South Asia. These initiatives have not been successful. In the USA, Shree Yogeesh's initiates are not of South-Asian origin, and his organization attracts mostly non-Jain westerners. In the UK, the establishment of a separate mendicant order within the diaspora, with customs and injunctions tailored to a Western context and Jain diasporic needs, was theorized by Natubhai Shah in 1996 (Shah 1996: 23–33), but the *Western Order of Jainism* he proposed has not come into being.

Existing lineages and subgroups have addressed international travel in different ways. The *Amarmuni Sampradāy*, led by Shri Chandanaji Maharaj, who is as yet the only *sādhvī* to have risen to the rank of ācārya, remains the only lineage where mendicants retain their rank and place in spite of occasional international travel. Others have addressed this issue in another way. Instead of lifting the ban on mechanized travelling for fully ordained monks and nuns, *Ācārya* Tulsi of the Śvetāmbara Terapanth tradition established a separate intermediate order of *samaṇ* and *samaṇīs* (male and female partially initiated mendicants) in 1980. Although these monks and nuns take most of the same vows of regular mendicants, they do not take vows prohibiting travel or the use of electricity. *Samaṇīs* are typically involved in education, teaching classes (on Jainism but also philosophy and languages) at Jain *pāṭhśālās* as well as at universities (for example SOAS in London, Ghent University in Belgium, and Florida International University in the USA). Other subgroups have similarly strengthened intermediate orders who do not take vows limiting travel, such as the *bhaṭṭārakas* in Digambara Jainism.

Gurus as Global Spiritual Guides

In addition to occasional travelling monks and former monks discussed above, lay gurus have come to prominence in India as well as in the diaspora. Considered self-realized by their followers, they are invested with considerable religious authority and treated with devotion. Shrimad Rajchandra Mission Dharampur, led by Rakesh Zaveri 'Gurudev' (°1966), is the most widespread, but Shree Raj Saubhag, with an ashram in Sayla in Gujarat and led by Nalinbhai Kothari 'Bhaishree' (°1943), also has several disciples in the UK. Both groups base their teachings on the work of the late nineteenth-century lay philosopher Śrimad Rājchandra, whose writings, together with those of the current guru, are studied by followers in regular reading groups. A personal relationship with the guru is actively encouraged and cultivated. The prominence of these lay gurus and the organizations that formed around them derives from the growing number of followers who attend reading groups and other activities, but also, especially in the case of SRMD, from organizations' involvement in religious education and charity events that attract significant numbers of attendees who may not consider themselves followers of the guru.

Constructing Digital Bridges

> *What I miss here is the contact with sādhvīs. We don't get to be in their presence, hear them speak, or seek their advice. I like to look for their pravachans on YouTube. Listening to them relaxes me and makes me feel [hesitates ...] connected somehow.*
>
> *Interview, T., Ann Arbor (USA)*

The diasporic presence of mendicants and mendicant-like figures has a profound impact on Jains outside South Asia. Such figures are instrumental in setting up diaspora organizations, like JAINA and the SCVP school, and they have contributed to the affirmation of the diaspora as an integral part, instead of a far periphery, of the Jain world (Flügel 2012: 978; Long 2009: 79–80). However, the mendicant presence in the Jain diaspora remains limited. Parallel to the rise in physical presence of Jain mendicants and mendicant-like figures in the diaspora, another process has unfolded which further increases lay–mendicant interactions in the diaspora as well as in India. The rise of digital media from the 1990s onwards has brought about new ways to access materials about Jain monks and nuns, as my respondent above clearly appreciates. Computer-mediated communication technologies enable new modes to connect with mendicants from anywhere across the globe. These developments have required a negotiation of the traditional rules in a way similar to the reassessment of travel restrictions for mendicants.[19]

Some groups and organizations, including several described above, maintain an elaborate digital presence, but many groups that uphold the absolute injunction against overseas travel also make allowances for technology. The use of microphones and recording materials, once rare, has become widespread, leading to a proliferation of images but also audio and video lectures in different types of media. The use of mobile phones and computers by mendicants is gaining popularity, enabling year-round individual and group communication with lay devotees, irrespective of geographical location (telephone calls, WhatsApp messages, emails, and comments on social media). This represents an important shift in opportunities for lay–mendicant interaction. Without such channels of communication, lay Jains seeking to interact with mendicants would have to follow them around or encounter them by chance, as monks and nuns lead a wandering existence for most of the year. Only during the four-month rainy season retreat, when mendicants would be sedentary and stay in a pre-selected town or village, was it easier for lay followers to find them and seek guidance (Vekemans 2019). Although computer-mediated interactions lack some features of in-person encounters, they add to the feeling of rapprochement between the lay and mendicant community. Just like the loosening travel restrictions discussed previously, this negotiated media presence can be especially impactful for Jains living outside India.

Studying the *Sādhū* Who Came for Lunch: A Vernacular Religion Perspective

Online and in-person encounters with Jain mendicants and mendicant-like figures in the USA, Belgium, and the UK ran counter to my expectations. These expectations were based on prescriptive, doctrinal readings of Jainism, and further fed by recurring tropes about the radical absence of mendicants in the diaspora and the resultant themes of loss and isolation. Such themes are found in scholarly work and textbooks, but they also appear in Jain discourses on diaspora. Indeed, they are quite common in the interviews I conducted. Unpacking the reasons behind this apparent incongruity is crucial to finding a research perspective that recognizes the feeling of isolation from the mendicant community, while also taking into account the growing presence of mendicants and mendicant-like figures and computer-mediated communication with mendicants in the diaspora as authentic and engaged forms of religious practice.

Regarding explanations of mendicant absence in scholarly work on Jainism, John E. Cort's 1990 article 'Models of and for the Study of the Jains' points out the scholarly preference for the doctrine of Jainism, rather than the individual religious practice of Jains, as a subject of study. While doctrine-focussed studies are not factually wrong, their emphasis leads to a severe restriction in the scope of subsequent studies, with little positive attention to Jainism as it is lived (Cort 1990: 44).

Discussing popular Hinduism, C.J. Fuller makes a similar remark, showing how even in the discipline of anthropology, the yardstick of orthodoxy is frequently used to measure, and find wanting, religious lives and practices (Fuller 2004: 27). This all-too-common analytical mistake has a real impact on the way both academic and non-academic understandings of culture and religion are constructed. In our case, real-life practices and interpretations not conforming to the orthodox ideal, such as travelling or video-chatting Jain mendicants, have often been overlooked by scholars, and denigrated as peripheral, borrowed from other traditions, inauthentic, or corrupt by both scholars and Jains themselves.

Indeed, the expectations of a radical absence of mendicants created or at least reinforced by scholarly literature are further fed by Jains bemoaning the impossibility of authentic contact with the mendicant community outside South Asia. The reason for the pervasive presence of such narratives of absence and separation in discussions and descriptions from within the diaspora Jain community is complex. In some cases, lay Jain respondents also present prescriptive accounts of what Jain practice should be rather than descriptive accounts of Jain practice. However, the feeling of being cut off from the mendicant community, of absence—sometimes even deprivation—expressed by some of my respondents is sincere. In fact, it is as sincere as the jubilant pride evident in the voicemail message I received informing me a *sādhū* was coming for lunch at my respondent's house. The simultaneous presence of these two sentiments reminds us that the lay–mendicant interactions discussed above are a relatively recent phenomenon, with an uneven geographic spread. Moreover, the options available may not meet the spiritual needs of every individual. Jains living in more remote areas may not have the opportunity to seek out such interactions. Similarly, though computer-mediated communication with mendicants is possible regardless of geographical location, not all lay people have the necessary skills to avail of this opportunity.

To account for, and be able to productively study, the inherent diversity of belief and praxis in Jainism, Cort recommends concrete and practice-based case studies, using what may be called a lived religion perspective (Cort 1990). Moreover, the cases under discussion here demand an approach to religion that explicitly allows for diversity and even contradiction of belief and practice on an individual as well as a collective level, for both lay people and figures traditionally invested with religious authority. Primiano's discussion of vernacular religion as a theoretical and methodological framework can be particularly useful here. Like Cort and Fuller, Primiano critiques approaches that measure religious practices against an imagined or constructed 'pure' core. He then proposes vernacular religion as an alternative that gives due attention to the individual as well as the context (Primiano 1995: 42). Moreover, he emphasizes that every religious actor, both lay and clergy/mendicant, develops their own set of individual meanings, interpretations, beliefs, and practices (Primiano 1995: 47). Taking on this vernacular perspective allows us to simultaneously recognize the anger expressed by devotees in India and Chitrabhanu's decision to travel and teach abroad as valid expressions of religious expression and belief. Similarly, it enables us to approach the attitude of devotion exhibited by my respondent towards the *sādhū* who came for lunch and the feeling of deprivation from mendicant contact expressed by others as two authentic iterations of Jain practice and belief. Stepping away from an abstract notion of orthodoxy, we can now make sense of such apparent contradictions as not mutually exclusive, but rather existing as separate vernacularizations which draw from and interact with Jain doctrine and ideals in different ways.

Conclusion: Accepted Absence and Negotiated Presence

A detailed assessment of the impact of these online and in-person diasporic lay–mendicant interactions that have stayed under the scholarly radar will require more research. An approach based on case studies of religion as it is lived, taking a vernacular religion perspective, can account for the internal oppositions and tensions of these encounters. Moreover, such a perspective also guards against rash judgements based on dichotomies of orthodox/heterodox or India/diaspora.

Although care should be taken not to over-estimate the presence of Jain mendicants outside South Asia, my own experiences in places with large Jain communities, such as London, indicate that regular in-person interactions with *samaṇīs* and lay teachers, as well as occasional encounters with gurus and mendicants, have become normalized. In-person interactions between lay Jains and the different types of Jain mendicants and mendicant-like figures indicate that both parties conceptualize these encounters and their role in them as sincere and invested Jain religious practice. The exchanges display the same dynamics of devotion and care reciprocated with religious and worldly guidance and teaching that are considered typical for lay–mendicant interactions in India. When consuming digital content featuring mendicants (a typical example being YouTube videos of sermons) or communicating with monks and nuns via mobile phone, WhatsApp, or email, the situation is somewhat, if not radically, different. Although in-person contact is generally preferred, these digital interactions are a meaningful part of religious life and practice for many Jains today.

Lay Jains in the diaspora are mostly aware of rules traditionally inhibiting overseas travel and use of technology by mendicants. Many in the diaspora voice a deep respect for those sects and lineages that do not deviate at all from the traditional injunctions and appreciate the exemplary function of such mendicants as epitomes of Jain values and detachment. However, this does not lessen their respect for smartphone-wielding and travelling mendicants, semi-initiated orders, and gurus. Religious authority figures that travel and spend time in the Jain diaspora are revered and inspire devotion within and beyond the borders of their own subsect, and they are sometimes even preferred by next-generation diasporic Jains seeking advice. These young(er) Jains argue that an awareness of the context within which youth in the West are expected to function better enables mendicants to take up a role of guide and advisor in both spiritual and worldly affairs (Vekemans 2019).

The diminished importance of (hereditary) sectarian affiliation among second- and third-generation Jains in the diaspora, spurred in part by the ongoing push towards a non-sectarian Jainism started by Chitrabhanu and Sushil Kumar in the 1970s and emanating from a.o. JAINA, has further enabled a more individual, pick-and-choose type of Jain religious practice. Attending events organized by different groups and interacting with gurus, *samaṇīs*, and mendicants whenever the opportunity presents itself is increasingly considered normal, even a sign of religious interest and spirituality. The line-up of speakers for the opening ceremony at the biannual JAINA convention in July 2021 illustrates this.[20] After some statements by the organizers emphasizing the need to be 'just Jain,' rather than identifying primarily as belonging to a given sect or group, announced speakers included such non-traditional mendicant figures as Acharya Shri Dr. Lokesh Muniji (independent travelling monk), Acharya Shri Chandanaji (travelling *sādhvī* of the *Amarmuni Sampradāy*), Pujya Gurudev Shri Rakeshbhai (living guru of the Shrimad Rājchandra tradition), and Shri Charukeerthi Bhattaraka Swamiji (*digambara bhaṭṭāraka*). This line-up underscores the importance of these travelling mendicants and mendicant-like figures to diaspora Jainism.

Notes

1 The research presented in this chapter was made possible by Research Foundation Flanders (FWO), grant number 12T7320N.
2 The number of Jains outside India is not definite. Based on estimates made by researchers, as well as Jain community leaders, it is assumed that between 150,000 and 300,000 Jains live outside India. An estimated 30,000 live in the UK. The numbers of Jains in North America are estimated as low as 50,000 (Dundas 2002, Jain 1998) and as high as 150,000 (Jain 2011). There are further Jain communities in a.o. Belgium, Hong Kong, Japan, Dubai, and Kenya.
3 Materials for this chapter are drawn from a decade of research into various aspects of Jainism—especially Jainism and migration and Jainism and digital media—including ethnographic fieldwork in Jain communities in India, Belgium, the UK, and North America (2013–2019). This research was conducted at the University of Ghent in Belgium, also funded under varied grants from The Research Foundation – Flanders (FWO).
4 For a robust introduction into Jainism, Jain doctrine, and Jain philosophy, refer to Babb (2016), Dundas (2002), or Cort (2001).
5 The five core values of Jainism are non-violence (*ahiṃsā*), non-attachment (*aparigraha*), not stealing (*asteya*), truth (*satya*), and celibacy (*brahmacarya*).
6 For example, *ahiṃsā* requires the layperson eat only vegetarian foods. The same principle applied to a mendicant prohibits the use of electricity and requires the use of a broom to gently shoo away small creatures that might otherwise be crushed beneath the mendicant's feet.
7 For an introduction to Jainism as organized and practiced in the diaspora, see Banks (1992), Flügel (2012), Vallelly (2002, 2004), Donaldson (2015), Shah (2011), and Vekemans (2019, 2021).
8 Some Jains in the diaspora actively seek a more full experience and enactment of the traditional lay–mendicant relationship as part of their own religious or spiritual development. When respondents designate the interactions they seek as 'authentic', they refer to the fact that India remains the heartland of the tradition and the only country where mendicant orders and mendicants follow the traditional rules in their original context. Sometimes the interactions between visiting diaspora Jains and mendicants in India are limited to a short conversation and a devotional touching of the feet. However, spiritually inclined members of diaspora communities occasionally travel to India to stay and travel with a group of mendicants for prolonged periods of time. The increased democratization of air travel from the end of the 1970s onwards has made this type of travel more feasible for those diaspora individuals seeking to interact with monks and nuns in a traditional setting. Even so, long stays require an amount of determination, planning, money, logistics, and stamina that make such journeys impractical, if not impossible, to many Jains.
9 The suffix *–jī* is commonly used in Hindi to mark respect.
10 The Śvetāmbar Terāpanth is a Sthānakvāsī mendicant lineage founded in the eighteenth century by Ācārya Bhikṣu, and still unified under one ācārya. They founded an order of intermediate-level novice mendicants called *samaṇ* (m.) and *samaṇī* (f.). These 'half-initiated mendicants' take most of the vows full mendicants take, but do not have to lead a peripatetic life, and they are allowed to travel, handle money, and provide their own food if necessary. This enables them to study at universities, visit Jain communities in the diaspora, etc. At the moment, *samaṇs* are very rare, whereas there is a significant number of *samaṇīs*. After some time, in consultation with the ācārya of their lineage, they take full initiation and become peripatetic mendicants.
11 Important guru-led movements in the twentieth and twenty-first centuries centre on the figure of Shrimad Rājchandra (°1867, ×1901), who was a friend and advisor to Mahatma Gandhi. Srimad Rajchandra Mission Dharampur (SRCMD) and Shree Raj Saubhag in Sayla have a significant following in the diaspora.

12 With different degrees of knowledge about traditional strictures of monastic life, organizations and individuals outside India had approached Jain mendicants with invitations and requests, conflicting with mendicant ideals. Spiritual seekers and interfaith organizers in the USA and Europe did not fully realize why their inviting initiated monks to participate in events outside South Asia was problematic. Jain communities and individuals outside South Asia who send invitations to spend *cātur-mās* (the sedentary rainy season) among them were most definitely aware that rules would have to be reinterpreted to make such a visit possible. However, recognizing their own needs, and perhaps wanting to subscribe to the tradition of the *vijñaptipatra* (invitation letters sent to invite monks to spend the rainy season), they continued to extend their invitations anyway.
13 https://www.asian-voice.com/News/International/In-memory-of-Gurudev-Shri-Chitrabhanuji.
14 The inclusion of Hindus and Jains in one organization and/or place of worship is quite common in the South Asian diaspora in North America. In places where the Jain community is too small or spread out to make a Jain centre or temple feasible, a Jain shrine is included into a Hindu temple. Although Jainism is generally considered to be a separate tradition, the cultural and ritual practices of Jainism and Hinduism are sufficiently similar to make such Hindu–Jain collaborations possible.
15 The first North American Jain nun to be ordained into Shree Yogeesh's lineage, the Siddha Sangh, was Sadhvi Siddhali Shree, formerly a US Army Iraq veteran (siddhalishree.com). Since her initiation in 2008, two other North American disciples of Yogeesh have been initiated.
16 Lokesh Muni (°1961), based in Delhi, first left the Terapanth order in which he was originally ordained for the Manmalji order, but later he resigned from all his functions entirely (*Ahimsa Times*).
17 Shree Jinchandraji Maharaj (Bandhu Triputi Muni www.jinjimaharaj.com; see also http://www.jainpedia.org/themes/practices/monks-and-nuns/mendicant-lifestyle/contentpage/6.html?tx_contagged%5Bsource%5D=default&tx_contagged%5Buid%5D=6&cHash=d2110767a5e2332729500b678a73830a).
18 The term 'independent' is used on the website www.jainsamaj.org, where Sushil Kumar and Lokesh Muni are listed as belonging to category of 'śvētāmbar – Independent sect.'
19 Traditionally, Jain mendicants do not make use of modern technology. The reason for this is dual. First, upon entering the monastic state, Jain mendicants forsake all worldly possessions (to the exception of the bare essentials such as robes, a water pot, and a brush). Ownership of a personal computer or smartphone is impossible. Second, the use of electricity, considered a form of fire, is seen to inherently involve violence. In their bid to live in accordance with the principle of *ahiṃsā*, the use of electrical appliances is minimized or avoided entirely (Cort 2001: 55).
20 https://www.jainaconvention.org.

Works Cited

Babb, Lawrence A. 2016. *Understanding Jainism* (Indian edition). Mumbai: Hindi Granth Karyalay.

Banks, Marcus. 1992. *Organizing Jainism in India and England*. Oxford: Clarendon Press.

Cort, John E. 1990. "Models of and for the Study of the Jains." *Method & Theory in the Study of Religion*, Vol. 2, No. 1, pp. 42–71.

Cort, John E. 2001. *Jains in the World: Religious Values and Ideology in India*. Oxford: Oxford University Press.

Detige, Tillo. 2020. "Digambara Renouncers in Western and Central India, c. 1100–1800." In Knut Jacobsen (ed.) *Brill's Encyclopaedia of Jainism*. Leiden: Brill.

Donaldson, Brianne. 2015. "Jains in America: A Socially Engaged Second Generation." *Pantheos Public Square* (July 1). www.patheos.com/topics/future-of-faith-in-america/eastern-religions/jains-in-america-brianne-donaldson-07-01-2015.html.

Dundas, Paul. 2002. *The Jains* (2nd ed.). London: Routledge.

Federation of JAINA. 1994. *Jain Digest Special Issue: Crusader of Peace and Non-Violence.* Vol. 6. USA: Federation of Jaina.

Flügel, Peter. 2012. "Jainism." In Helmut K. Anheier and Mark Juergensmeyer (eds.) *Encyclopaedia of Global Studies.* Vol. 3, pp. 975–979. Thousand Oaks: Sage Publishing.

Fuller, C.J. 2004. *The Camphor Flame: Popular Hinduism and Society in India.* Princeton and Oxford: Princeton University Press.

Jain, Sulekh C. 1998. "Evolution of Jainism in North-America." In Sagarmal Jain and Shriprakash Paney (eds.) *Jainism in a Global Perspective*, pp. 293–300. Varanasi: Pārśvanātha Vidyāpīṭha.

Jain, Kailash Chand. 2010. *History of Jainism: Vol. 3 Medieval Jainism.* Delhi: D.K.

Jain, Prakash C. 2011. *Jains in India and Abroad, A Sociological Introduction.* New Delhi: ISJS.

Kumar, Bhuvanendra. 1996. *Jainism in America.* Tempe: Jain Humanities Press.

Kumar, Satish. 1992. *No Destination: Autobiography of an Earth Pilgrim.* Devon: Green Books.

Long, Jeffrey D. 2009. *Jainism: An Introduction.* London and New York: I. B. Tauris & Company Limited.

Primiano, Leonard Norman. 1995. "Vernacular Religion and the Search for Method in Religious Folklife." *Western Folklore*, Vol. 54, No. 1, pp. 37–56.

Rosenfield, Clare. 1981. *Gurudev Shree Chitrabanu: a Man with a Vision.* Mumbai and New York: Divine Knowledge Society/Jain Meditation International Center.

Salter, Emma. 2002. *Raj Bhakta Marg: The Path of Devotion to Srimad Rajcandra. A Jain Community in the Twenty First Century.* Doctoral thesis, University of Wales.

Shah, Bindi V. 2011. "Vegetarianism and Veganism: Vehicles to Maintain Ahimsa and Reconstruct Jain Identity among Young Jains in the UK and USA." In Manish A. Vyas (ed.) *Issues in Ethics and Animal Rights*, 108–118. New Delhi: Regency Publications.

Shah, Natubhai. 1996. "Western Order of Jainism." *Jain Journal*, Vol. 31, No. 1, pp. 23–33.

Vallely, Anne. 2002. "From Liberation to Ecology: Ethical Discourses among Orthodox and Diaspora Jains." In Christopher Chapple (ed.) *Jainism and Ecology*, 193–213. Cambridge: Harvard University Press.

Vallely, Anne. 2004. "The Jain Plate: The Semiotics of the Diaspora Diet." In Knut A. Jacobsen and Pratap P. Kumar (eds.) *South Asians in the Diaspora: Histories and Religious Traditions*, 3–22. Boston: Brill.

Vekemans, Tine. 2019. "Roots, Routes, and Routers: Social and Digital Dynamics in the Jain Diaspora." *Religions*, Vol. 10, No. 4, 252.

Vekemans, Tine. 2020. *Jains in Belgium.* In K.A. Jacobsen (ed.) *Encyclopaedia of Jainism.* Brill. https://doi.org/10.1163/2590-2768_BEJO_COM_045011.

Vekemans, Tine. 2021. "Lost and Found, Centre and Periphery: Narratives of the Jain Diasporic Experience Online." *South Asian Diaspora*, Vol. 13, No. 1, pp. 65–80. https://doi.org/10.1080/19438192.2020.1773137.

Villalobos, Eric Daniel. 2021. "Yatis in Contemporary Mūrtipūjaka Śvetāmbara Jainism." *Centre of Jaina Studies Newsletter*, Vol. 16, pp. 26–28.

Wiley, Kristi L. 2006. *The A to Z of Jainism.* New Delhi: Vision Books.

3

WHAT MAKES FOLK BUDDHISM?

Alyson Prude

> My mother died when I was a baby. My father wanted to know if she was suffering [in the afterlife], so he would go to Kulu where there was a *delog* (Tibetan *'das log*). He would ask about my mother: "What kind of suffering is she experiencing?" He would ask, and the *delog* would look. He would give her my mother's name and where she'd lived. The *delog* would search for her and bring back messages.
>
> If your father and mother have done good things, they'll go to the Buddha realm. If they've done bad things, they'll go to hell. Like that, the *delog* summons them. And if they wonder, "Who is it that's asking about us?" she tells them your name. Then they send messages like, "Eh, that's my daughter. These are the people in my family. My house is in this kind of place." Then the *delog* delivers the messages.
>
> *Hyolmo laywoman*
> *Kathmandu*

> After you've finished all the rituals, then you go a second time. "Did it help or not?" Say, for example, [the *delog* told you that] your father is in hell. You recited *mani* and you did all the rituals that the *delog* told you to. Then you can ask her, "How is he doing now? Is he out of hell or not?"
>
> *Tibetan lama*
> *Kathmandu*

Delogs—people believed to be dead who then inexplicably return to life with stories of postmortem realms—offer a case study for how "lived," "religious," "folk" Buddhism is distinguished from "normative," "elite," "institutional" Buddhism. When *delogs* revive from their death journeys to share stories about the karmic consequences of positive and negative deeds, they reinforce orthodox

DOI: 10.4324/9781003257462-5

Buddhist values and cosmology. When *delogs* prescribe merit-making rituals to benefit the deceased, they contribute to the authority and financial stability of Buddhist monastics. Yet despite the corroboration and support that *delogs* offer official Buddhist institutions and recognized Buddhist authorities, *delogs* and their practices are not always regarded as legitimately Buddhist by scholars or by their communities. Instead, they are categorized as "folk" Buddhism.[1]

What is folk Buddhism? In English-language scholarship, folk Buddhism has indicated at least four distinct, yet often overlapping, types of rituals, ideas, and Buddhists. First, it has described Buddhist practices of "magic," tales of miracles, and beliefs in otherworldly gods and spirits (Swearer 2022 [1987]). This folk Buddhism encompasses the supernatural aspects of the Buddhist tradition that are rejected by modernist Buddhists (McMahan 2009). Second, like the synonymous categories of "lived" and "popular" Buddhism, folk Buddhism has alluded to non-normative, unofficial, or unorthodox beliefs and activities (Cuevas 2007, Swearer 2022 [1987]). Folk Buddhism, in this usage, designates any practice or principle that may circulate widely throughout Buddhist societies but which deviates from the Buddhism articulated in philosophical treatises and canonical texts. Third, as with "shamanic" and "brahmanical" Buddhism (both of which will be explained below), folk Buddhism has referred to elements of the Buddhist tradition speculated to have non-Buddhist origins (Davis 2016, Pommaret 1989, Samuel 1997, Swearer 2022 [1987]).[2] In this case, any custom or concept that predates the historical Buddha Śākyamuni or that may have been assimilated from a non-Indian cultural context constitutes folk Buddhism. These three characterizations of folk Buddhism point to a collection of rituals and beliefs that, although they may be ubiquitous throughout Buddhist cultures, are often the domain of low-status lay practitioners. This is the fourth connotation of folk Buddhism: the Buddhism of ordinary, everyday Buddhists.

The *delog* phenomenon offers a useful case study for investigating folk Buddhism as a conceptual category because it exemplifies all four understandings of folk Buddhism listed above. First, a *delog*'s messages from and about the dead are *miraculous*. *Delogs* relay detailed, personal information about people they have never met and places they have never visited. They describe events they did not witness and report the location of hidden objects. Second, to awaken from death contradicts Buddhist conceptions of the rebirth process as one-way and irreversible. There is no satisfying philosophical or physiological explanation for a body that has been unresponsive, cold to the touch, and without discernable breath or heartbeat for several days to return to life. Third, there are no references to *delogs* in Indian Buddhists texts, indicating that the origins of the *delog* tradition lie in *non-Buddhist* Central Asian soul-journeying practices or Chinese tales of anomalous events. Finally, even when *delog* narratives are employed by Buddhist elite to teach and generate donations, *delogs* themselves are often *not held in high esteem*.

The following sections examine these four usages of folk Buddhism, not to make a normative claim about how folk Buddhism should be characterized but to elucidate ways "folk" has been used in Buddhist contexts. The various implications of folk Buddhism share a pejorative assessment of a particular idea, ritual, or person's characterization as fully and properly Buddhist. "Folk" Buddhism, in other words, indicates "bad" Buddhism.

Folk Buddhism Deals in Magic and Miracles

> When the *delog* was young, maybe twenty- or twenty-five-years-old, she told people about money hidden in a faraway village, a Hindu village. She had met the man whose money it was when she was in the *bardo*.[3] People took a message to the [dead man's] family in the Hindu village. They organized a group and dug in a field behind the family's house to look. They found the money! From then on, people believed in her.
>
> *Hyolmo grandmother*
> *Kathmandu*

> I heard about someone who had died. The person encountered the dead and met the Dharma King, Lord of Death.[4] When the person revived and told what had happened, no one believed their story. But the person had an earring to prove it. The earring wasn't gold or silver or any other metal that is found on this earth. Somehow it was in the person's ear without it having any kind of opening; there was no way to take it on or off.
>
> *Tibetan laywoman*
> *Xining*

In his entry for the *Encyclopedia of Religion*, Donald Swearer identifies "magical intent" and the attribution of "supernatural powers" as defining characteristics of folk Buddhism. Prayers to bodhisattvas, like Kṣitigarbha and Avalokiteśvara, to rescue beings from unfortunate rebirths are, per Swearer, folk Buddhism. Legends that describe the "magical prowess" of highly realized adepts, like the Buddha's disciple Maudgalyāyana, are folk Buddhism. Likewise, accounts of the Buddha displaying supernatural feats of flying and foretelling the future and the recitation of Buddhist scriptures for purposes of well-being and protection (Pali *paritta*) are instances of folk Buddhism. Despite being part of the Pali Canon, *Jataka* tales describing past lives of the Buddha and the *Stories of Hungry Ghosts* (*Petavatthu*) are folk Buddhism. Although all have been "amalgamated into orthodox ritual activity" and their "content reflects the highest ethical and spiritual ideals of the normative tradition," Swearer considers these to be instances of folk Buddhism because they incorporate non-rational, empirically unproven/unprovable ideas and practices (2022 [1987]).

Mysterious, "magically" obtained knowledge is a fundamental feature of *delog* practice. During my 2008 fieldwork in Nepal, I visited a village where, the previous year, a disabled young man had mysteriously disappeared. No one had been able to determine where he had gone or what might have happened to him.

After months of searching, the villagers consulted the local *delog* who declared that the young man's mother had killed him and buried his body in the dirt floor of their house. The mother refused to let anyone enter the house, but one day when she was away, the *delog* and a group of villagers went to the home, and the *delog* led everyone to the precise spot where the corpse was buried. Upon exhumation of the body, the mother was arrested and interrogated, and it was revealed that she and her son had argued. In her anger and frustration that he would never be able to work, she had beaten him on his head, accidentally killing him. As a result of the *delog* exposing her crime, the woman was sentenced to ten years in prison.

The means by which *delogs* obtain information, i.e., dying and returning to life, is equally "magical." There is no doctrinal way to explain a *delog* reviving from death. Per Buddhist teachings, once a person has died, consciousness transitions to its next life. There is no philosophical avenue for reversing course and reviving in the body that has been left behind as a corpse. As described in the authoritative *Bardo Thödrol* (*Bar do thos grol*), popularly known in English as the *Tibetan Book of the Dead*, once a person passes through the *bardo* of dying (*'chi kha'i bar do*) and enters the *bardo* of reality (*chos nyid bar do*), the body has undergone the "most subtle inner dissolutions" of physical elements and breath, such that a person is irreversibly dead (Thondup 2005: 49–51). When consciousness emerges from the *bardo* of reality into the *bardo* of becoming (*srid pa'i bar do*), the stage of transition toward the next birth, the path back to the previous life has vanished. Himalayan Buddhists attempt to explain the anomaly of *delogs* in different ways: it was not the *delog*'s karmically determined time to die; the Dharma King, Lord of Death (gShin rje chos rgyal, Sanskrit Yamarāj), chose the *delog* to be his messenger to the human world; the *delog* was brought back to life by a god (*lha*). Theorizing a *delog*'s return from death by invoking supernatural beings and powers, however, does not render the *delog* phenomenon any less miraculous. It is because the *delog* journey and the narratives it engenders defy rational explanation that, per Swearer's view, the *delog* tradition relies on "magic" and thus falls squarely in the category of folk Buddhism.

Swearer's delineation of folk Buddhism limits "normative" Buddhism to rational philosophy and corresponds with what Flanagan labels "naturalistic" Buddhism:

> Imagine Buddhism without rebirth and without a karmic system that guarantees justice ultimately will be served, without nirvana, without bodhisattvas flying on lotus leaves, without Buddha worlds, without nonphysical states of mind, without any deities, without heaven and hell realms, without oracles, and without lamas who are reincarnations of lamas.
>
> *(2011: 3)*

He answers the question, "What would be left?" with "Buddhism naturalized." Buddhism naturalized would be a tradition from which the "incredible superstition and magical thinking," the "mind-numbing and wishful hocus pocus" would be erased (2011: 3). It would be a Buddhism shorn of what Swearer identifies as folk elements.

Swearer concedes that "magical" beings, powers, and events are present in the earliest Buddhist sources and recognizes that "Buddhism has had a folk or popular dimension since its inception" (2022 [1987]). So why limit "normative" Buddhism to rational ideals and practices? Sam van Shaik argues that magic—ritual practice that is "not based on theories"—is an integral part of the Buddhist tradition (2020: 8). Describing Burmese ritual practices aimed at lengthening life or controlling rebirths so that a person will be alive when the future Buddha Maitreya appears, van Shaik asserts that "magical" practices cannot "be convincingly explained away as later accretions or non-Buddhist 'folk' religion, since they draw on magical practices and terminology present in the Buddhist scriptures" (2020: 100). The use of spells (Sanskrit *dhāraṅī* and mantra), mandalas, and other forms of "Buddhist magic, as much as Buddhist ethics and meditation, has been central to the transmission of Buddhism… across Asia," he writes (2020: 102). Gregory Schopen (1988) has made a similar argument about "superstitious" Buddhist practices, namely, that they originate with the monastic Sangha, the Buddhist institution responsible for recording and maintaining the doctrinal corpus.

Because "magical" and "superstitious" rituals and events, like the appearance of an earring made of extraterrestrial metal, are part and parcel of the Buddhist tradition, singling them out as folk Buddhism signals merely that an author or speaker does not find them personally compelling. Folk Buddhism is thus implausible and unconvincing Buddhism.

Folk Buddhism Is Questionable and Unreliable

> How could someone die and return to life? I mean, it's not in any Buddhist texts.
>
> *Tibetan university student*
> *Xining*

Asian scholars have long called attention to the fact that, all too often, Euro-American scholars and practitioners have thought "that they are 'more knowledgeable' about Buddhism, that they practice 'real' Buddhism, as opposed to 'folk' Buddhism" (Duerr and Mushim, cited in Hsu 2016). It is important, therefore, to ask if Asian Buddhists make similar distinctions? Is there an emic category corresponding to folk Buddhism? In fact, Himalayan Buddhists are skeptical of anomalous events and evaluate religious phenomena and specialists, including *delog*s, using criteria and terminology that parallel those used by non-Asian scholars.

Geoffrey Samuel posits the term "shamanic Buddhism" to describe aspects of Tibetan Vajrayāna in which "a practitioner can relate directly to the sources of power and authority" (1993: 34). He includes *delog*s in this category because, instead of relying on book learning and oral teachings, *delog*s undergo a death journey during which they see and speak with the dead face to face. Like shamans who send their souls out of their bodies to travel to the spirit world, a *delog*is consciousness leaves the body to meet and interact directly with the dead. Both shamans and contemporary *delog*s undertake out-of-body journeys repeatedly. Some *delog*s die on a regular schedule, determined by the phases of the moon. Others' deaths are less routine, occurring whenever they are directly summoned by a bodhisattva or the Lord of Death to collect messages and missives. As a result of their ongoing visits to the lands of the dead, *delog*s can be consulted about the status of the deceased in the same way that someone might approach a shaman for information about the spirit world.

In the 1970s, Robert Paul reported that Sherpas in Solu-Khumbu preferred the services of a Buddhist lama to those of a shaman.[5] A lama's ceremonies "conform to the written books, which cannot lie" and are consistent and standardized (1976: 147). A lama's Buddhist rituals, that is, do not vary based on personal whim. Shamans, on the other hand, forego written texts and enjoy significant flexibility in their performances. They are free to improvise and adapt based on their direct encounters with spirits. It is spirits themselves, not any human institution, which initiate shamans through experiences of altered states of consciousness, including possession, trance, and extreme illness. As a result, shamans are "anomalous," and "one can never be sure if a shaman really sees the gods... or whether it is all an act" (147). A lama's power, however, "is certifiable, having been bestowed in an institutionalized way" (147). Lamas, therefore, are granted more trust and authority than shamans.

Despite the shamanic character of many Vajrayāna practices, Himalayan Buddhists are suspicious of *delog*s for many of the same reasons Sherpas are skeptical of shamans. In 2008, a Hyolmo elder dismissed his village's *delog* with the following critique:

> She had an older brother who could read and write a little. He must have listened to what people said, people who'd been to India and Burma and talked about those places. For example, the *delog* once said she met Jawaharlal Nehru, and he was stuck in the *bardo*. She said his obstacles (*bar chad*) would be removed only when his bridge project was completed... She must have heard about such things from her brother.

"It's all just cheating and lying," the elder insisted. Likewise, a Tibetan writer I interviewed in Kangding distinguished between true Buddhist adepts and questionably Buddhist ritualists based on how the person in question acquired their ability to, for example, see the future or communicate with the dead. He designated people who had engaged in intensive meditation and study or who were experiencing the results of exceptional karma created in past lives as "representatives of Buddhism." He declined to designate those who relied mechanically on ritual protocol or a physical object, such as a mirror, or whose bodies were possessed by spirits as religious (*chos*).[6] "Because we cannot understand how they attain their information, how can we be sure that they are not mere tricksters?" he asked.

Some lay Buddhists I encountered in my fieldwork compared *delogs* to spirit mediums, diviners, and other prognosticators and questioned whether or not such figures were authentically Buddhist.[7] According to a university student in Xining, practices of divination belong to the realm of "folk religion" (*dmangs chos*) which "is not really religion" but more accurately "tradition" (*rigs gnas*).[8] Also in Xining, a retired professor insisted that what I meant by "*delog*" was actually a case of spirit possession.

> [The person] is possessed by an evil spirit (*gshed ma*)... a ghost (*yi dwags*). They're seized by a demon (*'dre gzung*). According to folk belief (*dmangs srol*), it's not an evil spirit; it's a human consciousness. According to the scholarly tradition, it's an evil spirit; it's not actually a human consciousness... There was a girl who had this kind of experience. A middle-aged man died... His last words were: "I'm leaving some money. Give some to a lama and the rest to monks for rituals." After he died, the girl had a dream. In her dream, she saw the man. He told her that his money hadn't been used like he intended. He said that the lama had kept the money and not done any rituals for him.

The man continued speaking through the girl for several months until she was brought to the local monastery where a fire offering (*sbyin sreg*) succeeded in exorcising the spirit. "The man talked a lot through that girl. It was really strange," the professor concluded.

The professor's refusal to entertain the idea that *delog* was different from spirit possession reflects a widespread view that messages from the dead are "strange" and should be treated skeptically. As a result, the credibility of *delogs* is constantly questioned. Although the *delog* phenomenon confirms and supports many normative Buddhist teachings, *delogs*' unconventional methods and lack of institutional identity are met with suspicion and may be considered less than fully Buddhist. They are "folk" Buddhist.

Folk Buddhism Is Impure and Inauthentic

> His *delog* journeys only take three hours because he flies. He hops across mountain peaks and fence posts. Sometimes it only takes him half an hour to return from the dead.
>
> He instructed me to write his name in my notebook and draw a circle around it. The circle is to represent the hole, the round place in the sky he passes through when he goes *delog*. From up there, he looks down through

> the hole and sees everything. Things down here look very small and far away when viewed from up there.
>
> *Fieldnotes*
> *Nuwakot District, Nepal*

When "folk" designates unorthodox practices and practitioners that are not entirely Buddhist, the term overlaps with understandings of folk Buddhism as a mixture of Buddhist and non-Buddhist components. Samuel (1997b) uses "folk" to distinguish pre-Buddhist, and by implication non-Buddhist, rituals from practices clearly introduced to Tibetan societies as part of the dissemination of Indian Buddhism. He lists agricultural festivals, worship of Tibet's autochthonous deities, and ceremonies aimed at healing, avoiding misfortune, and communicating with the spirit world as examples. John Holt's ethnography of Cambodian *pchum ben* rituals documents "modernist" monks who criticized the popular ceremony in which merit is transferred to the deceased on the grounds that it is "a practice of ancestor veneration… not really found in the canonical Pali *Tipitaka*, and therefore is not essentially Buddhist" (2012: 11). The disapproval that many Theravada monks express toward certain Buddhist practices parallels scholars' characterizations of folk Buddhism as having non-Buddhist origins.

To label *delog*s folk Buddhists in this sense is to imply that the origin of *delog* practice lies outside the Buddhist tradition. Does it? A search for the genesis of *delog*s leads in multiple directions. One possible origin lies in Chinese accounts of the anomalous and miraculous (Ch. *zhi guai*). In this literature's return-from-death subgenre, people find themselves wrongly summoned to the underworld only to be sent back to finish their allotted lifespans. The *Mingxiang ji*, compiled in the 5th c., contains many such tales. In one, on the fourteenth day of the first month of the year 426, a man named Li Dan died of an illness. Surprisingly, "the area below his heart did not grow cold," and he revived seven days later (Campany 2012b: 195). Dan reported being summoned to the court of a magistrate and shown the "earth prisons" (Ch. *diyu*) where "he saw crowds of sinners receiving painful retribution, moaning and crying out" (195). Three years later, Dan died again. On his second visit to the realm of the dead, Dan was given messages by "some of the imprisoned sinners" (195). They asked Dan to tell their relatives about the bad things they had done while alive and to request their families perform acts of merit on their behalf. The dead told Dan their names, and when Dan revived, again after seven days, he was able to locate all the relevant people. This is a typical *delog* tale.

The Cambodian phenomenon called *bhlyk* is another parallel to *delog*s. People who experience *bhlyk* report being "seized by large, dark-skinned demons in the service of Lord Yama. . . [who] bring the person to stand in front of Yama, where he looks her name up in his ledger. He discovers that she has not yet reached her proper time and sends the person back to the surface, sometimes with the knowledge of her true and future time of death" (Davis 2016: 40). Consistent with many *delog* stories, as well as Chinese accounts of the anomalous, corpses that are actually *bhlyk* retain a slight degree of warmth, such that "the body is not as cold as a true corpse" (40). During his fieldwork, Erik Davis met a middle-aged man convinced that his wife would return to life. Awaiting her return, he obstructed funeral proceedings for a full day by lying prostrate on top of her corpse.

Françoise Pommaret names indigenous Central Asian shamans who embarked on soul journeys to visit the dead as likely precursors to *delog*s. "It is highly probable that the ancient pre-Buddhist Tibetans knew about this practice [of shamans traveling to the realm of the dead] from their contacts with the Turco-Mongol populations," she writes (1997: 499). Based on her reading of literary accounts and her interviews with *delog*s in Bhutan, she explains *delog*s as "akin to shamans, but shamans who have been Buddhicized in such a way and for such a long time that they have lost the memory of their shamanistic origin" (508). This theory of *delog*s as Himalayan shamans in Buddhist guise suggests a process of acculturation whereby what was originally a non-Buddhist practice became absorbed into a Tibetan Buddhist context. With the development of the *Bardo Thödrol* literature, first-hand reports of people who had traversed the intermediate state between lives became useful to members of the Buddhist establishment. Coincidentally or not, written narratives of *delog* journeys arose in tandem with the *Bardo Thödrol* texts (Cuevas 2008). Samuel proposes a historical process by which *delog*s and related shamanic specialists "carried out an adjunct role" to lamas and "helped to replicate Buddhist values at the level of village or pastoralist encampment" (1997a: 848). *Delog*s, in Samuel's estimation, are thus the offspring of shamans who were coopted into the formal Buddhist system, their rituals and purpose modified, when necessary, to conform to normative Buddhist teachings.[9]

An analogous process can be observed today in the recognition of *delog*s by reincarnate lamas. At a large monastic encampment in eastern Tibet, I met a *delog* who explained that although she underwent her first death experience at age fifteen, she did not know she was a *delog* until several years later when she met a charismatic lama who told her that she was. She declined to tell me about her *delog* experiences, referring me instead to the written account of her death journey, which, incidentally, was penned by a monk. She recommended that should I have questions after reading her story, I address them to the resident monks. My impression was that she was concerned lest her memory not conform to the normative *delog* standard established and monitored by her encampment's religious authorities.[10] In other words, it seems that *delog*s' reports of their return-from-death experiences are still being managed, and likely edited, by monks who ensure that the stories (and *delog*s) are sufficiently Buddhist.

The origin of *delog*s is impossible to determine. Supernormal abilities and rituals—such as clairvoyance, mediumship, and divination—by which people discern the fates of the deceased are found across the world. Reports of people reviving from death are ubiquitous across cultures and religious traditions, speaking to a universal human desire to know what happens at death and be assured that loved ones are not suffering. Perhaps *delog*s are the Tibetan instantiation of a transcultural phenomenon known in English as a near-death experience

(NDE), one additional avenue by which Himalayan Buddhists satisfy the universal human need for information about the dead (Becker 1985, Carr 1993, Sogyal 1993). In this case, categorizing the *delog* tradition as "folk" Buddhism signals only that it did not originate as a uniquely Buddhist practice.

Folk Buddhism Is Marginal and Low Status

> *Delogs* appear among poor, uneducated, un-religious people. They're sent to educate people and teach them right from wrong.
>
> *Hyolmo monk*
> *Kathmandu*

> *Delog* is a very difficult subject. It's very difficult in the monastery. If I told you anything, I would just be repeating lies. *Delog* is a topic for laypeople's gossip.
>
> *Tibetan lama*
> *Kathmandu*

Some of the most well-known images of hell in ancient China come from scrolls used by traveling lay storytellers who narrated the legend of Maudgalyāyana's hell journey. These itinerant preachers ranged across China and Central Asia, and their "preaching sessions are known to have taken place as much outside of state-supported Buddhist temples as inside them" (Campany 1988: 432). These evangelists' sermons are categorized as an instance of folk Buddhism, but not for reasons already discussed. It is not that hell realms are empirically unverifiable; hells are a fundamental element of the Buddhist cosmos. It is not that the content of the preachers' narrations diverged from normative Buddhist values; the stories exemplified Buddhist morals. It is not that Maudgalyāyana's origins lie outside the Buddhist textual tradition; Maudgalyāyana (Pali Moggallāna) was one of the Buddha's foremost disciples. The performances of itinerant storytellers are called folk Buddhism because the "preachers often came from outside the ranks of the officially ordained clergy" (Campany 1988: 432).

The same is true for *delogs*. *Delogs* are labeled folk Buddhists, not because of their work relaying messages from the dead, but due to their typical identity as uneducated, rural laywomen. This usage of "folk" to reflect social status is apparent in the context of Buddhist elite who also report about the dead. At a large Buddhist encampment in eastern Tibet, I learned of monks who, as a result of their realization (*mkhyen pa*) and clairvoyance (*mngon shes*), could see the deceased in meditation. These monks delivered good and bad news mirroring that provided by *delogs*. The monks, however, were not considered folk practitioners; they were highly revered teachers of Buddhist doctrine and meditation. Even when high-ranking Buddhists experience a physiological death and return to life, Buddhist masters are rarely known as *delogs* (Prude 2020). Tulku Thondup illustrates this point when he describes the death experience of Tibetan master Do Khyentse Yeshe Dorje (mDo mkhyen brtse ye shes rdo rje, 1800–1866). Despite becoming ill with chicken pox and "expir[ing] and remain[ing] dead for fifteen days," Do Khyentse's experience "cannot really be classified as a delog account" (2005: 163). The reason Do Khyentse is not a *delog* is that otherworldly journeys of "great adepts… are usually categorized in Tibetan Buddhist literature as pure visions or enlightened activities, not as delog experiences" (2005: 163). The very word "*delog*" implies a low-status person.

These examples illustrate another meaning of folk Buddhism. What makes both the Chinese tradition of itinerant Buddhist storytelling and the Himalayan practices of *delog*s folk Buddhism is the lack of prestige of the people involved. Laypeople who are illiterate, poor, rural, or female "[find] themselves embedded in culture (with a small 'c')," whereas members of the male monastic Sangha and other Buddhist elite are "bearers of Culture (with a capital 'C')" (Daniel 1996: 359). The latter, including lamas and monks, bear official, institutional approval for their visions and rituals and thus practice legitimate Buddhism (singular). The former, including "the women, the shepherds, the serfs and peasants, the poor, the popular and the public," practice various folk Buddhisms (plural) (359). Folk Buddhism vis-à-vis normative Buddhism is, in this view, not a matter of orthodoxy or orthopraxy but a question of the social background and religious standing of the people involved.

Davis shows how modernist, reformist Cambodian Buddhist monks designate their own practices and preferences as "Buddhist" and contrast these with the "Brahmanical" (Khmer *brahmaṅya-sāsanā*), the designation for all elements of Cambodian religion they do not approve. In the monks' usage, "Brahmanical" does not reflect origins in Indian Hindu rituals but includes the religious traditions of indigenous Cambodian highland ethnic groups. "Brahmanical," for the monks, indicates "institutional" and "moral" (not "cosmological") deviation from normative Buddhism. In other words, the difference between "true" Buddhism and "Brahmanical" or folk Buddhism lies not in the particular deities and spirits propitiated or in the teleology or philosophy that underlie a ritual; it lies in the esteem in which the Buddhist elite view the practice or practitioner in question. The self-serving nature of the distinction between "Buddhist" and "Brahmanical" is evident in the way modernist Cambodian monks insist they "exist outside of the everyday world's hierarchy and therefore must be offered the highest respect within that same hierarchy, as an expression of morality" (2016: 18). Paul reports a similar reasoning regarding Sherpa shamans. A shaman's work "is not guided by any particular formal moral or ethical code, as is the monk's," and "[a shaman's] power is not acquired or used in conjunction with any formal or institutional training or study, nor does it correspond to any high position on any social or religious hierarchy" (1976: 147–148). As a result, a shaman's rituals are ranked lesser than those of monks in Sherpa Buddhist society because "to have an ordinary fellow wielding such power" contradicts Sherpa socio-religious conventions (148).

When a Hyolmo *delog* located money buried in a distant Hindu village, even the local lamas are said to have respected her by putting her to sit at their head when they performed rituals in the monastery. The laywoman who told me this story interpreted the monks' ceremonial deference as an indication that the Buddhist authorities accepted the *delog* as authoritative. A reincarnate Tibetan lama assured me that *delogs* are legitimate but hinted at a fraught relationship between *delogs* and Buddhist institutions when he criticized *delogs* as "very proud." His reluctance to accord *delogs* the respect that he would another lama or to discuss *delog* stories within the confines of his monastery reveals how those in power hold ordinary practitioners in check. If an incarnation of a Buddhist master encounters and reports about the dead, his experience is said to result from meditative accomplishments and is endorsed as an example of normative Buddhism. If a non-specialist, by contrast, awakens with messages from the deceased, her reports, if they are legitimated at all, are viewed with apprehension by members of the monastic Sangha. Lest they challenge the power of the Buddhist establishment, they are designated folk Buddhism. A folk Buddhist is thus a Buddhist with no institutional power.[11]

The Buddhism of Ordinary People

> Drolma (Sgrol ma, Sanskrit Tārā) herself comes and tells me, "It's time for you to go," and then it happens on that day at that time. Otherwise, things like rainbows appear. A while back, when it was time, a Chinese man helped me take this photo… The cloud came toward me, right in front of me. I thought that I would die [i.e., go *delog*] then. My heart was going *tuk*, *tuk*, *tuk*, *tuk*… I thought, "Oh, now it's time to die. I should finish what I need to do." That evening, there were rainbows above my house and over the roof were clouds with rainbows around them.
>
> *Female* delog
> *Golok*

Attention to the *delog* phenomenon, including *delogs*' death journeys, the role that *delogs* play in their communities, possible origins of the *delog* tradition, and the suspicion with which *delogs* are viewed by many Himalayan Buddhists helps to clarify the meanings and connotations of "folk" Buddhism. In some instances, *delog* practice is called folk Buddhism because *delogs* and their reports cannot be explained in rational, naturalistic terms. "Folk," in these cases, is employed to disparage belief in miracles, supernatural beings, and other sorts of "magical" things. Other times, *delogs*' extraordinary claims to have visited and returned from the postmortem realms are regarded as folk Buddhism because they contradict orthodox Buddhist teachings. The miracle that *delogs* assert does not square with textual descriptions of the death process as irreversible. In still other cases, *delogs* are deemed folk Buddhists due to their assumed non-Buddhist origins.

"Folk," in this usage, signals impure, adulterated Buddhism. Finally, when a rural nomad who has never learned a single letter of the alphabet, much less engaged in Buddhist philosophy or meditation, encounters a bodhisattva and reads signs in cloud formations, she claims authority that the Buddhist elite may be hesitant to grant. In these instances, folk is a pejorative label those in power use to distinguish things that ordinary people do from their own official activities.

Delogs' methods and messages are anomalous, and their journeys take place outside of institutional boundaries and independently of formal Buddhist training. Yet *delogs*' reports demonstrate the truth of essential Buddhist teachings, namely the doctrines of karma and rebirth. *Delogs* contribute to the didactic and economic needs of Buddhist monastics by describing what happens at death and warning about the negative consequences that result from evil deeds, consequences that may be ameliorated by making offerings to the local monastery. *Delogs*' extraordinary abilities to communicate with and about the dead help the living navigate their worries and grief when someone dies, filling a need that all Buddhists are liable to feel at some point in their lives. Bifurcating Buddhism into folk and not-folk variants thus creates a boundary that is observed only in theory. Linh writes that whereas a "binary opposition may occur within the sangha imagination in an urban setting," a division between folk and non-folk is "questionable… in rural communities where everyday interaction and practice are often not as static" (2017: 401). Even in metropolitan contexts, highly literate, male monastics, i.e., the Buddhist elite, do and historically have participated in and promoted folk Buddhism (Lewis 2002, Schopen 1988–1989).

What does differentiating folk Buddhist practices, beliefs, and actors from normative rituals, ideas, and specialists accomplish? The implications of "folk" examined here differ, but all serve to denigrate or dismiss the Buddhist person or practice to which they refer. The most prevalent meaning of folk Buddhism is simply unsatisfactory, insufficient, "bad" Buddhism. Yet, the pejorative implications of folk Buddhism are inconsistent and, when taken together, encompass all Buddhists in their scope. Does the designation "folk Buddhism," then, hold any value? I suggest folk Buddhism signals something or someone is challenging the status quo: a novel and unique Buddhist expression is circulating; a compelling experience defies existing explanations; a normative interpretation is being contested; the power of the male elite is at risk. Folk Buddhism is interesting Buddhism.

Notes

1 The *delog* phenomenon and details of *delog* practice are described in more detail in Pommaret (1989) and Prude (2014, 2016, 2020).

2 This essay does not attempt to provide an exhaustive overview of scholarship addressing the dichotomy between "folk," "popular," "lived" and "institutional," "elite," "orthodox" as it has been employed and criticized in Buddhist Studies. I cite only a handful of sources that relate to the *delog* tradition by way of dealing with death rituals and/or aspects of the Himalayan variations of Buddhism of which *delogs* are a part.

3 The *bardo* (*bar do*) is the intermediate state between lives, as posited in Mahāyāna and Vajrayāna Buddhism.
4 The Dharma King, Lord of Death, is called Shinje Chögyal (gShin rje chos rgyal) in Tibetan and Yamarāj in Nepali.
5 Paul uses the term "shaman" to refer to "*pen-bu*" (*bon po*), "a non-clerical curer who heals by entering into trance or altered state in the course of which he journeys to the other world, manages to make direct contact with the gods for purposes of discovering the supernatural source of illness and its possible cure, and may [*sic*] also exhibit other oracular powers" (1976: 144). In contemporary Nepal, Sherpas and Hyolmo refer to *bonpos* as *jhākris* when speaking Nepali. Paul's depiction of Sherpa shamans also incorporates people called "*hla-wa*" (probably *lha ba*, usually spirit mediums) and "*min-dung*" (*mig mthong*, "seeing with the eyes").
6 See also Ekvall, 1963.
7 There are many types of and words for diviners in Tibetan. Three commonly used terms were *mo ba*, *phra mo*, and *jo mo*.
8 Waldo defines *dmangs* as "1) [ordinary] people; 2) populace, multitude, masses, public; 3) vulgar; 4) popular, folk" (Dharma Dictionary). The word *chos* is more complicated and multivalent. It is the word used to refer to the Buddhist "religion." More generally, it can refer to any "tradition," "particular doctrine," "knowable thing," or "system of morality" (Dharma Dictionary).
9 Davidson (2017) uses the term "historical erasure" to describe the process whereby marginal practices are coopted by a "dominant paradigm" and then, whether intentionally or not, their origins forgotten. He suggests magical elements of Buddhist Tantra originated with low-status, non-sectarian practitioners who engaged in the rituals for personal profit. Once incorporated into elite Buddhism, the history of the spells and mantras was effectively erased by simple omission from textual sources.
10 See Prude (2020) for a discussion of the ways monks and other representatives of institutional Buddhism exert control over who is and is not recognized as a *delog*.
11 I am referring to Tom Wolfe's oft-cited definition of "cult": "A cult is a religion with no political power" (1979: 43).

Works Cited

Becker, Carl. (1985). Views from Tibet: NDEs and the *Book of the Dead*. *Anabiosis: The Journal for Near-Death Studies* 5(1): 3–20.

Campany, Robert Ford. (1988). "Having Once Died and Returned to Life": Representations of Hell in Medieval China. *Harvard Journal of Asiatic Studies* 48(2): 433–464.

———. (2012a). Repertoires and Contestation: A Case Study Based on Buddhist Miracle Tales. *History of Religions* 52(2): 99–141.

———. (2012b). *Signs from the Unseen Realm: Buddhist Miracle Tales from Early Medieval China*. Honolulu: University of Hawai'i Press.

Carr, Christopher. (1993). Death and Near-Death: A Comparison of Tibetan and Euro-American Experiences. *The Journal of Transpersonal Psychology* 25(1): 59–110.

Chökyi Nyima Rinpoche. (1991). *The Bardo Guidebook*. Kathmandu: Rangjung Yeshe Publications.

Cuevas, Bryan. (2007). The Death and Return of Lady Wangzin: Visions of the Afterlife in Tibetan Buddhist Popular Literature. *The Buddhist Dead*, ed. Bryan Cuevas and Jacqueline Stone. Honolulu: University of Hawai'i Press, 297–325.

———. (2008). *Travels in the Netherworld*. Oxford: Oxford University Press.

Daniel, E. Valentine. (1996). Crushed Glass, or, Is There a Counterpoint to Culture? *Culture/Contexture*, ed. E. Valentine Daniel and Jeffrey Peck. Berkeley: University of California Press, 357–375.

Davidson, Ronald. (2017). Magicians, Sorcerers and Witches: Considering Pretantric, Non-sectarian Sources of Tantric Practices. *Religions* 8: 1–33.
Davis, Erik. (2016). *Deathpower: Buddhism's Ritual Imagination in Cambodia*. New York: Columbia University Press.
Dharma Dictionary. *Rangjung Yeshe Wiki*, hosted by the Tsadra Organization. Online at: https://rywiki.tsadra.org (accessed 10/15/2021).
Ekvall, Robert. (1963). Some Aspects of Divination in Tibetan Society. *Ethnology* 2(1): 31–39.
Flanagan, Owen. (2011). *The Bodhisattva's Brain*. Cambridge: The MIT Press.
Holt, John. (2012). Caring for the Dead Ritually in Cambodia. *Southeast Asian Studies* 1(1): 1–73.
Hsu, Funie. (2016). We've Been Here All Along. *Buddhadharma*. Winter 2016. Online at: https://www.lionsroar.com/weve-been-here-all-along/ (accessed 7/31/2022).
Lewis, Todd. (2002). Representations of Buddhism in Undergraduate Teaching. *Teaching Buddhism in the West*, ed. Victor Sōgen Hori, Richard Hayes, and James Mark Shields. London: RoutledgeCurzon, 39–56.
Lihn, Mai Bui Dieu. (2017). Review of *Deathpower: Buddhism's Ritual Imagination in Cambodia* by Erik W. Davis. *Pacific Affairs* 90(2): 400–402.
McMahan, David. (2009). *The Making of Buddhist Modernism*. New York: Oxford University Press.
Paul, Robert. (1976). Some Observations on Sherpa Shamanism. *Spirit Possession in the Nepal Himalayas*, ed. John Hitchcock and Rex Jones. Warminster: Aris and Phillips, 141–151.
Pommaret, Françoise. (1989). *Les Revenants de l'Au-Delà dans le Monde Tibétain*. Paris: Centre National de la Recherche Scientifique.
———. (1997). Returning from Hell. *Religions of Tibet in Practice*, ed. Donald Lopez. Princeton: Princeton University Press, 499–510.
Prude, Alyson. (2014). Kunzang Drolkar: A *Delog* in Eastern Tibet. *Eminent Buddhist Women*, ed. Karma Lekshe Tsomo. Albany: SUNY Press, 2014, 169–184.
———. (2016). Women Returning from Death. *Revue d'Etudes Tibétaines* 36: 5–28.
———. (2020). A Reexamination of Marginal Religious Specialists: Himalayan Messengers from the Dead. *Journal of the American Academy of Religion* 88(3): 779–804.
Samuel, Geoffrey. (1993). *Civilized Shamans*. Washington, DC: Smithsonian Institution Press.
———. (1997). Some Reflections on the Vajrayāna and Its Shamanic Origins. *Les Habitants du Toit du Monde,* ed. Samten Karmay and Philippe Sagant. Nanterre: Société d'ethnologie, 325–342.
Schopen, Gregory. (1988–1989). On Monks, Nuns and "Vulgar" Practices. *Artibus Asiae* 1/2: 153–168.
Sogyal Rinpoche. (1993). *The Tibetan Book of Living and Dying*. San Francisco, CA: HarperSanFrancisco.
Swearer, Donald. (2022 [1987]). Folk Religion: Folk Buddhism. *Encyclopedia of Religion*. *Encyclopedia.com* 28 July 2022. https://www.encyclopedia.com/environment/encyclopedias-almanacs-transcripts-and-maps/folk-religion-folk-buddhism (accessed 7/28/2022).
Thondup, Tulku. (2005). *Peaceful Death, Joyful Rebirth*. Boston: Shambala.
van Shaik, Sam. (2020). *Buddhist Magic*. Boulder: Shambhala.
Wolfe, Tom. (1979, December). Tom Wolfe's Seventies. *Esquire* 92: 40–48.

4

WHY A FOLK RELIGION MAY NOT EXIST AMONG FOLLOWERS OF AN ABRAHAMIC FAITH

The Case of Sunni Egypt

Hasan El-Shamy

Moslems in Egypt pride themselves that their faith is the faith of the original or basic life (*din al-fitrah*). This characterization of their faith signifies that there is no organized clergy and that laymen or even simpletons are in constant touch with God. Therefore, they can issue fatwas that legitimize or condemn issues that are not definitively treated in the formal faith. These *fatwa*s are considered binding on the entire population.

Although the folk-belief practice system in Egypt derives its credibility from formal religion, it does not totally stem from, nor agree with, the formal sacred dogma of ecclesiastic religion. Egyptian folk beliefs and practices represent real behavioral patterns, patterns that influence the thoughts, feelings, and actions of individuals and tradition-bound groups in their daily living. In many respects, the folk-belief system is the real culture, contrasted to the ideal culture. In this respect, I apply the concept of a folk motif as "a unit of measurement", and I use this motif for content analysis to demonstrate the folksy nature of the widely recurrent concepts I will be presenting. Such motifs are the very content of folk culture and practice. Motifs are listed in footnotes throughout this chapter, the numbers corresponding to earlier published research on the topic.[1] Such folksy motifs may contradict sacred dogma, but they also draw upon aspects of formal religion that may often be overlooked.

When dealing with Sunni Islam as a cognitive system with its numerous subsystems, all these subsystems cohere around the concept of legitimacy (*al-shar*^{C}*iyyah*) that is, being in harmony with the formal religion. A direct line of beliefs threads together the formal and the informal, regardless of the perceived legitimacy. Now, in 2023 CE, there is reasonable concordance between the ecclesiastical institution and the formal political institutions.

The areas of the formal and informal beliefs may seem separate, but they are interconnected in the manner of a vicious circle, even among the educated elite.

DOI: 10.4324/9781003257462-6

These beliefs mingle with one another, reaffirm one another, and contradict one another. These cognitive and behavioral belief-clusters defy change, despite their recurrent disastrous results at the individual and national levels. Just two examples of this vicious circle-manner are (1) beating of a person to death to extract an evil spirit and (2) summoning the soul of a dead president to find out how a national conflict will turn out.

The Abrahamic Faith

Manifestly, Islam professes that it is *munzal*-faith (divinely revealed or *din-samawi*); it is the *khatam* phase—the final, concluding, seal phase—of the Faith that Ibrahim (Abraham), "the father of God's Messenger", established some two millennia B.C.E. Islam's main objective is to set its two predecessors, namely Judaism and Christianity, on their original, divine right path, despite being corrupted by such problems as alterations, military conquests, and loss of compassion for the weak and the poor, etc. Islam is defined as the faith for "the poor and the brokenhearted" (Cox 78).

After centuries of religious conflicts, these three systems of faith—Islam, Christianity, and Judaism—have arrived at a stage that may be viewed as uneasy peace or "detente". Consequently, the Egyptian political system, represented by the "parliament", recently established a new law labeled *'izdira' al-'adyan*, which literally means "[displaying] contempt toward religions"; according to this law, insulting or even criticizing any religion is considered a crime. The law is, however, confined to the three Abrahamic systems of faith, not extending to non-Abrahamic or indigenous faiths.

Belief systems shared by social groups reveal multiple questions, which are nuanced by the three faiths practiced by Egyptian people. What are the criteria for a belief system to be considered a religion, whether designate formal or folk? And do belief-practice issues, specifically those cited below, qualify to be religious or are they merely folk elements surviving from an ancient past?

In his *Religion: An Anthropological View* (1967), Anthony F.C. Wallace identifies four systems of faith labeled "cult institutions" that distinguish what may be viewed as a "religion". These systems are reckoned according to a hierarchical structure regarding "who" performs rituals in these four "cult institutions" and for whom the rituals are performed—i.e., who are the clients. From the perspective of Islam, these institutions are as follows:

1 Individualistic. The ritual is performed by the layman, e.g., luck cult, or pleading with deity for help for oneself. This is an infinite, typical daily occurrence habitually undertaken by virtually all members of a population, including pleading for God's help or simply mentioning His name, even while committing a sin.[2]
2 Shamanistic. Performers of magic rituals and diviners work for laymen, e.g., the fortuneteller cult, faith healer cult. An example, though not Islamic, is

the American movie "The Exorcist". In this movie, one actor is a healer, and the one possessed person is a client.

3 Communal. Lay officials act as priests to perform for groups at prescribed times. An example is the American movie "Ghost BUSTERs".[3]
4 Ecclesiastical. Professional clergies are organized into bureaucracy, denominations, sects, and so forth. The clergy perform rituals, such as the national anthem or the blessing of the troops, for their constituents, e.g., Islam, Christianity, and Judaism clergy folk.

Wallace also designates four types of systems of faith or religions based on the four cult institutions designated above:

1 Shamanistic: incorporating only one cult institution.
2 Communal: incorporating the individualistic, shamanistic, and the communal.
3 Olympian or polytheistic: incorporating all cult institutions in addition to belief in numerous gods.
4 Monotheistic: incorporating all four cult institutions around belief in one God. Consequently, Islam is to be defined as a monotheistic religion that pivots around the belief in one supreme creator (i.e., theo-centric).

Meanwhile, a folk ritual such as the folk "*zikr*" (*dhikr*)—song and dance praising the holy—or the *zar*—a dance and song appeasing a harmful possessing *jinni*—are folk practices not included above. Yet, these may not be viewed as a component of "folk religion", as demonstrated below. Both *zikr* and *zar* are, in fact, based on and centered around formal Islamic dogma, represented by al-Azhar and its scholastic institutions.[4]

The *thawabit* of Sunni Islam (Fundamentals, Non-Negotiables), i.e., "The Actual Elements of Koran's Message" and Authenticated Hadith

The typical Moslem lives in a world regulated by the choice between two opposites: *al-ẖaram* vs. *al-ẖalal*, translated as the illegitimate vs. the legitimate.[5] By contrast, religious authorities designate certain aspects or rituals (^{C}*ibadat*) of Islam to be God-given—they are in the Koran, the very words of God—and, also, Prophet Muhammad's *hadith*, the tradition constituted by his authenticated sayings and deeds and acts. These five aspects or rituals (^{C}*ibadat*) are listed below, and being legitimate, they are not subject to change or alteration. Political calls for reconsidering these—especially prayers, fasting, and pilgrimage—or considering radical changes to them consequent to modern life are emphatically rejected, and such reconsiderations are often condemned as blasphemous.

1 Testimony/Witness (*shahadah*): declaration of faith
2 Prayers (*s̲alah*): five times daily

3 Annual religious alms, tithe(*zakah*): "1/4 of 1/10" of property, meaning 1/40th of property
4 Fasting (*ramadan*): from dawn to sunset during the lunar month of Ramadan
5 Pilgrimage to Mecca (*hajj*): once in a lifetime, which may be compared to ^{C}*umrah*/(visiting Mecca outside the required pilgrimage)[6]

In addition to these rituals, several other salient entities are considered sacred, including commemorations of holy events, which are celebrations accompanied by additional prayers, chants, melodic-chants, and musical `*inshad* (hymning), that include performing *muwashshahs*, *dhikrs*, and so forth. These commemorations include the following three events. First, the Coming of the Prophet and Islam: prophet Mohammad was born 571 C.E. The Prophet's Birthday (*moolid en-nabi*) is celebrated against interdiction by fundamentalists, whose latest charge (2022) is that the production of sugar dolls made only for this occasion mostly for children—in the form of a horseman, a girl in bridal attire, and so forth—is "Idol Worshipping".[7] Second, *hijrah*, the flight from Mecca to Medina in 622 C.E. And third, *'Isra'* and *Mi^{C}raj*, the ascent to heavens, around the year 621 (1 H.). The ascent to heavens has recently been reaffirmed. Though, as recently as 2022, an outcry developed over the wide publication of the view that the trip was either only "spiritual" or fabricated.[8]

See *zikr/dhikr*, below.

Saints and Sainthood

Associated with the firm belief of a prophet's "miracle": (Mot., V210.0.2, "Miracles manifested (by God) at hands of His Messengers (and Prophets). (mu^{C}jizât)" is that of saints and their Karamat (miracle-like manifestation). Theologians argue: "Whatsoever was a karamah for a saint, is a mu^{C}jizah for His [(God's)] Prophet," (Nabhani (al-) 1962, I, p. 11.), and that "sainthood is a less specific type of prophethood." (1962, I, p. 86).

Formal Islamic institutions accept the principle of sainthood but condemn the development of cults (Cibâdat) around the person believed to be a saint. (See NOTE NO. 13- Digwi (al-) Yusuf: 1931, "fatwa on "karamat al `awliya`/(Saints' Miracle-ike Manifestations)". Also, See: El-Shamy: Humanities 2018, 7, 67. 9/ July/2018, (Segment: 3.2.2. Shared Sacred "Islamic", "Coptic" and "Jewish" Narratives (Saints and Sainthood).

For theologians, the cornerstone for the acceptance of the sainthood principle is "rationality". For all good believers, "rationality"is a function of the being specified in the Koran, Prophet's tradition and precedents—the truthfulness of which is taken literally. Rationality and, consequently, credibility, are also functions of the source, i.e., the person who reports the account. Contemporary commentators on the supernatural in religious literature (i.e., the miraculous) typically state that had it not been for the sources to which the reports are attributed, all of whom are truthful and irreproachable, it would have been hard to believe these occurrences (Motif: U90$, "Credibility depends on characteristics of source").

An example of how a "reliable" source can fail is illustrated by modern academic and artistic injection of false data that seems logical. Koran specifies that Prophet Moses and his servant came to "majma^{C} al-Bahrayn"/("The Confluence of the Two Seas") they found "one of our servants" (Q 18:60, and 18:65), with no mention of Al-Khidr, which was injected into the situation despite the clarity of the Koranic verse. https://islamicreminder.org/the-story-of-musa-moses-and-al-khidr

Thus, "saints" have issued fatwas and given advice often with dire consequences. A recent case was reported in 2017, in which a common 55 years-old "pious" man wishes to become a *shaikh* (saint). Villagers tried to accommodate his wish. When he died, and entombed, his followers, thirty-five days later, sought the government permission to move his corpse to his home so that it would be his shaikh's-tomb (d*arih*). Tragically, the saint-to-be turned out to have been alive but actually died only a few hours before exhuming his corpse.

(http://www.youm7.com/story/2017/2/9/"أهالى قرية بقنا .«كرامات بعد الممات
ينقلون جثمان متوفى بعد 35 يوم من دفنه إلى ضريح باسمه بسبب رؤية.. أهالى «المقربية»: وجدنا
الجثمان كما هو دون تحلل أو تهتك.. ويؤكدون: الشيخ محمد كان زاهدا فى الدنيا
(الخميس، 09 فبراير 2017 12:38).

Also see, Shamy (El-), Hasan 2009 *RAFE*, Appendix No. 38 "The Generating of a Saint for a `Saint-less' Community: A Dead Person Demands Recognition".

Sects in Islam

There are three sects into which a Muslim may claim membership: Sunni, Shiite (which is scarce in Egypt), and Kharijite/Kharijites. These are not to be confused with "schools" of jurisprudence (*madhahib*). At present, the title "Kharijites of modern times" refers to al-Qaida (*al-Qa^{C}idah*), whose name may literally be translated as The Base. This and other extreme groups currently include the "Moslem Brotherhood" and other *takfiriyyin* "judging others, including governments, as disbelievers/unbelievers". These others, non-*takfiriyyin* including governments, must be fought.[9]

The Grand Shaikh al-Tayyib approved a new civil law criminalizing the issuing of *fatwa*s without authorization from *dar al-`ifta'*, which is the [Central] Department for *fatwa*-issuing. This negates the principle of *din al-fitrah*, which is the faith of the original or basic life, establishing that layfolk can pass judgment on issues not definitively treated in the formal faith. Unqualified self-appointed *fatwa* generators are currently legally prosecuted. Thus, both the civil and the ecclesiastical systems are linked.[10]

Formal Islam and Supernatural Entities Other Than God

There are several beliefs required for being a Moslem, and these beliefs include supernatural entities other than God, specifically angels, Satan, and *jinn*. *Jinn*, in fact, have effects on Muslims' social lives. Some formal *fatwa*s have recently stated that *jinn* do not interfere in the lives of Adamites; however, the belief in *jinn*'s existence and entanglements with humans is deeply rooted in the patterns of daily behavior of Moslems and Christians alike.[11]

Beliefs in Envy and the Evil Eye (h*asad*) are widespread. Vivid images of belief in *el-*^{C}*ain*, the [malicious] eye, are encountered universally in Egypt and the rest of the Arab world, among both Muslim and Christian. These images appear not only in the form of physical amulets on children, vehicles, and other objects of material culture, but are found in folk art and songs. Formal religious institutions (Al-Azhar and Dar al-`ifta`) accept the belief and provide advice to ward off their effects.[12]

Belief in Magic: Upper and Nether, White/Light/*nûrani*/ and Black/Sorcery/*shaytani*[13]

Koran lists the beliefs in the teaching of magic, in breathing into knots to actuate magic, and in envy; therefore, formal Islam unequivocally recognizes the validity of such beliefs and associated practices (Q113: 5, 2:102, and so forth).

Harnessing the Jinn and Minor Angels

Apart from using religious services—such as reciting verses from the Koran to exert pressure on the angels, jinn, Satan (*al-shytan*, *`Iblis*), or devilish demonic beings(*al-mutashaytinah*)—magical procedures (*sihr*) are present in every community, regardless of social class.[14] For early Moslem jurists, whose opinions still carry weight, until the present time, not all practices labeled magic were considered to be magic from a judiciary (*shri*^{C}*ah*) standpoint. Different penal codes were devised for the various types of magic. For example, "Imam" Mohammad ibn Idris al-Shafi^{C}i (A.D. 767–820), founder of the *Shafi-madhhab*, one of the four recognized orthodox schools of Sunni Islamic jurisprudence,[15] stated:

> [I]f a person is accused of having learned *sihr* (magic/witchcraft"), we would ask him, "Describe your magic for us." If he describes what would constitutes kufr/(unbelief, being infidel)--as [for example], that which people-of-Babel had believed concerning al-*taqarrub `ila*/(venerating) the Seven Planets, that person is an "infidel"; but if [that person's description of "magic"] does not constitute infidelity, he would become an infidel [only] if he believes that [true magic] should be allowed (*`ibahatah*, i.e., considered legitimate).[16]

Thus, according to the Shafi^{C}i *mathhab*/(School), it is possible for a person to interact with *jinn* and similar supernatural beings.

In another contrary viewpoint, a human being may not trespass on the *jinn* sphere or interact with a *jinni* in any manner. Violation of these boundaries may result in causing madness and loss of religious faith. The fact that God granted

Prophet Solomon power over *jinn* was in response to Solomon's prayer to be granted kingship that had not been allowed before, nor would be given after, to any one after himself (Q 38:35). Solomon's case is therefore unique and may not be extended to any other human being.[17]

Yet, in real social life, seeking to control jinn by magic dominates among all social classes.

Other Forms of Worship Through Song and Dance: The zikr/dhikr (and zar)

Formal orthodox Islam, while endorsing the principle of *dhikr* ("remembrance") of God and His names as a means of worship, frowns upon its popular practice, viewing that practice as an indignity to the faith and to the individual. Consequently, the ritual, as practiced by Sufis and non-Sufis, is ecclesiastically condemned to be *bid*^{C}*ah munkarah* ("irreverent innovation" or deviant fad), and therefore sinful. However, orthodox Muslims tolerate Sufis and their ways, whereas fundamentalists censure them for being interested mainly in ^{C}*alam al-ghayb* (the transcendental world of the unknown) and ^{C}*ilam al-ghayb* (occult knowledge).

The Sufi ritual of *dhikr*, though deviant, is regarded with less disdain than the *zar*. Those who practice folk *zikr* base their faith on Koranic texts that invite "the mentioning of God", but *zar* is unequivocally condemned as sheer disbelief. In the recent past, participants in *zikr* circles were mostly peasants, carpenters, mechanics, grocers, vendors, lower clerks, and others of fairly low social ranks.[18] By contrast, in the 1900s, the participants included members of the urban middle and upper classes such as government ministers, university professors, engineers, and medical doctors. Women *zikr* circles emerged, and they are gaining popularity. In its current expanded format, *zikr* circles overlap with the modernized "public" forms of *zar* rituals that seek to appease—not expel--possessing-jinn, who are labeled *`asyad*. Although dissociation is a climax sought in both the *zar* and folk *zikr*, possession and consequent climaxing are not manifestly presumed to be a factor from which relief is sought. However, the two rituals, regardless of their different rationales, contribute to the partaker's state of mental health.[19]

Zar Appeasing the Possessing Spirits: A Sacrilegious Ritual

The *zar* ritual is a means, usually held periodically, to appease a special category of jinn who cause sickness for a human being. Formal religious institutions view the *zar* cult as lying outside the bounds of the legitimate or permissible or even tolerable. These institutions condemn individuals who practice it, proclaiming them as guilty of *kufr*, meaning sacrilege, disbelief, or being infidels. In a reply to concerned readers of *fatwas* inquiring about "the religion's [Islam's] stand" on the zar, an Azharite authority, a member of the "Council of Senior Ulama"(Anonymous: 1940–1941), summed up the situation when he reiterated formal religious beliefs stating that harm can indeed be caused to humans by Satan or the *jinn* by the *mass*, the touch, of Satan and by evil *jinn* in the form of *rih*, the "wind", also used euphemistically as "mild supernatural illness", who would *yadkhulu/* (enter into or possess) the human body; these beings can cause insanity and epilepsy. The *zar* puts humans in close contact with such dangerous entities. Having emphasize the existence of Satan and Jinn, he concluded:

> This is the observable tangible [fact] the denier of which may be considered mukabir ([intransigent/*muta^{C}annit*] arrogantly insisting on correctness of own views in spite of incontrovertible evidence to the contrary) and denier of that which is witnessed by the eye. [. . .]. True believers and the pious try to heal through sacred Koranic and other sacred texts.

A *fatwa* declared that formal Islam condemns the *zar* for being a cult (^{C}*ibadah*), namely that endorses the veneration of supernatural entities other than God, and this violates numerous sacred prohibitions (*muharramat*/tabus). Among these are the following ten situations:

1. Simulating a ^{C}*ibadah* (worship),
2. Offering a *qurban* (sacrifice) to a spirit,
3. Killing a living creature illegitimately for purposes other than those permitted by God,
4. Circumambulating/(*tawaf hawla*) the sacrifice [thus treating it as if sacred],
5. Drinking blood or covering the human body with blood,
6. Drinking liquor, "if the possessing *jinni* [zar-spirit] is supposed to be the one who is drinking it",
7. Boasting,
8. Erotic dancing,
9. Immodesty of mixing of men and women in compromising positions, and
10. The destruction and wasting of goods.[20]

All these practices are forbidden by Islamic law (*shari^{C}ah*). They range from being viewed as cardinal sins (*kaba'ir*), such as in the cases of simulating a worship (*kufr*) or sheer disbelief (tabus nos., 1, 2, 4, p. 102) extending to being considered as *sagha'ir*/(minor sins), as in the case of conspicuous consumption and destruction of goods (tabu no. 10), held to be merely disdainful.

In spite of unequivocal condemnation and prohibition, the *zar* cult not only persists but is spreading vertically, to more social classes, and horizontally, to more regions and culture areas. Recent reports reveal that members of Western-educated groups, including females, holding high governmental offices participate in *zar* rituals.[21] It should be pointed out that the ritual referred to in the report is the "popularized" public form that may be characterized as pseudo-*zar* or public-*zar*. Yet, after the advent of the Islamic fundamentalism tide, beginning in the 1970s, the practice of the true-*zar* has become less overt in public.

Most practitioner *shaikhs* of the public-*zar*, with some justification, deny that the activity they conduct commercially is a *zar* at all; they insist on calling it *zikr*, remembrance, praising God, and they may also use the terms *daqqah* (beat) or simply *galsit tafariḫ* (a gathering for merry-making). These *zar*-like gatherings are held regularly on a specific weekday and are open to all. For a small fee, anyone may join in the *tafqir* (ritual dance) when her/his *nida* (musical call/beat) is played.[22] More than one participant may simultaneously reach the dissociative stage in which a possessing spirit manifests its presence. Each participant receives some attention from friends, other participants, or the troupe leader (the shaman-*shaikh*, or his assistants). Thus, as a modernized ritual, the public-*zar* lacks a number of healing conditions characteristic of the traditional true-*zar*: 1) the diagnostic phase in which the zar-priestess (*kodyah*) lives with client and observes her family and personal affairs, 2) sacrificial offering and related applications of blood rituals, including physical massage with or without blood, 3) uncontested centrality of the possessed person (as the "bride" of the zar), 4) direct involvement of members of the family of the afflicted, and 5) the conspicuous consumption of goods and drugs—including alcohol. There may also be consequent reorganization of the community so that the afflicted may be accommodated.

During a public-*zar* ritual held every Tuesday evening at a shaman-*shaikh*'s home in a village in the Nile Delta, I (the present writer) asked him about the clients who were present, and he stated the following, defensively:

> I do not know the name of any of those persons who are here; I don't know where they come from, nor what ails them. I am like a [medical] doctor; the *zubûn* (client, customer) comes, pays the `fizîtah'/(i.e., `visit,' a doctor's fee), and participates [in the *táfqir*/(ritual dancing)]. When the client is satisfied, he or she leaves. I do not ask about where they come from or where they go to [. . .] Ladies may come together, if one of them requires attention, they are the ones who would take care of one another.[23]

In many respects, the modernized public-*zar* resembles the Euro-American "discotheque" or psychedelic musical activities that have emerged in westernized, Egyptian urban centers. The popularized *zar*, however, is practiced within the context of traditional beliefs about the supernatural. The public-*zar* (and *zikr/dhikr*) share with the true-*zar* the vital function of allowing expenditure of pen up energies in a manner that communal ethos and puritan religious edicts do not accommodate. Such dissipation of energy and resulting exhaustion have preventive and therapeutic effects for individuals. Numerous recent studies on the *zar* were based on observing these public, less personalized, commercial enterprises. The findings of such studies should not be automatically extended to the traditional true-*zar* ritual.[24]

Public-zars are usually conducted by male practitioners, assisted by three or four assistants and musicians, including flutists, drummers, or tambourine players. Typically, one of the troupe members is a female. In the present case, the female assistant was the main practitioner's elder sister, a divorcee, in her mid- or late thirties, named Nagafah. She played the drum and attended to emergency situations when an unaccompanied female required close physical contact of a delicate nature. The public-*zar* differs from the true-*zar* where a female priestess is the uncontested leader, aided by other assistants, one of whom may be an *'odyah*, effeminate male *zar* practitioner. Within such non-individualized context, G. Sengers (2003) quotes one an informant: "These days, . . . the zar is no longer concerned with the asyad ... , but songs are sung for Allah and the saints". However, Sengers declares,

"I do not agree with those researchers who say that changes take place in the life of the women because an important network is created by the zar, which allows them to make new relationships operating outside their daily lives". I have never noticed the women who attend the *zar* together later visit each other in daily life, too; the ritual community does not extend to a social community outside ritual.

More rigorous analysis of actual performances of *zar* rituals reveals how *zar* characters mirror human sentiments vis-à-vis their human counterparts, especially in terms of brother–sister frequency of occurrence. It may be viewed as a process in which the projection of sentiments that are unsafe to express openly may be expressed. Yet, the so-called Brother–Sister syndrome is a phenomenon suppressed in all branches of Arab-Islamic social sciences and the arts despite its blatant and intense dominance in daily lives of the populations of the Arab World.

A defensive mechanism is demonstrated by its archetypal nature and recurrence in the projective guises such as the lists of *zar-`asyad* writers. All lists of the true-*zar* spirits illustrate familial ties because they occur within the context of the performance of the brother–sister ties that dominate these ritual lists; yet such ties and this brother–sister relations are ignored by major field studies. (For an example, see Shamy (el-) 1976, "... Mahfouz's Trilogy".

Exorcism: Expulsion of a Harmful Spirit

A shaman-*shaikh* may apply other procedures to get rid of an evil supernatural being; these cast it out of a living creature, be that creature a human being or domestic animal. This process may involve ejecting, extracting, humiliating, or killing that intruding being.

> A jinni-woman fell in love with the virtuous son of an authoritarian father and inflicted physical and emotional harm on the son. Modern medical treatment was unable to heal him; and the fundamentalist religious father refused to resort to traditional *mashayikh*-healers [(for only "God is the Healer")]. Through the intervention of neighbors, the father agreed to only watch a shaman-*shaikh* (exorcist) negotiate the terms of the jinn-woman's (not to be confused with *ginniyyah* as water-spirit) exiting the son's body, not via the eye as ordinarily done, but via a small cut to be made on the

> son's pinky toe. This mild outcome was accomplished by threatening the possessing spirit with resorting to the king of the supernatural domain ("kingdom") from which she came.[25]

Exorcism has been reported in some form in all Islamic countries. In a case from Palestine (Barghûthi (Al-): 1979. No. 48, p. 174), the possessing spirit escapes because of a threat to shame it/him with being sexually violated. In another case, a saint's legend—reported in the 13th century H./mid-19th century A.D. (Nabhani, (Al-): 1962: II, p. 164)—describes his healing of a possessed woman.

> A woman suffering from recurrent seizures—believed to be caused by jinn-possession—was taken to a shaikh/"saint" near the city of Nablus for a saintly cure. During the trip she had an epileptic seizure but in spite of her seizure, her husband had sexual intercourse with her as he was accustomed to doing. Upon their arrival to the "saint" and before telling him of what happened, he informed them that the possessing jinni causing the seizures fled because of that sexual intercourse and will never return. Thus, the woman was healed.[26]

Conclusion

Virtually without exception all cases of human interaction with supernatural beings cited above, especially minor beings, are integral parts of formal Islam as ecclesiastically codified. Consequently, the concepts of "Folk Islam" or "Vernacular Islam" are inapplicable to their occurrences in the daily lives of Sunni Moslems in Egypt. For this reason, my work (El-Shamy: 2009) is labeled Religion among the Folk, rather than Folk Religion/Islam or Vernacular Religion/Islam, in Egypt. Religious practices considered folk are performed among and by the folk, but it is not an essential mode or, alternatively, an alternative or corrupt form of Islam; this is especially true because these religious practices considered folk are integral parts of formal Sunni Islam as ecclesiastically codified.

Notes

1 **Note: the sign $ stands for a new motif generated by Hasan El-Shamy. (In lieu of §). *Folklore annotation*, motifs are placed within quotation marks (""), and tale-types are Italicized.**
2 Motifs, V59.0.1.2$, "God hears all prayers from those who call (plead with) Him and answers them;" J1362.1$, "Person accused of performing religious duties, and then committing major sins ('boring holes in earth [so as to tunnel into houses and rob]')."
3 In upper Egypt, the notables of a village contracted a shaman-*shaikh* to rid their village of the effects of evil magic fixes (^{C}*amalat*)—as he had done in a neighboring village. The *shaikh* supposedly located and "neutralized" 41 fixes.
4 *Nûr el-Islam Review. Majallt al-Azhar,* issued first in 1930. Vols. 7–43 (1936–1972), published by "*Mashyakhat* al-Azhar."

5 Mot., C1.1$, "*al-haram*: sacred (religious) tabu. 'The illegitimate' (illicit, 'not permitted')—opposite of: *al-halal* (the licit or legitimate, permitted by God)."

6 Mot., V3.5$, "Required pilgrimage". Cf., V85.0.1.2$, ^{C}*umrah*: minor pilgrimage to Mecca outside the prescribed time. For a summation of similarities between Islam and Christianity, see Cox: 1981, 75.

7 On the dolls, see, https://ph.news.yahoo.com/egyptians-celebrate-prophet-mohammads-birth-miss-sugar-dolls-174027712.html', (edited by Lena Masri and Kirsten Donovan)'.

In mid-2022, the present writer--surly--read in one of the daily newspapers the fundamentalist declaration, aimed at the present government, that such these sugar dolls are idols, hence, they constitute idol worship; (unfortunately, he was unable to relocate the report). This extreme fundamentalist attitude is reproduced in neighboring North Africa (see: https://observers.france24.com/en/20131106-sugar-dolls-tunisia-religious-hardliners.

8 Mot. V215.5$, "Prophet Mohammad's ascent to Heavens via Jerusalem and return to earth (al-'Isra` wa al-Mi^{C}raj)". For a detailed description of the sacred events, see Hasan, Muhammad Sa^{C}id 1977; also see,Vuckovic, Olson, Brooke: 2005. The Egyptian media, particularly Ibrahim Issa, aroused wide anger by questioning the miracle of "the Ascension of the Prophet" Muhammad, may God bless him and grant him peace, to heaven. Al-Azhar's first response to Ibrahim Issa's "skepticism" of "Al-Isra and Al-Miraj" 2/19/2022, 9:29:41 AM.

9 Jahiz, (Al-): 1938–1945. Abu ^{C}Uthman ^{C}Amr Ibn Bahr, an early Arab Intellectual from Basra, b. 775, d. 868. He was a rationalist belonging to Mu^{C}tizali School. His liberal views—expressed especially in his book *al-hayawan*(The animal)—presented the following Themes/(Motifs) that have contemporary relevance: V357.3.1$, "Kharijites (*khawarij*) waged the first sectarian war in Islam"; W5.1.1$, "Kharijite's asceticism: exaggeration of others' namely, sins, disregarding the fact that God hates injustice even to the most unjust of people; and A102.16.3$, God hates injustice even to the unjust (of all people). For details, see Shamy (el-): 2018/2021, p. 89 n. 295. Section 3.3.1. in Shamy (el-): 2018, characterizes al-Jahiz as "the First Folklorist". He advanced the view that Moslems attitudes toward women stem from the sacred Koranic accounts of the creation of Adam and his primacy See, Thackston 1974, p. 50, No. 44. "Eve's Recompense". Ironically, Al-Jahiz's *'I^{C}tizal*, i.e.,rational positivistic views caused him no real harm (but reticule) during his time. Today, this rational approach is condemned as disbelief (*kufr*).

10 An example of the fatwas issued by unqualified religious public figures exemplifies the confusion their deductive logic causes by attributing hypothetical merit to drinking Prophet's urine. See Motifs: D1002.0.1$, "Excrements of 'holy man' works wonders ('holy shit')"; D1846.5.3$, "Invulnerability through saint's excreta (urine)"; and V141.3$, "Healing power of sacred relic (shirt, cloak, etc.)". See https://www.discovermagazine.com/the-sciences/drinking-muhammads-urine.

11 So deeply rooted is the belief in jinn that it permeates all levels of Moslem and Christian societies. A study shows that there is a charlatan (*daggal*) for every 214 Egyptian citizens in Egypt. See, Aamer, Adel. https://www.youm7.com/story/2017/3/28/-لكل-دجال -240مصريا-مواطنا

The manager of a major sports club, who is at the top of Egypt's western/civil educated elite, claims that the decisive victory of his local Egyptian competitor is due to the services of a Maghrebian shaman-*shaikh*, who enlists the services of *jinn*. He promised to open the "locked door" in his club's favor by the Koran. Jinn & Soccer: محمود مصطفى -الوفد بوابة -قاهرة10/20/17. (site used on 20/09/2022; subsequently [reported] "Unavailable"). Compare, www.theguardian.com › football › 2016. Mortada Mansour blames sorcery for Zamalek African Champ. Also, recently, a report of an Egyptian physician in England poisoned his colleague in a "dangerous perversion of the Islamic 'Ruqya' ritual so as to exorcise an evil spirit from him".

https//www.BBC.com/news/uk-england-humber-58116324. (Doctor Hossam Metwally poisoned partner in … - BBC News).

12 Motifs, D2071, "Evil Eye. Bewitching by means of a glance"; D1273.0.6$, "'*raqwah*'/ *ruqwah*: charm containing sacred words renders invulnerable (protects)". For examples of actual life experiences concerning the effect of the application of this belief, see Shamy (el-): 1980, "The Stone in Bed", no. 45, p. 182 and "The New Car" no. 46, p. 183. See also, Digwi (Al-). 1941.,"*al-hasad wa al-ruqyah minh*" (The Evil Eye …).

13 The formal stand of Islamic institutions is founded on a Koranic verse speaking of "*mass-un min al-Shaytan*/(touch by Satan) (Q 2:275, 114: 4). See Digwi (al-) 1941, pp. 161–162; and Husayn, S: 1970??, pp. 93–94. Motifs, D1$, '*sihr* (magic, sorcery)': controlling (coercing, harnessing) the supernatural and the natural by means of supernatural agents other than God and His Powers"; cf. A170.1$, "Miracle. Supernatural deed or manifestation by God"; and D1784.1$, "Magic results from breathing into a knot".

14 Karm (al-), 'Usamah: 1990. See also n. 13 above.

15 The Shafi^{C}i madhab is the most prevalent in Egypt. The three other *madhahib* are: the Maliki, founded by Anas ibn Malik (ca 715–95 A.D.); the Hanafi, founded by al-Nu^{C}man ibn Thabit, nicknamed AbuHahifah (700–767); and the Hanbali founded by Ahmad ibn Hanbal (780–855). The latter, which claims the smallest numerical following, is recognized as the most strict and rigid; the common expression (a proverbial simile): "to be *hambali*" signifies being too dogmatic, inflexible, or intolerant.

16 As quoted in Digwi, (al-), Yûsuf: 1941, "*ta^{C}allum al-sihr* (The Learning of Magic)", pp. 490–491; also see Kouly (al-), Fawqiyyah: 1978.

17 Husayn, S. "n.d./[1970??]" *al-Jinn/Ginn*. Husayn sets two categories of criteria for judging *sihr*/magic: (1) "knowledge-wise", according to which a believer that magic functions without God's command is a *kafir*/unbeliever, and (2) "practice-wise", according to which magic is strictly forbidden except in the case of a bewitched person that must be saved/healed, with the stipulation that what is of *al-^{C}za'im* (incantations) is well known, since ignorance of the Hebrew language in which the incantation must be is unknown to the general public (S. Husayn, pp. 91–92).

18 Motif, V93.0.1$, "*dhikr/`zikr'* as Sufi worship (involving dance and chant). Koran cites *dhikr* (Q 13:28) in the sense of mere mentioning of God. However, folk "*zikr*"/ *dhikr* which goes beyond the mere mentioning is often viewed as *bid^{C}ah* (deviant fad) (see Anonymous: In *al-Azhar*, Vol. 31, p. 377). The principle is that "every *bid^{C} ah* (deviant intrusion/innovation/fad) is a *dalalah* (misguiding/corrupting act), and every *dalalah* is to Hell". Some writers view the ritual as merely *makrûh*/disliked (Mot., C3$, "*al-makrûh* ('the disfavored', 'the disliked' [by God]): almost-tabu, merely tolerated—not the preferred way (for Moslems)"; see Shuqayri (al-): 1969. On the characteristics of the musical aspects of *Zikr/dhikr*, see Hartmann 1894; Faruqi (Al-) 1975; Lane 1973/1836; Waugh 1989. A recent fatwa views music as legitimate: https://sailanmuslim.com/culture- heritage/fatwa-on-music-by-the-grand-mufti-and-shaykh-of-al-azhar-shaykh-jad-al-haq-ali-jad-al-haq.

19 Motifs: V1.2.1.1$, "za rituals as veneration (worship) of jinn"; F385.2.1$, "Possessing jinn placated by supplications (song, dance)"; V93.1$, "Ecstasy (trance) through religious dancing (*dhikr, 'zikr'*)"; F956.7.7.3$, "Venting anger (stress) by shouting (loud 'singing,' 'quarrelling,' etc.)"; and V93.0.1$, "*dhikr/'zikr'* as Sufi worship (involving dance and chant)".

On the effects of "exhaustion", see Shamy (el-): 1972/1970, "Mental Health . . .", p. 18, n. 4. For a brief description of the entertaining aspect of *zikr*, see Amin, Ahmad (a distinguished historian and educator): 1953, p. 389, where he describes a performance by a troupe of the "Mawlawiyyah" Sufi-brotherhood of "whirling dervishes" (pp. 384–386). Amin expresses his own pleasure with the atheistic aspects of the ritual as a dance. Also see Burton: 1984, Vol. 2, p. 28, n. 1. For a detailed description of a "zikr" performance on the occasion of the Prophets Birthday, see Lane: 1973/(first published 1836), pp. 444–453.

20 An Azharite authority ("Member of the Council of Senior Ulama") of Al-Azhar in: Al-Azhar/Nour el-Islam Review, Vol. 11, No. 6, pp. 342–343. El-Shamy (el-): 2009, p. 23, n. 64. Motifs, F385.2.4$, "Possessing zar-jinn placated by appeasing (mollifying) person whom they possess"; F950.0.2$, "Hallucinatory drugs used to induce state of altered consciousness in exorcism rituals"; F950.0.2.1$, "Drug-induced illusion (hallucination)"; V93.2$, "Ecstasy (trance) through sacrilegious dancing (zar-ritual)"; C851.1, "Tabu: using food for unworthy purpose"; and C793$, "Tabu: destruction of property (e.g., food, land, clothing, etc.)" (no. 6). Besides the sacrifice, alcoholic beverages, or drugs (hashish, opium), the true-zar requires additional edibles such as nuts, fruits, crackers, and the like to be placed on a tray that sits on a low-rise table. This element is labeled *kursi-e-zar*/(the zar-chair/stool): Shamy (el-): 1980, "The Possessed Husband and his Zar", No. 41, pp. 175–178, 284–285. Elaborate procedures required for conducting a true zar, see n. 4, above. These include the zar-priestess (*shaikhah*) living with the afflicted for days, observing the surrounding social condition and her patterns of behavior and of those around her. Then, the *^{C}arûsit-ez-zar* must be the uncontested center for the entire procedure from beginning to end and beyond. Sample of a true-Zar *nida* (call) as chanted by Hesain Abu . . ., of the village of Kafr el-Zytoon, to the tunes of flue, tambourine and open drum:

> Ya Safinah f-el-bahr ^{C}awwamah
> O Safinah/(Ship), you are a swimmer in the sea
> bahariyyah f-el-bahr ^{C}awwamah
> Sailors/(marines) are swimmers in the sea
> wi muluuk el-mayyah f-el-bahr ^{C}awwamah
> And the water kings/(spirits) are swimmers in the sea!
> Etc.

21 *Al-Ahram*: (February 16, 1971), p. 3. Professional women in zar (university graduates) constituted 8%; meanwhile, the study indicated that nonliterate women who are typical zar-users were beginning to visit psychiatrists.

22 Vendors of religious objects and services eschew the use of the words "price", "cost", or "fee" to refer to what they expect a consumer would pay; the word "wahbah" (lit.: donation, grant) is preferred. In 1969, the admission fee ordinarily ranged from 10 to 25 piasters (quarter of a pound) for the entire session; in 1982, it was roughly three times that amount; and in 2000, the fee became from 5.00 to 10.00 pounds (there are 100 piasters to a pound). At the beginning of the 2000s, the fee was much higher, and some practitioners charge per *tafqirah* ([joining in] one ritual dance to a beat ("*nida*").

23 Shamy (el-): 2009, p. 102 n. 336. Informant: '*shaikh*' Hesain Abu-. . ., 35, the son of the village of Kafr el-Zaytûn's senior shaman-*shaikh*; a practitioner himself. Tape-recorded in April 1969 and May 1982. A sample of the public Zar's *nida* as chanted to the accompaniment of flue, tambourine, and open drum in 1969 and 1982 is as follows:

> Hobb el-Hasan wi el-Husain fi muhgatqti sakin /
> The love of el-Hasan and el-Husain (Prophet Mohammad's grandsons) resides in my *muhgah* (the innermost seat of love in a heart.
> lakin hobb en-nabi, bi-y'al'al/(yuqalqil) es-sakin
> But the love of the Prophet loosens what is dead still.
> Ya mustafa, ana min gharamak ma b-nam el-lail
> O Chosen-one, due to my love for you, I don't sleep at night /
> Sa^{C}ah b-mdahak , wi sa^{C}a b-'ahlam bik ya zain lakeen hob en-nabi, bi-y'al'al/(yuqalqil) es-sakin
> But the love of the Prophet loosens what is dead still /

Ya mustafa, ana min gharamak ma b-nam el-lail
O Chosen-one, due to my love for you, I don't sleep at night /
Sa^{C}ah b-mdahak , wi sa^{C}a b-ahlam bik ya zain, /

For a while I praise you, and for a while I dream of you, O beautiful-one.

24 Mot., F956.7.2.1$, "Curative effects of strenuous physical activity (till exhaustion)". Accounting to (K.), a middle-aged childless woman, the zar–*'asayad* who possess her, she cited 28 possessing characters (*ital.* added for sister-to a-brother): (1) Littmann's List Sister: 6 Occurrences. (2) El-Shamy's List Sister: 10 Occurrences. (3) Shummay's/Fawwaz's List Sister: 9 Occurrences.

25 Motifs, W4.4$, "Piety: believing that only God heals"; F361.17.10$, "Jinniyyah (fairy) takes revenge on man who slights her love"; F405.15$, "Spirit leaves when exorciser threatens to resort to its government (king)"; and F405.14.1$, "Possessing spirit leaves body of possessed person via wound (made by exorciser)".

26 Barghuthi (Al-): Motifs: F405.14.3$, "Possessing spirit leaves when it is violated sexually (disgraced, humiliated)". Nabhani (Al-): D2065.1.1$, "Epilepsy from possession by jinn"; F304.7$, "Jinni violates human woman (girl)"; D2161.3.8.1.1$, "Epilepsy cured by coition"; and V223, "Saints have miraculous knowledge".

Works Cited

Aamer, Adel. 2017, 28, Mar دجال-لكل-240-مواطنا-مصريا...https://www.youm7.com/story/2017/3/28/ Adel (2017). Youm7 Daily: Cairo.

Ahram (Al-). (February 16, 1971), p. 3. "Professional Women in zar (University Graduates Constituted 8 Percent); Meanwhile, the Study Indicated that Nonliterate Women Were Beginning to Visit Psychiatries".

Al-Azhar, Vol. 11, No. 6, pp. 342 43. See, *Nour el-Islam Review.*

Amin, Ahmad. 1953. *qamûs al-^{C}adat wa al-taqalid wa al-ta^{C}abir al-misriyyah (Dictionary of Egyptian Customs, Traditions and Expressions)* (Al-nahdah: 2nd ed.: Cairo).

Anonymous. An Azharite authority (Member of the "Council of Senior Ulama") of Al-Azhar. In: *Al- Azhar/Nour el-Islam Review*, Vol. 11, No. 6, (1940–41) pp. 342–343.

Barghûthi (al-), ^{C}Abd al-Latif M. 1979. *hikayat jan min Bani Zayd (Jinn Tales from Bani Zayd [Palestine])* (Jerusalem).

BBC. Broadcasting House in London (London, U.K.).

Cox, Harvey. 1981. "Understanding Islam: No More Holy Wars". In: *The Atlantic Monthly.* (Boston: 1857 ff., Jan. 1981, pp. 73–80.

Digwi (al-) 1931. Yusuf. fatwa on "karamat al `awliya`/(Saints' Miracle like Manifestations)". In: *Nûr al-Islam*, Vol. 1, No. 10 (1931), pp. 764–770.

Digwi (al-). 1941. "al-hasad wa al-ruqyah minh"(The vil Eye and the Incantation/Charm Against it). In: *al-Azhar*, Vol. 12, No. 8, pp. 161–162.

Faruqi (Al-), Louis Ibsen. 1975. "Muwashshah: A Vocal Form in Islamic Culture." In: *Ethnomusicology*, Vol. 19, No. 1 (January), pp. 1–29.

Fawwaz. 1893. Zaynab. See Shumays, below.

Goldziher, Ignaz. 1955. Vorlesungen über den Islam (Readings in Isalm), Andras and Ruth Hamori, trs. pp. 238–240 (no. 6). M.Y. Mûsa: 1955, tr.,ed. of the Arabic edition under the title al-^{C}aqidah wa al shari^{C}ah fi al-Islam/(Belief and Religious Law in Islam) (al-Khangi: Cairo).

Hartmann, Martin. 1984. "Über die Muwashshah. genannte Art der Strophengedichte bei den Arabern." In: *Acte reintalists* (Geneva), Vol. 2, pt. 3, pp. 47–67 (Ktaus reprints-Nendeln-Leichtenstein, 1972).

H̲asan, Sa^{C}id Muhammad. 1977. *haqa'iq al-Isra' wa al-Mi^{C}raj (Facts about the 'isra' and the mi^{C}raj)* (Cairo: S.M. Hasan).

Husayn, Sayyid ^{C}Abdallah. 1970??. *Al-ginn/(jinn): In Mentioning all the Conditions of the Jinn* (Cairo: al-H̲alabi).

Karm (al-), 'Usamah. 1990. *h̲iwar ma^{C} a al-ginn. 'asra^{C} t̲uruq li ^{C}ilag al-'amrad̲ al-musta^{C}s̲iyah bi al- Qur'an/(Discourse with Jinn. The Fastest Methods for Treating Hard to Cure Incurable Illnesses with Koran)* (Cairo: Madbûli).

Kisa'i (Al-), Muhammad ibn ^{C}Abdallah. 1922. *Qis̲as̲ al-'anbiya' (Vita Prophetarum).* Isaac Eisenberg, ed. (Leiden, the Netherlands: Brill).

Kouly (al-), Fawqiyyah. 1978. "Islam Prohibits Magic and Contact with Jinn, and [Secular] Law Considers These Acts Crimes of Impostery." *Al-Ahram* (Sep. 8), p. 11.

Lane, Edward William. 1973. *An Account of the Manners and Customs of the Modern Egyptians* (New York: Dover, 1973/first published in 1836).

Littmann, Enno. 1950. *Arabische Geisterbeschwörungen aus Ägypten* (Leipzig: Otto Harrassowitz).

Mahfouz, Nagib. 1960, [Tripartite novel] = B.Q. = *Bayna al-Qas̲rayn*; Q.Sh. = *Qas̲r al-Shawq*; S. = *al-Sukkariyyah* (Cairo, 1956–1960). [Should have been titled: "Brother and Sister in Mahfouz's Trilogy"].

Majalt [i.e., *Majallat*] *al Azhar,* issued first in 1930. Vols. 7 43 (1936-72). published by Mashyakhat al-Azhar (Cairo, 1938ff.).

Masri, Lena, K. Donavan, 2018, Egyptians-celebrate-prophet-mohammads-birth-miss-sugar-dolls-174027712.html'.

Nabhani (al-), Yûsuf Isma^{C}il. 1962. *Jami^{C} karamat al-`awliya`/(An inclusive collection of saints' karamt)* I. ^{C}A, ^{C}Awad, ed. (Cairo: al-H̲alabi).

Sengers, Gerda. 2003. *Women and Demons: Cult Healing in Islamic Egypt* (Brill).

Shamy (El-), Hasan M. 1972/1970. "Mental Health in Traditional Culture: A Study of Preventive and Therapeutic Folk Practices." In: *Psychiatry and the State*, Mark C. Kennedy, Ed. (Petersborough, : Trent University Press 1972), pp. 13–28.

———. 1976. "The Traditional Structure of Sentiments in Mahfouz's Trilogy: A Behavioristic Text Analysis." In: *Al-'Arabiyya: Journal of the American Association of Teachers of Arabic*, Vol. 9 (October), pp. 53–74. [Should have been titled: "Brother and Sister in Mahfouz's Trilogy"].

———. 1979. Brother and Sister. Type 872★: A Cognitive Behavioristic Analysis of a Middle Eastern Oikotype. Folklore Monograph Series, No. 8 (Bloomington, IN).

———. 1980. *Folktales of Egypt: Collected, Translated and Annotated with Middle Eastern and [sub-Saharan] African Parallels* (Chicago: University of Chicago Press).

———. 1982. "Belief Characters as Anthropomorphic Psychosocial Realities," (with a résumé in Arabic). In: *al-kitab al-sanawi li-^{c}ilm al-'igtima^{c} (Annual Review of Sociology),* published by Department of Sociology, Cairo University, Vol. 3, pp. 7–36; Arabic Abstract, pp. 389–393.

———. 2005. "Sister and Brother, Motif: P253". In: *Archetypes and Motifs in Folklore and Literature: A Handbook.* Jane Garry and Hasan El-Shamy, Eds. (M.E. Sharpe), pp. 349–361.

———. 2009. *Religion among the Folk in Egypt* (Westport, CT; London: Praeger).

———. 2011. "Motif". In: *The Cambridge Encyclopedia of Language Sciences*, Patrick C. Hogan, gen. ed. (Cambridge: Cambridge University Press), pp. 530–531 (El-Shamy's name is not listed in the "INDEX".].

———. 2013. *Beyond Oedipus: The Brother-Sister Syndrome as Depicted by Tale-Type 872★: A Cognitive Behavioristic, Demographically Oriented, Text Analysis of an Arab Oikotype* (Bloomington, IN: The Trickster Press).

———. 2018. "Folklore of the Arab World". *Humanities* 7(3), 67; doi:10.3390/h7030067.

Shumays, ^{C}Abd al-Mun^{C} im. 1971. "al-zar masrah ghina'i lam yatatawwar/(The Zar: A Lyric Drama That Did Not Evolve)." In: *al-Funûn*, No. 17 (Cairo), pp. 72–83. [The primary data given by Shumays is derived from Zaynab Fawwaz's 1893 study.]

Shuqayri (al-), ^{C}Abd al-Salam Khidr. 1969. *al-sunan wa al-mu^{C}taqdat al-muta^{C}alliqah bi-al-`adhkar wa al-ṣalawat* (Prophet's Traditions and Deviant Fads in Remembrances and Prayers) (Cairo).

Thackston, W. M. 1978. *Tales of the Prophets of al Kisa'i*. Translated from Arabic with notes by: W. M. Thackston, Jr (Boston: Twayne Publishers).

Vuckovic, Olson Brooke. 2005. *Heavenly Journeys, Earthly Concerns: The Legacy of the Mi^{C}raj in the Formation of Islam* (New York: Routledge).

Waugh, Earle H. 1989. *The Munshidin of Egypt: Their World and Their Song* (Colombia: U. of South Carolina Press).

APPENDIX

This "Appendix" for the present chapter in Borkataky-Varma and Ullrey may appear superfluous. However, it places every theme treated in this chapter in the proper context of the folk-belief practice system. Examples are the traditional practice of communicating with the dead via séance cited below as II.E. *er-roah* (The Soul) and *en-nafs* (The Self/[psyche]), which is the parent category of II.E.1. *Cafrit* (Ghost, cf. spook/revenant), which is the parentcategory of; and II.E.2. Summoning the Soul (Séance). From these topics a systemic continuum for this practice can be established.

Various other topics from the "Bird's Eye View" below explain themes in the chapter and continue assert a systemic continuum. *Zikr* (*dhikr*) is typically paired with the *Zar* in daily life and shown to be a subdivision under a category different from Zikrs, namely I.A. Allah (i.e., God) and I.A.1 *zikr* (Remembrance [of God]). Meanwhile, *Zar*—dealing with a special category of possessing-*jinn*, who neither appear in any other belief-practice function (e.g., leading to treasure, carrying a person) nor can be evicted/eliminated—is placed under II.C. *Jinn* as Components of the Individual: Supernatural Counter-spirits and Siblings, including the following: II.C.1. The *Qarin* and *Qarinah*: A Human's Counter-spirit, Correlative, or Spouse; II.C.1a. The *'Ukht* (Sister), and *'Akhkh* (Brother); II.C.2. The Cult of Supernatural Illness, Possession, and Healing; and II.C.2a. *'asyad* ez-zar (*zar* spirits/possessing-*jinn*). Although categories II.C, II.C1, and II.C1a don't appear in the present study, their presence is essential for the fullness of the *Zar* context.

Magic is a topic of particular interest. Magic, *sihr* comes under, Harnessing the Jinn and Minor Angels: II.B.3. *sihr* (magic): *sihr-súfli* (nether magic, sorcery), *halb en nugûm* (milking the stars); *shabshabah* ([magic through] use of slipper); II.B.3.a. *sihr Cúlwi* (upper magic or folk para-religious ritual). Although the Koran lists the beliefs in the effects of magic, in "breathing into knots to actuate magic" and in envy together, each pertains to a different category of the belief-practice system.

The former belongs to the category of II.B.3. *sihr*(Magic): *sihr-súfli* (Nether magic, Sorcery).

Finally, Viii. Mechanical Associations within the supernatural. Only Edward Westermarck (1926) reported from Morocco the belief that a jinni accompanies the malicious glance to the envied object causing it harm. Yet, such a belief has not been found elsewhere. The typical belief sets the effect of the malicious glance within "Mechanical Associations" found in VIII.C. *el-hasad* ([Malicious] Envy) and *el-*^{C}*ain* (The [Evil] Eye) [which—in a broader context—would lead to Motifs: Z138.4.1$, "Evil Eye acts independently of owner‘s will"; Z138$, "Body organ (member) personified"; F1042$, "Mania: compulsion--uncontrollable (involuntary) behavior"; and Z138.4$, "Eye personified"]. The same argument may be advanced vis-à-vis other *takfiriyyin/(al-Qa*^{C}*idah*, Moslem *'awliya* and Coptic *shuhda*, etc.

Thus, the "Appendix" provides critical information for assessing a belief's systemic connection and leads to additional data that may cast more light on its possible interpretations.

A prototype of the present work presented as an appendix below was first introduced at the IX International Congress of Anthropological and Ethnological Sciences, held at Chicago, Illinois in September 1973, and it is a part of "The Brother–Sister Syndrome" theory advanced by the present writer. The manuscript for the work was expanded and made available to students at Indiana University and elsewhere in successive mimeographed pre-publication editions (1974, 1975, 1984, 1997) as a textbook in my Middle Eastern folklore classes taught from 1974 to 2011. Segments of the system were published in Hasan El-Shamy, "Belief Characters as Anthropomorphic Psychosocial Realities". In: *al-Kitab al-sanawi li-*^{C}*ilm al-'igtima*^{C} *(Annual Review of Sociology)*, Department of Sociology, Cairo University, Vol. 3 (1982), pp. 7–36, Arabic Abstract, pp. 389–393. The outline depicting the general structural schema of this system was published along with relevant motifs in 1995 in Hasan El-Shamy, *Folk Traditions of the Arab World: A Guide to Motif Classification*, 2 vols. (Bloomington: Indiana University Press, 1995), Vol. 1, pp. 443–444.

This bird‘s eye view of the full belief-practice system for "religion among the folk in Egypt" is, to the best of my knowledge, the only system of its kind in this field (Islam). For a typical example of what other Islam scholars perceive to be the view of the world, the following website is an example: https://www.google.com/search?q=Worldview+in+Islamic+diagram+of+worldview. It is also reflected in Anton M. Heinen's *Islamic Cosmology: A study of AS-SUYÛTI'S al-Hay`a as-saniiya f i l-hay`h as-sunniya . . .* (Beirut: 1982). Similar literary views appear on the web dealing with how the physical (God created) world is structured and viewed. Actually, El-Shamy was the first to introduce the intricate concept of "World View" in "African Religion and World View". In: in *Africa*, (IU Press, 1976), pp. 208–220.

Religion among the Folk-Belief Practice System

Table (A Bird's Eye View)—phonetic guides to pronunciations are kept.

I Creation and Cosmology

I Allah and Creation

I.A *zìkr* (Remembrance [of Allah (God)])

I.B Cosmology

I.B.1 Creation of *al-qadàr, el-qismàh/en-naṣîb* (Destiny, Kismet): *al-qalàm* (the Pen), *al-làwḫ al-màḫfûz* (The Safeguarded Tablet)

I.B.1a *al-^{C}àrsh* (The Throne), *al-ḫàyyàh* (The Viper), *es-samawat* (Heavens), Nûn–the Whale [(named Lûtiya)]

I.B.1b. Establishment of Night, Day, and Related Temporal Phenomena

I.B.2 Paradise, Hell, Isthmus–The Straight-path, The Lote-tree of the Extremity

I.C Heavenly Bodies

I.D *el-'Arḏ* (Earth)

I.E *el-ḫigab* (The Veil, Barrier)

I.F *al-bàrzàkh* (The Isthmus, Purgatory)

I.G *Sidràt al-Muntaha* (The Lote-tree of the Extremity)

II Supernatural Beings

II Supernatural Beings

II.A *malâykàh* (Angels)

II.A.1 Other Categories of Angels

II.A.1a Angels as Components of a Person (Self/Psyche, etc.)

II.A.1b Nakir and Nakîr, The Two Interrogative Angels [(grave trial)]

II.A.2 Eblîs and Other Fallen Angels

II.A.2a Harût and Marût [(angles sent to Earth, seduced by a female)]

II.B *el-ginn* (The Jinn, cf. fairies)

II.B.1 *gìnniyyât* (Female Jinn)

II.B.1a Unstratified Female Jinn

II.B.2 Influencing/Harnessing the Jinn and Minor Angels

II.B.2a *fàtḫ el-màandàl* (Oracle, detective-divination via jinn)

II.B.3 *sìḫr* (Magic): *sìḫr-suflî* (Nether magic, Sorcery)–*ḫàlb en-nugûm* (Milking the stars); *shàbshabàh* ([Magic through] use of Slipper)

II.B.3.a *sìḫr ^{C}ulwî* (Upper magic) or Folk Para-religious Ritual?

II.C Jinn as Components of the Individual: Supernatural Counter-spirits and Siblings

II.C.1 The *Qarîn* and *Qarînàh*: A Human's Counter-spirit, Correlative, or Spouse

II.C.1a The *'Ukht* (Sister), and *'Akhkh* (Brother)

II.C.2 The Cult of Supernatural Illness, Possession, and Healing
   II.C.2a 'asyâd ez-zâr (zâr spirits/possessing-jinn)
II.D Zoological Supernatural Beings
II.D.1 ghîlân (Ogres) and Similar Creatures/Beings
II.D.2 Supernatural Animals: The Mare and the Stallion
   II.D.2a The "Earth's Animal" "Dàbbàt el-`ard̲" (the "earth's animal").
II.D.3 Supernatural Reptiles
II.D.4 Supernatural Birds
II.D.5 The Cat and other Creatures with Ties to the Supernatural—(Ant, Bee, Mantis)
II.E er-roah̲ (The Soul), and en-nàfs (The Self/[psyche])
II.E.1 ^{C}àfrît (Ghost, cf. spook/revenant [also seldom used to describe a powerful jinni])
II.E.2 Summoning the Soul (Seance)

III AL-'INCE (Humans)
III.A Social Stratification in 'ince Society
III.B Specific Classes
   III.B.1 rusùl (God's Messengers) and `anbiya (Prophets) and their Associates
   III.B.2 s̲ahabàh (The Prophet's Companions)
   III.B.3 Saints: Moslem `awliya ("God's Favorites") and Coptic shuhada ("Martyrs")
      III.B.3a S̲ûfî Brotherhoods and Other Religious Organizations
III.C en-nâs (People), and [implicit] Folk Theories of Personality

IV Deified Humans
IV The Arch-saints
   IV.A el-`arba$^C$àh el-`qt̲âb (The Four Axes [of Earth]/Arch-saints)
   IV.B el-Khidr (The Green-one), St. George, Elijah
   IV.C Imam ^{C}Alî
   IV.D Organization among Arch-Saints
      IV.D.1 The Concept of Power and the Right to Rule: The Parallel Government
      IV.D.2 ed-dîwân (the Divan/Council), and the Cult of Martyrdom
   IV.E jihad Rightous-struggle and Greater Martyrdom

V Powers and Abstracts
V.A Sacred Powers
   V.A.1 God's Power
V.B al-^{C}ìlm, (Knowledge, Gnosis)
   V.B.1 Sources of Knowledge and Truth
   V.B.2 Instructive Dreams
V.C Concepts and Abstract Forces
   V.C.1 barakàh, (Blessing/Grace/Benediction)
   V.C.2 la^{C}nàh, ghad̲ab, nìqmàh: ([God's] Curse, Anger, Wrath)

VI Nonsacred Forces and Concepts

VI.A Temporal Forces, Quasi Powers of Fate: *ez-zamàn/ez-zamân* (Time), *ed-dàhr* (Time-epochs), *el-`ayyâm* (Days), *el-^{C}îshah* (Life/[living]), *ed-Dùnya/Dinya* (World, Life)

VI.B Chance: *hàzz/bàkht* (Luck), *zàhr* (Dice), *el-yâ-nasîb/lutarìyyàh* (Lottery), *tâli^{C}* (One's place in the horoscope), and *suàdfàh* (Accident, Chance)

VI.C Learning of the Unknown: *el-kàff* (Reading the palm of the hand), *el-fingan/fingal* (Reading the residuals in a coffee cup), Divination through *el-ràml* ("[Cutting] sand") and *el-wadà^{C}* (Sea shells), and et-tâ-*lì^{C})* (One's horoscope)

VIC1 Soliciting God's Choice (*`istkhârah*), and Bibliomancy (fath el-kitâb)

VI.D Risks and Gambles: *mi`aysàh/"muqâyasàh"* (Risk taking, Venturing), *muqâmarah* (Gambling, or taking a gamble), *'ìstibyâ^{C}* (Venturing all, including one's own life, out of desperation)

VII. Anti-Sacred Forces

VII Eblis (Satan), Other "satans". Cf. *shàrr* (Evil)

VIII Mechanical Associations within the Supernatural

VIII.A *khuzà^{C}balât* (Superstitions)

VIII.B *mushâhràh* or *kàbsàh* (Loss of Fecundity, Induced Barrenness, Infertility)

VIII.C *el-*hasàd ([Malicious] Envy) and *el-^{C}ain* (The [Evil] Eye)

VIII.C.1 *el-^{C}ain* (The Eye)

VIII.C.2 *el-kelmàh* (The Word)

PART II

Spirit Beings and Deities

5

GODDESS TREES IN THE FOREST OF BLISS

Local Place and Translocal Space in a City of Pilgrims

David Gordon White

Varanasi: A Tale of Two Cities?

The capital city of the ancient kingdom of Kāśī, Varanasi did not emerge as a major pilgrimage destination until the early second millennium CE, when glorifications (*māhātmyams*) of holy places began to be featured in the compendia of Hindu theism known as the Purāṇas.[1] Prior to that time, the sole comprehensive guide to South Asia's *tīrtha*s had been that included in the third book of the great *Mahābhārata* (MBh) epic, a work dating from between 200 BCE and 400 CE. There, among the hundreds of pilgrimage sites noted in its extensive survey, the MBh devotes a single verse to Varanasi as a place where the fruit of honoring the bull-bannered god Śiva and bathing at the Kapila pool is equivalent to that obtained through the performance of a royal consecration (*rājasūya*).[2] An early version of the *Skanda Purāṇa* preserved in an 810 CE Nepalese palm-leaf manuscript is likely the earliest work to provide an expanded account of the city's holy places. However, its portrayal of Varanasi as a heavily wooded "garden of the gods" populated by yogis, Pāśupatas, and other ascetics, does not highlight the devotional practices praised in nearly all later *māhātmyams*.[3] Rather, it is the fruit of yogic practice that is underscored.[4] In the succeeding centuries, *vārāṇasī māhātmyams* running to several chapters would appear in well over a dozen Purāṇas.[5] The longest such glorifications are those embedded in two of these, the *Skanda* and *Brahmavaivarta Purāṇa*s. Titled the "Kāśī Khaṇḍa" (KKh) and "Kāśī Rahasya," respectively, these are quite late, dating from the fourteenth and sixteenth centuries, respectively.[6]

A number of encyclopedic works (*nibandha*s), some predating these Puranic sources and authored by illustrious residents of Varanasi, also provide extensive accounts of the holy city's many bathing places and shrines. The earliest of these, and the template for all that have followed, is Lakṣmīdhara's "Examination

DOI: 10.4324/9781003257462-8

of the Holy Pilgrimage Sites" (*tīrtha-vivecana*), which comprises the eighth volume of his massive ca. 1110 CE "Wish-fulfilling Tree of Righteous Actions" (*Kṛtyakalpataru*) (Aiyangar v, liv–lv). A chief minister of the Gāhaḍvāla king Govindacandra and the most eminent scholar-statesman of his time (Aiyangar xvii–xviii, xlii, lv, lxx), Lakṣmīdhara's survey of the *tīrtha*s of the Hindu ecumene, which was heavily weighted toward this, the Gāhaḍvāla "power base" of Varanasi (Bakker 38–39), listed no fewer than 462 major bathing places and shrines throughout the city, most of them Śaiva as evidenced by the *-īśvara* endings of their names.[7] This was altogether appropriate since Śiva had long been the city's Great God (Mahādeva). In 1193 CE, Varanasi and the entire kingdom would fall to the armies of Islam, with the following centuries seeing mosques rising out of the wreckage of the city's holiest temples. Yet, as Hans Bakker has observed, "the ruin of old Vārāṇasī was just the required condition to stimulate the Hindu imagination," that imagination taking the form of the KKh's construction of a "timeless Vārāṇasī . . . on a grand scale" (Bakker 43). Twelve thousand verses in length, the work catalogs the merits of visiting and venerating 1000 of the city's temples and bathing places, many of them long since vanished at the time of its compilation.[8] Authors of later digests, expanding on content found in these works, would further promote the city's greatness, devoting as many as two-thirds of their discussions of the *tīrtha*s of the entire Hindu world to Varanasi or Kāśī alone (Aiyangar lix).

In the course of its six "Muslim centuries," the holy city's temples were destroyed six times over (Eck 83). When in the late eighteenth century, the British ushered in a time of relative peace, that virtual Varanasi of *māhātmyam* nostalgia would, through the patronage of wealthy merchants and princes, gradually (re)emerge. Yet, even as new temples with old names were rising across the skyline of the holy city—concentrated especially around Viśvanāth, Śiva's greatest temple—the glorification of Varanasi's past would actually climax, albeit in a new medium, in 1876. This was the year in which Kailashnath Sukul, patriarch of one of the city's most illustrious families, would produce a great stylized "picture map" titled *Kāśī Darpaṇa*, the "Mirror of Kāśī." This remarkable document depicts the city as a circular mandala enclosing some 1200 named sites, both ancient, as authenticated in the *Purāṇa*s, and modern, as represented in the new temples that were springing up all over.[9]

Kailashnath's legacy was carried forward into the late twentieth century when his grandson, Kubernath Sukul, published an exhaustive digest of Varanasi's temples and *tīrtha*s in his 1977 Hindi-language *Vārāṇasī Vaibhav* ("Varanasi's Grandeur"). Patterned after Lakṣmīdhara's "Examination of the Holy Pilgrimage Sites" and the KKh, which he cites extensively, Sukul's work has a twofold purpose: to uncover and describe to the extent possible the major temples and *tīrtha*s named in those two works (Sukul 1977: 361–368 [Appendix *ka*]), and to provide a highly detailed contemporary street guide to the city's "most celebrated" (*suvikhyāta*) holy sites. A total of some 780 sites are cataloged in this guide, of which nearly half are Śiva temples. Of the remaining entries, drawn from the two aforementioned works and various Purāṇas, many are listed as "vanished" (*lupt*) (Sukul 1977: 380–408 [Appendix *ṅa*]). In this respect, Sukul's is a record of a Varanasi of the Hindu imagination. Sukul's *māhātmyam*-based methodology has been uncritically adopted by a number of the world's leading specialists, writing in the English medium.[10] Diana Eck, whose authoritative 1982 volume *Banaras, City of Light* is dedicated to Sukul, was guided by him in her dissertation research there in the early 1970s.[11] Niels Gutschow, author and photographer of the lavishly illustrated 2006 *Benares, The Sacred Landscape of Vārāṇasī*, speaks in his foreword of Sukul's powerful influence on his own vision of the city (Gutschow 7). He also praises his "co-pilgrim" Rana P. B. Singh, who has emerged as the most prolific of all scholars charting the city's sacred geography, as well as Kedarnath Vyas, about whom he writes that

> he did not need to carry maps because his topographical knowledge was stunningly perfect. Both the map that provides orientation in this world as well as the map that refers to the inaccessible world beyond visible realities is carried in his mind. With an exceptional pace he moved through the narrow lanes of Benares to arrive at any place we wished to find that stands for "religious translocality".
>
> *(Gutschow 10)*

Like Gutschow, Eck identifies her principal informants as "the brahmins of Banāras, especially those who are the knowledgeable keepers of the tradition and who act as interpreters of myth and *māhātmyam*" (Eck xv), accessible to non-specialists through written sources alone:

> From childhood . . . pilgrims have known of Kāshī, not through the diaries of travelers, but through a type of traditional literature called *māhātmya* . . . These *māhātmyas* are not descriptive statements of fact about an *ordinary city* (my italics), but statements of faith about a sacred city. Kāshī is the whole world, they say. Everything on earth that is powerful and auspicious is here, in this microcosm.
>
> *(Eck 22–23)*

Axel Michaels, who together with Gutschow published a short German-language guide to Benares (Gutschow and Michaels 1993), discusses the implications of these statements of faith, according to which the entire Hindu universe is present, immanent and invisible, at once within and beyond the boundaries of the sacred city-in-the-world: "[In] pilgrim texts and city eulogies . . . Kāśī appears . . . in bright light, as a field of cosmic forces, as a sacred Maṇḍala enclosing the whole universe as a place of perfect purity, liberation, and redemption" (Michaels 289).

All of the sources reviewed to this point were created for the edification of people from other places. These are pilgrims who, relying on guides to a Varanasi from another time, further rely on (mainly) hereditary pilgrimage priests (*paṇḍās*) to guide them through the many ritual acts required of them during their brief sojourn in the holy city. Then, having satisfied their ancestors and ensured their own salvation beyond death, most of them return to their own places, scattered across the Indian subcontinent and the wider world.

Pilgrim's guides are portable, transferrable across space either in the form of a text carried in a pilgrim's (or scholar's or tourist's) luggage or lodged in their hearts and minds. All refer to a space that transcends both geographical and temporal boundaries, a universe in microcosm whose most salient features—temples and shrines that no longer exist, gods from across the entire Indian subcontinent—are often invisible to the naked eye. This, according to Gutschow, is the advantage of the "picture map": "[C]artographic maps rarely created a sense of translocality, which is characteristic of the 'picture maps' of Benares" (Gutschow 18).

But this translocal, universal, "all-Indian" vision of an exclusively Hindu Varanasi is not shared by all who pass through the city's labyrinthine lanes or walk the magnificent *ghāṭs* of its riverfront. The "ordinary city" of Varanasi is currently home to well over a million residents, people from every social group and religious persuasion whose transactions with their gods are far more often local than translocal, a fact acknowledged by Eck (xv–xvi). While they will occasionally worship at the great temples of Śiva and other supreme beings of translocal Hindu theism as pilgrims do, Banarsi-wallahs will more generally interact with gods that are closer to home, gods they petition for succor and meaning in their everyday lives: family gods, lineage gods (*kuladevatās*), chosen gods (*iṣṭadevatās*), and gods of the place (*grāmadevatās*) embedded in the cityscape.

Although undocumented in the literature of "official" Hinduism, these local deities' humble shrines—often simply called their "places" (*sthāns*)—are far more numerous than the city's temples, visible and invisible, of translocal renown. We know this because they have been documented through the very sort of maps that Gutschow eschews on the specific ground that they fail to convey a "sense of translocality." In 1824, the earliest extant cartographic map of Varanasi was drawn up by the British Orientalist and administrator James Prinsep, who presented his data in two ways: statistically, in his tabulation of census data and cartographically, in his representation of the city's urban landscape. Paired with the comprehensive data of his 1832 census (Prinsep 470–498), Prinsep's remarkably detailed "sixty-four-inch map" provides an early, accurate tableau of the city's demography. As noted in the introduction to his census, the baseline category for mapping and tabulating Varanasi's population was the *mahallā*,[12] a well-defined gated enclave of houses and shops. Instituted by the same Delhi Sultanate whose imperial forces had sacked the city in 1194 CE,[13] Varanasi's *mahallā* system is mainly organized along the lines of caste, craft, ethnicity, religion, language, or regional origins. These have remained vibrant features of the city's social and religious life down to the present day.[14]

In Prinsep's time, there were 369 *mahallās* in the city, of which one, named "Terhee Neem," was situated in the modern-day Godaulia neighborhood, a short distance inland from Varanasi's principal ghats and bordered on its eastern edge by the famed Shri Vishvanath-ji ki Galli, the north-south lane leading to the great Viśvanāth temple. According to Prinsep's survey, this *mahallā* harbored five "ruins" and three temples (*shiwalas*) (Prinsep 480, 489). Later maps offer greater detail. On "Sheet No. 12" of the 1929 "Benares City" map of the Dashashwamedh and Chauk police wards, the borders of the *mahallā* (hereafter transliterated as Terhi Neem) remain unchanged; however, this map reveals the presence of no fewer than ten individual temples or temple groupings there (Figure 5.1).

Most recently, in a statistical and cartographical survey published in 2018, Christian Haskett numbered Varanasi's temples at 3,347, and, classifying them on the basis of their relative size, identified 175 as "large," 644 as "medium," and 2,034 as "tiny" or "small," while noting that "of the 523 remaining sanctuaries, we also located 157 trees that were identifiable as temples, in addition to and apart from the several hundred temples of all sizes that were built around trees."[15] Amidst the high concentration of mainly "medium" and "tiny" temples clustered in the map quadrant in and around the Terhi Neem *mahallā*, Haskett's map indicates that three of these are "tree temples."[16]

I have presented these statistical and cartographic data for two reasons. First, the image they offer of Varanasi's religious landscape has nothing in common with those provided by "official" sources, from the Sanskrit-language *māhātmyams*

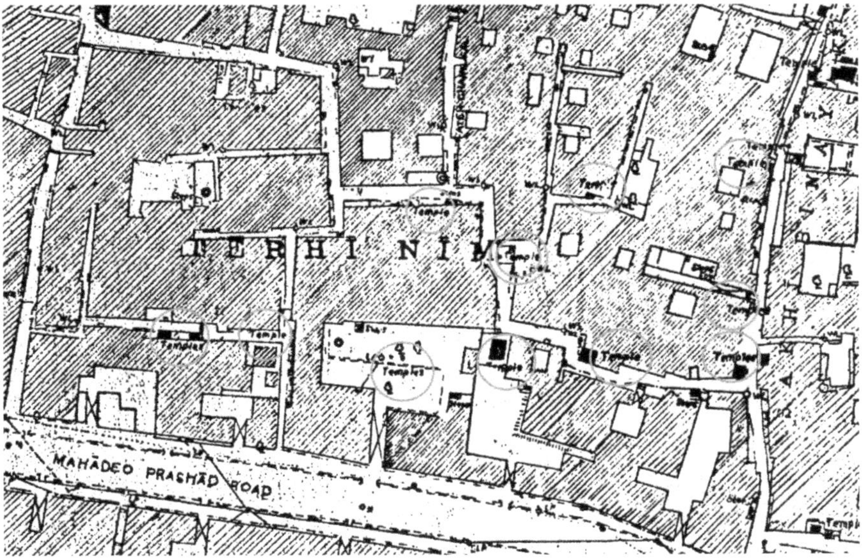

FIGURE 5.1 Detail, " Dashashwamedh and Chauk police wards," sheet 12. Temples are circled in grey; the "Saṅkaṭ Nāśinī Vijaya" Durgā temple is twice circled in grey.

down through Kailashnath Sukul's "picture map," his grandson Kubernath's Hindi-language guide, and the majority of books and chapters written by Indian and foreign scholars over the past decades.[17] Not a single one of the Terhi Neem *mahallā*'s many diminutive shrines appears in these sources, because even though situated a short distance from the Shri Vishvanath-ji ki Galli and several of the city's "most celebrated" temples, none figure in guides for pilgrims translocating through the city's sacred space.

The urban fabric of the Terhi Neem *mahallā* has not changed since Prinsep's time. I know this because a rough sketch I made of its lanes in the winter of 1999 shows the same layout as recorded on both his 1824 map and the 1929 "Benares City" map.[18] My sketch was prompted by my "discovery" of a small Durgā temple enclosing a margosa (*Azadirachta indica*), a tree known throughout north India as the neem. According to the Hindi-language signage in the neighborhood, the first member of this *mahallā*'s name is *ṭaiḍhahī*. Anglicized as Terhi, the word is likely derived from the Hindi adjective *ṭeḍhā*, "crooked, twisting." While the neem I photographed there that winter was somewhat gnarled and bent, such is not an unusual feature of these trees. Furthermore, given the rapidity with which neems grow, the specimen I photographed could not possibly have dated from over two centuries prior, whenever it was that the eponymous *mahallā* was first laid out, or first received that name (National Research Council 23, 26–27). There is no way of knowing when the Ur-Terhi Neem tree would have taken root and been recognized as the goddess of the place, or whether its original location corresponded to that of the Durgā shrine I photographed. Today Varanasi's cityscape landscape is dotted with neem trees, some quite massive and many receiving worship; however, none other of these have lent their names to the neighborhoods over which they preside (Figure 5.2).

The neem tree shrines that I visited and photographed in 1999 were documented in a short study published in 2004. All identified with or as goddesses, these are scattered across the city and its environs, including one located (1) in the Gol Ghar neighborhood, a short distance south of the modern Varanasi Town Hall and the great Kāl Bhaironāth temple; one situated at the (2) Kamaccha crossroad, named Śāyarī Mātā but also identified on its signage as a "Neem Mother Junction" (*nīmā māī tirāhā*); one named "Crossroad Goddess" (Caura Devī) in (3) Nagwa, at the far southern end of the city; and one named Mother Śītalā (Māṃ Śītalā) (4) in the hamlet of Mitim, located in large neem grove across the Ganges River from Nagwa, some two kilometers to the east of the town of Ramnagar (Figure 5.3).

These neem shrines are found in particularly high concentrations in the (5) Chet Ganj and Benia *mahallā*s, located in a northwestern quadrant of the city not absorbed into Varanasi's urban fabric until the turn of the twentieth century. One of these, the much-frequented shrine of the "Pacification Goddess" (Śānti Devī), is, in spite of its neem tree's relatively diminutive size, eye-catching in its design, inasmuch as its boughs emerge through a set of round holes in its conical roof.[19] A rustic painting on a nearby wall represents the goddess Śītalā—one

FIGURE 5.2 Nīm tree and surrounding wall of "Saṅkaṭ Nāśinī Vijaya" Durgā temple, Terhi Neem *mahallā*, Varanasi. Photo by the author.

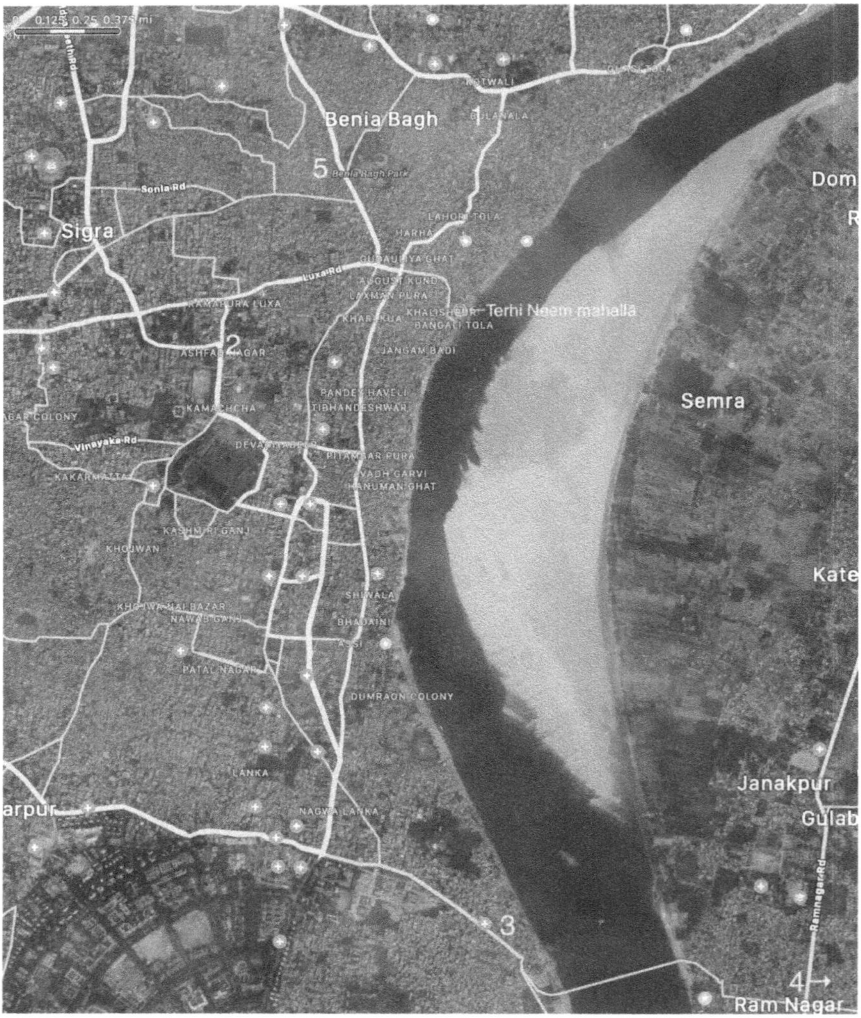

FIGURE 5.3 Distribution of Varanasi tree shrines discussed in this study. Image generated by Google Maps: https://www.google.com/maps/@25.2951182,82.9849072,17798m/data=!3m1!1e3!5m1!1e4

of the two goddesses most commonly associated with neem shrines in north India (Haberman 2013: 137–152)—seated on her traditional donkey mount (Figure 5.4).

A short distance to the southwest of Śānti Devī, a set of marble plaques affixed to the shrine of the "Neem Mother (Nīmā Māī) Temple" provide a chronology of sorts for the development of tree sanctuaries. The first of these, dated 1959, describes improvements made to the raised platform of the shrine's inner sanctum. Two additional plaques, dated 1979 and 1995, document the repair

FIGURE 5.4 Wall painting of goddess Śītalā, Chet Ganj, Varanasi. Photo by the author.

or renovation (*jīrṇoddhara*) of the temple by the "Kali Mahal Preservation and Development Association."[20] A list of donors and officers shown on one of these attests to a rather wide cross section of Varanasi society, including as it does the names of brahmins (Khare, Dixit), of an individual from the cattle-raising Yādav community dominant in the Chet Ganj *mahallā* (Singh 1996: 130), as well as of a Muslim (Saiyyad Itarat Husain), two lawyers (*aidvokeṭ*), and two persons from the Sikh community (Gopi and Lallu Sardar). Also indicated on one of the plaques are the place of residence of certain of these donors, with all hailing from the Kali Mahal or adjacent neighborhoods. No trans-locating pilgrims these, but rather the people of the place sheltering beneath their local goddess tree (Figure 5.5).

Like the Durgā temple in the Terhi Neem *mahallā*,[21] the gradual development of the Nīmā Māī shrine encapsulates the evolution of a local tree shrine into a translocal goddess temple. On the one hand, its current structure mimics that of the classical north Indian temple style, albeit on a humble scale, comprising a platform, pavilion (*maṇḍapa*), and inner sanctum (*garbha gṛha*), with the neem itself standing as its tower (*śikhara*).[22] On the other, the installation of worship images of several of the gods of official Hinduism in its sanctum (Hanumān, Durgā, Gaṇeśa) and pavilion (Śiva) attests to an initiative on the part of the temple association to translocalize its Neem Mother into the Great Goddess of official Hinduism. While still named for a tree, which is entirely unadorned, the temple's goddess is now venerated as an anthropomorphic image in the shrine's inner sanctum.

These three sanctuaries' surrounding walls hark back to the earliest stage of temple development in South Asia, as articulated in the opening verses of the circa fifth-century CE Pali-language commentary on the Buddhist *Dhammapada*. Here, a childless householder named "Much Gold"

> seeing on the roadside a branching leafy "Lord of the Forest" (i.e., a great tree) [thought to himself], "This [tree] must be haunted by a powerful *devatā*." So, he had the area underneath the tree purified, a surrounding wall erected, [and] sand spread out; and having hoisted up and adorned the Lord of the Forest with flags and banners, he joined his hands together [and vowed]: "If I should receive a son or a daughter, I will pay you great honor." So saying, he went on his way.[23]

One may characterize this as the initial phase of temple development: the "clothing" of a tree in bolts of cloth and the erection of a railing or wall around its base. The successive installation of a slab altar at the foot of the tree prefigures the masonry platform of later temples, with the following step—the erection of a small shed beneath or around the trunk of the tree itself—being the forerunner of the *śikhara* (Figure 5.6).

These phases of development, which may be viewed *in media res* at various neem shrines throughout and around the city, are also documented on coins and bas reliefs from the beginning of the Common Era.[24] A most vivid example is a

FIGURE 5.5 Nīmā Māī Temple, Chet Ganj, Varanasi. Photo by the author.

FIGURE 5.6 Caura Devī temple, rear view, Nagwa, Varanasi. Photo by the author.

bas relief carved into the second-century BCE "Katra Architrave" housed in the Mathura Museum, which depicts a rudimentary shrine, likely Hindu (Quintanilla 2007, 48–49), enclosed by a rail fence (*vedika*) to the right of which there stands a tree whose branches are hung with garlands and whose trunk is girdled by strips of cloth (Figure 5.7).

This image may be compared to the modern-day shrine situated in the hamlet of Mitim, mentioned above. Here, a neem tree hung with a cloth skirt and a silver mask is enclosed by a masonry shrine, on whose platform the words "Mother Śītalā" are inscribed. Standing close by is another neem, its trunk also draped in a bolt of the red- and yellow-colored cloth favored by Hindu goddesses (Figure 5.8).

A common feature of Varanasi's neem shrines, which may be viewed as an additional intermediate phase in their development, is the presence of masks installed to facilitate *darśan*, the exchange of gaze that occurs between devotee and divinity in worship. *Darśan* is impossible without a face and a set of eyes to gaze upon, and so an increasing number of these shrines will have a mask affixed to the trunk of the tree, at eye level. A most elaborate development of this trend is that observed at the Śānti Devī temple in Chet Ganj. Here, worshipers may take *darśan* of no fewer than seven masks, with that of Śītalā enclosed in a tiny white marble shrine.[25] This use of masks is not unique to the city's neem shrines. Images of many of the great translocal gods of Varanasi are enhanced in much

FIGURE 5.7 "Katra Architrave," detail. Government Museum, Mathura, Uttar Pradesh. Photo by John C. Huntington, Courtesy of the John C. and Susan L. Huntington Photographic Archive of Buddhist and Asian Art.

the same way, their faces being represented as lovely repoussé masks since at least the mid-nineteenth century (Sherring 166) (Figure 5.9).

Worship of Varanasi's neem trees does not require the mediation of a temple priest (*pūjārī*) or specialist. Furthermore, the masonry structures built around the city's most elaborate neem shrines are not necessarily the principal objects of worshippers' attentions, as in the case of the "Crossroad Goddess" (Caura Devī) in Nagwa. Here, the four-sided hypaethral sanctum that encloses the trunk of the great tree is empty of recognizable worship images, and shows little sign of activity. However, the base of that tree, which emerges from the shrine's outer surrounding wall at street level, receives frequent attention. Here, a great burl—a sort of eruption of the goddess from the heart of her tree—is venerated on a regular basis, its surface adorned with flowers, colored powders, burnt joss sticks, and the patina left by years of contact with worshipful hands (Figure 5.10).

The Crossroad Goddess's temple is a frequent halting place for local wedding processions, at which time offerings are made together with a petition for a happy and fruitful marriage. Such pragmatic requests—for children, life, and well-being—have defined tree worship for well over 2000 years. As evidenced in the *Dhammapada* commentary quoted above, this dynamic is an ancient and oft-repeated one.

In this, the prime impulse or rationale for worshiping these local neem goddesses differs from that of pilgrims to the holy cities of translocal Hinduism, which more often stems from otherwordly concerns: the fate of their ancestors and their own eternal salvation.

FIGURE 5.8 Māṃ Śītalā shrine and cloth-draped neem tree, Mitim village, Ramnagar, Varanasi District, Uttar Pradesh. Photo by the author.

Convergences and Synergies

What are we to make of these data? Is Varanasi's a tale of two cities, a metaphysical Varanasi and a physical Varanasi, the one a virtual utopia mediated by representatives and representations of official Hinduism, and the other a concrete *topos* shared among local humans and local gods? Is it appropriate here to speak of a dichotomy

FIGURE 5.9 Masks on trunk of neem tree, Śānti Devī temple, Chet Ganj, Varanasi. Photo by the author.

FIGURE 5.10 Neem burl, Caura Devī temple, Nagwa, Varanasi. Photo by the author.

of official versus vernacular religion, the one sanctioned by scripture and the other unsanctioned, the one specific to Hindus and the other multicultural, the one spatially and temporally unbounded and the other rooted in a specific place? If we were to limit our inquiry to the contemporary scene alone, these would appear to be two different planes of existence. However, when South Asian tree worship both within and beyond Varanasi is viewed through the prism of history, the two are seen to converge. In his penetrating study of "religion of the place" as observed in a medieval Buddhist monastery, Richard Cohen argued against a two-tiered model that would distinguish "'true' Buddhism, founded in pure philosophy . . . from a 'lesser' Buddhism that involves . . . the worship of spirits or deities." Rather, as he put it, "local spirit cults [are to] be conceived as essential to Buddhist traditions in Asia" with "*place* (my italics) set[ting] the idiosyncratic and indigenous on par with the translocal and universal, the here and there with the everywhere" (Cohen 361).

Leonard Primiano had already taken the same general position a few years earlier, when he argued that the "vernacular" is the normative, default mode of religious life, over and against official religion, which is only normative for an elite sliver of society (Primiano 35–76). While most people will engage with this or that aspect of official religion at specific moments in their lives—on holy days, during life cycle rites, while on pilgrimage, and so forth—such engagements will be transitory diversions from the flow of their vernacular religious life. Pilgrims upon returning home will reconnect with the local gods of family, lineage, and place, while the elite religious specialist who had earlier guided them through the "official" Varanasi will salute his neighborhood goddess tree when he passes her by and venerate his ancestors during the autumnal "Fortnight of the Fathers." At the same time, local actors are seen to adopt translocal idioms, identifying their local neem goddess with Śītalā, Durgā, or the Great Goddess, and making architectural and iconographic additions to their shrines that mimic "classical" north Indian temple styles. They too are shuttling between the local and the translocal, between the vernacular and official lifeworlds of South Asian religion.

Official Hinduism has never shown much interest in trees, tree shrines or tree worship. The rare mentions of trees in the Vedas generally involved those whose woods were optimal for the fashioning of sacrificial implements: ladles, spoons, and fire drilling sticks. In this last case, it was the woods of the "male" *aśvattha* and "female" *śāmī* trees that were employed. Best known in north India under their modern Hindi names of *pīpal* (Ficus religiosa) and *nīm* (neem), their pairing has survived down to the present day in a number of widely observed ritual contexts, most especially in the custom of "tree marriage" (Biardeau 49–56, 87, 197, 224, 255–256, 265, 288–291; Boulnois 15–16, 104). As for forests, a late Rigvedic hymn to Araṇyāṇī, the "Lady of the Wilderness," portrays her domain as a generally forbidding place.[26] In later literature, forests would come to be considered sacred not because they were the dwelling places of the gods, but because they were the haunts of holy men—renouncers, hermits, ascetics, and so forth. They were, however, also the natural habitats for certain classes of spirit deities, often called rākṣasas or yakṣas, who were generally cast as threatening, sometimes flesh-eating, beings. They are so portrayed in the MBh's tale of a riddling yakṣa whose massive body resembles a palmyra palm, and of a man-eating rākṣasa named Hiḍimba who dwells in a sal tree (White 2021: 142–143, 159–160).

This inauspicious legacy likely accounts for the paucity of sacred trees, groves, and forests recommended as pilgrimage destinations in the MBh's voluminous *tīrtha-yātra-parvan*. Of these, none are located in the Varanasi region;[27] however, several Varanasi *māhātmyam*s refer to a great forest tract situated to the south of the city's ancient core, known by the name of the "Forest of Bliss" (Ānandavana, Ānandakānana). Myths from the *Matsya* and later Purāṇas identify this as the site of the domestication or "Śaiva-ization" of yakṣa worship. Harikeśa, the son of a powerful yakṣa lord, comes to the Ānandavana to devote himself to Śiva, who, impressed by his extreme austerities, makes him the leader of his minions (*gaṇa*s) in the city and installs him at the gate to his principal temple (Eck 199–200). This is in fact a variation on an oft-repeated theme concerning the urbanization of these forest deities.

The early Buddhist record not only made tree worship a central focus of religious practice, but also highlighted Varanasi as a place where said worship occurred. In its tale of one of the Buddha's prior births as a prince of Varanasi, the "Dummedha Jātaka" describes a crowd that regularly gathered at the foot of a banyan tree on the outskirts of the city to petition the devatā that had "come forth" (*nibbatta*) in that tree for sons, daughters, glory and wealth. The same tale describes the offerings made to the devatā, which included flowers and fragrances as well as the flesh and blood of sheep, goats, cocks, swine, and the like.[28] The MBh attests to similar appetites on the part of "crones" (*vṛddhikā*s) that, arisen in trees, were worshiped by persons desiring children.[29] Another Jātaka, the "Sutasoma," also features a prince of Varanasi paired with a tree deity, this time female and called a yakkhī. In this birth, the Buddha heals both the man and the yakkhī of their addiction to human flesh.[30]

These tales of yakṣa carnivores notwithstanding, early Buddhist attitudes toward trees and tree worship were strongly positive, as evidenced in both scripture and iconography, with the future Buddha himself appearing as a tree deity (*rukkha-devatā*) over forty times in the *Jātaka*s (White 2021: 241, note 83). Three of the major events in his life—his birth, enlightenment, and death—all occur beneath trees inhabited by tree deities: a sal (*śāla*, Shorea robusta) tree at the time of his birth and death, and a sacred fig (*aśvattha*) at enlightenment (Nugteren 145–163). This, the Bodhi Tree itself, was so venerated by the Mauryan emperor Aśoka that he dedicated his reign to it on no fewer than three occasions (Nugteren 202). It remains the case, however, that *rukkha-devatā*s most often bore feminine names in the Jātakas and other Buddhist tales (Viennot 104),[31] a legacy that has continued down to the present day, inasmuch as the great majority of tree deities receiving worship in modern Varanasi and greater South Asia are female.

Representations of trees and tree worship were ubiquitous fixtures of early Buddhist iconography, appearing on hundreds of bas reliefs from across the Indian subcontinent. Certain of these sculptures confirm both the ancient scriptural and modern-day ethnographic records, showing that the principal aim of the worship of tree deities was and remains the desire for healthy children.[32] An emblematic example is a stele from the first-century BCE Buddhist monastery of Amaravati in Andhra Pradesh (Figure 5.11).

Three fig trees are depicted here, of which two, standing on raised platforms, are enclosed by railings. A couple is shown placing an infant at the foot of one of these, while a kneeling figure who has placed two swaddled infants on a low platform is shown praying to a figure not seen due to damage to the sculpture. The accompanying inscription reads *bahu'puta-cetiya vesālakāni chetiyāni*, "Multiple Children Tree Shrine [and] the Sacred Trees of Vaiśālī." According to commentators, a great banyan at Vaiśālī was worshiped, precisely, by persons desiring sons (Ghosh and Sarkar 171). This bas relief is a depiction of the presentation of newborn infants to the tree deities whose intervention had made their birth possible. Still a common practice today (White 2021: 119–121), Māyāvatī made just such a presentation following the birth of her son, the future Buddha. This is memorialized on another Amaravati bas relief, which shows her presenting the child to a forest deity, who has literally "come forth" from the trunk of the tree to behold the newborn savior.[33]

Buddhism disappeared from north India nearly a thousand years ago; however, the veneration of trees as (the haunts of) *grāmadevatā*s has persisted down to the present day in sanctuaries across the entire subcontinent.[34] The worship of tree deities has also been enshrined, albeit in a subliminal way, in the mythology and iconography of certain of the major gods of official Hinduism. Prominent among these is Kṛṣṇa, whose play (*līlā*) in the Vṛndāvana or Braj forest was inspired, as Charlotte Vaudeville has argued, by a pre-existing yakṣa cult in the Mathura region.[35] More relevant to the present study is Śiva's relationship to

FIGURE 5.11 "Multiple Children Tree Shrine, Sacred trees of Vaiśālī," detail, Amaravati, 1st. c. BCE. Amaravati Site Museum, Andhra Pradesh. Photo by John C. Huntington, Courtesy of the John C. and Susan L. Huntington Photographic Archive of Buddhist and Asian Art.

yakṣas and tree worship. In its "catalogue of yakṣas," the *Mahāmāyūrīvidyārā-jñī-sūtra*, a Buddhist work dated to circa 400 CE, identifies Mahākāla, one of the names of Śiva, as the "yakṣa" of Varanasi (Takubo 19; Lévi 3). Like devatā, yakṣa was long a generic term for "deity," and so this moniker need not be taken at face value. However, as Gritli von Mitterwallner has shown, several elements of the iconography of early Śiva lingams were likely adapted directly from sculptural representations of yakṣas (Mitterwallner 12–31). In the light of his findings, a second-century CE bas relief from the Mathura region, long identified as a lingam, may well be an image of a yakṣa shrine, with the anatomically correct phallus surmounting a platform beneath a tree belonging not to Śiva, but rather to a yakṣa fertility deity (Figure 5.12).

However, even after such phallic images came to be identified specifically as Śiva lingams, their associations with trees remained operative, as evidenced in both Gupta-era coinage and the configuration of modern-day neem shrines. As Jean Boulnois has noted, lingams are invariably placed at the foot of neem trees in modern-day south India (Banerjea 122, 135; Boulnois 104). This aligns with Whitney Sanford's observation concerning contemporary yakṣa practice in Braj: "most yakṣa worship occurs outside on a platform (*cabūtarā*) under a neem tree" (Sanford 102).

Here, I believe it is appropriate to make a historical argument concerning the relationship between vernacular and official religion in South Asia. As we have seen, the antecedence of the former over the latter was openly acknowledged by the early Buddhist community, which made no secret of its savior's relationship to the tree deities that preceded and applauded his coming into this world, and which continued to venerate the subcontinent's indigenous devatās for several centuries. Prior to the emergence of the Buddhist savior figures known as *bodhisattvas*, these objects of popular worship were effectively the sole gods of

FIGURE 5.12 Tree shrine with yakṣas and platform surmounted by phallus, detail, Bhuteśvara, ca. 200 CE. Government Museum, Mathura. Photo by John C. Huntington, Courtesy of the John C. and Susan L. Huntington Photographic Archive of Buddhist and Asian Art.

official Buddhism. The Hindu situation was and remains more complex. The centuries around the beginning of the Common Era were precisely those in which "classical" Hindu theism emerged, with the cults of such non-Vedic gods as Śiva in particular being sanctioned in the MBh and the Puranic canon. These textual developments were but one facet of what Alexis Sanderson (41–44) has rightly called "the Śaiva Age" (circa fifth to thirteenth centuries CE), a period in which royal patronage spurred the formation of powerful Śaiva religious orders, the construction of royal temples to Śiva, the formulation of specifically Śaiva ritual programs, and so forth. Polytheism being a zero-sum system, accepting tree deities and other devatās as authentic gods outside of his entourage would have undermined the Great God's supremacy, an unacceptable situation.

A hallmark of Hindu ideology as expressed through myth is an identification of antiquity with legitimacy and superiority. This is the message of the most widely disseminated narrative of Śaiva mythology, found in both scripture and sculpture. The plot of the myth of the "manifestation of the lingam" (*liṅgodbhava*) is driven, precisely, by an argument that has erupted between the three supreme male gods of Hindu theism concerning "who came first." When neither Viṣṇu nor Brahmā is able to find the beginning or end of Śiva's lingam, they grudgingly acknowledge his primordiality and supremacy.

The Śiva of Hindu myth is eternal. He precedes the universe that he created, and he will outlive the universe that he will destroy. Varanasi has a special place in this article of faith as well. Called Avimukta ("Not Forsaken") in several *māhātmyams*, Varanasi is the place where the Great God's lingam was first established on earth, and the place where he will remain even as the entire universe is annihilated at the end of the current age, its three hills being held above the final conflagration on the tips of his trident (Eck 28). According to this mytho-logic, Varanasi's tree shrines did not come into being until long after Śiva took up residence in the city shortly after the beginning of time. However, whereas Śiva is eternal, his images and temples, the sole hard data that we have for his presence on earth, are not. Tree shrines predate the earliest Śiva lingams, lingams whose original placement, morphology, and iconography attest to their emergence out of the altars proper to pre-existing yakṣa and devatā cults. In this respect, the relationship between official and vernacular religion through history tracks with that of the historical present: the vernacular is always already there whenever the official manifests itself. Vernacular South Asian religion is the historical background out of which official Hinduism emerged and the lifeworld with(in) which it continues to evolve.

Notes

1 In this study, all contemporary place names (Varanasi) and names of persons (Sukul) are given without diacriticals. All other proper names (of gods, mythical places, people and places from the past, etc.) are given with diacriticals. Words found in the Oxford English Dictionary (e.g., neem, sal, lingam) are given in their English spelling, rather than in standard Hindi or Sanskrit transliterated form (*nīm*, *sāl*, *liṅgam*).

2 MBh 3.82.69, in Dandekar (1971: 505). The *tīrtha-yātra-parvan* occupies chapters 80–153 of the epic's third book, the *Āraṇyakaparvan*.
3 *Skanda Purāṇa* 29.4–59, in Bakker and Isaacson 2005. In this, the Purāṇa echoes an account given by the seventh-century Chinese Buddhist pilgrim Hsuan Tsang: Bakker (1996: 35).
4 SP 29.60-116 goes on to describe Śiva as a *mahāyogin* venerated there by semi-divine yogis: Sanatkumāra, etc.
5 On the earliest of these, see Smith (2007: 85), n. 6.
6 While most scholars date the 12,000-verse KKh to the thirteenth or fourteenth century, Smith (2007: 84, 100–104) argues rather persuasively for an eleventh-century date.
7 Of the 2525 verses of the "Tīrthavivecanakāṇḍa" (Aiyangar 1942: 264, note 2), over 1000 are devoted to Varanasi alone. The work lists a total of approximately 340 bathing places, temples, and lingams: ibid., lxx, 268–272 (Appendix B), 281 (Appendix D). However, Sukul's (1974: 168) tally comes to 462 sites, of which 397 are temples. He provides a synoptic listing (idem., 1977, pp. 361–368) of Varanasi's *tīrtha*s as recorded in both Lakṣmīdhara's work and the KKh. In chapter 16 of a "lost" recension of the *Liṅga Purāṇa* quoted by Lakṣmīdhara (Aiyangar 1942: 120–121), Śiva refers to "hundreds and thousands" of other lingams in the city.
8 Sukul's (1974: 165) tally of the KKh's mentions of temples and bathing places dedicated to Śiva and other gods and goddesses, comes to 1099. He notes, however, that among these the KKh stipulates that only 383 are "most important." Dimmers and Gengnagel's exhaustive on line "Alphabetical Index of *Kāśīkhaṇḍa*" lists over 1400 temples, shrines, *tīrtha*s, and *yātra*s.
9 Pieper (1979: 215); Gutschow (2006: 18, 55). This map has been reproduced in several works, including Pieper (1979: 216) (fig. 1), Singh (1993: 39), and Gutschow (2006: 57).
10 Sukul 1974 is written in English; however, it's treatment of the city's religious landscapes is far less exhaustive than the Hindi-language Sukul 1977.
11 Personal communication from Diana Eck, Varanasi, September 1974.
12 Prinsep (1832: 472).
13 Singh (1955: 8), Kanungo (2022: 20), and Yanagisawa and Funo (2018: 386). The original *mahallā*s were named after Islamic martyrs.
14 Yanagisawa and Funo (2018: 386–387).
15 Haskett (2018), par. 14.
16 Ibid., fig. 7.
17 They are absent from Lakṣmidhara's "Tīrthavivecanakāṇḍa" and the KKh and "Kāśīrahasya" mentioned above, as well as from Vācaspati Miśra's fifteenth-century *Tīrthacintāmaṇi* and Nārāyaṇa Bhaṭṭa's sixteenth-century *Tristhalīsetu*.
18 My thanks to Michael Dodson for Prinsep's map, and to Kiwamu Yanagisawa for the 1929 Benares City map, which they made available to me in the summer of 2021.
19 White (2004: 576–586). David Haberman, who carried out research on the same topic between 2006 and 2008, was apparently unaware of my obscure publication. Chapter 5 of his monograph (Haberman 2013: 132–159) covers much of the same material in greater detail, and notes the high concentration of neem shrines in this part of the city.
20 Prinsep's census (1832: 485) and map indicate that in the early nineteenth century, this *mahallā*, located on the western edge of the city, was mainly a place of gardens, and barely inhabited.
21 Saṅkaṭ Nāśinī Vijaya Durgā ("Victory to Durgā, Destroyer of Dire Misfortune") is the name by which the temple is known nowadays.
22 The *śikhara* ("peak") is most often identified as a mountain. However, as Kramrisch (1946: vol. 1, p. 207) and Boulnois (1989: 133) have suggested, a tree together with its surrounding railing was the archetype for these features of temple architecture.
23 *Dhammapada* 1.1.1, in Tatia (1973: 4).

24 Online: http://coinindia.com/galleries-agathocles.html; and http://www.hindujafoundation.org/antiquity-collection-listing.html?id=h7E1+qzqBq8qIvkbBciZag==. Accessed October 20, 2021.
25 Haberman (2013: 140–155) also writes extensively about the preponderance of masks in this context, providing several illustrations.
26 Ṛg Veda 10.146, in Jamison and Brereton (2014: 1632).
27 "Brahmā's *udumbara* [Ficus glomerata] tree" at Brahmavarta (MBh 3.81.58); the "Grove of Vyāsa" (3.81.77); "Arbor of Naimiṣa" (3.81.93): Saugandhika Forest (3.82.4); and Tuṅgaka Forest (3.83.43–44): in Dandekar (1971: 498–499, 502, 509).
28 Jātaka 50, in Fausböll (1877: 259). On the carnivorous yakṣas of Hindu tradition, and prescribed offerings to them, see White (2021: 241, notes 84, 91).
29 MBh 3.220.16, in Dandekar (1971: 696).
30 Jātaka 525, in Fausböll (1891: 177–181); translation and discussion in Holt (1996: 76–79). For an image, see White (2021: plate 19).
31 It would appear that fig trees (banyan, sacred fig) are the exception to this rule: like the *aśvattha/pīpal* in Hindu tree marriages, these are cast as male in early Buddhist scripture and iconography.
32 Like the modern-day Śītalā and the numerous Bhavānīs of north India, many yakṣīs of Buddhist legend were both protectresses and devourers of infants: Sutherland (1991: 141–145) and White (2021: 108–109).
33 Ibid., p. 105 (fig. 4.14). For an accurate interpretation of this scene, see Quintanilla (2017: 130–135). The Pali commentary to *Dhammapada* 2.1.6 (Tatia 1973: 173) describes a tree deity's "cleaving" (*pādalitvā*) of the trunk of his tree to reveal himself to his petitioners.
34 For images, see Huyler (1999: 95, 97, 103, 104, 107, 124–125, 129, 212, 218), White (2003: 56), and White (2021: plates 20, 22, and 23).
35 Vaudeville (1999: 26): "[Kṛṣṇa] was the great *yakṣa* of mount Govardhana and the protector of cowherds living in the area of Mathurā." Cf. Sanford's (2005) more nuanced treatment of the marginalization of the yakṣas of Braj to the benefit of official Krishnaite religion.

Bibliography

Aiyangar, K. V. Rangaswami, ed. *Kṛtyakalpataru of Bhaṭṭa Lakṣmīdhara*. Baroda: Oriental Institute, 1942.

Bakker, Hans T. "Construction and Reconstruction of Sacred Space in Vārāṇasī." *Numen* 43 1996: 32–55.

——— and and Harunaga Isaacson, eds. *The Skandapurāṇa. Vol. IIA. Adhyāyas 26–31.14. The Vārāṇasī Cycle. Critical Edition with an Introduction, English Synopsis & Philological and Historical Commentary*. Groningen: Egbert Forsten, 2005: Online: https://www.universiteitleiden.nl/binaries/content/assets/geesteswetenschappen/lias/skandapurana-project/transliteration/st029.txt.

Banerjea, Jitendra. "Siva and His Emblems on Early Indian Coins and Seals." *Indian Historical Quarterly* 16 1940: 118–142.

Biardeau, Madeleine. *Stories About Posts: Vedic Variations around the Hindu Goddess*. Translated by Alf Hiltebeitel, Marie-Louise Reiniche and James Walker. Chicago: University of Chicago Press, 2004.

Boulnois, Jean. *Le caducée et la symbolique dravidienne indo-méditerranéenne, de l'arbre, de la pierre, du serpent, et de la déesse-mère*. Paris: Maisonneuve, 1989.

Chandra, Moti. *Kāśī kā Itihās: Vaidik Kāl se Avārcīn Yug tak kā Rājanaitik-Sāṃskṛtik Sarvekṣaṇ*. Varanasi: Vishvavidyalaya Prakashan, 1985.

Cohen, Richard S. "Nāga, Yakṣiṇī, Buddha: Local Deities and Local Buddhism at Ajanta." *History of Religions* 37.4 1998: 360–400.
Dandekar, R. N., ed. *The Mahābhārata. Text as Constituted in its Critical Edition*, vol. 1. Poona: Bhandarkar Oriental Research Institute, 1971.
Dimmers, Michaela and Jörg Gengnagel. "Alphabetical Index of *Kāśīkhaṇḍa*." Online: http://www.benares.uni-hd.de/kkh-index.htm
Eck, Diana L. *Banaras City of Light*. Princeton, NJ: Princeton University Press, 1982.
Fausböll, Viggo, ed. *The Jātaka Together with its Commentary, Being Tales of the Anterior Births of Gautama Buddha. For the First Time Edited in the Original Pali*, vol. 1. London: Pali Text Society, 1877. Online: http://gretil.sub.uni-goettingen.de/gretil/2_pali/1_tipit/2_sut/5_khudd/jatak1ou.htm.
———, vol. 5. London: Pali Text Society, 1891. Online: http://gretil.sub.uni-goettingen.de/gretil/2_pali/1_tipit/2_sut/5_khudd/jatak5ou.htm.
Ghosh, A. and H. Sarkar. "Beginnings of Sculptural Art in South-East India." *Ancient India* 20–21 1964–1965: 168–177.
Gutschow, Niels. *Benares, The Sacred Landscape of Vārāṇasī*. Stuttgart: Edition Axel Menges, 2006.
——— and Axel Michaels. *Benares: Tempel und religiöses Leben in der heiligen Stadt der Hindus*. Köln: Dumont Buchverlag, 1993.
Haberman, David L. *People Trees, Worship of Trees in Northern India*. New York: Oxford University Press, 2013.
Haskett, Christian. "On Varanasi's Tiny Temples." *South Asia Multidisciplinary Academic Journal* 18 2018: 1–20. Online: https://doi.org/10.4000/samaj.4524
Holt, John Clifford. *The Religious World of Kīrti Śrī: Buddhism, Art, and Politics in Late Medieval Sri Lanka*. New York: Oxford University Press, 1996.
Huyler, Stephen P. *Meeting God: Elements of Hindu Devotion*. New Haven, CT: Yale University Press, 1999.
Jamison, Stephanie W., and Joel P. Brereton, trans. *The Rigveda: The Earliest Religious Poetry of India*, vol 3. New York: Oxford University Press, 2014.
Kanungo, Pralay. "Religion, Heritage, and Identity: The Contested Heritage-scape of Varanasi." In Supriya Chaudhuri, ed., *Religion and the City in India*, pp. 210–226. London: Taylor & Francis, 2022.
Kramrisch, Stella. *The Hindu Temple*, vol. 1. Kolkata: University of Calcutta, 1946.
Lévi, Sylvain. "Le catalogue géographique des yakṣa dans la Mahāmāyūrī." *Journal Asiatique*, 11th series 5 1915: 19–138.
Michaels, Axel. *Hinduism, Past and Present*. Translated by Barbara Harshaw. Princeton, NJ: Princeton University Press, 2004.
Mitterwallner, Gritli von. "Evolution of the Liṅga." In Michael Meister, ed., *Discourses on Śiva: Proceedings of a Symposium on the Nature of Religious Imagery*, pp. 12–31. Philadelphia: University of Pennsylvania Press, 1984.
National Research Council. *Neem: A Tree for Solving Global Problems*. Washington, DC: The National Academies Press, 1992. Online: https://doi.org/10.17226/1924.
Nugteren, Albertina. *Belief, Bounty, and Beauty: Rituals Around Sacred Trees in India*. Leiden: Brill, 2005.
Pieper, Jan. "A Pilgrim's Map of Benares." *GeoJournal* 3.2 1979: 215–218. Online: https://doi.org/10.1007/BF00257710
Primiano, Leonard. "Vernacular Religion and the Search for Method in Religious Folklife." *Western Folklore* 54.1 1995: 37–56.
Prinsep, James. "Census of the Population of the City of Benares." *Asiatic Researches* 17 1832: 470–498.

Quintanilla, Sonya Rhie. 2007. *History of Early Stone Sculpture at Mathura, ca. 150 BCE–100 CE*. Leiden: Brill.

———. "Transformations of Identity and the Buddha's Infancy Narratives at Kanaganhalli." *Archives of Asian Art* 67.1 2017: 111–142.

Sanderson, Alexis. "The Śaiva Age—The Rise and Dominance of Śaivism during the Early Medieval Period." In Shingo Einoo, ed., *Genesis and Development of Tantra*, pp. 41–349. Tokyo: Institute of Oriental Culture, University of Tokyo, 2009.

Sanford, A. Whitney. "Shifting the Center: Yakṣas on the Margins of Contemporary Practice." *Journal of the American Academy of Religion* 73.1 2005: 89–110.

Sherring, M. A. (Rev.). *The Sacred City of the Hindus: An Account of Benares in Ancient and Modern Times*. London: Trübner & Co., 1868.

Singh, Rana P. B. " Vārāṇasī: The Pilgrimage Maṇḍala, Geomantic Map & Cosmic Numbers." In Rana P. B. Singh, ed., *Banāras (Vārāṇasī) Cosmic Order, Sacred City, Hindu Traditions. Festschrift to Prof. R. L. Singh*, pp. 37–64. Varanasi: Tara Book Agency, 1993.

Singh, Reginald Lal. *Banaras: A Study in Urban Geography*. Varanasi: Lal Kishore, 1955.

Singh, Shashi Bala. "Settling Process and Spatial Pattern of Linguo-Cultural Groups in Varanasi City." *National Geographical Journal of India* 42.1–2 March–June 1996: 116–132.

Smith, Travis L. "Re-newing the Ancient: The Kāśīkhaṇḍa and Śaiva Vārāṇasī." *Acta Orientalia Vilnensia* 8.1 2007: 83–108.

Sukul, Kubernath. *Varanasi Down the Ages*. Varanasi: Bhargava Bhushan Press, 1974.

———. *Vārāṇasī Vaibhav*. Patna: Bihar Rashtrabhasha Parishad, 1977.

Sutherland, Gail Hinich. *The Disguises of the Demon: The Development of the Yakṣa in Hinduism and Buddhism*. Albany, NY: SUNY Press, 1991.

Takubo, Shuya, ed. *Ārya-Mahā-Māyūrī-Vidyā-Rājñī*. Tokyo: Sankibo, 1972. Online: http://gretil.sub.uni-goettingen.de/gretil/1_sanskr/4_rellit/buddh/mmayuvru.htm (input by Klaus Wille).

Tatia, Nathmal, ed. *Dhammapada-Aṭṭhakathā*, part 1. Nalanda: Nava Nalanda Mahavihar, 1973.

Vaudeville, Charlotte. *Myths, Saints, and Legends in Medieval India*. New Delhi: Oxford India, 1999.

Viennot, Odette. *Le culte de l'arbre dans l'Inde ancienne: Textes et monuments brâhmaniques et bouddhiques*. Paris: Presses Universitaires de France, 1954.

White, David Gordon. "The Goddess in the Tree: Reflections on Nīm-Tree Shrines in Varanasi." In Naval Krishna and Manu Krishna, eds., *The Ananda-Vana of Indian Art: Dr. Anand Krishna Felicitation Volume*, pp. 575–586. Varanasi: Indica, 2004.

———. *Dæmons Are Forever: Contacts and Exchanges in the Eurasian Pandemonium*. Chicago: University of Chicago Press, 2021.

Yanagisawa, Kiwamu and Funo Shuji. "How Mohallas Were Formed: Typology of Mohallas from the Viewpoint of Spatial Formation and the Urbanization Process in Varanasi, India." *Japan Architectural Review* 1.3 July 2018: 385–395. Online: https://doi.org/10.1002/2475-8876.12040

6

BHAIRAVA, HANUMĀN, AND THE DEIFIED DEAD

A Material Study of Vernacular, Official, and Folk Registers of Living Hinduism in Vārāṇasī, North India

Seth Ligo

Introduction

In the study of living Hindu traditions, multiplicity is to be expected. A single site, story, person, or deity can be important to multiple traditions, or to a single tradition in multiple ways. Paying attention to multiplicity and the many networks that pass through a single phenomenon enriches and illuminates our understanding of Hindu worlds as they actually exist and function—that is to say, as they are lived, rather than as they are prescribed or described in an abstract, ideal form. In the past, scholars of South Asian religions have often reduced multiplicity to a binary of 'little' and 'great' traditions[1] in an effort to make sense of variation within a religious system. This bifurcation tended to privilege the hierarchical, unitary, and textual 'great' traditions, of which 'little' traditions were incomplete, corrupted, or contaminated derivations. A matriarch's household ritual might, for example, have been seen as a modified and simplified version of a textually prescribed priestly rite.

The little/great model parallels the descriptive work of American Folk Studies pioneer Don Yoder, who traced the use of the label 'folk religion' as the binary complement of 'official religion' (69). Yoder's student Leonard Primiano famously challenged his teacher's reification of the folk/official divide, arguing that there was effectively only one religious register: the vernacular. Official religion, argued Primiano, is an abstraction, perhaps gestured toward but never actually lived in the real world. On the other hand, he contended that folk religion as the religious activity of the masses or as a counterpoint to official religion fails to recognize that individuals constantly negotiate and interpret their own beliefs and actions in response to specific contexts (Primiano 45–51).

The present study illustrates the importance of Primiano's call to focus on individual, contextual, vernacular religion while demonstrating the importance

DOI: 10.4324/9781003257462-9

of recognizing distinct folk and official registers. Here, I take folk religion not to be the generic religion of the masses, but of a particular, limited population—a folk. Official religion in my account is not an unrealized abstraction, but a concerted political and social effort to emphasize and homogenize select elements of a religious tradition. Awareness of these registers facilitates the present study of Bhairava—a protective Hindu deity who is terrifying yet also beloved—in the context of the north Indian sacred city of Vārāṇasī. Bhairava's correspondence with other protectors, namely the deified dead (former community members who have taken on supernatural status, here exemplary of the folk register) and the Hindu god Hanumān (here exemplary of the official register), demonstrates the complexity of vernacular religion, and the enduring utility of 'folk' and 'official' categories.

Vārāṇasī—A Multi-layered City

To understand vernacular religious processes of contextual negotiation and interpretation—what I will refer to as reckoning—in Vārāṇasī, we must first be aware of the city's own context and history as a sacred site in broader Hindu sacred landscapes. Jutting from the western bank of the Gaṅgā (Ganges River) in northern India, Vārāṇasī (a.k.a. Banāras or Kāśī) lies some twelve hours' road journey from New Delhi to the west, Kolkata to the east (each ~420 miles), and Kathmandu to the north (~220 miles; there are mountains), making it an important hub along routes connecting these political, economic, and religious centers. A tradition as variegated as Hinduism has no single heart, but Vārāṇasī—semi-submerged in a river that is a living goddess, cradled in the Ganges Basin, in the middle of the historical territories of the Pala and Gupta empires, and participating in trans-regional sacred networks (such as those of the *Jyotir Liṅgas* and the *Śakti Pīṭhas*)—is an important and thoroughly integrated feature of Hindu sacred geography. Though touted as timeless, this importance was first codified in the seventh- to ninth-century *Early Skanda Purāṇa*, which presents Vārāṇasī as a sort of crown jewel of north Indian sacred geography. In addition to featuring in broader networks of sacred sites, Vārāṇasī also came to incorporate those sites and networks by proxy, a process well under way by fourteenth-century addition of the *Kāśī Khaṇḍa* (*Section on Kāśī*, i.e. Vārāṇasī) to the *Skanda Purāṇa*. Today, the *Kāśī Khaṇḍa* and similar compendia are cited as authoritative registers listing the sacred mountains, rivers, cities, temples, and even continent-spanning pilgrimage routes present in the city by proxy. It follows that the potency and efficacy of those sites are also present, and it is commonly held that a pilgrimage to Vārāṇasī is effectively a pilgrimage to the entirety of Hindu sacred territory. Merely entering the city is said to remove the residue of one's past misdeeds, no matter how heinous. With one's karmic sebum sloughed, liberation is immanent.

Given Vārāṇasī's trans-regional—even global—importance, one might presume the city to be clearly structured and organized, its contents corresponding to precise descriptions present in the Purāṇas and other compendia, and its sacred geography demonstrative of Hindu theology and cosmology (see Singh's *Banāras Region, Towards the Pilgrimage Archetype*). This is overwhelmingly not the case (see Ligo). As noted above, Primiano argues that 'what scholars have referred to as "official" religion does not, in fact, exist,' meaning there is no individual or group that lives entirely, and exclusively, in keeping with religious ideals (45). We can extend this claim to posit that no city exists in complete conformity to ideal prescription. There are, however, efforts to quite literally construct an official sense of sacred space, and by extension an official Hinduism, in Vārāṇasī. Here the official is not an abstract ideal, but a curatorial program reflecting a certain religious and social reckoning, intended to assert a homogenous, pan-Indian Hinduism. Exemplary of such efforts is the Kāśī Viśvanātha Corridor, inaugurated by Prime Minister Narendra Modi, which carves through the city from the banks of the Gaṅgā to its most famous temple, Viśvanātha Mandir.[2] The corridor increases and directs pilgrimage traffic to reinforce a particular politicized understanding of the city: namely that the city has a single essence, and that it is the unrivaled, official heart of Hinduism. Modi was elected Prime Minister twice from the Vārāṇasī constituency, and this, along with his celebration of the corridor project, present him as champion of the country, the city, and by extension, official Hinduism.

But Vārāṇasī is also blanketed in hundreds of small shrines and temples, the majority of which focus on local deities, or local iterations of more mainstream gods and goddesses (see Haskett; Singh, *Banāras Region*). Despite the prominence in guidebooks and pilgrimage traffic of a few temples of trans-regional importance, it is these smaller shrines that constitute the vernacular religion of the residents of Vārāṇasī, and truly inform and shape its sacred landscape. Vernacular religion is not religion as it 'could' or 'should' be, but as Primiano puts it, '…religion as it is lived: as human beings encounter, understand, interpret, and practice it' (44). He is careful to note that the vernacular is not just a rebranding of the 'folk' (42), but rather a corrective to the limited scope of what can be addressed in the study of folk religion (51). With the 'official' disrupted and the 'folk' discarded, Primiano urges scholars of religion to acknowledge that the vernacular is all there is, and all there ever was. And yet the vernacular is never homogenous. What do we do with a highly diverse, coincidental religious context such as that of Vārāṇasī, where the vernacular—whether it be in language or architecture or religion—can change from one street to the next, and one generation to the next?

The following case study of Deurā village at the city's periphery, and consideration of Bhairava networks in Vārāṇasī more broadly, demonstrate the importance of recognizing at least three distinct but interrelated registers composing an expanded understanding of vernacular religion, registers we will refer to as folk, vernacular, and official. The vernacular is still preeminent, but it is broadly shaped by its interaction with the folk, and these folk and vernacular registers are made more distinct by interventions of the official, which wishes to co-opt them.

Bhairava, the Deified Dead, and Hanumān in Deurā Village

There is a site in Deurā village, on the southwestern edge of Vārāṇasī, where folk, vernacular, and official registers of lived religion clearly coincide. Adjacent to a large pond, the site is just inside the Pañcakrośī Yātrā, a pilgrimage route marking the border of Vārāṇasī's sacred territory (see Singh's *Toward a Pilgrimage Archetype*; Gengnagel's *Visualized Texts*). It is difficult to precisely date the site's three prominent features, but the relative chronology is clear. The newest and largest is a ~25-square-foot marble temple dedicated to Hanumān, a simian deity famous for his devotion and heroism in the great Indian epic the *Rāmāyaṇa*. A plaque records a consecration date of 2007. Significantly older and smaller is a shrine containing Unmatta (wild) Bhairava. About three feet square and five feet tall, the shrine is topped by a rectangular pyramid with slightly convex sides, and the whole structure is painted vermilion. This shrine form is very common, and appears throughout Vārāṇasī. A small placard identifies the shrine's occupant as the Unmatta Bhairava mentioned in the *Kāśī Khaṇḍa*, the addendum to the *Skanda Purāṇa* that lists sacred sites in Vārāṇasī. The third and oldest feature sits in the open: a four-foot-tall conical form with a small niche cut into one side, painted the same vermilion as the Unmatta Bhairava shrine. This is a *satī sthāla*—a place (*sthāla*) where a woman was ritually immolated on her late husband's funeral pyre, a process referred to as committing *satī*.[3] Such a death can be seen as extraordinary, heroic, and tied to a specific place, meaning instances of *satī* meet the criteria for the 'deified dead' who remain present in and connected to their communities post-mortem (Coccari 'Bīr Bābās of Banāras' 253; 'Protection and Identity' 132). *Satī Mā Kī Jay*, or Victory to Mother Satī, is written along the base below a sketch of a woman in white, the color of widowhood.

This site must be considered in relation to the nearby village of Deurā. Its proximity to water and placement just beyond the village's border makes it a viable site for cremation, and its position at the turnoff from a main thoroughfare that leads to the village proper makes it a site warranting protection. *Satīs*, like other instances of the deified dead, are historical persons who remain connected to their communities. They have the potential to terrorize or protect, depending on the quality of care offered by their community (Coccari, 'Protection and Identity,' 130, 132, 139). They are hyperlocal, unique deities, and it seems that this is Deurā's own *satī*, still actively propitiated for protection.[4] Tied to a single population, irreproducible, and non-transferrable, this *satī* and other instances of the deified dead are folk deities in a direct and literal sense.

The function of protection at this site extends to the presence of Unmatta Bhairava and Hanumān. Though neither is local or unique like the *satī*, both are protectors, especially of boundaries between the wild and the domestic. This, and their association with the liminality signaled by traditionally peripheral cremation grounds, makes their position here at this crossroads by a cremation ground on the perimeter of Vārāṇasī quite fitting (Lutgendorf 185, 238, 313). But at what register or registers of lived religion do they protect? If both are vernacular, are they equally so? The context, form, and presentation of these examples prove telling.

The Deurā instance of Unmatta is unusual among Bhairava *mūrtis* (enlivened statues) in Vārāṇasī. His spread and bent legs, and his hands clasped to his chest, are reminiscent of *bīr bābās* (heroic, potentially hazardous male instances of the deified dead) and other hyperlocal protectors. Two other *bīr bābās* appear along the roadway in the immediate vicinity of this site. It is likely that this *mūrti* was originally a *bīr*—perhaps paired with this *satī* in a protective dyad—before being reinterpreted as Unmatta Bhairava (cf. Coccari 139). The clearly later construction of his enclosing shrine[5] and application of a label referring to the *Kāśī Khaṇḍa* support the reading of this *mūrti* as part of a hyperlocal folk register that has now been included as part of the citywide vernacular register of the Pañcakrośī Yātrā.

Further, as Unmatta, this *mūrti* is one of the Aṣṭabhairava: eight Bhairavas that protect Vārāṇasī (Ligo; Sukula; Sarasvatī 132–133). But this Bhairava literally stands apart—he is significantly farther afield than any other of these eight. As such, he straddles—a posture suited to his stance—folk religion in Deurā and vernacular religion that stretches through Vārāṇasī. The Pañcakrośī circuit pulls this folk form into the city's orbit, and as a member of the Aṣṭabhairava, he extends vernacular sacred networks to the city's frontier. Ultimately, Unmatta Bhairava protects both Deurā and Vārāṇasī. The folk and vernacular elements of his role are distinct, but coincide in a manner that is mutually reinforcing rather than contradictory.

Unlike the hyperlocality of *satīs* and other instances of the deified dead, and the local and regional scope of Unmatta and other Bhairavas, Hanumān's association with the *Rāmāyaṇa*, the worship of Rāma, has resulted in traditions of representation and veneration spanning South and Southeast Asia. In the past few decades, Hanumān has experienced a striking rise in popularity in India (Lutgendorf 3–33).[6] In addition to appearing as an ideal devotee[7] and guardian of boundaries, he has become a guardian of Hinduism itself—a final distinction that has developed in conjunction with a rise in Hindu Nationalism (cf. Ray and Dube 181; Peabody 378; Alder).[8] The recent installation of his temple in Deurā coincides with this wave of increased interest in Hanumān, and the association with current political, national sentiments is affirmed by the names of two politicians—Radhe Shyam Gupta and Rajkumar Pal, both members of the BJP[9]—on the dedication placards to the temple. This is further aligned with Vārāṇasī as Modi's proclaimed home district, and the appearance of PM Modi himself in advertisements along the Pañcakrośī route which celebrate him as 'Blessed Narendra Modi, Prime Minister.' Here Hanumān is not only transregional: he is national.

If the case site in Deurā were treated as a nexus of vernacular religion without reference to 'folk' or 'official' differentiating registers, much of the history and dynamic interplay present there would be missed. Instead, I have presented three different strata, from the hyperlocal folk serving as foundation and anchor, to the official which reaches out nationally and even echoes internationally. The vernacular mediates and envelops these two, likely sharing taproots with the folk while offering both connection and challenge to the official. As we will see, Bhairava exhibits many elements we can consider folk while doing palpably vernacular work. At the same time, Bhairava offers an alternative to Hanumān, with his more ferocious, wild (*unmatta*), and potentially horrifying forms reminding us of the spectrum of supernatural presence in Hindu landscapes beyond the relatively sanitized,[10] circumscribed Hanumān that is deployed by those seeking to articulate and enforce a sort of official religion.

To be clear, my reference to these elements as 'strata' does not imply hierarchy, as the official is neither superior nor authoritative. Rather, this geological metaphor signals the chronological layering of these elements at this site in Deurā. It also reminds us that these upper, more recent, and here larger and more lavish stratum can obscure preceding or parallel elements, the consideration of which is crucial to the understanding of vernacular religion as a whole.

Bhairava, Hanumān, and Bīr Bābās—The Folk, the Vernacular, and the Official in Vārāṇasī

Having identified folk, vernacular, and official registers in the example of Deurā, the same framework proves useful to the analysis of sacred space and living religion in Vārāṇasī more broadly. While Deurā is the clearest conjunction of representatives of these three registers, there are clear coincidences throughout Vārāṇasī. These are signaled by the copresence of Bhairava, Hanumān, and/or *bīr bābās* (common instances of the deified dead). There is frequent parallelism in the placement and pairing of some of these figures. For example, Saṇkaṭ Mocan, Vārāṇasī's most famous Hanumān temple, lies just south of the Asi river, which serves as the city's southernmost border. Lāṭ Bhairava, standing on a platform believed to have been a major Bhairava temple, lies just north of the Varaṇā river, which constitutes the city's northernmost border. A bridge crossing the Asi river in the south is guarded by Sahodar Bīr Bābā, while just inside the confluence of the Varaṇā and the Gaṅgā to the north we find Bābā Bhainsāsura, a fusion of a *bīr bābā* and folk iteration of the buffalo demon famously slain by the goddess Durgā.[11] Both Hanumān and Bhairava appear in direct correspondence with *bīr bābās*. In the neighborhood of Baḍī Piyarī, 1008 Kāla Bhairava and Caukhaḍi Bīr Bābā appear shoulder to shoulder and share the same mask iconography. Not far from the Kāl Bhairav Mandir, the most trafficked Bhairava temple in the city, the shrine of Jhaṇḍī Bīr Bābā is decorated with an image of Hanumān subduing a demon. Inside, the *bīr* takes the place of the sun, with a small Hanumān leaping toward him.

Having noted these correspondences and coincidences, let us think about Bhairava's relationships with Hanumān and *bīr bābās* in greater detail. The association of Hanumān and Bhairava is not coincidental nor recent. Both have fangs, both wield clubs, and both straddle the boundary of the wild and the domesticated. They are therefore ideally suited protectors of boundaries between those worlds, between us and them, and between the 'sacred' space of a temple and the 'profane' space of a street outside. They guard goddess temples together in the Panjab, and appear at the edges of Rajasthani villages (Erndl 4; Lutgendorf 238). Jain mustachioed heroes Gaṇṭhakārṇ Mahāvīr (associated with Hanumān) and Nakoda Bhairava display strikingly similar iconographies. What sets these two apart, then, with Bhairava maintaining the full range of the vernacular, including the folk, while Hanumān becomes official? A material consideration of their iconography is instructive. Bhairava appears in a wide range of iconic and aniconic forms, many of which are described below. Though there are occasional aniconic Hanumān *mūrtis* slathered in tel-sindūr and representative of the folk register,[12] the majority conform to two types: heroic, standing Hanumān, and a leaping or flying Hanumān carrying Mt. Droṇagirī. This collapse of iconographic variety comports with the homogenization that is an intentional effect of the broader process of articulating Hanumān as an official, national presence.

While the rise of a national, official Hanumān might be the result of emic, even vernacular trends, it is also clear that there are nationwide efforts to assert an official Hanumān, defender of a nationalist Hinduism. An official reckoning of Hanumān is inherently a political tool, one that recasts the vernacular and folk while presenting a sanitized protector who has none of the potentially troubling, heterodox elements of Bhairava, *bīr bābā*, or *satī* traditions, as described in greater detail below. A compelling and explicit example of the displacement of Bhairava in favor of Hanumān appears in the context of the Jūnā Akhāḍā, or Old Regiment, a monastic, ascetic, and martial Hindu order dating back some nine centuries and originally called the Bhairavī Akhāḍā after their tutelary deity. Now, in their headquarters in Vārāṇasī, the largest and most lavish shrine is dedicated to Hanumān. The Jūnā Akhāḍā are often counted among mendicant groups active in the protection of national Hinduism, and conversations with members confirm their self-identification as protectors of Hanumān and 'Sanāntana Dharma,' a rebranding of Hinduism as the world's original, global religion.

Though the official register might wish to remake vernacular Hinduism according to its own reckoning, the example of Bhairava and his strong association with the folk register through examples of *bīr bābās* provides insight into other echelons of religious reckoning. It is common to find Bhairavas and *bīr bābās* appear alongside one another at crossroads and along borders, with some apparent overlap or reinterpretation of certain *mūrtis* themselves, as seen in the case of Unmatta in Deurā. Both Bhairavas and *bīr bābās* also participate in masking practices that obscure the line between these iconographic categories. The installation of pressed metal masks over *mūrtis*, frequently to provide a face for an otherwise aniconic form, seems to only happen with figures related to folk registers: Bhairavas, *bīr bābās*, and *devīs* (goddesses).[13] In the case of Bhairava and *bīrs*, the similarity is striking, as these masks usually depict wide-eyed, mustachioed faces, and are often iconographically identical. Many Bhairava sites, including Lāṭ, Daṇḍapāṇi, Rudra, and even Kāl, are instances of masks affixed to otherwise aniconic stone. The example of *Bābā* Baisāsura, mentioned above, also shares in this iconography, in this case the pressed metal mask appearing atop what is apparently a *bīr* cone.[14] This correspondence is not limited to Vārāṇasī: Koḍamdesar Bhairu (a variant of the name Bhairava) in Rajasthan is a large cone identical to those of *bīrs* and *satīs*, the aperture on the side having been identified as a mouth into which offerings are placed.[15]

The folk register is typified by hyperlocality and non-transferability. As we have seen, while there may be many instances of the deified dead that are similar in form and function, each is unique: each is understood to be the metaphysical repercussion of an historical person, and to have a relationship with a particular population, that is to say a particular folk. Even when a population is displaced, as happened in the case of the construction of Banāras Hindu University just to the south of Vārāṇasī, the *bīrs* remained in situ. To this day, members of these displaced populations regularly returned to tend to these metaphysical members of their communities (Mahanta).

Bhairavas demonstrate local specificity similar to that of the deified dead, and distinct from the more homogenous forms of Hanumān now common across India. While they share iconography with *bīrs* in Vārāṇasī, Bhairavas across South Asian landscapes are highly individual and easily recognizable. Famous instances of Kāl Bhairav in the cities of Kathmandu, Vārāṇasī, and Ujjain are strikingly different in their appearance, placement, and overall demeanor. In Vārāṇasī, there is frequent reference to a Purāṇic episode in which Bhairava severs one of Lord Brahmā's five heads, wanders outcaste for twelve years, and is liberated upon entry into the sacred city, demonstrating Vārāṇasī's sacred *kṣetra* (territory) removes the karmic effects of even the most heinous deeds. Once in the city, Bhairava becomes its guardian and regulator, as are *bīrs* for their communities. He is, in a sense, the *bīr* of Banāras (Vārāṇasī). Nevertheless, he maintains this tension of insider and outsider, of folk and urban, evident in his iconography and ritual veneration. Associated with skulls and cremation, and accepting of transgressive offerings, Bhairava is terrifying as his name suggests (Bhī+Rava, lit. Cry of Fear), and yet he is beloved. A description of some of the more transgressive rituals at an otherwise friendly neighborhood Bhairava temple illustrates the tension that Bhairava maintains, framing a final consideration of his role in the articulation of sacred space.

Baṭuk, Krodhana, and Unmatta Bhairavas

An example drawn from the most popular of Bhairava's neighborhood temples—that of Baṭuk (Little Boy) Bhairava in Kamācchā—illustrates the way in which his networks maintain folk elements while exemplifying vernacular religion. While Baṭuk is worshipped as any prominent neighborhood deity would be for the safety and flourishing of the surrounding population, a small ancillary shrine tucked away in the complex serves a specialized, crucial purpose. There, a sizable *mūrti* of Krodhana (Angry) Bhairava is flanked by a small statue and an empty sconce. The empty sconce echoes *bīr* traditions of leaving an empty space to signify the presence of a member of the deified dead. The small statue is identified as Unmatta Bhairava. Though Unmatta Bhairava in Deurā is labeled as the official site according to the *Kāśī Khaṇḍa*, this instance of Unmatta Bhairava in the Baṭuk Bhairava complex is an approved proxy featured in more contemporary pilgrimage guides, perhaps to skip the hours-long trip out to Deurā (Ligo 180). Here, we see a vernacular reinterpretation of the location of Unmatta Bhairava, and even a vernacular doubling. Rather than a simple shortcut, fabrication, or deviation from a textual tradition, this is an example of maintaining the folk within the context of the vernacular, functioning not for the sake of simplicity but as a sort of holographic or cinematic dual presence: as film and projection, each complete.

There is a further layer of interaction with Unmatta Bhairava in the Baṭuk Bhairava temple complex which is particularly fascinating: each Tuesday night, a Tantric *pūjā* (ritual worship service) is dedicated to him. Featuring the smallest Bhairava present in the complex, this *pūjā* ties everyday neighborhood religious life to a ritually, physically, and historically marginal tradition. The ritual in question involves the temporary reconsecration of the left side of the shrine space directly in front of this Unmatta Bhairava with *yantras* (empowered geometric diagrams) drawn on the floor with a combination of Gaṅgā water, white liquor, and *sindūr* powder. The *pūjā* involves hand gestures, the recitation of mantras, and consumption of the *pañcamakara*, five ritually taboo substances in direct tension with, and considered taboo by, purportedly normative, textual, 'official' Hinduism. Many ounces of white liquor are consumed in the process, and once the rite is completed, and the temporary sub-shrine disassembled, the *pūjārī* (ritual specialist) steps out into the alleyway—still well within the temple complex—for a cigarette. He insists that all other participants join him.

While Bhairava, even childlike Baṭuk, is known to accept alcohol as an offering,[16] the consumption of alcohol and the rest of the *pañcamakara*, even the smoking of cigarettes, would usually be highly inappropriate within the temple complex. On Tuesdays, this activity is not only accepted, it is expected. It is a vernacular reinterpretation of a prescriptive distinction between left- and right-handed paths, between the orthodox and the heterodox, between the mainstream and the marginal. While Bhairava's general acceptance of alcohol complicates the assertions of orthodoxy, this Tantric process intentionally complicates prescriptive norms. The location of Unmatta Bhairava in Deurā in a marginal cremation ground further ties this practice to left-handed Tantric practices. These practices, it has long been theorized, reflect indigenous practice that has found new purchase and meaning in a wider Hindu context. This would mean, then, that it reflects the influence of the folk in the vernacular. The vernacular, then, is not the category into which all lived religion falls, but rather the means by which folk and other elements are interpreted.

Conclusion

Bhairava, reproducing the folk and resisting the sanitized official, is positioned ideally to represent the vernacular. This may be changing in the case of certain Bhairavas, however: in mid-January, 2022, images of Kāl Bhairav dressed in a police chief's uniform 'for the good of the country' were circulated on Facebook. It is not clear whether this apparently novel presentation is a reflection of a longstanding association of Kāl Bhairav with the nearby police headquarters, or the result of increased national sentiment in the current political climate, particularly following visits by PM Modi to the temple. It is likely the result of both. Nevertheless, the distinctness of these three registers, and their utility even in assessing elements and currents in religious reckoning, stands. In arguing for the maintenance of folk and official strata in the consideration of vernacular religion I am not arguing for the reinstatement of the model presented by Don Yoder, with the folk being a derivative localization of the official. Rather, the official is a reduction, or flattening, of the folk. Official versions of Hanumān and Bhairava, sanitized and co-opted, would lose much of their range of representation and relevance. Understanding that the official is often a reduction and homogenization of the folk offers a corrective to misleading arguments that the folk and the vernacular are gestures of resistance to the official by marginalized, folk populations (contra Sax; Freeman).

I close with a consideration of the way even prescriptive, 'official' registers of religion are ultimately products of the vernacular.[17] In Vārāṇasī's Kāl Bhairav temple—the most famous Bhairava temple in the city and by some accounts one of the most important temples in all of Vārāṇasī—there is inscribed above the door to the sanctum sanctorum a Sanskrit verse in praise of Bhairava. Noticing some eccentricities in the Devanāgarī inscription, I asked my friend and interlocutor, Manoj, who keeps a stall in the temple and sells sacred souvenirs and blessings, what the inscription said. Glancing briefly to confirm I was indicating the inscription above the door, he looked directly at me and recited the verse perfectly, in clear Sanskrit. He cited it as coming from the *Skanda Purāṇa*. But there are at least two reasons to be curious about this claim. The first is that I have at least so far been unable to find that verse in any version of the *Skanda Purāṇa*. The second is that what he recited was not what was written above the door. To be sure, the verse he shared with me was what was *supposed* to be written above the door, but the actual inscription was laced with errant letters and ligatures, completely disrupting the meter of the verse and making it all but illegible. When I pointed this out to Manoj, he was surprised. He had always known what was written there, and never needed to read it. For him, the recited verse was what the inscription said. He had negotiated his religious context and extended his vernacular authority to fill the position of the inscribed, textual, architectural official.

Notes

1 The 'great' and 'little' dichotomy is often attributed to Robert Redfield, cf. *The Little Community* (1956), an ethnographic work on Mexican society. Mckim Marriott, a student of Redfield, applied these terms to Indian society in *Village India, Studies in the Little Community* (1955). Louis Dumont and David Pocock deploy these terms in their introduction to the journal *Contributions to Indian Sociology*, Vol. 1 (1957). Gananath Obeyesekere engages this discourse in his study of Sri Lankan Buddhism "The Great Tradition and the Little in the Perspective of Sinhalese Buddhism" (*Journal of Asian Studies* 22, 1963). Milton Singer continues the application of this dichotomy in the Indian context in *Structure and Change in Indian Society* (1968), and the framework is still used in 2021 (e.g. Banibrata Mahanta, "Transformed Heroes").

2 https://www.ndtv.com/india-news/what-is-kashi-vishwanath-corridor-project-explained-in-5-points-2648407; https://timesofindia.indiatimes.com/india/kashi-vishwanath-corridor-project-how-bjp-is-casting-pm-modi-in-hindu-queen-ahilya-bai-holkars-mould/articleshow/88247567.cms; https://timesofindia.indiatimes.com/india/pm-modi-inaugurates-kashi-vishwanath-dham-in-varanasi-key-points/articleshow/88250072.cms.

3 Named after the goddess Satī, who in Purāṇic mythology self-immolated due to great anger or shame, the practice of *satī* has a contested history and has been expressly illegal in India since 1829. Since 1987, it has been a criminal act to glorify the practice, but these historical sites are still actively venerated.

4 Vārāṇasī is also called the *mahāśmaśān*, or the great cremation ground, and *satī* stones can be found in many places throughout the city. These small stones typically feature male and female forms, and should not be confused with *satī sthālas*, which are large, conical, feature only the *satī*, and signal the continuing presence of the deified dead.

5 The feet of this *mūrti* are below the level of the shrine floor, suggesting the structure came later.

6 A YouTube video of the Hanumān Calisa, a praise song, has 2.5 billion views. https://youtu.be/AETFvQonfV8.

7 A role exemplified Hanumān's 'sacred heart' images in which he tears open his own chest to show Sītā and Rāma, objects of his perfect devotion, emblazoned upon his heart.

8 This can be observed in an uptick in militant Hanumān imagery, from calendar art to vinyl wraps for SUVs.

9 The Bharatiya Janata Party (Indian Peoples' Party), frequently aligned with Hindu Nationalism, to which PM Narendra Modi belongs.

10 Though these processes are often referred to as Sanskritization, that is to say put into keeping with 'official' register Sanskrit texts, they are usually more a process of sanitization, or comportment with current sensibilities of propriety, regardless of Sanskrit textual contents.

11 In this fusion, he appears to guard against himself while embodying protective and harmful potentialities of Bīr Bābās, as well as their frequent pairing with female sources of metaphysical power. cf. Coccari, "Protection and Identity," 139. This site also features a *satī* stone.

12 A mixture of oil and pigment. For related folk practices, see White.

13 Even goddesses associated with transregional exemplars of the divine feminine are still frequently tied to local, neighborhood, tree-centered goddess traditions and ritual practices. See the essay by David Gordon White in this volume.

14 The linking of Bhairava to Baisāsura is commonplace in Maharashtra. See Sontheimer, 26, 32.

15 https://goo.gl/maps/8b2u5BGgXenQoTkg8. There is a nearby stele of a male hero figure labeled Kālā Bhairu, at once eliciting Kāl Bhairav and other Bīr steles.
16 On his birthday, Baṭuk receives gift baskets containing Cadbury's bars and fifths of Johnnie Walker Black.
17 Purāṇas also make vernacular 'official.'

Works Cited

Alder, Ketan. "Explainer: What Are the Origins of Today's Hindu Nationalism?" *The Conversation*. Accessed December 9, 2021. http://theconversation.com/explainer-what-are-the-origins-of-todays-hindu-nationalism-55092.

Coccari, Diane. "The Bīr Babas of Banāras: An Analysis of a Folk Deity in North Indian Hinduism." Doctoral Thesis, University of Wisconsin, 1986.

——— "Protection and Identity: Banaras's Bir Babas as Neighborhood Guardian Deities" in Freitag, Sandria, ed. *Culture and Power in Banaras: Community, Performance, and Environment, 1800–1980*. Delhi: Oxford University Press, 2010.

——— "The Bir Babas of Banaras and the Deified Dead" in Hiltebeitel, Alf, ed. *Criminal Gods and Demon Devotees: Essays on the Guardians of Popular Hinduism*. Albany: State University of New York Press, 1989.

Cort, John E. *Jains in the World: Religious Values and Ideology in India*. Oxford University Press, 2011.

Erndl, Kathleen. *Victory to the Mother: The Hindu Goddess of Northwest India in Myth, Ritual, and Symbol*. New York: Oxford University Press, 1993.

Freeman, John R. "Shifting Forms of the Wandering Yogi: The Teyyam of Bhairavan." In *Masked Ritual and Performance in South India: Dance, Healing, and Possession*, edited by David Shulman and Deborah Thiagarajan. Michigan: University of Michigan, 2006.

Gengnagel, Jörg. *Visualized Texts: Sacred Spaces, Spatial Texts and the Religious Cartography of Banaras*. Ethno-Indology ; 7. Wiesbaden: Harrassowitz Verlag, 2011.

Haskett, Christian. "On Varanasi's Tiny Temples." *South Asia Multidisciplinary Academic Journal*, no. 18 (July 23, 2018).

Ligo, Seth. "Kāśī Kṣetra, Kāśī Maṇḍala: Digitally Mapping Evolving Interpretations of an Idealized Sacred City." *International Journal of Hindu Studies* 26 (2022): 161–188.

Lutgendorf, Philip. *Hanuman's Tale: The Messages of a Divine Monkey*. Oxford; New York: Oxford University Press, 2007.

Mahanta, Banibrata. "Transformed Heroes: The Bīr Bābās and their Religio-cultural Metamorphosis" in A. Singh, S. Tholia, and P.K. Patel, eds. *The Hero and Hero-Making across Genres*. London: Routledge India, 2021.

Marriott, Mckim (Ed.) *Village India: Studies in the Little Community. (Comparative Studies of Cultures and Civilizations*. Chicago: University of Chicago Press, 1955.

Obeyesekere, Gananath. "The Great Tradition and the Little in the Perspective of Sinhalese Buddhism." *The Journal of Asian Studies* 22, no. 2 (1963): 139–153.

Peabody, Norbert. "Disciplining the Body, Disciplining the Body-Politic: Physical Culture and Social Violence among North Indian Wrestlers." *Comparative Studies in Society and History* 51, no. 2 (2009): 372–400.

Primiano, Leonard. "Vernacular Religion and the Search for Method in Religious Folklife." *Western Folklore* 54, no. 1 (1995): 37–56.

Ray, Avishek, and Ishita Banerjee-Dube. *Nation, Nationalism and the Public Sphere: Religious Politics in India*. London: Sage Publishing India, 2020.

Sarasvatī, Daṇḍisvāmī. Nd. *Kāśī Gaurav*. Vārāṇasī: Śrī Māsṭar Khelāṛīlāl Śītal Prasād.

Sax, William Sturman. *God of Justice: Ritual Healing and Social Justice in the Central Himalayas*. New York: Oxford University Press, 2009.

Singer, Milton, and Bernard S. Cohn, eds. *Structure and Change in Indian Society*. Chicago: Routledge, 1968.

Singh, Rana P. B. 2002. *Towards the Pilgrimage Archetype: The Pañcakrośī YātrāātrBanāras*. Vārāṇasī: Indica Books, 2002.

Singh, Rana P. B. and Pravin S. *Banāras Region: A Spiritual & Cultural Guide*. Vārāṇasī: Indica Books, 2006.

Sontheimer, Günther-Dietz. *Pastoral Deities in Western India*. New York: Oxford University Press, 1989.

Sukula, Kailāsanātha. "Kāśī Darpaṇa" (1876). Vārāṇasī Research Project, 2001, http://benares.uni-hd.de.

Vyās, Kedarnāth. *Paṃcakrośātmaka Jyotirliṃṅg Kāśīmāhātmya*. Vārāṇasī: Kāśī Śodh Anusaṃdhān Saṃsthān, 2011.

White, David. "Filthy Amulets: "Superstition," "True Religion" and "Pure Science" in the Light of Indian Demonology." Translation of "Amulettes et lambeaux divines: superstition, vraie religion et science pure à la lumière de la démonologie hindoue." *Puruśārtha* 27 (2009): 135–162.

Yoder, Don. *Discovering American Folklife: Studies in Ethnic, Religious, and Regional Culture*. Ann Arbor, MI: UMI Research Press, 1990 [1976].

7

THERE IS SOMETHING IN ME

Narratives of LGBTIQ+ *Sangomas* (Traditional Healers) in South Africa

Rachel C. Schneider

This chapter examines the intersection of gender, sexuality, and folk religion in narratives presented by healers/diviners known as *sangomas* (traditional healers) in South Africa. Analyzing published narratives about and by lesbian, bisexual, and transgender *sangomas*, the chapter shows how these narratives reveal changing notions and emerging tensions regarding gender and sexuality in twenty-first-century South Africa. LGBTIQ+[1] people in South Africa often face hostility and violence. While most *sangomas* are assumed to be heterosexual, there are sangomas who identify as lesbian, gay, or transgender. LGBTIQ+ *sangomas* and those around them appeal to the power and authority associated with ancestral spirits in order to explain and legitimate same-sex desire and gender nonconformity in an often-hostile context, even as they reinterpret religious beliefs in light of LGBTIQ+ identities. I focus my analysis on Nkunzi Nkabinde's autobiography *Black Bull, the Ancestors and Me: My Life as a Lesbian Sangoma* (2008) supported by other first-person narratives of LGBTIQ+ *sangomas* published in edited volumes. These books, intended for an English-speaking public audience, draw upon interviews conducted in English or translated from indigenous languages such as isiXhosa or isiZulu.[2]

Sangomas are viewed by many South Africans as powerful subjects who occupy a liminal, or in-between, space between the natural world and the spirit world, between the ancestors and their community, and between male and female because they channel both male and female ancestors. Because of *sangoma*'s perceived sacred power, being a *sangoma* provides LGBTIQ+ persons with forms of social protection not necessarily available to other Black LGBTIQ+ people in South African society. However, *sangomahood* should not be seen simply as a mere strategy to address stigma; it is not a form of bad faith. Rather, religion, gender, and sexuality represent mutually constitutive and meaningful aspects of complex *sangoma* subjectivity (Pinn 2003), and this subjectivity is far from unified or stable. Indigenous African religious beliefs and practices help individuals

DOI: 10.4324/9781003257462-10

make sense of their gender and sexuality; in turn, gender and sexuality shape how individuals creatively interpret folk religion.

Indigenous African religions[3] are examples of folk religions because they arise out of indigenous ethnic communities in Africa; they present no systemized doctrines codified in texts nor centralized religious authority. Diffuse knowledge is passed to individuals through rituals and oral traditions. Deeply shaped by local contexts, and often interacting with other religious systems, indigenous religious traditions in Africa inform how individuals experientially interpret, believe, and practice in their everyday lives (Primiano 1995). Within indigenous religious systems, traditional healers/diviners are specialists who individuals seek out to discern causes of illness and suffering, individual and communal. Healers offer individuals prescriptions for healing based on the healers' connection to ancestral spirits.

In South Africa, *sangoma* is the term generally used to describe traditional healers/diviners, an English version of the Zulu term *isangoma*. Many *sangomas* also adopt the term "traditional healer" (Wreford 2008, x).[4] *Sangomas* typically undergo, or pursue, strict training and initiation into a guild of practitioners. Often, this training is proceeded by a period of suffering seen by the initiate as a "sign" of being chosen by deceased ancestors for their vocation (Reis 2000, 72). Accepting the call to *sangomahood* requires an individual to seek a trainer who confirms the ancestral call, and then the aspirant undertakes a period of arduous training, culminating in ritual initiation. In the work of divination, a *sangoma*'s "power and authority" is based on "claims to a specific association and communication with the spirit world" (van Dijk, Reis, and Spierenburg 2000, 7). The influence of ancestors and spirit entities enables *sangomas* to diagnose causes of sickness and misfortune for their clients and also to combat evil forces arising from human and inhuman entities (Reis 2000, 73). The divining process includes bone throwing, use of herbal medicine, and trance and trance-related activities such as drumming, singing, and dancing.

LGBTIQ+ Sangomas in South African Society

Even though South Africa is overwhelmingly Christian (86%)—and only a minority of people (5.3%) identify primarily with ancestral/tribal/animist or other traditional African religions—traditional healing practices continue to exist and be utilized ("General Household Survey" 2015, 3).[5] Many people across the southern African region, including *sangomas* themselves, combine belief in the power of Jesus or the Holy Spirit with ancestral beliefs. For example, they will pray to Jesus/the Holy Spirit and perform rituals to appease and solicit the help of ancestors (Morgan and Reid 2003; Podolecka 2021). That persistence of indigenous African religious beliefs is a testament to their enduring power despite repression by Western colonial powers and European Christian missionaries. At the same time, the colonial legacy of condemning indigenous African religion persists, actively. Many Christian churches in South Africa condemn traditional healing as "demonic" or "satanic" (Podolecka and Cheyeka 2021, 19). In a study of young men living in the urban area of Soweto, male youths also expressed concerns that *sangomas* are "fake" and only after people's money, comparing the paid work of *sangomas* negatively to churches where healing services are offered for free (Nyundu 2018, 5–6).

The majority of *sangomas* are assumed (or expected) to be heterosexual; therefore, *sangomas* who engage in same-sex sexual practices, express gender nonconformity, or self-identify as lesbian, gay, bisexual, transgender, intersex, or queer face additional hostility due to general anti-LGBTIQ+ social attitudes. Hostility is legitimated by appeals to Christianity, Islam, and general claims that queer sexuality is a Western "import" foreign to African culture and religion (Schneider 2018; Van Klinken and Chitando 2016; Chidester 2012, 205). Ironically, Western colonialism and European Christian missionary activity played a significant role in the stigmatization and criminalization of same-sex practices throughout Africa.

South Africa's 1996 Constitution prohibits sexual orientation discrimination, the first constitution in the world to do so. Regardless, LGBTIQ+ people, particularly Black women and those living in impoverished environments, face significant threats of violence (Reid 2022), including "corrective rape" whereby perpetrators justify sexual violence by claiming rape will "cure" victims (Makhaye 2021); forced sex is thought to confer heteronormativity.

Some LGBTIQ+ *sangomas*, however, claim that being a *sangoma* affords them protection from violence (Neilson 2014; Sam 1995). Nkunzi Zandile Nkabinde, a twenty-nine-year-old, self-identified lesbian *sangoma* who published the primary narratives examined below, explains why same-sex *sangomas* occupy a privileged position compared to other Black lesbians in contemporary South African society.

> Same-sex *sangomas* are powerful people at the center of African culture. They therefore occupy a special position in society in that they are respected and feared. *Sangomas* who are involved in same-sex relationships don't have the problem of being harassed by the community. Lesbian rape is a punishment and seen as necessary by thugs in order to teach visible lesbians a lesson. However same-sex *sangomas* are not raped as people are afraid of *sangomas* because of the power they believe *sangomas* have.
>
> *(Nkabinde and Morgan 2005, 232)*

Claims that social protection is afforded through *sangomahood* should not be overstated. Elsewhere Nkabinde describes fearing violence by being an "out" masculine-presenting Black lesbian, despite being a *sangoma* (Nkabinde 2008, 147–149). But Nkabinde's comments allude to how being a *sangoma* may mitigate stigmas surrounding queer sexuality in a hostile, possibly deadly, environment. A perceived connection to ancestral spirits makes *sangomas* liminal figures, meaning that they are "threshold people" who exist "betwixt and between" socially assigned conventions (Turner 2011, 95), which is only amplified by gender fluidity or queer sexuality. As ritual theorist Victor Turner argues, liminal figures are "necessarily ambiguous" because they "slip through a network of classifications" typically used to locate individuals in "cultural space." Their "ambiguous and indeterminate" attributes are associated with heightened sacred power, making liminal entities both revered and also seen as potential threats to the dominant order (95). While the liminal attributes of *sangomahood* may heighten the degree to which LGBTIQ+ *sangomas* are perceived as dangerous "others," the sacred power associated with liminality operates, unexpectedly, as protection: a cisgender male may think twice before making trouble, fearing supernatural repercussions for his actions.

From Secrecy to Visibility: The Importance of Narrative Activism

Same-sex sexual experiences among South African *sangomas* are historically shrouded in secrecy and taboo, which served a protective function for *sangomas* in a patriarchal, heteronormative cultural context (Mkasi 2016, 3). In the first, in-depth research on same-sex identified female *sangomas* (2000–2002), anthropologists Ruth Morgan and Graeme Reid document that all their informants used the term "lesbian" to identify themselves due to their attraction to women, but the meaning of the term lesbian was elusive, because those who adopted it avoided public visibility and activism (Morgan and Reid 2003, 383).[6] More recently, *sangomas* in urban contexts do publicly organize around LGBTIQ+ identities, though gay and lesbian *sangomas* report facing discrimination from community members and clients because of their sexual identities (Ntongana 2016).[7]

Increased use of sexual and gender identity categories such as lesbian and transgender by *sangomas* can be linked to the inclusion of sexual rights in the 1996 Democratic Constitution of South Africa. The prevalence of human rights discourses in South Africa and high levels of gender-/sexuality-based violence have additionally served as a catalyst for LGBTQI+ *sangomas* to seek to educate others and document their own stories: stories that challenge homophobic and transphobic discourses, and stories that imagine different ways to perform one's relationship to God, community, and ancestors. Increased visibility has occurred alongside concerted efforts by activist NGOs to document sexual and gender diversity in South Africa and Africa more broadly, producing ground-breaking, edited volumes featuring personal narratives of lesbian, bisexual, and transgender people, including *sangomas* (Morgan and Wieringa 2005; Morgan, Marais, and Wellbeloved 2009; Nkabinde 2008).

Nkunzi Zandile Nkabinde, a sangoma who published an autobiography titled *Black Bull, the Ancestors and Me: My Life as a Lesbian Sangoma* (2008), represents a primary example of organized efforts to shed light on the lives of LGBTIQ+ sangomas. Nkabinde is a diviner who identified first as a "lesbian sangoma" and later identified as a transgender man (Morgan 2018; Zabus and Kumar Das 2021). Nkabinde died in 2018, but Nkabinde's research, advocacy, and personal story continue to reveal how traditional healers experience intersections of spirituality, gender, and sexuality. Before he died, Nkabinde participated in the Gay and

Lesbian Archives (GALA)[8] project based in Johannesburg, which seeks to document the life stories of South African gays and lesbians—and his participation led to Nkabinde conducting field research to document stories of other sangomas, all featured in the edited volume *Tommy Boys, Lesbian Men and Ancestral Wives* (2005). Nkabinde, additionally, started a support group for LGBTIQ+ sangomas, the first of its kind.

Nkabinde saw his[9] research and writing as providing a celebratory and corrective intervention to the silencing and shaming of queer *sangomas* and Black lesbians.[10] Nkabinde notes that stories of queer *sangomas* are difficult to document because of the "heterosexual male *sangomas* who control our history and the information that is passed on from generation to generation" (Nkabinde and Morgan 2005, 232), but knowledge of same-sex sexual relationships and practices has always existed, if secretly, among *sangomas*. As such, Nkabinde's position as a *sangoma* allows entrance to knowledge difficult for Western researchers or non-*sangomas* to access. Nkabinde's autobiography and the narratives of *sangomas* he interviewed are precious sources. Expressing a complex relationship between spirituality, sexuality, gender, embodiment, and desire, LGBTIQ+-identified *sangomas* articulate a subjectivity that is *their own*. While such narratives should not be read uncritically, they index expressions of religion, gender, and sexuality that elude easy classification and challenge public erasure. As such, these narratives work to challenge secular categories about LGBTIQ+ identity, often used in transnational discourse, especially in the West, while offering alternate framings (Zabus and Kumar Das 2021). These narratives also function as a tool of activism by challenging dominant discourses in South Africa that argue homosexuality is antithetical to African culture and religion.[11]

Sexuality, Gender, and Ancestral Beliefs in *Sangoma* Narratives

Scholars have argued that indigenous religious and cultural frameworks in southern Africa historically offered opportunities for nonconformity to heteronormativity. In extensive research on the Shona people in Zimbabwe, historian Marc Epprecht argues that though an emphasis on heterosexuality and procreation was dominant in pre-colonial and colonial eras, "what we today would now term homosexual orientation or trans-gender identity was also not necessarily an offense but a respected attribute if caused by a certain type of spirit possession or manifest[ed] in certain ways. This would have included rare cases of physiologically ambiguous genitalia [...] as well as possession by benign spirits of the opposite sex" (Epprecht 2012, 520–521). Sprit possession, then, challenged everyday heteronormativity by providing possibilities for gender fluidity and same-sex relationships. If a man expressed feminine characteristics, this was attributed to a female spirit possessing a male body, and vice versa. Epprecht notes that "such explanations of cause removed the blame from an individual, and same-sex couples so possessed could live together as husband and wife without attracting opprobrium" (Epprecht 2012, 521). In such marriages, what happened in private was left unspoken. Sadly, these types of arrangements and religious interpretations of gender binary nonconformity were increasingly stigmatized or driven underground in the colonial period.

In contemporary South Africa, indigenous African religious interpretations of same-sex relationships and nonbinary gender reemerge in creative ways. The perceived power of ancestors enables *sangomas* to understand gender nonconformity and same-sex desires via indigenous African religion while simultaneously challenging heteronormative religious hegemony. In particular, a practice known as ancestral marriage is cited by LGBTIQ+ *sangomas* as a sign of indigenous religious-cultural accommodation, and even approval, of same-sex relationships. Ancestral marriage is a type of partnership whereby a *sangoma* takes a woman designated an "ancestral wife" to live with them. The physical companion is believed to be chosen by the ancestors, and often the *sangoma*'s family (or husband) will pay *lobola* [dowry] to the ancestral wife's family. Ancestral marriage relationships are not supposed to be sexual—rather, the ancestral wife is intended to assist the *sangoma* in their divination/healing work and domestic tasks. In some instances, however, this arrangement offers a private space for secret sexual relationships to develop between a *sangoma* and the companion.

Older, female *sangomas* who report having secret, sexual relationships with their ancestral wives attribute these relationships to the direction and desire of a dominant, often unmarried, male ancestor who influences/guides them. Hlengiwe—a lesbian *sangoma* in her fifties who lives in a rural area—is legally married to a man, but the legal marriage is not sexual. She is in a long-term, secret sexual relationship with her ancestral wife, insisting that "Muzi [the ancestor] chose her [wife]; I didn't have anything to do with." When possessed by Muzi, Hlengiwe says "I become a man," and she emphasizes that "I only have sex with Muzi's wife" (Nkabinde and Morgan 2005, 249) and not other women. Hlengiwe, then, identifies as a man when possessed by a male ancestor who uses her body for (hetero)sexual fulfillment. When not engaged in sex, Hlengiwe regards herself as a woman, and she affirms that she loves her wife.

Other *sangomas* believe their own sexual desires play a role in their choice of ancestral wife and sexual partner. Nkabinde describes fighting with dominant male ancestor, Nkunzi, because Nkabinde wanted to choose his own sexual partners and to keep his relationship with his ancestral wife non-sexual, but at times Nkabinde and his ancestor Nkunzi will desire the same woman sexually.

> Nkunzi [dominant male ancestor] loves women, especially young women. If I am with a woman of 21 or 22, normally Nkunzi will want to have sex with her. I will feel his presence as if someone is touching my shoulders and sometimes I see the legs and genitals of a man. [...] I have more power when Nkunzi is in me, especially when we both desire the same woman. When this happens, I change. I become so strong. He takes control of my body and even the sounds I make are different.
>
> *(Nkabinde 2008, 68)*

While Nkabinde states that the ancestor doesn't determine the choice of sexual partners, the ancestor's approval is important for the long-term success or failure relationship: "if he is not happy with my choice of woman, I will end up fighting a lot with that woman and eventually I don't even feel sexually attracted" (Nkabinde 2008, 69).

Zodwa—an eighteen-year-old, bisexual *sangoma* in an urban area—is involved in a secret, sexual relationship with her *sangoma* trainer. Zodwa attributes her sexual orientation to ancestor guides, including a grandmother who was "involved with another woman" in an ancestral marriage (Nkabinde and Morgan 2005, 239). Before entering training, Zodwa did not feel attracted to women. When asked if she believes that ancestors approve of queer sexuality, Zodwa states, "yes, they do agree because some of the *sangomas* took wives. You find that a person is a female, and she takes another female to be her wife. This has happened from ancient times; it's something that you are born with. If it wasn't allowed there wouldn't be so many *sangomas* like you (pointing at Nkunzi who is an out lesbian *sangoma*)" (Nkabinde and Morgan 2005, 240). In this way, the traditional practice of ancestral marriage is seen as a sign of ancestral approval of contemporary, same-sex relationships as well as an endorsing of modern conceptions of lesbian and bisexual identity.

"My ancestors helped me become who I am"

Zimbabwean theologian Edward P. Antonia discusses the long history of "transgender homosexuality" among diviners, defining transgender homosexuality as the "temporal and symbolic transformation of human sexuality through the corporeal individuation of the sexual ontologies of spirit beings" (Antonio 1997, 304). Female diviners who are possessed by male spirits will dress and behave like men ("male women"), and, likewise, male diviners possessed by female spirits will dress and behave like women ("female men"). Thereby, the *sangoma*'s gendered body, even if he or she is understood to be cisgender or heterosexual, may display gender fluidity when influenced by ancestral spirits.

LGBTIQ+ *sangomas*, however, articulate a far more complex relationship between embodiment, ancestral influence, and their own sense of sexuality and gender. Some *sangomas* ascribe transgender and same-sex experiences to the will of their dominant ancestor(s). Other *sangomas* insist their gender identity and sexual orientation have nothing to do with being a healer or their dominant ancestors, even as they describe how ancestors actively influence their embodied sense of gender and sexuality.

Thandi, a lesbian *sangoma* in her fifties in a rural area, is conventionally married to a man, but she also has had secret sexual relationships with various ancestral wives. Thandi felt sexually attracted to women from an early age and adopted the term lesbian as an identity. However, Thandi, born female, has also felt like a man from an early age. Though Thandi's sexual desires align with those of multiple heterosexual, male ancestral guides, Thandi attributes attraction to women and feeling "like a man inside" to be something "in me" before she entered training, so it is not entirely reducible to ancestral possession. Importantly, ascribing one's gender and sexuality as innate, or essential, to the self is more akin to how sexual orientation and gender identity are often understood in the West (Nkabinde and Morgan 2005, 247).

Likewise, Stallion, a younger, lesbian *sangoma* living in an urban area, understands their gender and sexuality to be independent from having a dominant male ancestor, because they identified as gay before becoming a *sangoma*; furthermore, their dominant ancestor is a baby boy, perceived as asexual. Stallion's self-described identity remains complex: "I am not a man and I'm not a woman. I'm a lesbian and I'm butch" (Nkabinde and Morgan 2005, 250). Here, Stallion rejects a fixed binary gender categorization but claims the identity category of "lesbian" because of a sexual attraction to women and "butch" by being the male-identified partner in same-sex relationships.

Nkabinde interprets his sexual and gender identity to be something separate from his ancestors, as something that belongs to him; he also believes his ancestors guided and supported the development of his sexual and gender identity. As Nkabinde explains:

> I feel my sexuality was with me from birth. It is not from my ancestors, but my ancestors supported me. When I was a child, I didn't have a choice about things like wearing a dress but as I grew up, I knew I must express the feelings that were inside me and do what was right for me. My ancestors helped me become who I am. They guided me knowing I was going to grow up the way I am. My sexuality is from childhood.
>
> *(Nkabinde 2008, 38)*

Assigned female at birth, growing up, Nkabinde remembers wearing men's clothes and being reprimanded by his mother: "I wanted to tell her, my mom, that there is something in me that makes me like this and I am free when I am like this," which Nkabinde attributes, in part, to the influence of his ancestor Nkunzi. In this way, Nkabinde tries to make space for his own sense of agency while accounting for the agency of a dominant ancestor who fulfills his own desires through Nkabinde's body. As Nkabinde reflects, "If Nkunzi [the ancestor] didn't want me to be a lesbian I don't believe I would have had these feelings. He would have given me a male partner and I would have been happy with that. Nkunzi accepts me as a lesbian. He understands my feelings. Nkunzi knew he was going to use my body long before I did" (Nkabinde 2008, 67). The relationship with Nkunzi is paramount for Nkabinde because his relationship with that ancestor makes divination work possible.

While Nkabinde's comments about Nkunzi may seem contradictory, they highlight tensions between modern ideas of gender and sexuality as intrinsic to an individuated self and indigenous understandings of a gendered self constructed through a network of relationships that for *sangomas* includes interactions with the living and the dead. Nkabinde finds freedom in the gender fluidity made possible by being a *sangoma*, especially in his Zulu ethnic group. Zulu culture maintains strict binary gender divisions in behavior, but Nkabinde explains that gender norms for *sangomas* are flexible: "I can dance like a woman and wear woman's clothes and dance like a man and wear a man's clothes" (Nkabinde 2008, 73). Being a *sangoma*, then, allows for a gendered subjectivity that is fluid and open to change. Femininity and masculinity are not reduced to or conflated with the body; these qualities are connected relationally to both a personal sense of gender and the gender(s) of ancestors.

The experience of embodying multiple entities with multiple genders and sexual desires in one body illustrates Judith Butler's argument that "as a mode of relation, neither gender nor sexuality is precisely a possession, but, rather, is a mode of being dispossessed" (Butler 2020, 24). In other words, bodily possession by spirits or ancestors renders a *sangoma*'s sexuality and gender never wholly their own. However, the experience of surrendering one's body to an ancestor is not experienced as repressive and may even feel liberating. Nkabinde writes that "Since I started to have the spirit of Nkunzi in me I hardly menstruate. I only menstruate when I have a female ancestor in me." This lack of menstruation is interpreted positively because "[a]lthough I love it when there is a female spirit in me, I have never learned to cope with menstruation or having breasts. [...] If I were rich, I would have an operation to remove my breasts" (Nkabinde 2008, 19). Nkabinde expresses reverence for feminine spirits, but he also expresses a desire to occupy a masculine body that aligns with his personal sense of gender and that of Nkunzi.

Nkabinde's reverence for Nkunzi, his dominant male ancestor, and, additionally, Nkabinde's participation in activist organizations, however, creates tension between traditional and modern ways of life. On the Zulu cultural practice of physically examining young women to see if they are virgins, Nkabinde sees how such practices are valuable because, from his ancestor Nkunzi's perspective, they are a way to preserve Zulu culture and keep authority in the hands of community elders, especially in the face of HIV/AIDS and pregnancy. But Nkabinde also sees how the human rights of girls are violated by these tests. This latter perspective, which critiques traditional practices as patriarchal and oppressive to women, emerged as Nkabinde publicly identified as a lesbian *sangoma* and began to interact with feminist and sexual rights organizations (Nkabinde 2008, 17). Tensions abound.

Some gendered articulations are also intentionally framed for public consumption. The back cover of Nkabinde's autobiography portrays him as a boundary-crossing exemplar, the publisher writing this tagline: "Nkunzi dances like a woman and slaughters like a man." Nkabinde is positioned as a figure who is seeking a middle path "of balance and integration between the living and the dead, the traditional and the modern" and who is "conscious of her constitutional rights as an urban young lesbian in a time of a relentless spate of hate crimes against township lesbians" while "simultaneously sensitive to the demands of the guiding ancestral voice of the traditional, rural Zulu patriarch whose name she bears." Nkabinde, then, is the perfect narrative subject for scholars and activists. Positioned as a "Zulu woman, a lesbian, and a *sangoma*" (Nkabinde 2008, 4), who later identifies as a transgender man, Nkabinde reflects progressive values through claiming the identity of lesbian while reflecting so-called traditional values as a Zulu and *sangoma*—as such, he is a figure who can lead the way to a decolonial future.

"I marvel how God created me"

As we see above, African indigenous religious frameworks are used to interpret gender and sexuality in twenty-first-century South Africa. While this is not always positive—it is not uncommon for family members to take a person feared to be gay or transgender to a *sangoma* to be cured from possession of an evil spirit—reverence for ancestral power and ancestral beliefs can provide a pathway for self-acceptance, social acceptance, and even spiritual integration. A 2020 newspaper article about Nthabiseng Mokoena, a genderqueer intersex activist who is Christian and a *sangoma*, describes the socially transformative possibilities provided by indigenous African religion. Nthabiseng reflects on their call to *sangomahood*: "I think it was the first time I could completely reconcile my gender expression, my intersex traits and my spirituality without any conflict, because within the realm of spirituality there are no set norms, like 'you have to be this or that:' there is a lot of fluidity" (Pikoli 2021). Similarly, when LGBTIQ+ *sangomas* speak of the support of their families and their communities in their process of coming out, this support is linked to the perceived presence of the ancestors.

A 2011 GALA sponsored book, *TRANS: Transgender Life Stories from South Africa* features a fascinating narrative by a twenty-one-year-old *sangoma* named Tebogo who describes himself to be a "FTM [female to male] transsexual." In a chapter titled "My Ancestor Was Living through Me" (Morgan, Marais, and Wellbeloved 2009, 119), Tebogo describes an early childhood awareness of being different: "When I was in standard 6, I started expressing my feelings. I could no longer suppress this thing: I preferred being male rather than female" (Morgan, Marais, and Wellbeloved 2009, 120). Tebogo didn't want people to know he was assigned female at birth, so he sought to hide his breasts and adopted a masculine name and dress.

When he was fifteen, Tebogo started training as a *sangoma* after receiving "the call" from his deceased great-grandfather, and he was relieved to find acceptance from his trainers: "It was obvious for all to see that I was different. The fact that I wore something to hide my breasts and I liked to talk to my girlfriends didn't worry my trainer. They are very few straight *sangomas* around. They just thought that I inherited my masculine ways from my ancestors, who were also male." Because of ancestral beliefs, Tebogo found a measure of acceptance from his family and community elders "because they could tell that perhaps my ancestors were making me play the role I played. My ancestor was living through me because he was male." Social acceptance allowed

Tebogo to then find a measure of self-acceptance: "my elders started accepting me because they believed my ancestors played a role in what I am. That made me believe it was the right thing" (Morgan, Marais, and Wellbeloved 2009, 121). A link to the ancestors also helped Tebogo woo his girlfriend, who felt strongly about not dating lesbians. He was able to convince her that he belonged in a different category, even though he didn't have language at this stage to describe what this category was: "I didn't see myself as a lesbian. I told her I was a man and at the same time I'm fulfilling tradition" (Morgan, Marais, and Wellbeloved 2009, 121–122).

Tebogo saw an Oprah episode in 2005 that focused on a man assigned female at birth who subsequently had a sex-change operation, which led Tebogo to contact a local NGO titled "OUT LGBT Well-Being." Tebogo wanted to learn more about sex-change procedures, and, through this organization, he encountered the term "transsexual" for the first time. Tebogo learned the difference between gender identity and sexual orientation and OUT explained he was "suffering from gender identity disorder." Tebogo was subsequently introduced to a transman who had successfully transitioned from female to male. Through his engagement with OUT, and another NGO called Gender DynamiX,[12] Tebogo decided it was necessary to transition via hormones and surgery. His choice to transition has been accepted by his family and community, though he notes his lesbian friends do not approve of his decision. "We don't see eye to eye, but they don't discourage or mislead me" (Morgan, Marais, and Wellbeloved 2009, 125). Tebogo has started working for Gender DynamiX to educate others about the experience of being transgender.

Tebogo's published narrative about his transgender journey includes a fascinating description of finding personal integration between Christian and indigenous African beliefs. Tebogo describes how he used to pray and preach as a child, but when he received the calling to *sangomahood*, he stopped identifying with Christianity because he didn't think one could be a *sangoma* and a Christian at the same time. Now, just as he is finding integration around his transgender identity, he has returned to Christianity and found spiritual integration as a *sangoma* and a trans man.

> I am very religious. I'm a Christian who's also a *sangoma*. I've been a Christian since standard 5. At times I marvel at how God created me. I used to preach at school, up until standard 10, and on the other hand be a *sangoma* and a trans man, and not a lesbian. At times I find my situation to be quite overwhelming, but I guess that's how things ought to be. [...] I'm a Christian, I know who God is, and I acknowledge his importance as well as his existence. My ancestors are a part of my culture and also part of my reason for existence. That's my heritage. So I think it's important that I respect my culture. I also read and comprehend the Bible. Therefore, I think I lead a healthy life. I am a true Christian.
>
> *(Morgan, Marais, and Wellbeloved 2009, 126)*

Here, Tebogo appeals to God as the Creator of his complex personhood, and he holistically links his identities as a Christian, a *sangoma*, and a trans man. Similarly, Stallion, a butch lesbian *sangoma*, describes how participation in the predominantly Black LGBTIQ+ affirming church, Hope and Unity Metropolitan Community Church, provides a space of inclusion, unlike other churches. Stallion is both a prophet in the church and a *sangoma*, and God and the ancestors work together to provide Stallion with spiritual power to divine the future (Nkabinde and Morgan 2005, 255).

The blending of Christianity and indigenous religion in LGBTIQ+ *sangoma* narratives foregrounds David Chidester's observation that in the "long conversation" between indigenous African religion and European Christianity, "mixtures rather than purity have been the rule" (Chidester 2012, 202), especially when it comes to how religious beliefs and practices are lived by everyday people. In particular, the narratives of LGBTIQ+ *sangomas* blur (or queer) "the convenient and misleading binaries of tradition/modernity, ancestor worship/Christianity, body/mind, man/woman and heterosexual/homosexual" (Stobie 2007, 54–55). While indigenous religious beliefs are not always accommodated by Christian churches, most *sangoma* express the conviction that a person can believe in God and the ancestors simultaneously.[13] This conviction invites us to think about the socially transformative potential of folk religion, which for many South Africans includes some elements of both indigenous African religion and Christianity. Increased visibility of LGBTIQ+ *sangomas* may inspire communities to interpret gender and sexual diversity among non-*sangomas* to be positive in relation to God and the ancestors. Given that South Africa is overwhelming Christian, this is a revolutionary dynamic. The story of a Black, non-*sangoma*, transsexual Zama indicates this positive interpretation; his brother supports his transition because "God is the only one who has a right to judge. If I see you, I see God because we are all created in His image" (Morgan, Marais, and Wellbeloved 2009, 192). Here, ancestral beliefs and inclusive Christian theology provide a pathway to positively interpret gender and sexual diversity.

Conclusion

Because *sangomas* occupy a liminal space, mediating between past, present, and future, the ways LGBTIQ+ *sangomas* narrate their experiences invite us to rethink the relationship between spirit, gender, and sexuality more broadly and to consider how individuals creatively negotiate and engage with indigenous African religions in postcolonial Africa. In recent years, activists have pushed to formally recognize indigenous religion and ancestral beliefs in South Africa amidst larger discussions about decolonization. In 2022, the Congress of Traditional Leaders in South Africa designated May 8 as Ancestors' Day, calling the government to make it a national public holiday. According to leaders, the holiday is intended for "reflection, prayer, [and] appeasement of our ancestors" and to "honour our forefathers and foremothers" (O'Regan 2022). But in the decolonial quest to elevate the status of indigenous religion, the experiences of LGBTIQ+ *sangomas* should not be erased. LGBTIQ+ *sangomas* assert the primacy of indigenous African religious epistemologies, even as they publicly challenge enduring gender binaries and heteronormativity *within* traditional African religion. In doing so, they provide a pathway for greater visibility and acceptance of gender and sexual diversity in South Africa that embraces, rather than eschews, indigenous religious frameworks.

Published narratives of LGBTIQ+ *sangomas* become sites where "the borders and boundaries of communal identities are formed," negotiated, and expanded to include emerging gender and sexuality identity categories (Gopinath 2005, 9). At the same time, we should not overlook the fact that *sangomas* draw on indigenous religion to interpret their sexual practices and desires in ways that often work to reinforce gender binaries, heteronormativity, and patriarchy.[14] For lesbian *sangomas*, belief in ancestral possession by a male ancestor works to legitimate them in the eyes of their community through an appeal to masculine authority. "For a woman who would otherwise experience the marginal status of being a lesbian, having a male ancestor speak and act through her gives her unquestionable authority in this particular social context" (Morgan and Reid 2003, 387). This observation has caused some scholars, and even *sangomas* themselves, to question whether or not Black lesbians claim a "spiritual calling" to attribute their sexual desires to a power they cannot control and avoid charges of homosexuality as un-African, resulting in discrimination (Gunkel 2010, 129–130). Such a functionalist analysis fails to acknowledge that *sangoma* livelihood depends on being able to provide concrete results through healing work, it is believed that one's power as a *sangoma* depends on an authentic connection with the ancestors. While theoretically, anyone can be LGBTIQ+, not everyone can be a *sangoma*. Thus, being a *sangoma* serves to legitimate one's gender and sexuality, but one's gender and sexuality are also given public validity through perceptions of sacred power.

Ultimately, first-person narratives of lesbian, bisexual, and transgender traditional healers in South Africa illustrate how notions of lesbian, bisexual, or transgender identity (and same-sex experience) are not easily separated from indigenous religious epistemologies and practices. Gender and sexuality, as discussed by *sangomas,* do not easily map onto secular notions of gender and sexuality in Western contexts, inviting us to consider new ways to understanding intersectional identities that include, rather than exclude, suprasensible experience and to recognize socially transformative potentials found in indigenous religion. Heightened public visibility of LGBTIQ+ *sangomas* demonstrates how indigenous practices are not "hermetically-sealed embodiments of tradition and culture" (Morgan and Reid 2003, 203); rather, such practices are dynamic and fluid, reflecting the dynamics and fluidity of gender and sexuality in South Africa and, perhaps, among all people.

Notes

1 LGBTIQ+, an umbrella acronym that encompasses lesbian, gay, bisexual, transgender, intersex, and queer identities, is often used in used in public discourse in South Africa. That being said, there are also indigenous frameworks that encompass gender fluidity and same-sex sexuality and vernacular identity categories tied to race, class, and ethnicity. Because of stigma and violence, same-sex practices are often cloaked in secrecy, which makes assigning and interpreting identity categories challenging. I use the term same-sex throughout this chapter to be inclusive of people who have had sexual experiences with or are attracted to someone of the same sex but who may not identify as gay, lesbian, or queer.

2 Using English signifies a desire to reach an educated and transnational audience. However, English is often the default "bridging" language between different ethnic/cultural groups. It dominates in business, government, and academic discourse in South Africa, which has eleven official languages. Therefore, the language of bridging is also one of cultural dominance that harkens back to South Africa's British colonial past. For a critical discussion of the complexities that arise when translating interviews with *sangomas* on gender and sexuality from isiZulu and isiXhosa to English, see Zabus and Kumar Das (2021).

3 Sometimes referred to as Traditional African Religion. I prefer the term "indigenous" because it avoids complications arising from using the term "traditional" in reference to contemporary practices. That being said, the term "traditional" points to the long historical lineages of practices on the African continent, which is why it is often juxtaposed with the spread of "modern" religions like Christianity and Islam in the nineteenth and twentieth centuries. Using the term "religions" versus "religion" indexes the fluidity of diverse traditions across space and time. Indigenous African Religion is very much a "lived" or "vernacular" religion in that it depends on circulation of knowledge among diffuse groups and individual ritual practices amidst everyday life. Practices and rituals are highly adaptable to both individual and community (*volk*) needs. While there are various levels of status and authority in indigenous African religions (within families, clans, and specialized groups such as an age-cohort or guilds of religious specialists), with urbanization, these frameworks have weakened, which allows individuals more freedom to adopt beliefs and practices that are perceived as beneficial to daily life. In the contemporary African context, indigenous African religions are often marginalized in relation to Christianity and Islam, which tend to be dominant and the primary religions of elites.

4 Traditional, in this term, does not mean an unmediated reproduction of pre-colonial customs, beliefs, knowledge, and ritual. As anthropologist Robert Thornton notes, the term "traditional" indexes localized knowledge forms perceived as distinctly African that are in dialog with modernity and negotiated within an increasingly westernized national and global context (Thornton 2017, 3).

5 A 2010 Pew Research Center study finds that nearly half (46%) of the adult general population in South Africa exhibit high levels of belief in and practice of African traditional religion, including belief in sacred objects, evil spirits, witchcraft, the protective power of ancestors, visiting traditional healers, and participating in rituals to honor ancestors (Pew Research Center 2010, 34).

6 Two of the *sangomas* also identified as bisexual.

7 A 2017 video conversation between gay and lesbian *sangomas* also discusses harassment and discrimination (StreetTalkTV 2017).

8 The group has since changed its name to GALA Queer Archive, dedicated to "the production, preservation and dissemination of information about the history, culture and contemporary experiences of LGBTIQ (Lesbian, Gay, Bisexual, Transgender, Intersex, Queer) people in South Africa" ("About the GALA Queer Archive" n.d.).

9 Out of a desire to honor Nkabinde's later identification as a transgender man, I will refer to Nkabinde throughout using the pronouns he/him, though at the time Nkabinde wrote his autobiography, he identified as a masculine lesbian woman.

10 Cultural studies scholar Henriette Gunkel notes that some *sangomas* who have secretive sexual relationships within ancestral marriages are angry at other *sangomas* for "outing" their practices in public, because it may bring increased scrutiny (Gunkel 2010, 130). At the same time, published narratives function as tools for activism, challenging hostility toward indigenous religion and challenging the broader heteronormative erasure of LGBTQI+ people in Africa.

11 It is not uncommon for family members to solicit the help of a *sangoma* to "cure" homosexuality because they believe that same-sexuality or gender binary nonconformity as the result of an evil spirit.

12 Gender DynamiX is a human rights organization promoting freedom of expression of gender identity, focusing on transgender, transsexual, and gender non-conforming individuals.

13 Morgan and Reid note in their research that all "the *sangomas* who we interviewed combine belief in a Christian God with direct experience of the ancestors, sing Christian hymns and communicate with the ancestors" (Morgan and Reid 2003, 381).

14 Ancestral marriage mirrors heterosexual marriage in that there is typically a male-identified and female-identified partner.

Works Cited

"About the GALA Queer Archive." n.d. GALA. Accessed May 26, 2022. https://gala.co.za/about/history/.

Antonio, Edward P. 1997. "Homosexuality and African Culture." In *Aliens in the Household of God: Homosexuality and Christian Faith in South Africa*, edited by Paul Germond and Steve De Gruchy, 295–315. Cape Town: David Philip.

Butler, Judith. 2020. *Precarious Life: The Powers of Mourning and Violence*. London: Verso Books.

Chidester, David. 2012. *Wild Religion: Tracking the Sacred in South Africa*. Berkeley: University of California Press.

Epprecht, Marc. 2012. "Religion and Same Sex Relations in Africa." In *The Wiley-Blackwell Companion to African Religions*, edited by Elias Kifon Bongmba, 515–528. Chichester: Wiley-Blackwell.

Gopinath, Gayatri. 2005. *Impossible Desires: Queer Diasporas and South Asian Public Cultures*. Durham: Duke University Press.

Gunkel, Henriette. 2010. *The Cultural Politics of Female Sexuality in South Africa*. London: Routledge.

Makhaye, Chris. 2021. "LGBTQIA+ People in South Africa 'Are Under Siege.'" *New Frame*, April 22, 2021. https://www.newframe.com/lgbtqia-people-in-south-africa-are-under-siege/.

Mkasi, Lindiwe P. 2016. "African Same-Sexualities and Indigenous Knowledge: Creating a Space for Dialogue within Patriarchy." *Verbum et Ecclesia* 37(2): 1–6.

Morgan, Ruth. 2018. "Legacy of a Lesbian Sangoma." *The Mail & Guardian Online*, June 6, 2018. https://mg.co.za/article/2018-06-06-legacy-of-a-lesbian-sangoma/.

Morgan, Ruth, and Graeme Reid. 2003. "'I've Got Two Men and One Woman': Ancestors, Sexuality and Identity among Same-sex Identified Women Traditional Healers in South Africa." *Culture, Health & Sexuality* 5(5): 375–391.

Morgan, Ruth, Charl Marais, and Joy Rosemary Wellbeloved, eds. 2009, *Trans: Transgender Life Stories from South Africa*, 119–128. Johannesburg: Jacana Media.

Morgan, Ruth, and Saskia Wieringa, eds. 2005. *Tommy Boys, Lesbian Men, and Ancestral Wives: Female Same-Sex Practices in Africa.* Johannesburg, Jacana Media.

Neilson, Susie. 2014. "Gay Sangomas Are Not Un-African." *Independent Online*, April 23, 2014. https://www.iol.co.za/news/south-africa/gauteng/gay-sangomas-are-not-un-african-study-1679062.

Nkabinde, Nkunzi, and Ruth Morgan. 2005. "'This Has Happened Since Ancient Times...It's Something We Are Born With': Ancestral Wives Amongst Same-Sex Sangomas in South Africa." In *Tommy Boys, Lesbian Men, and Ancestral Wives: Female Same-Sex Practices in Africa*, edited by Ruth Morgan and Saskia Wieringa. Johannesburg: Jacana Media.

Nkabinde, Nkunzi Zandile. 2008. *Black Bull, Ancestors and Me: My Life as a Lesbian Sangoma.* Johannesburg: Jacana Media.

Ntongana, Thembela. 2016. "Traditional Healers Show That Being Gay Is African." *GroundUp News*, August 15, 2016. http://www.groundup.org.za/article/traditional-leaders-show-being-gay-african/.

Nyundu, Tony. 2018. "'Sangomas Are After People's Money': Family and Community Discourses around the South African Youth." *Commonwealth Youth and Development* 16(2): 1–10.

O'Regan, Victoria. 2022. "Day of Reflection: Traditional Leaders Campaign for Another South African Public Holiday – To Honour Ancestors." *Daily Maverick*, May 6, 2022. https://www.dailymaverick.co.za/article/2022-05-06-call-for-another-south-african-public-holiday-to-honour-ancestors/.

Pikoli, Zukiswa. 2021. "Transformations: Pastor, Sangoma, Genderqueer Change Agent: The Journey of an Intersex Activist." *Daily Maverick*, November 24, 2021. https://www.dailymaverick.co.za/article/2021-11-24-pastor-sangoma-genderqueer-change-agent-the-journey-of-an-intersex-activist/.

Pinn, Anthony B. 2003. *Terror and Triumph: The Nature of Black Religion.* Minneapolis, MN: Fortress Press.

Podolecka, Agnieszka. 2021. "The Role of Lethuelas/Sangomas in Lesotho. 'Traditional' Beliefs, Spiritual Professions and Christianity among the Basotho." *Studies in African Languages and Cultures*, no. 55: 159–184.

Podolecka, Agnieszka, and Austin M. Cheyeka. 2021. "Ng'angas-Zambian Healers-Diviners and Their Relationship with Pentecostal Christianity: The Intermingling of Pre-Christian Beliefs and Christianity." *Journal for the Study of Religion* 34(2): 1–27.

Primiano, Leonard Norman. 1995. "Vernacular Religion and the Search for Method in Religious Studies." *Western Folklore* 54(1): 37–56.

Reid, Graeme. 2022. "Letter to South African Authorities Regarding LGBTI Murders and Assaults." *Human Rights Watch.* January 19, 2022. https://www.hrw.org/news/2022/01/19/letter-south-african-authorities-regarding-lgbti-murders-and-assaults.

Reis, Ria. 2000. "The 'Wounded Healer' as Ideology: The Work of Ngoma in Swaziland." In *The Quest for Fruition Through Ngoma: Political Aspects of Healing in Southern Africa*, edited by Rijk van Dijk, Ria Reis, and Marja Spierenburg, 61–75. Cape Town: David Philip.

Sam, Tanya Chan. 1995. "Five Women: Black Lesbian Life on the Reef." In *Defiant Desire*, edited by Mark Gevisser and Edwin Cameron, 186–192. New York: Routledge.

Schneider, Rachel C. 2018. "Gay Rights Comes to Africa?: Decolonization, Sexuality, and Africa." *The Marginalia Review of Books* (blog). August 17, 2018. https://themarginaliareview.com/religion-sexuality-and-postcolonial-desire-in-africa/.

Stobie, Cheryl. 2007. *Somewhere in the Double Rainbow: Representations of Bisexuality in Post-Apartheid Novels.* Pietermaritzburg: University of KwaZulu-Natal Press.
StreetTalkTV. 2017. *Sangoma's On Gender.* https://www.youtube.com/watch?v=IoOb4Dc4Mg0.
Thornton, Robert. 2017. *Healing the Exposed Being: The Ngoma Healing Tradition in South Africa.* Johannesburg: Wits University Press.
Turner, Victor. 2011. *The Ritual Process.* New Brunswick: Transaction Publishers.
Van Dijk, Rijk, Ria Reis, and Marja Spierenburg, eds. 2000. *The Quest for Fruition Through Ngoma: Political Aspects of Healing in Southern Africa.* Cape Town: David Philip.
Van Klinken, Adriaan, and Ezra Chitando. 2016. *Public Religion and the Politics of Homosexuality in Africa.* London: Routledge.
Wreford, Joanne Thobeka. 2008. *Working with Spirit: Experiencing Izangoma Healing in Contemporary South Africa.* New York: Berghahn Books.
Zabus, Chantal and Samir Kumar Das. 2021. "Hijras, Sangomas, and their Translects" *Interventions* 23(6): 811–834.

PART III

Performance and/or Ritual Praxis

8

SUFI FESTIVALS IN CONTEMPORARY MOROCCO

Authorizing and Performing Folk Religiosities

John C. Thibdeau

Sufism and Folk Islam in Morocco

Sufism (*al-taṣawwuf*) is a discursive, embodied, and material tradition that is integral to Islamic thought and practice (Figure 8.1). Emerging in the 9th and 10th centuries in Iraq and Central Asia, Sufism spread along the frontiers of the Muslim empires from South Asia to West Africa, embedding itself in social and religious fabrics of local populations (Green 2012). While its geographical and temporal diversity makes it hard to define without essentializing, Sufism involves the transformation of the individual's self-ego (*nafs*) through the cultivation of pious states (*maqamāt*) under the supervision of a guide (*murshid*) with the goal of eliciting an experience (*ḥāl*) of closeness with (*qurba*) and witnessing

FIGURE 8.1 *Mawsim* Mawlay Idriss II, Fes, Morocco. Photo by the author.

DOI: 10.4324/9781003257462-12

of (*mushāhada*) the divine. These experiences are often characterized as an annihilation of the self-ego (*fanā'*) that elicits an ecstatic state (*wajd*), and those who attained such states were able to acquire special knowledge (*ma'rifa*) and earn the status of 'friend of God' (*walī Allah*). Such experiences may be spontaneous, but they are also produced through rigorous adherence to and deployment of an ensemble of disciplinary practices including repetitive chanting of divine formulas (*dhikr*), collective ritual 'dances' (*ḥaḍra*), spiritual retreats (*khalwa*), and musical and poetic concerts (*samā'*). These practices can be performed in private, semi-private settings such as the Sufi lodge (*zāwiya*) or mosque, and public settings such as festivals. In Morocco, these festivals go by a variety of names including the *mawlid* – the celebration of the birthday of the Prophet Muhammad), *mawsim* – the celebration of a Sufi 'saint' (*walī Allah*), and the *mihrajān* – a genre of 'secular' festival centered on the performance of Sufi music as culture. This chapter examines these festivals as spaces for the performance of folk religiosities.

The academic study of Sufism has tended to approach it through the lens of mysticism on the one hand, and folk and/or popular Islam on the other hand (on 'folk Islam' see Hadaway 2021 and Musk 1989). As mysticism, Sufism is approached through historical and textual analysis, often focusing on a golden age of Persian and Arabic Sufi literature in the 12th–14th centuries that subsequently deteriorated with the popularization of Sufism. In this process, the mystical tradition of Sufism declined into 'popular Sufism' – or 'folk Islam' more generally – characterized by beliefs and practices that were seen as survivals of local religious customs and traditions. These included belief in saintly figures (*awliyā'*) that could perform miraculous deeds (*karamāt*), spirits (*jinn*), and spirit possession, as well as practices like the visitation of shrines (*ziyāra*) to seek intercession or blessings (*baraka*). Such beliefs and practices became the subject primarily of anthropological inquiry which then constructed an image of 'folk Islam' as distinct on the one hand from the high literary mysticism of the Middle Ages and on the other hand from the orthodox legalism of the religious scholars (*ulamā'*). As a pervasive element of Moroccan religious life, this popular Sufism was used in explanatory binaries that differentiated urban and rural, literate and illiterate, and scriptural and folk types of Islam against one another (Geertz 1968, Gellner 1969, Munson 1993, Hammoudi 1997).

The perception of Sufism in Morocco as a distinct type of Islam was reinforced by modern scholars and movements within Islam that criticized such practices as illegitimate innovations (*bid'a*) (Sirreyeh 1999). Specifically, practices of visiting shrines and seeking intercession are seen by some Muslims as forms of idolatry (*shirk*) that elevate individual saints to excessive status. What is deemed *bid'a* by internal Muslim critics was often labeled 'folk Islam' by external scholars, and in the process, a host of practices were assessed negatively relative to a normative vision of Islam. In other words, a variety of Sufi practices became equated with 'folk Islam,' which was in turn rendered as non-normative, antinomian, and inauthentic. Consequently, the term 'folk Islam' has been critiqued on the grounds that imposes an artificial hierarchy, it assumes a monolithic version of Islam as textual and legalistic, and it fails to recognize the diversity and dynamics of internal contestation embedded within Islamic traditions (Mahmood 2005, Zaman 2012). Underlying the critique of 'folk Islam' is the recognition that power, as the internal ability to use legal tools such as *bid'a* and as the external assertion of colonial control and management of populations, operated to produce a category that was closely tied to class relations. Some alternatives to folk Islam include terms like multiple *islams*, vernacular Islam (Flueckiger 2006), and local Islam (Mohammad 2013). While I find these contributions incredibly insightful, I propose 'folk religiosity' as an alternative to draw attention to festivals in Morocco as polyphonic sites for the performance of piety by diverse people.

As sites for the performance of folk religiosities, festivals are polyphonic spaces and times where individuals engage and experience their traditions in distinctive ways alongside one another. In thinking of festivals in this way, I follow anthropologist Samuli Schielke who differentiates between 'festivals' and 'festivities' where the latter is 'the practice, the experience, the act of entering an extraordinary, temporary set of social relations and roles' (Schielke 2012, 55). Consisting of multiple and at times conflicting festivities (including pieties) experienced and performed by diverse people and conditioned by competing claims to authoritatively define proper modes of Islamic practice, Sufi festivals in Morocco are not expressions of a pre-existing 'folk religion,' but they are sites for the performance of folk religiosities, that is, personalized forms of pious practice.

In addition, this framing shifts attention away from Islam in the abstract or geographically based forms of Islam and considers the things that Muslims – as people living in complex global societies – practice, discuss, and believe. Rather than focusing on sets of beliefs or practices, however, 'folk religiosity' seeks to elucidate the embodied forms of piety that permeate daily life, from styles of dress through forms of social interaction to the enactment of rituals. 'Folk religiosity' also points to the discourses and dynamic structures of power that not only authorize certain forms of religious knowledge and practices but also constructs the possibilities for pious subjectivities upon which forms of religiosity are predicated.

For example, the place of Sufi festivals has once again shifted as the Moroccan state has sought to sponsor Sufism as a component of Moroccan religiosity to combat the influence of what it considers to be radical and foreign interpretations of Islam. Within that context, the state has deployed an array of strategies from educational and institutional reform domestically to policies of spiritual diplomacy regionally, but one creative strategy that exploits Morocco's existing sacred geography is its support of Sufi-related spiritual and cultural festivals. These festivals have operated as an important part of Morocco's state strategy of sponsoring Sufism by 'staging the sacred,' which has, in turn, transformed these practices into a symbol of cultural identity and instrument for 'tuning the nation's' public religiosity. The most notable of these is perhaps the Fes Festival of World Sacred

Music (Kapchan 2008). Sufi festivals in Morocco have undergone a series of shifts, and instead of being a representation of a static 'folk Islam,' it is better to see it as a space where people can perform varieties of pious practices that is nonetheless constrained and informed by structures and discourses of power in local and global contexts.

Sufi Festivals in Morocco

One of the prominent festivals in Morocco is the celebration of the Prophet Muhammad's birthday. While many Muslims throughout the world critique this practice as an illegitimate innovation (*bid'a*), it is celebrated as an official holiday in Morocco. Much like the Eid holidays, it is a time for reflection and religious practice in addition to food and festivities. Religious practices often include the recitation of poems in praise of the Prophet Muhammad, a genre known as *madih*. Sufi orders often host large gatherings to perform recitations of Sufi poetry (*samā'*) and group rituals (*ḥaḍra*) for local communities while also providing them with food and tea. As such, it often brings together a mixture of disciples, quasi-disciples, and local people that bring divergent experiences and expectations. In addition to celebrations of the Prophet's birthday, Sufi festivals in Morocco include annual celebrations of Sufi saints. Often hosted by Sufi orders, the *mawsim* as a genre of Sufi festival provides space for the performance of Morocco's diverse folk religiosities. The diversity of Sufism in Morocco is reflected on the one hand in the distinctive styles of *mawlid* festivals held by individual Sufi orders, and on the other hand by the multiple festivities on display at a single festival. In this section, I will discuss four examples: the *mawlid al-nabī* of the Karkariyya, the *mawlid al-nabī* of the Budshishiyya, the week-long festival of Sidi Ali bin Hamdouch held around the time of *mawlid al-nabī*, and the *mawsim* of Mawlay Abd al-Salam bin Mashish held by the Alawiyya.

For the Karkariyya Sufi order, the celebration began as men dressed in multicolored patchwork robes called *muraqqa'a* slowly filled the tent behind the lodge. Women were directed inside where they would perform their own sets of rituals. Taking seats on carpets laid on the ground, the event opened with a series of salutations and prayers upon the Prophet Muhammad, Shaykh Fawzi, and King Mohammed VI before a small group of disciples began singing poetry. As they sang, unaccompanied by instruments, members of the local community dressed in ordinary clothes began to filter in, taking seats around the outside. Gradually, the singers modulated their singing, increased their volume, and quickened their tempo until the shaykh gave the signal for the disciples to rise to their feet. Forming a large circle and clasping hands, the disciples began rocking forward and backward chanting the name '*Ḥayy*' (a reference to one of God's names). Slowly accelerating over the course of an hour, the singers and the shaykh led the group nearly to the point of exhaustion before stopping abruptly. This sequence was repeated three times in total. As the disciples performed the ritual, the local

FIGURE 8.2 *Ḥaḍra* at Prophet's Birthday, Karkariyya, Al-Aroui, Morocco. Photo by the author.

spectators took out cell phones and recorded, some joining in at various points as well (Figure 8.2).

Once the ritual cycles were completed, everyone sat while the shaykh's father performed a supplication. Performing in a strained, emotional voice on the verge of weeping, he honored the Prophet Muhammad, Shaykh Fawzi, and blessed the king of Morocco as many members of the audience broke into tears. Afterward, disciples took turns presenting poetry or other artistic endeavors. After the ritual cycles had been completed and prayers were completed, disciples distributed large plates of food – roasted chicken with vegetables. Instinctively, everyone formed groups of 8–10 people and began digging into the food as is a custom in Morocco. Once the food was finished and most of the locals had left, the disciples formed groups based on where they were from and Shaykh Fawzi invited them up to renew their allegiance. Sitting under a large portrait of King Mohammed VI, disciples repeated a set of phrases related to the 'pledge of the tree' (Q 48:18). In addition to disciples renewing the *bay'a*, some locals sought blessing from the shaykh, placing money on the rug in front of him and receiving a brief prayer in return (Figure 8.3).

Taking the analysis of 'folk religiosity' suggested here, the first thing to highlight is the diverse constituency in attendance. Not only were the disciples themselves global in composition (Morocco, Algeria, Senegal, France, Germany,

FIGURE 8.3 Individuals seeking blessing from Shaykh Fawzi, Karkariyya, Al-Aroui, Morocco. Photo by the author.

Spain, Egypt, Yemen), but there were also people from the community with distinctive ties to Sufism. While some came to receive the blessing of Shaykh Fawzi, others came to watch the spectacle and others came for the food. There was no single 'folk' represented at the festival; rather, it was a composite space in which individual people engaged with the performances on different terms. Secondly, the means for performing piety drew on a range of traditional and innovative practices. The *muraqqaʿa*, for instance, is an important component of the ethical education of disciples as a means to cultivating modesty and humility, and in the Karkariyya, this is adapted as a colorful robe. In addition, the performance of *Conference of the Birds* in French integrates a Persian classic of Sufi literature with the 'vernacular' of the French disciples in the context of Morocco. In other words, it is not a local style of performance but is instead a cosmopolitan manifestation. Finally, with the repeated recognition of the king as well as his presence presiding over the proceedings in the form of his portrait, the celebration reinforces not just an allegiance to the shaykh, but also to Morocco. This is even more poignant when you look at the image above in which the act of allegiance to the shaykh is literally overseen by the king.

The following night, I drove with several acquaintances I met at the Karkariyya *mawlid* across northeastern Morocco to the town of Madagh where the prominent Budshishiyya host their annual *mawlid* festival.While the Karkariyya numbered in the hundreds for its celebration, the Budshishiyya had thousands of attendees. It also boasted a much more substantial infrastructure with mausoleums for the previous shaykhs and a huge assembly hall. Outside the hall, banners were hung depicting the king and the country's motto 'Allah, Al-Malik, Al-Waṭan' (God, King, Country). There were rows of stalls selling food and merchandise and a separate tent for the concurrent conference being held on the topic of 'spiritual diplomacy.' Entering the assembly hall, thousands of people were seated on the floor as a long line of people lined the walls around the outside. They were waiting to meet the shaykh, who incidentally had just inherited leadership of the order that year after the passing of the former leader. Walking down the line, I asked people what they were waiting for. They responded in a variety of dialects, which I was able to translate through the help of my acquaintances. They explained that they were waiting to meet the shaykh. I asked them what precisely they would do, and they said they'd offer money in exchange for a blessing (*tabarruk*).

Compared to the Karkariyya, which was less than an hour drive away, the *mawlid* of the Budshishiyya was a different world. Despite their proximity, the transnational makeup of the attendees, their respective relations with the government, and the differences in spiritual methods created distinctive festive environments. While the Bushishi celebration included some locals, it drew a much larger international audience, and perhaps more noticeably a more upper-class Moroccan population. People who had the means traveled from across Morocco to the northeast corner for the annual festival, and this was also demonstrated in the sums of money given – the minimum I heard at the Budshishi was 400 dirham (about 40 dollars) versus 40 dirham average at the Karkariyya. This difference is suggestive of broader claims made in scholarship that the Budshishiyya reflects a bourgeois spirituality that allows Moroccans to reconcile wealth and piety. Differences also existed in performance practices as the Budshishiya did not hold a public ritual (*ḥaḍra*) and do not have the same dress practices. Also, although the Budshishiyya emphasize the motto that they are not an order of '*tabarruk*' (seeking blessing), hundreds of people still stood in line to get the blessing of the shaykh. The movement away from '*tabarruk*' is reflective of broader reform trends that are informed by global critiques of Sufism, but the continued presence of the practice for some, but not others, reflects how individuals can enact their own styles of religiosity alongside one another in the festival context. Finally, while both give a prominent place to the king, in many ways he was kept outside of the assembly hall for the Budshishiyya, potentially reflecting the division of the event into a religious celebration and an academic conference. In other words, rather than reinforcing political legitimacy through the allegiance as reflected in the Karkariyya, the Budshishiyya relied on the conference as a contribution to Morocco's current efforts to sponsor Sufism as a form of public piety that underpins practices of spiritual security and diplomacy, which was the theme of the conference.

Much like the *mawlid*, the *mawsim* is also targeted by some Islamic groups as an illegitimate innovation (*bid'a*) that incorporates deviant practices, superstitions *(khurafāt)*, and idolatry. Due to the global influence of groups that are critical of Sufis and their associated practices, a process that has a long history, some Sufi groups present reformed versions of these festivals – as is the case with the Alawiyya – while other instances are transformed into performances of cultural and national heritage – as is the case with the Sidi Ali festival. In other words, these festivals should not be seen as arising out of or expressing inherent aspects of Moroccan Islam; rather, the styles of religiosity they reflect and represent take shape through ongoing local, national, and global debates and dynamics of authority in Muslim societies. In the next two cases, I will be considering the *mawsim* of Sidi Mawlay Abd al-Salam bin Mashish, held by the Alawiyya in August 2018, with the week-long festival of Sidi Ali bin Hamdouch in which myriad Sufi orders and other cultural groups take part.

The Alawiyya order was formed in the early 20th century under the leadership of the Algerian Sufi master Ahmad al-Alawi (d. 1934) and traces its lineage through the Shadhiliyya order to Mawlay Abd al-Salam bin Mashish (d. 1227). Seen as one of the founding saints of Moroccan Sufism, pilgrimages to Mashish's shrine atop Jabl Alam in northwest Morocco have been commonplace for much of Moroccan history, at one point even being recommended in place of the Hajj during periods of political instability in the 14th and 15th centuries. It has therefore been a site of continued religious and political significance, and the Alawiyya, as a Sufi order with roots in the region, draws on this tradition in its contemporary *mawsim*.

In August 2019, I attended the Alawiyya *mawsim* of Mawlay Abd al-Salam bin Mashish. On the first night, we attended a small gathering of *dhikr* late into the evening where I was introduced to members and leaders of other branches of the Alawiyya in Morocco. Over a few hours, people arrived in the tent before the *dhikr* segued into poetic recitations – *samāʿ* – then into a series of prayers and invocations. After the tent reached capacity – several hundred in all – the branch leaders instructed everyone to begin the ascent to the top of the mount, about a mile up the road and a steep climb, especially in the heat of the summer. At the top of the mountain, there was a small village with a few restaurants, souvenir shops, and small markets (*hanuts*). We sat at one of the cafes for a pot of Moroccan tea as we caught our breath before proceeding to the assembly station. Passing underneath another banner reading 'God, King, Country,' we entered a small parking area beneath a newly renovated mosque and a paved pathway up the final few hundred meters to the tomb of Mawlay Mashish. In the pathway, several of the older disciples formed the front of a procession – about eight people wide – and began singing songs of praise from Mashish's collection as well as other well-known litanies. They continued singing as we waited for the current leader of the Alawiyya – Shaykh Khalid bin Tunis – to join the group after his visit to the mosque. The crowd behind the singers began to grow as the hundreds of people in attendance packed together in a long procession line, attempting to make their way forward as Shaykh Khaldi descended the steps from the mosque. Moroccan officers in uniform framed the crowd as a dozen Moroccan flags flew overhead, and Shaykh Khalid made his way to the front of the procession. Slowly, the group ascended the pathway as disciples pushed their way to the front to touch, shake hands, or kiss the hand of Shaykh Khalid (Figure 8.4).

The tomb itself was modest with a large tree overshadowing an open-air garden (*rawḍa*) in front of the tombs and people immediately began vying for seats under the tree or in the shaded garden. During this time, I also had the opportunity to talk with different people and ask them why they had come. There were a mix of reasons. One man in his twenties had come with his mother who was sick from Marrakech. They believed that visiting the tomb itself would provide healing for her. Another pair of teenage girls from France indicated that they had come with their families and that this was part of their vacation in Morocco since their families were originally from Morocco. Others were members of the Alawiyya's NGO known as AISA (Shaykh Alawi International Association) based in Europe, and this trip was seen as part of their larger project of bridging cultural and religious differences between Europe and Muslim societies. Such views were of course in addition to many of the devoted disciples who view Shaykh Khalid as a living saint (*walī*) and teacher whose guidance has the capacity to ensure happiness in this life and the next (Figure 8.5).

Back in the tent, a line of singers performed *dhikr* then *samāʿ* until the final prayer of the day. After the prayer, Shaykh Khalid gave a short lecture discussing a topic that he had presented recently – mathematics and religion. Presenting

FIGURE 8.4 *Mawsim* Mawlay Abd al-Salam bin Mashish, Alawiyya, Jbal Alam, Morocco. Photo by the author.

FIGURE 8.5 *Du'a* at tomb of Mawlay Mashish, Alawiyya, Jbal Alam, Morocco. Photo by the author.

first in Arabic then in French, he outlined his vision of Islamic reform and the ability for Sufism to pave the way for an enlightened modernity, rich with spirituality and morality. Following the lecture, the singers began performing once again, but quickly ascended in volume and tempo until the disciples were invited to stand and form a circle to perform the *ḥaḍra*. All at once, a few dozen disciples shot to their feet, grabbed each other's hands, and began swaying while chanting the phrase 'Ḥayy.' One of the branch leaders stayed in the center of the circle to facilitate, keep tempo, and at times restrain individuals who were demonstrating ecstatic behaviors. They continued with a slow acceleration for about forty minutes before reaching a crescendo and then virtually collapsing to the ground. The session closed with a supplication and followed by a large meal of roast chicken and vegetables served to groups of eight to ten people on the floor of the tent.

After the meal, some individuals stayed in the tent to pray, while others made their way back to the houses or rooms they had rented. I stood outside the tent with several of the branch leaders as they answered questions and helped make arrangements for many of the disciples and pilgrims. While one was attempting to provide directions to a visiting family, an 'enraptured' disciple (often referred to as a *majdhūb*) kept interrupting the conversation, much to the annoyance of the branch leader, who eventually turned to the disciple and said 'Sufism is entirely *adab*' (*al-taṣawwuf kulluhu al-adab*). Intended as interdiction and reminder of his inappropriate behavior, the phrase seemed to work as the *majdhūb* wandered off into the night. This moment, however, brings together three distinct experiences of the festival (four if you include my own) where one is seeking to elicit an ecstatic experience, one is attempting to organize an event, and one is attempting secure lodging for his family (and one who is attempting to think through the work that festivals do in constructing religious subjectivities). The experience for each, as well as the religious work done in the festival space, is quite distinct for each individual and therefore reflects not a single 'folk religion' that is on display. Rather, it shows the festival as a site for the multifaceted encounter of distinctive styles of piety.

Taken as a whole, the Alawiyya *mawsim* represents a broader trend in 'reformed' Sufi practices that eschew controversial practices, such as the inclusion of musical instruments and the outward displays of ecstatic experience (*wajd*). While certainly local in its use of a popular Moroccan saint and his repertoire of prayers and hymns, it maintained a transnational aspect in the participants, use of language, and ritual performance styles. Those who attended also displayed different modes of attachment to Shaykh Khalid. Some related to him as a saint filled with *baraka* that could heal or bestow blessings while others saw him as a social reformer and critic and consequently as a kind of spiritual-civic leader. Even within the same order, therefore, there are multiple manifestations of the master–disciple relationship, and, at the festival, Shaykh Khalid embodies distinctive modes of sainthood that make possible the performance of multiple pieties. Finally, both national and international politics play themselves out in the *mawsim*. On the one hand, the presence of Moroccan authorities, the plethora of Moroccan flags, and the banner with Morocco's national slogan all serve as reminders of the event as Moroccan and taking place under the auspices of the king. Unlike the Karkariyya and Budshishiyya, however, no portraits of King Mohammed VI were visible anywhere in the event, suggesting a less direct connection to national politics. In fact, Shaykh Khalid does much of his work in Europe, serving on France's Council of Muslim Faith and working with the United Nations through his international NGO. Stradling the Mediterranean in this fashion, Shaykh Khalid is in some ways able to operate as a socio-political critic, often subtly critiquing policies of the Moroccan government itself. In summary, the *maswim* reveals folk religiosities that can be analyzed when specific attention is paid to the people, the styles of performance, the modes of piety enacted, and the dynamics of power.

Finally, the Sidi Ali festival, as it is popularly known, combines the *mawlid al-nabī* celebration with the *mawsim* style of festival in that it is a week-long event scheduled to take place during the period surrounding the Prophet Muhammad's birthday but includes processions and rituals in honor of a specific saint – Sidi Ali bin Hamdouch (d. circa 1722) – whose tomb is in the town in the mountains north of Meknes. A site of pilgrimage for a couple of centuries, today the festival brings together several Sufi orders. These include the Hamadsha, which derive their name from Sidi Ali, the Aissawa, and the Gnawa. Since the three explicitly incorporate Sufi practices and discourses to varying degrees, the Sidi Ali festival blends a cultural festival atmosphere in which these groups perform as popular musicians with a religious festival atmosphere in which they perform piety through music and ritual practices. However, what generally binds these three groups together is not only their use of musical instruments but also the professionalization of the musicians that will perform in both sacred and secular contexts. Most notable in the music is the use of polyrhythms that infuse music with a distinctive West African sound that accompanies Arabic melodic poetry called *malhun*. In addition to the musical aspect, the orders are connected to ritual practices associated with exorcising *jinn*, snake charming, and self-mortification practices (on Hamadsha, see Crapanzano 1973). While the musical styles and ritual practices are different and there is great variation even within each group, because of their musical performances and ritual practices these three groups are often glossed as 'popular' Sufi orders.

In December 2017, I attended the Sidi Ali festival with a group of friends from Fes. During the festival, local branches of each group come to Sidi Ali and set up temporary residences, renting out an apartment or setting up a tent where they will perform nightly religious musical concerts called a *layla* (lit. night). In addition, each local branch of the Hamadcha leads a procession through the town that ends in the tomb of Sidi Ali. The procession itself is quite a spectacle as the musicians and their followers attempt to weave their way through the crowds and narrow streets of the village. Along the way, many individuals will enter trance-like states leading to practices of self-mortification that tend to leave a trail of blood on the ground through the village. In addition to processions, during the day many of the troupes will perform individual *ḥaḍra* rituals. Forming a circle and using music to elicit trance-like states, individuals may start to dance and move erratically, often whirling their heads wildly, or perform controlled acts of self-mortification such as passing skewers through tongues or cheeks.

In addition to the daily events that take place in public, these groups also host nightly *laylas*, that is, small musical concerts with a sequenced set of rituals. One night during the festival, I attended a *layla* held by the Aissawa. Arriving early in the evening, we ate a small meal with the hosts who were renting the small ground-floor apartment. The apartment had one main room with a small kitchen, bathroom, and small bedroom at the back. I joined the musicians in the back room for a couple of hours as people slowly began to fill the room outside. Talking about the music and the various performances during the day, the musicians were quite explicit in their status as members of a Sufi order, not just musicians. In this vein, we discussed their founding saint, Muhammad al-Hadi bin

Aissa (d. 1526), at length. As this specific band was from Meknes, they had great reverence for this founding saint and performed often at his tomb in Meknes. Discussing the music and rituals, the leader of the group argued it was because of their own piety and devotion to the saint, that is their intimate relationship with him, that they were able to display and transmit *baraka* to others through the music. The *baraka* was in this sense made possible by the saint but also required devotion from the individual. The *baraka* bestowed certain powers on the musicians – particularly their leader – that included the ability to cure people from possession of *jinn* or protect others from harm. I asked what other types of powers this might bestow, and the leader said potentially the power over life and death, at which point he took a chicken that was in the room, rolled it onto its back in his hands, and laid it on the floor. The chicken then went limp, not moving, until he snapped his fingers, and the chicken came 'back to life.' Throughout the *layla*, I moved between the back room and the main room to watch parts and then discuss them with the musicians who took turns. At one point, one of the members in the back room took out a large knife and began preparing for the portion of the ritual in which he would slice his tongue and stomach. In the back, he listened to the music as he worked himself into a trance under the supervision of the leader. As he exited the room, I followed him and was able to find a spot on the floor as the crowded room made space for him. Over the next fifteen minutes, he would dance and stop to cut his tongue or stomach before returning to the back room. After he finished, a woman in the crowd rose to her feet and began shrieking and writing as she whipped her hair around wildly. The musicians changed rhythms immediately and a shift occurred in the atmosphere as the ritual of sonic exorcism began. Through an interactive call and response of the rhythms and the woman's movements, the woman was led to a cathartic release that saw her collapse on the floor. The concert would last into the early hours of the morning and as we exited the apartment, we saw the first rays of the sun emerge over the tomb of Sidi Ali.

While many of the extravagant practices can still be found, in general, the festival has become much more controlled and organized in the past few years, largely as a product of the state's approach to festivals as sites of tourism. In the process, what was once a more organic performance context in which the performers and audience were integrated and interactive has become a staged production of an artistic heritage consumable for domestic and international audiences. In doing so, even though for the practitioners themselves these are expressions of religiosity, the staging of them as objects of national and cultural heritage transforms their significance in Moroccan public life. As such, the intervention of state authorities in the staging of the festival has functioned on the one hand to commodify the event for global markets and on the other hand to 'folklorize' these practices, thereby effectively differentiating them from the 'proper' religious practices associated with groups like the Budshishiyya (Figure 8.6).

FIGURE 8.6 Tomb of Sidi Ali bin Hamdoush, Sidi Ali Festival, Sidi Ali, Morocco. Photo by the author.

Conclusion

The discussion above analyzed Sufi festivals as polyphonic sites for the performance of piety by diverse people. Even though these festivals all draw on local traditions, their form is also shaped by the dynamics of power and authority that authorize and constrain their performance. In Morocco, the state has invested in these festivals and in the process has sought to transform Sufism from 'folk Islam' into a feature of normative Moroccan religiosity. While such bureaucratization of the festivals restricts and homogenizes certain aspects of the festive experience, the Sufi festival in Morocco remains a place where diverse groups of people perform competing and contrasting modes of piety, making it difficult to speak about either the 'folk' or 'Islam' in the singular. I, therefore, proposed the term to highlight that these personal aspects of religious practice and performance are not a distinct type but are an integral aspect of all religious traditions. Folk religiosities are not a category distinct from non-folk religiosities; instead, they are the myriad mechanisms through which traditions are enacted in daily life.

Despite their controversial status, festivals have been crucial for this enactment. Thinking about 'folk Islam' in this context is therefore not to reference a specific set of practices and beliefs that are contrasted with others; rather, it points attention to the ways in which Islam is performed, enacted, embodied, and debated in the daily lives of Muslims as they encounter local, national, and global discourses and representations of Islam. Folk Islam is in this sense an ever-present aspect of 'Islam,' whether global or local, scriptural or ritual, urban or rural, elite or popular, formal or informal.

Works Cited

Crapanzano, Vincent. *The Hamadcha: A Study in Moroccan Ethnopsychiatry*. Berkeley: University of California Press, 1973.

Flueckiger, J.B. *In Amma's Healing Room: Gender and Vernacular Islam in South India*. Cambridge: Cambridge University Press, 2006.

Geertz, Clifford. *Islam Observed: Religious Developments in Morocco and Indonesia*. Chicago: University of Chicago Press, 1968.

Gellner, Ernst. *The Saints of the Atlas*. Chicago: University of Chicago Press, 1969.

Green, Nile. *Sufism: A Global History*. Chichester: Wiley-Blackwell, 2012.

Hadaway, Robin. *The Muslim Majority: Folk Islam and the Seventy Percent*. Nashville: B&H Academic, 2021.

Hammoudi, Abdellah. *Master and Disciple: The Cultural Foundations of Moroccan Authoritarianism*. Chicago: University of Chicago Press, 1997.

Kapchan, Deborah. "The Promise of Sonic Translation: Performing the Festive Sacred in Morocco." *American Anthropologist* vol 110, no. 4, 2008, pp. 467–483.

Mahmood, Saba. *Politics of Piety: The Islamic Revival and the Feminist Subject*. Princeton: Princeton University Press, 2005.

Mohammad, Afsar. *The Festival of Pirs: Popular Islam and Shared Devotion in South India*. New York: Oxford University Press, 2013.

Munson, H. *Religion and Power in Morocco*. New Haven: Yale University Press, 1993.

Musk, Bill. *The Unseen Face of Islam*. Kent: Monarch Publications, 1989.

Schielke, Samuli. *Perils of Joy: Contesting Mulid Festivals in Contemporary Egypt*. Syracuse: Syracuse University Press, 2012.

Sirreyeh, Elizabeth. *Sufis and Anti-Sufis: The Defense, Rethinking and Rejection of Sufism in the Modern World*. Richmond: Curzon, 1999.

Testa, Alessandro. "Rethinking the Festival: Power and Politics." *Method and Theory in the Study of Religion* vol. 26, no. 1, 2014, pp. 44–73.

Zaman, M.Q. *Modern Islamic Thought in a Radical Age: Religious Authority and Internal Criticism*. Cambridge: Cambridge University Press, 2012.

9

MANTRAS FOR "EVERY GOD AND GODDESS"

Vernacular Religious Ritual in the Literature of Sabhapati Swami

Keith Edward Cantú

There is an important feature of yogic literature that has received no scholarly treatment to date, namely the incorporation of a wide variety of mantras for a range of gods, goddesses, and planetary deities in the Tamil vernacular literature of Sabhapati Swami (ca. 1828–1923/4), a nineteenth- to twentieth-century Tamil yogin with ties to the esoteric milieus of his time. Modern yoga in South Asia from the colonial period onward is often perceived to depart from its historical connection with the formalities of vernacular ritual in many contexts, a perception partly due to Swami Vivekananda's modernization of yogic teachings, the efforts of the Theosophical Society, and later an emphasis on physical body culture and exercise (Singleton 2010, De Michelis 2008). Nevertheless, a wide variety of ritual forms remained popular in vernacular contexts of yoga that predated and were contemporary with this modernization. I present here an alternative story that shows how yoga in the Tamil vernacular context of Sabhapati Swami's literature maintained an intrinsic connection with not only mantras but also an accompanying ritual apparatus that was deeply intertwined with festival traditions connected at shrines for the Tamil Siddhars and so-called "Swamigals."

For the past century, Sabhapati Swami has remained a largely forgotten yet enigmatic figure, not only in the fields of yoga studies but also in esotericism, a field that has its own contours and links to alternative religious movements originating both in and outside of Europe (Cantú 2020, 2021; Asprem and Strube 2020; Hanegraaf 2015). Born in Velachery, then a small temple village south of colonial Madras, present-day Chennai, Sabhapati was educated at a Scottish missionary school in his early childhood yet remained deeply connected to Śaiva temple culture via his family's service to Velachery Chidambara Swamigal (Vētacirēṇi Citambara [Periya] Cuvāmikaḷ, d. 1858), a Tamil Vīraśaiva guru in the line of Kumara Devar (Kumāratēvar) (Cuvāmikaḷ 2014, Cantú 2023). His three surviving hagiographical accounts state that he had a vision of the transcendent

DOI: 10.4324/9781003257462-13

Śiva (*civam*) who guided him to travel to the Pothigai Hills, a mountain range on the border with what was then Travancore (modern Kerala), specifically to the hermitage of Agastya, a legendary amalgamation of the Vedic rishi and founder of the Tamil Siddhars, who were revered as poets, alchemists, and yogins (Zvelebil 1992, Appendix 3; Venkatraman 1990). While it is difficult to account for what transpired at this hermitage, it is clear that he engaged with a network of yogins who were interested in revitalizing earlier traditions of the medieval Tamil Siddhars (Tam. *cittar*, < Skt. *siddha*),[1] a group that gradually, by Sabhapati's time, were better known as Swamigals (*cuvāmikaḷ*, < *svāmin* + Tamil plural/honorific suffix *kaḷ*) on account of their connection to Tamil Vīraśaiva movements.[2] The hagiographies of Sabhapati Swami—or Sabhapati Swamigal (Capāpati Cuvāmikaḷ) as he was known by Tamils—claim that his new guru, a semi-legendary and centuries-old figure named Shivajnanabodha Rishi (Civañāṉapota Ruṣi, < Śivajñānabodha Ṛṣi), instructed him to take his message to the rest of South Asia. While it is unclear just how many temple complexes he actually visited in North India, we know that by 1879 and 1880 CE, he was spending his time between the Kangra Valley of Himachal Pradesh and Lahore in the British Punjab (now in Pakistan). In Lahore, he met with Shrish Chandra Vasu (Śrīś Candra Basu, 1861–1918), then a Bengali student at Government College Lahore and budding legal advocate whose father had migrated to the Punjab from what is today Bangladesh. Shrish Chandra edited and helped to publish the first edition of Sabhapati's lectures, by that time a common format for presenting material by traveling speakers of reform movements (Jones 1976). Shrish Chandra published these lectures, predating Swami Vivekananda's own published lectures on Rājayoga by over fifteen years, along with extra material (Swami 1880), and he was also involved in its Bengali translation. He likely helped Sabhapati arrange his meeting with the founders of the Theosophical Society, namely Helena P. Blavatsky (1831–1891) and Henry S. Olcott (1832–1907), who remained friendly but ultimately very distant on account of their disbelief (at least publicly) over Sabhapati's claim to have physically flown to the semi-legendary Mount Kailasa (Cantú 2021, Baier 2016).

Sabhapati became largely forgotten by the Theosophical Society, and his relationship with Shrish Chandra Vasu appears to have gradually faded by the end of the nineteenth century, yet he did not disappear from the historical record. Sabhapati instead turned his attention more directly to the temple culture of Tamil vernacular ritual practice, especially the use of mantras, or sacred formulae. By "vernacular" I mean customs popularly accessible and open to members of all castes, often connected with natural environments, landscapes, and things (e.g. stone, metal, water, flowers, and leaves), and grounded in religious customs and traditions as accessible through a local language. This accords with the notion of religious folklife as popular culture, which is arguably "an extension of or development from the older traditional forms of culture" (Yoder 1990), and are forms that are re-processed via new forms of media and in a language that the majority of the population could understand. My use of adjectives like "folk" or "popular" or "vernacular" as such are ultimately predicated on language, that is, a common language of the people. While Sanskrit (often verging into a late form of the Tamil-Sanskrit hybrid language *maṇippiravāḷam*, < Skt *maṇipravāla*, "pearl and coral") provided the linguistic foundation for most of Sabhapati's religious teachings from the outset, it is clear from his works on mantra for Tamil audiences that he gradually began to much more consciously employ vernacular language in his guidance on holidays and the rituals surrounding local religious festivals. As a result, his later works came to reflect a fluid interface between both Sanskrit and Tamil vernacular religious worlds. Using the adjective "vernacular" with regard to Tamil is less problematic since it continues as a spoken language of the people, despite its rich classical history, but the Sanskrit vernacular remains less understood. In this context, it refers to the ways in which Sanskrit terms were rendered popularly accessible via the Tamil script as verbal forms, philosophical concepts, and mantras.

The best example of this interface is Sabhapati's four-part pamphlet *Cakalākama tiraṭṭu* ("A Compilation of All Āgamas"), the first part of which was published in 1894. This work presents Hindu ritual observances of a wide array of holidays assigned to Tamil months (Yōkīsvarar 1894). These include annual celebrations and astrological events, most of which are celebrations intended for the general public, in this case Tamil speakers since the work is in Tamil with essentially no English. It is a valuable record of what kinds of rituals were taking place on a regular basis at the Konnur "Meditation Hall," which is Sabhapati's own English translation for the *maṭālayam* (< Skt. *maṭha* + *ālaya*) that he established between Konnur and Villivakkam, villages to the west of Madras, after returning there in the 1890s. These celebrations included prominent observances like Shivaratri (*civarāttiri viratam*, < Skt. *śivarātri*) and Vinayaga/Ganesh Chaturthi (Tamil *viṉāyakacaturtti*, < Skt. *vināyakacaturthī*),[3] but also relatively less-common festivals and local observances that may reflect Sabhapati's travels outside South India (e.g. "Dol" or "the Observance of Lord Kedar").[4] The full list is as follows, imparting an impression of the contents and connection with Tamil vernacular religion:

1 "Monthly worship rites to be carried out at shrines to Śiva" (*civālaya mātapūjai*, < Skt. *śivālaya mātapūjā*)
2 "The Observance of Vinayagar's Chaturthi" (*viṉāyaka caturtti viratam*, < Skt. *vināyaka caturthī vrata*)
3 "The chaturthi observance for [removing] difficulties" (*caṅkaṭa caturtti viratam*, < Skt. *saṃkaṭa caturthī vrata*)
4 "Arudra Darisanam," lit. "Vision of Ārdrā [Nakṣatrā]" (*āruttirā taricaṉam*, < Skt. *ārdrā darśana*)
5 "The (winter) solstice" (*caṅkirānti*, < Skt. *saṃkrānti*)
6 "Dol, or the Festival of the Holy Swing" (*ṭōḷ allatu tiruvūcaluṟcavam*)
7 "Diwali (Narak Chaturdashi)" (*tīpāvali (narakkā caturttaci)*, < Skt. *dīpāvali (naraka caturdaśī)*)

8 "The Observance of Lord Kedar [of Kedārnāth tīrtha]" (*kētārīsvarar viratam*, < Skt. *kedārīśvara vrata*)

9 "Rules for the Lamp of the Lunar Asterism of Krittika [Dīwālī or Dīpāvalī]" (*kārttikai nakṣattira tīpaviti*, < Skt. *kr̥ttikā nakṣatra dīpavidhi*)

10 "The Instrument of Pradosham" (Mpvl. *piratōṣakāraṇam*, < Skt. *pradoṣakāraṇa*)

11 "The Observance of Monday [in the month of Karthika]" (*cōmavāra viratam*, < Skt. *somavāra vrata*)

12 "The Festival of the Float" (*teppōṟcavam*)

13 "Worship rites for the Vision of the Bliss of the Supreme Śakti" (*parācatti ānanta taricaṉap pūjai*, < Skt. *parāśakti ānanda darśana pūjā*)

14 "The Observance of the Friday of Vinayagar (*vināyaka cukkiravāra viratam*, < Skt. *vināyaka śukravāra vrata*)

15 "The Observance of Vinayagar's Shasthi"[5] (*vināyakacaṣṭi viratam*, < Skt. *vināyakaṣaṣṭhī vrata*)

16 "The Observance of Angaraka's Chaturthi" (*aṅkārakacaturtti viratam*, < Skt. *aṅgārakacaturthī vrata*)

17 "The Observance of the Friday of Subramaniar" (*cuppiraṇiyar cukkiravāraviratam*, < Skt. *subrahmaṇya śukravāravrata*)

18 "The Observance of Skanda's Shasthi [sister or bride]" (*skantacaṣṭi viratam*, < Skt. *skandaṣaṣṭhī vrata*)[6]

19 "The Observance of the Krittika [Nakshatra]" (*kiruttikai viratam*, < Skt. *kr̥ttikā vrata*)

20 "The Observance of the Thiruvathira [Nakshatra]" (*tiruvātirai viratam*, < Skt. *śrī ārdrā vrata*)

21 "The Great Festival of the Five Actions" (*pañcakiruttiya makōṟcavam*, < Skt. *pañcakr̥tya mahotsava*)[7]

22 "The Observance of Umamaheswara" (*umāmakēsvara viratam*, < Skt. *umāmaheśvara vrata*)

23 "The Observance of Night of Shiva" (*civarāttiri viratam*, < Skt. *śivarātri vrata*)

This legacy of festival observances has survived to the present. The current "Shrine of Sri Sabhapati Swami and Ananda Ananda Swami" (Śrī Capāpati Cuvāmi maṟṟum Āṉantā Āṉanta Cuvāmikaḷiṉ Cannitāṉam) on Red Hills Road in Villivakkam regularly holds religious festivals advertised via WhatsApp and Telegram, events that are often combined with folk dancing and music. One of the most regular of these, which was also practiced in Sri Sabhapati Swami's time according to *Cakalākama tiraṭṭu*, is a Tamil-specific "evening worship" (*piratōṣam*, < Skt. *pradoṣa*) on auspicious nights for Śiva (often held bimonthly on the thirteenth day of the lunar fortnight), connected with the myth of the churning of the ocean of milk (see Figure 9.1).

The festivals presented by Sabhapati in his pamphlets were not only to be observed in a highly organized fashion on specific days of the year, but they also were connected to an elaborate system of mantras, in this context Sanskrit sacred utterances in both the Tamil and Devanagari scripts, to be recited every

FIGURE 9.1 A pamphlet in Tamil on *piratōṣam* (< Skt. *pradoṣa*) in the collection of the Shrine of Sri Sabhapati Swami and Ananda Ananda Swami in Villivakkam. Photo by Keith E. Cantú.

day. In other words, the ritual attitudes cultivated on non-festival days (i.e. in daily ritual practice) inform these special observances, even those that are connected to dance, music, and ritual. The demand for further guidance on these proper ritual attitudes and associated mantras is reflected in another of Sabhapati's pamphlets published four years later and entitled *Cātaṉāppiyāsāṉupava upatēcam* (< Skt. *Sādhanābhyāsānubhava upadeśa*, "Guidance on the Exercises and Practices of the Rites," Svāmikaḷ 1898). This work, published in Vellore, a city west of Chennai, included such topics as "Guidance on the Order of Ceremonies that Must Be Carried Out in the Morning" (*kālaiyil ceyyavēṇṭiya aṉuṣṭāṉaviti upatēcam*), "Śaiva and Vaiṣṇava Assignments of the Limbs and Assignments of the Arms" (*caiva vaiṣṇava aṅkarnniyācam, karnniyācam*), "Meditation on the Recitation of the Gāyatri [Mantra]" (*kāyattiri jepattiyāṉam*), "Guidance on the Mantras for Recitation of Every Deity" (*carvatēvatā jepamantiraṅkaḷiṉ upatēcam*), and "Guidance on the Sacrifice and Meditation of the Nine Celestial Bodies" (*navakkirakattiyāṉam yākam upatēcam*). This latter guidance on the nine celestial bodies (< Skt. *navagraha*) reflects engagement with a specific folk ritual practice, prominent in a wide variety of local Tamil temples, of circumambulating stone fixtures of the celestial bodies clockwise so as to remove astrological defects (*doṣas*) that affect one's potential for success in life (see Figure 9.2).

Emphasis on mantra as central to religious practice and the observance of popular festivals is not in and of itself a marker of vernacular religion; such an emphasis will also readily be found in Hindu elite temple contexts across South Asia. However, Sabhapati's emphasis is unique, for he imbued his pan-Indian teachings on mantra with what I would call a distinctly Tamil vernacular "flavor." This flavor is reflected in at least three qualities that distinguish his teachings from the way mantras were presented to audiences in North India. First, his entire system is framed in the yogic mythology of Agastya, who as stated above was a Vedic rishi whose eponymous mountain is on the border between Kerala and Tamil Nadu, and who is considered the legendary founder of the

FIGURE 9.2 A stone installation of the nine celestial bodies at Sri Devi Ellaman Thirukoil (Śrī Tēvi Ellammaṉ Tirukkōvil) in Adyar, Chennai, just south on Damodharapuram Main Road from the headquarters of Theosophical Society. Photo by Keith E. Cantú.

community of Tamil Siddhars, yogins, physicians, and alchemists whose tumuli (*jīvacamāti*, < Skt. *jīvasamādhi*, although the compound appears to be unattested in Sanskrit sources) are scattered across South India. Second, the mantras were published in the vernacular script of Tamil with explanatory notes for Sanskrit terms, allowing his teachings to be widely understood by his local audience. Third, the mantras connect with musical tones (*svaras*) to make their recitation popularly accessible, inviting local participation and intersecting with the world of Tamil devotional music.

The first two of the above three qualities, as well as Sabhapati's elaborate system of mantras as a whole, is most clearly articulated in his second book-length Tamil work (Cuvāmikaḷ 1913), the all-too-extended title of which was *Carva māṉaca nittiya karmānuṣṭāṉa, carva tēvatātēvi māṉaca pūjāttiyāṉa, pirammakñāṉa rājayōka niṣṭai camāti, carva tīkṣākkramattiyāṉa, cātaṉā appiyāca kiramāṉucantāṉa, caṅkiraha vēta tiyāṉōpatēca smiruti* ("Inspired Treatise on the Instructions of Meditation, as Compiled from the Scriptures, on Every Mental Ceremony to be Performed Daily, on a Mental Ritual Meditation for Every God and Goddess, on the Steadfast Composition in the Yoga of Kings that is the Gnosis of Brahman, on Every Meditation on the Sequences of Initiation, and on an Inquiry into the Sequence of the Practice of the Rites"). Amid this lengthy title is also found an important claim: there are mantras and meditations for "every god and goddess" (*carva tēvatātēvi*, < Skt. *sarva devatādevī*). Sabhapati may have known this is an exaggeration as some local Tamil deities seem to be missing (e.g. Ellaman or Karuppu Sami), or the claim could relate to his philosophy that these gods and goddesses are found within various parts of the yogic body and/or are all part of a transcendent Sarveśvarar or "God of All." In any case, the main work was published by the Office of Shanmuga Vilasa Press (Ṣaṇmuka Vilāsa Piras Āpīc) in the Puttur (Puttūr) area of Tiruchirappalli (formerly Trichy), today an important metropolis in Tamil Nadu, with portions also published by "Sivarahasyam Press, P. T." in Madras; little is known about either publishers. The work was registered with the Madras Record Office, in which the catalog entry is shortened to "Mantira Sangraha Veda Dyanopadesa Smriti," an Anglicization of *Mantira caṅkiraha vēta tiyāṉōpatēca smiruti*; the head word being the Tamil word mantra (*mantiram*) stresses its main feature as a work on mantra. The scope of the work is large and contains mantras to an entire pantheon of gods and goddesses as well as instructions in both Tamil and English on Śivarājayoga (see Cantú 2023).

This work also contains a diagram, even a map of sorts, depicting Agastya, Sabhapati's semi-legendary guru Shivajnanabodha, and Sabhapati himself with the title Guru Father Rishi (see Figure 9.3). The diagram is appropriately titled "the diagram of the tradition of succession between guru and student on the mountain called Mount Agastya, the Southern Kailasa" (*takṣaṇakailāca akastiyācala parvata kurucişya pāramparaiya paṭam*). The three yogins are depicted meditating in caves (Mpvl. *kukaikaḷ*, < Skt. *guhā*) at the confluence of the Thamirabirani River and two other (possibly legendary or "yogic") rivers, the Amrita

FIGURE 9.3 "The diagram of the tradition of succession between guru and student on the mountain called Mount Agastya, the Southern Kailasa." Agastya is pictured on the left, Shivajnanabodha Rishi in the center, and Guru Father Rishi (Sabhapati Swami) on the right. Diagram published in Cuvāmikaḷ 1913.

River (Mpvl. *amirutanati*) and the Siddhi River (Mpvl. *cittinati*). These form a "triple-braided" (Skt. *triveṇi*) confluence that mirrors the revered confluence of the Ganges, Yamuna, and (subterranean) Saraswati in present-day Prayagraj.

Recurrent references to Agastya are perhaps Sabhapati's most explicit link to Tamil vernacular religion, given Agastya's direct connection to the Siddhars. In the early twentieth century, the rishi also played an important role in the Dravidian language movement as the legendary founder of the Tamil language (Weiss 2009). Sabhapati was writing before this movement gained momentum, and as a result was probably more interested in using the symbolic capital of Agastya's power and authority as a primal guru (*ātikuru*, < Skt. *ādiguru*) of yoga.[8] The text asserts itself to be "a scripture on the mantra of Agastya's hidden guidance" (*akastiyar kuptōpatēca mantira vētameṉal*). As with many of these sections of "guidance" (*upatēcam*, < Skt. *upadeśa*), the actual content of this section consists only of the following prose poem (Cuvāmikaḷ 1913, 3):

> Listen, O world! Listen, even if you won't listen. The giver of liberation and individuated bliss (*muktikaivalliyam*), the great and undying Agastya Rishi [pronounced] the truth and mystery of the scriptures as a hidden instruction. How much has this man been gracious unto me, he who is called the blessed Shivajnanabodha Rishi? Have I not pronounced these also daily as the instructions of this collected scripture, O expanse of the world?[9]

This poem firmly grounds the rationale for the use of mantras in this entire "collected scripture" on mantra in the Tamil vernacular mythology of Agastya and Sabhapati Swami's semi-legendary guru Shivajnanabodha Rishi. The importance of Agastya was also reflected in Sabhapati's publication of a lost work entitled *Aṭukkunilai pōtam*, "The Order of the State of Awakening," a series of verses attributed to Agastya that appear to derive from extant manuscripts known by the same title.

Agastya also figures prominently in Sabhapati Swami's Tamil-language hagiography, composed by Shivajnanaprakash Yogishwara (Civakñāṉappirakācayōkīsvara, dates unknown), and also appears in his English-language works. One legend asserts that Agastya is still living and appears once in every fifty years, and a second legend refers to Agastya founding a temple that Sabhapati frequented before establishing his meditation hall (Cuvāmikaḷ 1913, 13 [of hagiography section]):

> He then approached the city of Chennai and is in Holy Konnur in Villivakkam. In ancient times Agastya established a pilgrimage bathing site of Agastya and a temple of Agastya at a forest of bael trees (*vilvavaṉam*, < Skt. *bilvavana*) where he slew the asuras Vatapi and Ilvala. He instituted a large pool, called the Offering Pool (Yākakuṇṭam, < Skt. *yajñakuṇḍa*), and made an offering (*yākam*, < Skt. *yajña*) upon coming to Holy Konnur. He approached the large pool, and was in his gnostic vision of the past, present, and future (Mpvl. *tirikāla ñāṉatiruṣṭi*, < Skt. *trikālajñānadr̥ṣṭi*) while on the ground in steadfast devotion. While in his steadfast devotion, he also established a hermitage and abode of instruction (*maṭālayam*, < Skt. *maṭhālaya*) after a short time. He dwelled there in that place and made offerings at the great lake called the Offering Pool. On the ground at the north side of this Pool of Offering was where the Lord of All (Carvēsvara, < Skt. Sarveśvara) had given the vision of his dance (*naṭaṉam*, < Skt. *naṭana*) of five activities (Mpvl. *pañcakiruttiyam*, < Skt. *pañcakr̥tya*) to Agastya, and where his disciples had gone to perform worship rites to 1,008 lingas and 108 shaligrams.[10]

Holy Konnur (Tirukoṇṇūr, also just Konnur or Connoor) was a village in the Saidapet Taluk of Chingleput District that today has been almost entirely subsumed within the northwest Chennai suburb of Villivakkam (Villivākkam); a Vijayanagara-era temple called Arulmigu Agatheeswarar Temple (Aruḷmiku Akastīsvarar Tirukkōyil) still exists at the site. A published pamphlet about this sacred site (*talam*, < Skt. *sthala*) in Tamil, entitled *Vilvāraṇyat tala purāṇac curukkam* ("Summary of the Legend of the Sacred Site of the Bael Forest"), refers to both the bael forest and to the same destruction of Vatapi and Ilvala by Agastya in Villivakkam (Tāsar 2000, see Figure 9.4). The earliest known mention of this story appears to be in the third book (Skt. *parvan*) of the Mahābhārata epic, entitled the "Āraṇyakaparvan," chapter 99 according to Sørensen's order (1904, 237, 720) and chapter 97 according to Sukthankar's numbering of the *parvan*

FIGURE 9.4 *Vilvāraṇyat tala purāṇac curukkam* ("Summary of the Legend of the Sacred Site of the Bael Forest"). I am grateful to Chitra Selvakumar for mailing me a copy of this work after we met at the temple in February 2020.

(Sukthankar 1942, 339–341; see also Zvelebil 1992, 238 and Appendix 3). The prominence of the story of Agastya's ingestion of the two "demon" (Skt. *daitya* or *āsura*) brothers Ilvalan and Vātāpi—the latter of whom even has an ancient temple site named after him in Badami, Karnataka—provides a compelling example how the Sanskrit mythos of Agastya became intertwined with Tamil and other South Indian vernacular legends, including a temple named after him in Konnur (Figure 9.5).

Sabhapati's literature is not just connected to the Tamil legends of Agastya, but also employs vernacular languages and scripts. Throughout his Tamil works are found mantric formulae and instructions for their application, all in the Tamil script, just as his (heavily Sanskritic) Hindi and Telugu works and Bengali translation—not fully considered in this chapter for the sake of space—contain instructions in the Devanagari, Telugu, and Bengali scripts, respectively. The Sanskrit rendered in these scripts would not always have been understood to his

FIGURE 9.5 A line of *śivaliṅgas* worshipped with flowers along the outer courtyard of the Arulmigu Agatheeswarar Temple. Photo by Keith E. Cantú.

audience, so Sanskrit terms are often accompanied by additional notes to explain or clarify meaning in vernacular languages (see, for example, Figure 9.6). While there is certainly a rich tradition of interpreting Sanskrit terms in manuscript commentarial traditions and vernacular translations from Sanskrit, the presence of a list of terms giving Tamil equivalents for Sanskrit terms was very rare at this time for a non-academic published work. This concern to "localize" teachings and make them accessible to various regions of India, in other words, opened the door for Sabhapati to willingly blend his Sanskrit-based teachings on yoga and mantra with vernacular religious worlds. Such a phenomenon of localization to fit a given vernacular-language audience can be usefully contrasted with Sanskritization as a means to make a local text intelligible to an educated audience all across South Asia.

Sabhapati's Tamil works contain vernacular instructions for how these mantras are to be used in the observation of rituals (Cuvāmikaḷ 1913, 4):

> It is necessary to meditate according to the summary of this teaching, and this is the sequence: having recited the mantra for bathing in the morning and taken a bath, sit in a solitary place. While reciting the rules for the sequence of daily ceremonies using your mouth, at that time also meditate with your mind. This should start at six o'clock in the morning and

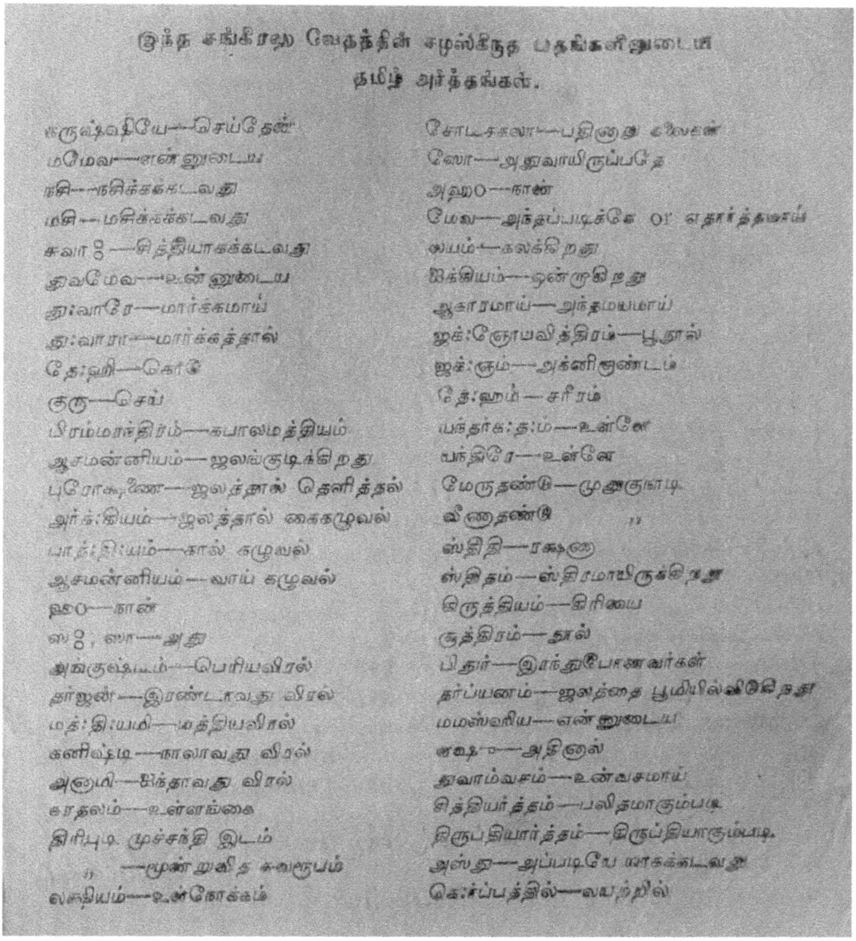
இந்த ஸங்கிரஹ வேதத்தின் ஸமஸ்கிருத பதங்களினுடைய
தமிழ் அர்த்தங்கள்.

FIGURE 9.6 Part of a list giving Dravidian Tamil equivalents of Sanskrit words (Cuvāmikaḷ 1913).

be finished at seven o'clock. Then after seven o'clock up to eight o'clock recite with your tongue the worship rites to be performed mentally, while also meditating on them in your mind. After finishing this you should go to work according to your circumstances. Then, at night from seven o'clock to eight o'clock one should recite the meditations for the royal yoga (*rājayōkam*, < Skt. *rājayoga*) and the meditations for the sequence of initiation, and while doing so meditate with your mind. With this you will be finished. In this way you will receive absolute purity, happiness now and in the hereafter, the fruits of desire and dispassion, the absorption of mind, wealth, offspring, trade for one's crops, employment, the knowledge of devotion, and liberation.[11]

Notice the sequence of times, which allows for anyone who is employed with other activities to perform the mantras along with their ritual practices, not just full-time male or female ritual specialists (i.e. *pūjārins* or *pūjārinīs*). Another possible indicator of a connection with a popular level is the promise that performing these rites daily will not only bring one the attainment of soteriological goals but also lead to certain tangible results (*bubhukṣu*, "desiring [this-worldly] enjoyment" instead of *mumukṣu*, "desiring liberation"): wealth, offspring, and the "trade for one's crops" (*payir varttakam*).

Another interesting feature of Sabhapati's vernacular instructions is his combination of physical practices, such as bathing and marking oneself with ashes, with practices of mental interiorization, such as meditative concentration. For example, among other instructions are found: (1) "Three small concentrations for the mind" (*maṉētiriciṉṉa tāraṇam*), (2) "Guidance on all the ceremonies, mantras, and meditations" (*carvāṉuṣṭāṉa mantira tiyāṉa upatēcam*), (3) "Guidance on the mantras for bathing" (*sṉāṇa mantira upatēcam*), (4) "Guidance on the mantra for the three marks of ash" (*viputi tiricūrṇamantira* [*upatēcam*]), (5) "Guidance on the binding of the eight directions" (*aṣṭatikapantaṉa upatēcam*), (6) "Guidance on the nine celestial bodies" (*navakkiraha upatēcam*), and (7) "Guidance on (mental) formulation" (*caṅkalpa upatēcam*). It is clear from these instructions that the contents make use of an elaborate Sanskrit technical vocabulary on mental formulation (*caṅkalpam*, < Skt. *saṅkalpa*) and meditative cultivation (*pāvaṉai*, < Skt. *bhāvanā*), while their language simultaneously connects it to Tamil vernacular rituals happening all around the margins of formal temple environments.

The body of practices that Sabhapati Swami builds with these mantras moreover spans the sectarian boundaries of Śaiva, Vaiṣṇava, and goddess worship, and it includes a whole pantheon of gods and goddesses. These include (1) "guidance on the [mantras for] the praise for all gods" (*carvatēvatārccaṉā upatēcam*), (2) "guidance on the [mantras for] the praise of all goddesses" (*carvatēviyārccaṉā upatēcam*), (3) "guidance on the recitation of the five-syllabled mantra of the God of All" (*carvēsvarar pañcākṣarajapa upatēcam*), (4) "guidance on the five-syllabled mantra of the Goddess of All" (*carvēsvari pañcāṭkṣara upatēcam*), (5) "guidance on the five-syllabled mantra of Viṣṇu" (*viṣṇū pañcākṣara upatēcam*), (6) "guidance on the eight-syllabled mantra of Viṣṇu" (*viṣṇū aṣṭākṣara upatēcam*), (7) "guidance on the five-syllabled mantra of the great Śiva and Śakti" (*mahācivacakti pañcākṣara upatēcam*), (8) "guidance on the five-syllabled mantra of the guru" (*kuru pañcākṣara upatēcam*), (9) "guidance on the five-syllabled mantra for every god and goddess" (*sarvatēvatātēvi pañcākṣara upatēcam*), (10) "guidance on the five- and sixteen-syllabled mantra of Gaṇapati" (*kaṇapati cōṭaca pañcākṣara upatēcam*), and (11) "guidance on the six-syllabled mantra of Subrahmaṇya" (*cuppiramaṇiyar ṣaṭākṣara upatēcam*) (Cuvāmikaḷ 1913, 30). This concern to transcend various sectarian and deity-based boundaries of Hinduism was popular in South India during Sabhapati's lifetime, and was not only promoted by the Theosophical Society in Adyar but also even earlier by Tamil Vīraśaiva authors (Steinschneider 2016) and informed by the antinomian folk legacy of the Siddhars (Zvelebil 1996).

The last connection with Tamil vernacular discourse in Sabhapati's writings is the connection between mantra and sound. While the theoretical framework of mantras and their meditation is undoubtedly Sanskritic and elite, the application of vocalizing Tantric mantras and seed-syllables in Sabhapati's yogic teachings helped to bridge his vernacular world with the elite temple contexts in which the Vedas and other scriptures were recited and intoned (cf. Gerety 2021). Sabhapati's literature accordingly outlines the contours for a kind of religious, vernacular music practice that developed out of the early modern reception and performance of the musical expressions of the Tamil Siddhars, songs that to this day are held up as an exemplar of Tamil folk religious identity (Zvelebil 1973). The Siddhars, who as mentioned above were connected to the legends of Agastya, were not just *yogin*s and *yoginī*s but also composers of songs that are still performed in many temple contexts today alongside the more established performances of the songs of the Vaiṣṇava Āḻvārs and Śaiva Nāyaṉmārs (Peterson 1989; Zvelebil 1973).

Sabhapati's trilingual work in English, Tamil, and Sanskrit contains vivid descriptions about how each of the Tantric *cakra*s or lotuses (*kamalam*, < Skt. *kamala*), which Sabhapati translated into English as "faculties," is "created as puffing and swelling as bubbles" (Yogiswer 1890, 158). Each of these lotuses corresponds to what Sabhapati calls "Divine words" (*pījamantiram*, < Skt. *bīja-mantra*, lit. "seed-mantras" or "seed-spells"). For example, there are five such words (or "seed-syllables") in the case of the "Kundali [Skt. *kuṇḍalī*] of elements or Mooladharum [*mūlādhāra*]." Each of these words has what Sabhapati translates as "Spirit" (*tēvatamsam*, < Skt. *devatāṃśa*, lit. "part of a deity"), which dwells in what he calls a "bubble" (an idiosyncratic translation of *kamala*, lit. "lotus"): the "Spirit of the syllable *om*" creates ether in the center, and the "spirits" of *va*, *ca*, *śa*, and *sa*, respectively, create air, fire, water, and "mud" (i.e. earth). These words create five faculties (*tattva*s) that accordingly contain "sins, vices, impurities and unholiness" which "must be purified by silent and dumb meditation" (*maunajapatiyāṉam*, < Skt. *maunajapadhyāna*, lit. "meditation of silent [mantra]-recitation"). The impurities of these faculties arise on account of *māyā*, what Sabhapati translates as "delusion," analogized with "impure water." The "pure water," by contrast, is the divine word or seed-spell of each Spirit that, when daily recited by the practitioner, can wash away the impurity and cause the *tattva* to eventually be re-absorbed into the transcendent Śiva.

Sabhapati's hagiographies mention he was celebrated during his lifetime as a Tamil poet, and his works include lyrical songs and poetic compositions; it is no surprise that the aforementioned practices on mantric seed-syllables were not just a cosmological abstraction but also linked to the theory and practice of intoning musical *svara*s or "tones." The mantras are linked to phonetic sounds that comprise lyrical music. The student is instructed to think beyond the bliss that arises from singing musical lyrics and to meditate on the sounds from which these lyrics are molded, the theory of which somewhat resonates with the *Saṅgītaratnākāra* of Śārṅgadeva (Kitada and Śārṅgadeva 2012). These tones in turn correspond to cosmogonic "inherent natures" (*svarūpam* or *cuvarūpam*, < Skt. *svarūpa*) invoked using sounds. The vowels (*svara*) are the starting point of the practice, which then develops to include the labial and nasal humming associated with syllables like *am*, *nam*, *oṅ*, and *ram*. This then gives way to the "bliss" of *na*, *ma*, *ci*, *va*, *ya* (< Skt. *namo śivāya*), or the Śaiva five-syllabled mantra (Skt. *pañcākṣaramantra*), which are then all integrated in the *praṇava* or syllable Om.[12] We return finally to the "gamut of the Vedas" (*vedasvara*), which are what Sabhapati calls "Spiritual sounds" (*piraṇavasvarasaptalaya saṅkītam*, < Skt. *praṇavasvarasaptalaya saṅgīta*, lit. "music of the seven-fold absorption in the sounds of the syllable Om"). This seven-fold absorption in sound (Mpvl. *saptalayam*) are the seven *svara*s plus their octaval resolution (Mpvl. *ca*, *ri*, *ka*, *ma*, *pa*, *ta*, *ni*, *ca*, < Skt. *sa*, *ri*, *gā*, *ma*, *pa*, *dhā*, *ni*, *sa*), the notes of which form the basis for musical improvisation in Indian modes or *rāga*s, including the Tamil vernacular songs of the *Tēvāram* and those of the Tamil Siddhars.

As Primiano concluded in his survey of the importance of vernacular religion and folklore, research need not be limited to consideration "not only about *how* and *what* people have said, sung, or expressed religiously, but about the substance and objects of those beliefs in themselves whether natural or supernatural" (1995, 52). To this point, I would add that, in this case, it is not even just about "beliefs" but also ritual practices that lead to living dispositions and ways of perceiving the world. Further analyzing the expressions and rites of Tamil vernacular religion as expressed by an author like Sabhapati Swami, his predecessors, and his followers, can provide a critical window into these dispositions and show the diversity of teachings even among published authors on yoga in the modern period.

Notes

1 In this and subsequent references to technical terms, I will first give the Tamil transliteration according to standard diacritical practice, followed by a transliteration from Sanskrit when applicable.
2 For various ways in which scholars have framed the contours of this group, some more convincing than others, see R. Venkatraman (1990), Zvelebil (1996), Weiss (2009), Mallinson (2019), and Ezhilraman (2015). For consideration of their place in the wider pan-Indian context of the Siddhas, see White (1996) and Linrothe et al. (2006).
3 "Chaturthi" (*caturtti*, < Skt. *caturthī*) is the fourth day of a lunar fortnight after a new or full moon.
4 The festival of Dol Purnima (Bng. *dol pūrṇimā*)/Dol Yatra (Hnd. *dol jātrā*) is sometimes celebrated with a swinging palanquin.
5 "Sasthi" (Mpvl. *caṣṭi*, < Skt. *ṣaṣṭhī*) is the sixth day of a lunar fortnight after a new or full moon. It can also refer to the name of an important childbirth goddess who is honored on the sixth day of the lunar month, and the sixth day after childbirth.
6 See White (2006, 40–34) for more on this observance.
7 The five actions are "creation" (*ciruṣṭi*, < Skt. *sṛṣṭi*), "maintenance" (*titi*, < Skt. *sthiti*), "destruction" (*caṅkāram*, < Skt. *saṃhāra*), "the darkening of the soul by the deity" (*tiropavam*, < Skt. *tirobhava*, lit. "disappearance," "vanishing"), and "favor" (*aṉukkiraham*, < Skt. *anugraha*).

8 For a history of various "Agastyas" in Tamil literature, see Appendix 3 of Zvelebil 1992.

9 *kēḷīrulakīr kēṭṭaikkēṭuttu kēṭilā muktikaival liyantarum*
māḷāta yakastiyaruṣi mākupta tōpatēcamāvētarahasciyōṇmaiyai
yāḷāveṉaiyāṇṭa yaruṭ civakñāṉa pōtaruṣiyeṉak karuḷ iyavāṟē
nāḷāyuraittēṉ nāṉuñ caṅkirahavētōpatēcamāyulakuyyavē.

10 *vilvavaṉattil ātiyil akasttiyar vātāpi, vilvāpiyacurāḷ aikkoṉṟu akasttiyāralayamum, akasttiya tīrttamum stāpittu ipperēri ye:ṉpatil yākakuṇṭam erpaṭutti yākañceytupōṉa tirukkoṇṇūriṟkuvantu pērērikku yaṭutta nilattil niṣṭaiyilirukkumpoḻuthu taṉ tirikāla ñāṉatiruṣṭiyil, tāṉ niṣṭaiyilirukkumiṭam akasttiyaruṣi koñcakālam maṭālayayācīrmam eṟpaṭutti, vacittupōṉayiṭamāyum, pērēri avar yākañceytayākakuṇṭamāyum inta yākakuṇṭavaṭapuṟanilattil akastiyarukku carvēsvarar taṉ pañcakiruttiya naṭaṉa taricaṉam koṭuttatāyum,* 1008 *liṅkaṅkaḷ ai* 108 *cālikkirāmaṅkaḷ ai taṉ ciṣyarkaḷ pūjittu pōṉatāyum.*

11 *inta upatēca kuṟippiṉpaṭi tiyāṉam paṇṇavēṇṭiyak kiramam kālaiyil snāṉamantirattaiccolli snāṉ añceytu or taṉiyiṭattiluṭkārntu nittiyakkiramayaṉuṣṭāṉa vitikaḷ ai vāyiṉāl vācittukkoṇṭē appoḻ utē maṉatiṉāluntiyāṉittukkoṇṭē kālaiyil* (6) *maṇimutal* (7) *maṇikkuḷḷ āka ceytu muṭittuviṭṭu appoḻutē* (7) *maṇikkumēl* (8) *maṇikkuḷḷāka māṉacakiriyāpūjaikaḷaiyum vākkāl vācittukkoṇṭē maṉatiṉāl tiyāṉittukkoṇṭē ceytu muṭittuviṭṭup pirakuyavāḷavāl toḻiluk kuppōkavum. irāttiri* (7) *maṇimutal* (8) *maṇikkuḷḷ āka rājayōkat tiyāṉaṅkaḷaiyum, tīkṣākkiramattiyāṉaṅkaḷaiyum, vācittukkoṇṭē maṉatāl tiyāṉittukkoṇṭē ceytu muṭikkavum. itaṉāl carvacutti, ihaparacukam kāmyiya niṣkāmmiyapalaṉ, maṉō[l]ayam, taṉam, cantāṉam, payir varttakam, uttiyōkam, paktikñāṉam muktikkiṭaikkum.*

12 For a dated but useful translation of Tamil verses pertaining to these syllables, see Pope (1900, xxxix–xlii). For more analysis of the mantra in Tamil Śaiva-specific contexts, see Winch (1975, 72–75). For other contexts in which Om is linked to sound and yoga, see Gerety (2021).

Works Cited

Asprem, Egil, and Julian Strube, editors. *New Approaches to the Study of Esotericism*. Brill, 2020.

Baier, Karl. "Theosophical Orientalism and the Structures of Intercultural Transfer: Annotations on the Appropriations of the Cakras in Early Theosophy." *Theosophical Appropriations: Esotericism, Kabbalah and the Transformation of Traditions*, edited by Julie Chajes and Boaz Huss, Ben-Gurion University of the Negev Press, 2016, pp. 309–354.

Cantú, Keith. "'Don't Take Any Wooden Nickels': Western Esotericism, Yoga, and the Discourse of Authenticity." *New Approaches to the Study of Esotericism*, edited by Egil Asprem and Julian Strube, Brill, 2020, pp. 109–126.

———. *Like a Tree Universally Spread: Sri Sabhapati Swami and Śivar jayoga*. Oxford University Press, 2023.

———. "Sri Sabhapati Swami: The Forgotten Yogi of Western Esotericism." *The Occult Nineteenth Century: Roots, Developments, and Impact on the Modern World*, edited by Lukas Pokorny and Franz Winter, Palgrave Macmillan, 2021, pp. 347–373.

Cuvāmikaḷ, Capāpati. *Carva māṉaca nittiya karmānuṣṭāṉa, carva tēvatātēvi māṉaca pūjāttiyāṉa, pirammakñāṉa rājayōka niṣṭai camāti, carva tīkṣākkramattiyāṉa, cātaṉā appiyāca kiramāṉ ucantāṉa, caṅkiraha vēta tiyāṉōpatēca smiruti*. Ṣaṇmukavilās Piras, 1913.

Cuvāmikaḷ, Citampara Periya. *Upatēca uṇmai, ciḷakka uraiyuṭaṉ*. Vēḷaccēri Makāṉ Patippakam, 2014.

De Michelis, Elizabeth. *A History of Modern Yoga: Patañjali and Western Esotericism*. Reprint, Continuum, 2008.

Ezhilraman, R. *Siddha Cult in Tamiḻnādu: Its History and Historical Continuity*. Pondicherry University, 2015.
Gerety, Finnian. "Sound and Yoga." *Routledge Handbook of Yoga and Meditation Studies*, edited by Suzanne Newcombe and Karen O'Brien-Kop, London, 2021, pp. 502–522.
Hanegraaff, Wouter J. "The Globalization of Esotericism." *Correspondences*, vol. 3, 2015, pp. 55–91.
Jones, Kenneth W. *Arya Dharm: Hindu Consciousness in 19th-Century Punjab*. University of California Press, 1976.
Kitada, Makoto, and Śārṅgadeva. *The Body of the Musician: An Annotated Translation and Study of the Piṇḍotpatti-Prakaraṇa of Śārṅgadeva's Saṅgītaratnakara*. Peter Lang, 2012.
Linrothe, Robert N., et al., editors. *Holy Madness: Portraits of Tantric Siddhas*. Rubin Museum of Art; Serindia Publications, 2006.
Mallinson, James. "Kālavañcana in the Konkan: How a Vajrayāna Haṭhayoga Tradition Cheated Buddhism's Death in India." *Religions*, vol. 10, no. 4, 2019, pp. 1–33.
Peterson, Indira Viswanathan, editor. *Poems to Śiva: The Hymns of the Tamil Saints*. Princeton University Press, 1989.
Pope, G. U. *The Tiruvāçagam, or "Sacred Utterances" of the Tamil Poet, Saint, and Sage Māṇikka-Vāçagar*. The Clarendon Press, 1900.
Primiano, Leonard. "Vernacular Religion and the Search for Method in Religious Folklife." *Western Folklore*, vol. 54, no. 1, Jan. 1995, pp. 37–56.
Sanderson, Alexis. "The Śaiva Literature." *Journal of Indological Studies*, no. 24 & 25 (2012–2013), 2014, pp. 1–113.
Singleton, Mark. *Yoga Body: The Origins of Modern Posture Practice*. Oxford University Press, 2010.
Sørensen, Søren. *An Index to the Names in the Mahābhārata*. Williams and Norgate, 1904.
Steinschneider, Eric. *Beyond the Warring Sects: Universalism, Dissent, and Canon in Tamil Śaivism, ca. 1675–1994*. University of Toronto, 2016.
Sukthankar, Vishnu S. *The Āraṇyakaparvan (Part 1), Being the Third Book of the Mahābhārata the Great Epic of India*. Poona, 1942.
Svāmikaḷ, Ñāṉakuru Yōkīsvara Capāpati. *Koṇṇūr kñāṉa kurumaṭālaya tapācīrmattiṉuṭaiya ñāṉakuru yōkīsvara capāpati svāmikaḷ aṉukkirakitta cātaṉāppiyāsāṉupava upatēcam*. Natasun & Co. and V.N. Press, 1898.
Swami, The Mahatma Giana Guroo Yogi Sabhapaty. *Om. A Treatise on Vedantic Raj Yoga Philosophy*. Edited by Siris Chandra Basu, "Civil and Military Gazette" Press, 1880.
Tāsar, Aruṭkavī Śrī Tēvī Karumārī. *Vilvāraṇyat tala purāṇac curukkam*. Iḷaiñar Aruṭpaṇi Maṉṟam, 2000.
Venkatraman, R. *A History of the Tamil Siddha Cult*. Ennes Publications, 1990.
Weiss, Richard S. *Recipes for Immortality: Medicine, Religion, and Community in South India*. Oxford University Press, 2009.
White, David Gordon. *Kiss of the Yoginī: "Tantric Sex" in Its South Asian Contexts*. University of Chicago Press, 2006.
———. *The Alchemical Body: Siddha Traditions in Medieval India*. University of Chicago Press, 1996.
Winch, Mary Elizabeth. *The Theology of Grace in Saiva Siddhanta, in the Light of Umapati Sivacharya's Tiruarutpayan*. McMaster University, Apr. 1975.
Yoder, Don. "Folklife Studies in American Scholarship." *Discovering American Folklife: Studies in Ethnic, Religious, and Regional Culture*, UMI Research Press, 1990, pp. 43–61.
Yogiswer, The Mahathma Brumha Gnyana Mavuna Guru Sabhapathy Swamy. *Om. The Cosmic Psychological Spiritual Philosophy and Science of Communion with and Absorption in*

the Infinite Spirit, or Vedhantha Siva Raja Yoga Samadhi Brumha Gnyana Anubuthi, Second Book. Karnatak Press, 1890.

Yōkīsvarar, Ñāṉakuru Capāpati. *Amcumati cūriyamūrttikkup pōtitta cakalākama tiraṭṭu*. Printed by N. Kupusawmy Chettiar at the Duke of Edinburgh Press (Part I-A and Part I) and by C. Murugesa Mudalyar at the Hindu Theological Press (Part I-C and Part I-D), 1894.

Zvelebil, Kamil. *Companion Studies to the History of Tamil Literature*. Brill, 1992.

———. *The Poets of the Powers*. Rider, 1973.

———. *The Siddha Quest for Immortality*. Mandrake, 1996.

10

OBSERVING BUDDHIST PRECEPTS BY DIVINATION

Practices According to *Zhanchajing*

Xingyi Wang

> I deem that in the final [dharma] period, for those who aspire to pure precepts, aside from the method of *Zhancha* divination[1] there is no other path.
>
> 予念末世。欲得淨戒。捨此占察輪相之法。更無別途。[2]
>
> –Ouyi Zhixu 蕅益智旭

Introduction

Is divination (Chi. *zhanbu*), ubiquitous in the folk-religious landscape in East Asia, compatible with Buddhist practice on the ground? If so, what motivates Buddhist practitioners to seek confirmation of the divine by throwing dice? We may answer the above questions by examining practices surrounding *Zhancha shan'e yebao jing* (Sūtra on the Divination of the Requital of Good and Evil Actions, hereafter *Zhanchajing*), an indigenous apocryphal text produced in sixth-century China.[3] This seemingly non-Buddhist practice prescribed by *Zhanchajing* was accepted in medieval Chinese, Korean, and Japanese monasteries, and it became an important source of religious inspiration for Buddhist clerics in the late imperial period. The practice appeals to Buddhist practitioners as a testimony of one's karmic retribution, even though early Buddhist catalogs cast doubt on its authenticity. *Zhanchajing* gained legitimacy through endorsement of canon compilers and its eventual canonization.

Recent scholarship on divination practice on the silk road has greatly advanced our understanding of the complex and evolving relationship between non-Buddhist and Buddhist practices.[4] On the one hand, we have Buddhacization—transforming supposedly non-Buddhist practice as Buddhist practice—of multiple divination traditions on the silk road; on the other hand, long-standing Chinese numerical trigram divination traditions found its way

DOI: 10.4324/9781003257462-14

into Chinese apocryphal Buddhist texts. We are now at a better position to appreciate the nuanced divination practice within Buddhist communities.

The main body of the chapter concerns Ouyi Zhixu's (1599–1655, hereafter Ouyi) engagement with the divination practice prescribed by *Zhanchajing*. I argue that the *Zhanchajing* contains a dialogical aspect that serves as a central form of communication with the divine for the sake of affirming either karmic purification or the power of faith. When conventional ways of practice were conceived of no longer guaranteed enlightenment, the divination prescribed in *Zhanchajing* became a reliable resource for Buddhist masters. Combined with the monastic repentance ritual, divination was further adapted for the needs of those who seek confirmation of rebirth in Amitābha's Pure Land, a paradisiacal place in Buddhism. Understanding the fate of *Zhanchajing* is not only meaningful in terms of how the text has been accepted in the Buddhist catalog and canon. More importantly, it shows that divination, a popular practice for the "ordinary and ignorant," once theorized and combined with Buddhist precepts and Pure Land practice, was transformed into a reassuring tool for communication with the divine.

Zhanchajing, A Text of Divination

Given that Buddhist doctrine clearly rejects divination, one may reasonably doubt how could a text on divination be accepted by Buddhist community. Leonard Norman Primiano have long argued that the dualistic treatment of folk religion vis-à-vis "official" religion "residualizes the religious lives of believers and at the same time reifies the authenticity of religious institution as the exemplar of human religiosity."[5] Therefore, Primiano advocates the use of the concept of "vernacular religion," a theoretical hybrid of fields studying religion, which "highlights the power of the individual and communities of individuals to create and re-create their own religion."[6]

On similar notes, a univocal reaction to divination within Buddhist communities is not attainable; also, in modern ethnography, we see all sorts of divination practices used by Buddhists.[7] Hence, a more suitable question should be how divination *became* a legitimate and lived Buddhist practice, as "folk-religious aspects of sectarian religion," in Don Yoder's words.[8] The legitimacy of *Zhanchajing* is tied to the issue of canonization in Buddhist catalogs compiled in China. Early catalogers were also aware of the dubious characteristics of the text, and they cast doubt on its authenticity. As Kyoto Tokuno has shown, the compiler of a catalog often determined the fate of a text in circulation.[9] Fajing's (n.d.) *Zhongjing mulu* (594), Fei Changfang's (n.d.) *Lidai sanbao ji* (597), and Daoxuan's (596–667) *Datang neidian lu* (664) agreed that *Zhanchajing* is less likely a translation from Sanskrit than a piece written in China.[10] Fajing designates *Zhanchajing* under the category of "scriptures of doubtful authenticity," while Fei Changfang and Daoxuan classified it as Buddhist apocrypha. Fajing went so far as to not only criticize all texts containing divination of good and bad omens not only as spurious and fallacious, but he also suggests that these texts should be put to sleep to save the world from calamity.[11]

In Fei Changfang's catalog, a divination practice associated with *Zhanchajing* indicates that in the early circulation of the text, Buddhist monks and laypersons were attracted to the divination of throwing dice to reveal one's karmic status. According to the record, some reported this practice as heresy to the government of Canton in 593. As a result, the government consulted Buddhist masters including the previously mentioned Fajing. Since *Zhanchajing* is absent from all previous Buddhist catalogs, and the practice apparently deviates from other Buddhist texts, Fajing and other masters considered that "one should not follow the divination practice." [12] This episode ends by the emperor's order that texts such as *Zhanchajing* should not be in circulation.[13]

The popularity of *Zhanchajing* seems to go against the initial judgment of Buddhist historians and the Sui Wen emperor. It first gained legitimacy through the text's recognition in a Buddhist catalog produced in 695 during Empress Wu's reign,[14] and was vindicated by Zhisheng's influential catalog finished in 730.[15] Rejecting Fe Changfang's earlier judgment as unconvincing, Zhisheng argued,

> how could one, by means of one's own limited view, not allow [another] person's extensive view? There are eighty thousand dharma gates, and the principle is approached by multiple paths. If this text is not from the Buddha, how could it reveal such profound meaning?[16]

Zhisheng presented a compromising view that digressed from philology of his time, which authenticates a text based on an affirmed translator, time, and conformity to authoritative doctrine, and carved a space allowing alternative practice consistent with Buddhism.[17] Since *Kaiyuan shijiao lu* is the root catalog for the compilation of the Buddhist Canon in the Northern Song, *Zhanchajing* was sequentially designated canonical in all Buddhist canon editions since.

We should not over-estimate the importance of authoritative endorsement over the intrinsic adaptability to Chinese Buddhist practice. *Zhanchajing* acquired multiple alternative names in Zhisheng's catalog, testifying to its popularity and wide circulation in monastic and lay practice.[18] Endo Junichiro and Ikehira Noriko have argued there are noteworthy overlaps between Zhiyi (538–597) and *Zhanchajing*'s repentance ritual, indicating both may draw from common textual sources, or the author of *Zhanchajing* integrated Zhiyi's method of repentance, that became increasingly popular in the Sui-Tang era.[19] Moro Shigeki has identified that the popular practice of repentance resembles descriptions of such practice in Chan and Pure Land texts.[20] Overall, the popularity of the divination method on the ground and *Zhanchajing*'s sophisticated Buddhist theories, undistinguishable from other Buddhist sūtras, prompted its acceptance in the canon.

Regarding the classification of apocryphal texts in East Asian Buddhism, I concur with Funayama Tōru's and others' reflection that it is less possible to draw a definitive and mutually exclusive line between a translated text and a Chinese-produced text, mainly for a Chinese-produced text often incorporates the style, vocabulary, framework, and discourse of translated and vernacular texts, and a translation text has to borrow from indigenous literary tradition to make itself understandable.[21] *Zhanchajing* is a work that absorbs and appropriates multiple practical and theoretical Buddhist and non-Buddhist traditions. It does not follow the general model of combing of Indian-originated Buddhist elements and indigenous Chinese elements; instead, this text is a marriage of Indian-originated Buddhist components, supposedly non-Buddhist divination, and indigenous Chinese touches.

The Emerging of Zhancha Divination

Fei Changfang's early assessment discloses an assumed connection between the divination of *Zhanchajing* and popular practices of throwing two two-sided flat leather dice, each with "good" and "evil" to receive an immediate read of one's karmic status. However, a close reading of *Zhanchajing* reveals that the popular version of divination was not identical to the prescription in the sūtra, which contains a detailed method of divination, including how to make wooden dice in four-sided rectangular cuboid with two sharp ends. The divination process includes throwing wooden dice in three rounds. The first round uses a set of ten dice, corresponding to ten kinds of wholesome/unwholesome deeds; the second throw of three dice helps determine the intensity of karmic result of the first round; and the third throw of six dice reveals the answers for questions regarding karmic retribution in past, present, or future lives.[22] The two-leather-dice divination practice is accompanied by practices to eliminate the evil karma called *tachan* (repentance of stūpa) and *zipu* (throwing one's body to the ground).[23] The repentance in *Zhanchajing*, however, is more ritually complicated.

Recent scholars such as Brandon Dotson (Dotson et al. 2021) have made exciting process toward identifying that Zhancha divination shares roots with early Chinese indigenous practices and imported non-Buddhist practices through the silk road. Not only is the divination technique of wooden wheels used in Zhancha divination distinctive from yet closely related to the four-sided rectangular dice (Skr. *pāśaka*) discovered along the silk road, but it also shares the same overriding concern and ritual process with the text of *Divination of Maheśvara* (*Moxishouluo bu*).[24] In the third round of Zhancha divination, the process of bearing in mind a question about karmic retribution while throwing the dice, adding up numbers on dice, and receiving an oracle-like interpretation to the question with 189 possible variations resembles that in *Divination of Maheśvara*. Moreover, the use of a signature blank side to indicate the number zero suggests a potential connection with the indigenous *Stalk Divination* (Chi. *shifa*) and the Empowered Draughtsmen Divination Method (*Lingqi bufa*).[25] Therefore, *Zhanchajing* represents a syncretic effort as the Buddhacization of multiple divination traditions on the silk road with long-standing Chinese numerical trigram divination traditions.

Esther-Maria Guggenmos (2018) discusses "temple oracle" in three distinctive modes that have been pervasive in Buddhist monasteries and popular religion into present day. Based on its characteristics, Guggenmos conceives Zhancha divination as a practice-oriented integration of vernacular religion and Buddhism.[26] This divination practice is used to accurately discern the intensity of imperfection in the ten wholesome (four verbal, three bodily, and three mental) deeds.[27] By adding a temporal dimension, the practice also provides specific answers regarding karmic retributions in past, present, and future lives. With repeated practice, improvement of karmic status can be measured. The repentance ritual in *Zhanchajing* provides a manageable solution to resolving the tension of knowing one's fate and making a visible change to the status quo; the text promises the success of such methods for loyal practitioners. Even the dullest and most sinful are promised the opportunity to gain a purgative karmic stage with a diligent 1000-day period of practice.[28] Blurring the boundary between cleric and lay, *Zhanchajing* innovatively makes a self-consistent and self-sufficient purification practice for all.

Ouyi and *Zhanchajing*

Zhanchajing is attractive for its clear eschatological tune. Ouyi's writings confirm the framing narrative of the *Zhanchajing*, which anticipates the historical moment of entering the degenerative age of the dharma (Chi. *mofa*) in the future (approximately 1500 years after the nirvana of the historical Buddha, aka around the eleventh century). As the future in the sūtra became the reality, *Zhanchajing* offers a rare positive approach to communication with the divine for people who live in chaotic times.

A significant shift from the Tang dynasty (618–907), which occurred in the Northern Song dynasty (960–1127), is that there was a consensus that Buddhism has entered this degenerative period. In early Tang, the renowned Buddhist master Daoxuan (596–667) was still debating whether human endeavors might postpone this inevitable process. Daoxuan considered Zhancha divination as "superficial and only practiced by the shallow and mundane,"[29] indicating that those who excel at the profound Buddhist doctrine and practice have no such need to fathom fate by divination. Unlike Fajing, Daoxuan was not completely against divination. He acknowledged that since dreams—merely "illusive signs and imagination"—are worthy to be relied on, the results of the throwing the dice seem more direct and assuring, plus the mind of one pursuing such a practice no doubt deserves approval.[30] Daoxuan's limited endorsement of divination may have eased the anxiety of later Buddhist masters such as Zhanran (711–782), Chengguan (737–838), Yanshou (904–975), Zhili (960–1027), Yuanzhao (1048–1116), and Ouyi (1599–1655); all of these were convinced that they lived in a despairing age of dharma when conventional practices could no longer guarantee enlightenment.

Ouyi anchored himself in a syncretic approach encompassing precepts observation, meditation, and doctrinal study, with a soteriological orientation of rebirth in the Pure Land. What has not yet fully captured the attention of scholars is the relationship between Ouyi's abrupt change of monastic identity and his divination practice, which occurred in tandem with the composition of three consecutive commentaries on *Zhanchajing*, including a detailed divination ritual instruction, a sentence-by-sentence exegesis, and an elaboration on the profound meaning of the sūtra.

To respond to the reality of the final dharma age, Ouyi justified the use of divination as a valid Buddhist practice by distinguishing from mundane use, i.e., that mundane divination is not based on the "single realm of truth." He argues that although mundane divination claims that everything is a manifestation of one's mind, it resorts to either erroneous cause or to no cause.[31] Since Zhancha divination is accompanied by doctrinal instruction on the correct teaching of cause and effect, there is no reason to reject divination as a category. Compared with the above-mentioned defense of *Zhanchajing*, Ouyi delivered a confirmative argument, distinguishing valid "Buddhist divination" from secular superficial divination.

In his three commentaries on *Zhanchajing*, Ouyi verified the importance of daily observance of precepts and rejected the antinomian, superficial application of Buddhist doctrine. For example, he criticized those who

> by misunderstanding the idea that sentient beings and the Buddha are equal, do not rely on practice; or who hearing that the nature of debauchery, anger, and ignorance is the nature of Buddha, unscrupulously indulge in greed and hatred, without a sense of shame and guilt.[32]

Ouyi asserted that people who had accumulated unwholesome karma are not fit to practice meditation before purification through repentance.[33] Following Daoxuan's previous judgment on Zhancha divination, Ouyi further prioritized divination results in terms of certainty and accuracy over other auspicious signs such as seeing luminosity, having dreams with good signs, and smelling miraculous scent.[34]

Beyond the built-in purifying model of *Zhanchajing*, the text appeals to Ouyi for a specific reason: *Zhancha* divination facilitated and marked Ouyi's eventual *break* from the progressive model of purification, meditation, and enlightenment. After he was introduced to *Zhancha* divination by a lay follower and together with his familiarization with the Vinaya canon, Ouyi became increasingly uncertain about his own monastic status, possibly because he could not gain a pure sign from Zhancha divination after many years. In her monograph on Ouyi, Beverley McGuire has examined a volitional text by Ouyi dated 1633. Volitional text is a genre of writing contains resolution and action plan, favored by numerous religious and secular practitioners in East Asian history. In this 1633 piece, Ouyi made eight possible precept/monastic statues into lots (Chi. *jiu*) and then vowed to use lots drawing as a means to inquire about his current monastic status.[35] My reading differs from McGuire's. Philologically speaking, the volitional part was written in an optative mood and future tense, describing the divination ritual he was going to conduct; Ouyi never did and had no reason to disclose the result of his divination in a volitional text.[36] The lots drawing divination ritual created by Ouyi, in the mode of direct communication between him and the divine, serves as a remedy for the uncertainty created when Ouyi received the full monastic ordination by self-ordination in front of Yunxi Zhuhong's (1535–1615) stūpa, not by the proper *prātimokṣa* ordination ritual. We only discover the result of the lots drawing divination in a retrospective letter in which he mentions that he only maintained the status of *bodhisattva-śrāmaṇera* (with bodhisattva precepts and *śrāmaṇera* precepts),[37] suggesting he did not uphold the full precepts and was not qualified as a fully ordained monk.[38] The lots result brought enormous agony to Ouyi, as it declares his total failure as a Buddhist monk. At this point, *Zhancha* divination, the source of anxiety, became his only rescue, though not in the expected way of allowing him to make spiritual progress by purification as the sūtra promises.

Zhancha divination operates like the lots divination by revealing one's karmic status in the ten wholesome deeds. However, as mentioned above, Zhancha divination gives a much more accurate description than status in kind, by which the practitioner can determine precisely whether one has perfected the deeds, and when karmic retribution will come in fruition. For Ouyi, Zhancha divination was effective not because it uncovered his progress in the purification of unwholesome karma, but because it operated in the opposite fashion.[39] After diligent practice in pursuing the sign of purification for twelve years, Ouyi boldly claimed that he was *not able* to observe any precepts. He proclaimed, "[I have] decisively made up the mind that I will completely abandon *bodhisattva-śrāmaṇera* [precepts] and all pure precepts, only to become a Buddhist follower taking the three refuges."[40]

While we discern an idiosyncratic application of Zhancha divination in Ouyi's case, it simultaneously suggests two profound implications in the context of East Asian Buddhism: one, a tendency of denying self-ordination as a valid way to gain full-fledged monastic status, and the other, a breaking away from the progressive model of purification. The first appears self-denying, or at least contradictory in Ouyi's case. As directly recommended in *Zhanchajing*, "receiving the bodhisattva precepts, namely the three categories of precepts, through self-ordination, is then called completely receiving the *prātimokṣa* precepts of renunciation. One is called bhikṣu or bhikṣuni."[41] A salient example for the endorsement of self-ordination by *Zhanchajing* is that before the Vinaya master Jianzhen's (688–763) arduous journey to Japan in 753 (when there were no qualified Vinaya masters to confer the *prātimokṣa* precepts), the Japanese Buddhist community used to receive full ordination based on self-ordination, and they used *Zhanchajing* as the essential proof text to validate the practice.[42]

Another example comes from the Korean Vinaya master Chin-p'yo's (n.d.) biography. Chin-p'yo received guidance to follow the *Zhanchajing* through a revelatory vision of Maitreya, the future Buddha. By Zhancha divination, Chin-p'yo gained two sequential affirmative answers (number 8 and number 9) from the third round showing he "newly received the wondrous precepts" and "additionally received full precepts."[43] At the end of Chin-p'yo's biography, Iryŏn (1206–1289) quoted Fei Changfang's previously discussed episode, but he followed it with his own defense of the authenticity of *Zhanchajing*. Iryŏn pointed out that, as I have shown above, there is an apparent inconsistency between the popular practice and Zhancha divination.[44] Referring to the fact that *Zhanchajing* has been successfully listed in Buddhist catalog, Iryŏn focused on those who rejected the sūtra, accusing them of "holding the flax and abandoning the gold."[45]

Deviating from the instructions of *Zhanchajing* and conventional practices such as found in Japan and Korea, Ouyi was extremely cautious about endorsing the method of self-ordination as a proper way to receive *prātimokṣa* precepts while embracing divination practice. He did not accept *Zhanchajing*'s prescription of self-ordination, likely due to his own self-ordination that did not stand the test of the lots divination he created, and also because he was not able to gain a pure sign of Zhancha divination as promised by the sūtra. He vowed not to confer Buddhist precepts to anyone,[46] an unusual decision for a Buddhist master. Unlike the conferral of bodhisattva precepts, he suggested that one must first receive a pure sign (which is extremely difficult to acquire) before seeking self-ordination.[47]

Breaking away from the purification model, Ouyi appears disheartened in his resolution to abandon all precepts; however, intentional move should not be understood at face value. This exceptional claim rather showed that Ouyi had arrived at a critical moment, namely the "breaking the cauldrons and sinking boats."[48] His urgency at seeking a breakthrough experience from the progressive model testifies that Ouyi had moved forward in the path of spiritual growth. In 1645, one year after he wrote the letter about his decision of abandoning all precepts, Ouyi received a pure sign by constantly "worshiping Buddhas and practicing Zhancha divination."[49] At this point, though, Ouyi was not at all relieved by the pure sign. Having abandoned the precepts, he could not evaluate this attainment by the previous progressive practice. Ouyi perceived the pure sign as a mere gift out of Buddha's compassion, not as his personal achievement. He conceived himself as having created numerous unwholesome karmas right after receiving the pure sign. Like a person falling into a cesspool, Ouyi considered the only pure part of his body as pure eyes—pure eyes of correct dharma.[50]

The negative assertion of Ouyi's impure precepts status and his inability to maintain purity by divination has simultaneously consolidated his aspiration for rebirth in the Pure Land. Ouyi argued that "if not speedily seeking the pure practice [to gain rebirth in the Pure Land], how can one once for all leave saṃsāra?"[51] Ouyi's conversion to the Pure Land conformed to the overarching narrative of the degenerative age of the dharma, in which achieving enlightenment on one's own power is extremely difficult, if not impossible. His close disciple recalled him concluding, "In previous years, I single-mindedly sought to restore the practice of the bhikṣu. In recent years, I have single-mindedly aspired to have a rebirth in the west."[52] This transformation coincides with *Zhanchajing*'s strong sense of eschatology, and it assures the destination of rebirth in the afterlife.

Through the hands of Ouyi, a communal dimension of salvation in the Pure Land is incorporated into the originally individualized Zhancha divination. Although *Zhanchajing* is not designated to a singular Pure Land as a preferred afterlife destination, it prescribes chanting the Buddha's name to gain rebirth in a desired Buddha-land. Ouyi considered it karmically mature to devote oneself to gaining rebirth in Amitābha's Pure Land and his devotional practice toward the Pure Land, like many predecessors including Yunxi Zhuhong, always contained a communal aspect. As observed in volitional texts of Ouyi, many were composed for the communal practice. The aspiration to the Pure Land is not one man's achievement, but a collective endeavor, as one often needs the assistance of multiple co-practitioners' chanting during the deathbed ritual. Extending the merit to all sentient beings, Ouyi kept whoever suffered in his volitional text based on *Zhanchajing*, wishing "those in the northern and southern part of the Yangtze River and in China, who recently suffered in the military chaos, to eliminate [karmic] debts and to be liberated from hatred."[53]

Conclusion

Divination's mode of existence and overlap in Buddhism is worthy of further reflection. What do the historical moments that discussed in this chapter tell us about the relationship between the invisible but omnipresent folk religion and well-documented monastic practice? Religious Studies now questions and challenges reliance on, or prioritization of, doctrinal and orthodoxy materials from intuitional religions. When the category of folk/vernacular/lived religion became the container of anything and everything out of institutional practice, it obscures dialectical interactions and complexities. I suggest no naïve abandonment of doctrinal materials, nor denying the distinction between the two, but rather nuancing how scholars should approach available sources, to appreciate the complex dynamics of Chinese religions without presuming a dualistic view. Folk practices have been "absent" but also "preserved" by the doctrinal text. In Fei Changfang's assessment, the popular divination practice attempts endorsement derived from an authoritative text. When the authenticity of the text is in question, the defenders of the text find justification in ubiquitous practice. Outside his scholastic training, Ouyi was taught about Zhancha divination by a lay person. Ouyi found inspiration in divination's ability to give affirmative results, and he wrote commentaries to further promote divination practices in his community. The practice of divination is present through these exceptional textual moments, when the two encounter, converge, and mutually enhance each other. Today Zhancha divination remains a favored practice, the result of constant interactions between doctrine and practice.

Notes

1 The specific term used here should be translated literarily as "sign of wheel," indicating the result by means of wooden dice used in the divination.
2 Epilog of *Zhacha shan'e yebaojing yishu*, X.21.371.455a3-4.
3 It is generally accepted that *Zhanchajing* was produced between 570 and 590 in China, while several scholars such as Fujii Shigetoshi, based on inter-textual evidence, have presented the hypothesis that *Zhanchajing* was produced in Korea. Mochitsuki Shinkō is the first scholar who studied *Zhanchajing* together with Wakening of Faith (*Dacheng qixin lun*) and concluded *Zhanchajing* was composed first. Kashiwagi Hirō concluded that *Zhanchajing* was composed later than the *Wakening of Faith in the Mahāyāna* (*Dacheng qixin lun*).
4 See Brandon Dotson, Constance A. Cook, Zhao Lu, *Dice and Gods on the Silk Road: Chinese Buddhist Dice Divination in Transcultural Context* (Leiden: Brill, 2021).
5 Leonard Norman Primiano, 1995, 39.
6 Primiano, "Afterward: Manifestations of the Religious Vernacular: Ambiguity, Power, and Creativity." *Vernacular Religion in Everyday Life* (Routledge, 2012), 394–406.
7 See Stephen F. Teiser (1995), Adam Yuet Chau (2005), and Kenneth Dean (2011).
8 Don Yoder, *Discovering American Folklore: Studies in Ethnic, Religious, and Regional Culture* (Ann Arbor: UMI Research Press, 1990), 76.
9 Kyoko Tokuno, "The Evaluation of Indigenous Scriptures in Chinese Buddhist Bibliographical Catalogues." *Chinese Buddhist Apocrypha*, ed. Robert E. Buswell (Honolulu: University of Hawaii Press, 1990), 31–74.
10 Daoxuan, *Datang neidian lu*. T.55.2149.279a28-b13. Daoxuan copied this passage from Fei Changfang's *Lidai sanbao ji*. T.49.2034.106c8-22.
11 *Zhongjing mulu*, T.55.2146.127c16-17.
12 Fei Changfang, *Lidai sanbao ji*, T.49.2034.106c9-22.
13 Fei Changfang, *Lidai sanbao ji*, T.49.2034.106c9-22.
14 *Dazhou kanding zhongjing mulu* (Catalog of Buddhist sūtra compiled in the great Zhou Dynasty, T.55.2153).
15 *Kaiyuan shijiao lu* (Catalog of Buddhist teaching in the reign title Kaiyuan, T.55.2154.)
16 *Kaiyuan shijiao lu*, T.55.2154.551a19-21.
17 I do not rule out the possibility that Zhisheng affirmed the decision made by Empress Wu's catalog out of political consideration; however, we should not forget that Zhisheng finished his catalog in 730 when the political legacy of Empress Wu (reign 690–705) would have ceased to be a primary concern.
18 Chen Ming. 1999. "'*Zhancha shan'e yebaojing' de liuchuan yanjiu*." *Nanya yanjiu* 1:60.
19 Endo Junichiro. 2000. "*Sensa zenaku gyōhōkyō to chigi no zanhō*." *Chisan gakuho* 49: 95–125; Ikehira Noriko. "*Sensatsu zen aku kōhō kyō no seiritsu to denpo ni tsuite*." *Tōdai no shūkyō*, ed. Yoshikawa Tadao (Kyoto: Hōyūshoden, 2000), 355–380.
20 Moro Shigeki identified that the popular practice of repentance resembles the description in texts such as *Guanfo sanmeihai jing* 觀佛三昧海經, Shandao's Pure Land practice, and *Chan miyao fajing* 禪密要法經. "*Sensakkyō no seiritsu to juyō—naze uranai ga hitsuyō to sareta no ka*." *Nihon bukkyō gakkai nenpō* 77:140–141.
21 Funayama Tōru. 2002. "*Kanyaku to chūgoku sanjutsu no aita—kanbun butten ni tokuyūna keidai o megutte*." *Bukkyo shigaku kenkyū* 45(1):1–28.
22 Beverley Foulks McGuire has a detailed description of the three-round divination process. See *Living Karma: The Religious Practice of Ouyi Zhixu* (New York: Columbia University Press, 2014), 34–35.
23 Lien-sheng Yang suggested the practice of zipu might have roots in the Taipingdao movement in the Han dynasty. See "*Daojiao zhi zipu yu fojiao zhi zipu*." In *Bukkyō shigaku ronshū: Tsukamoto Zenryū shōju* (Kyoto: Kyoto University, Jimbun kagaku kenkyūsho, 1961), 962–969.

24 Brandon Dotson, Constance A. Cook, Zhao Lu, *Dice and Gods on the Silk Road: Chinese Buddhist Dice Divination in Transcultural Context* (Leiden: Brill, 2021), 42: 156–160.
25 Ibid., 159–160.
26 Esther-Maria Guggenmos, 2018. "Qian Divination and Its Ritual Adaptations in Chinese Buddhism." *Journal of Chinese Religions*, 46(1): 60.
27 The ten wholesome deeds are not killing, not stealing, not committing adultery, not lying, not speaking harshly, not speaking idly, not being greedy, not being angry, and not having erroneous views.
28 *Zhanchajing*, T.17.839.904a27-28.
29 *Xu gaosengzhuan*, T.50.2060.700a19-21.
30 *Xu gaosengzhuan*, T.50.2060.700a26-29.
31 *Zhancha shan'e yebao jing yishu*, X.21.371.426a13-16.
32 *Zhancha shan'e yebao jing yishu*, X.21.371.453b5-6.
33 *Zhancha shan'e yebao jing xingfa*, X.74.1485.578c12-14.
34 *Zhancha shan'e yebao jing xingfa*, X.74.1485.582a16-17.
35 Beverley Foulks McGuire, *Living Karma: The Religious Practice of Ouyi Zhixu* (New York: Columbia University Press, 2014), 31.
36 "*Qian anjuri gong jiu wen*" 前安居日供鬮文, *Ouyi dashi quanji*, vol.16, 10305–10310.
37 "*Yu liaoyin yiqie zisu*" 與了因一切緇素, *Ouyi dashi quanji*, vol.17, 10973–10975.
38 "*Qian anjuri gong jiu wen.*" *Ouyi dashi quanji*, vol.16, 10307.
39 My reading clearly differs from Whalen Lai (1990) who sees that Ouyi's continuous practice finally yield to the sign of purification.
40 "*Yu liaoyin yiqie zisu.*" *Ouyi dashi quanji*, vol. 17, 10974–10975.
41 *Zhanchajing*, T.17.839.904c16-18.
42 Sōshō宗性, *Enryaku sōroku* 延暦僧録, *Nihon kōsōden yōmonshō* 日本高僧伝要文抄, BZ.101.69.
43 *Kanyaku sangoku iji* (Tōkyō: Akashi Shoten, 1997), 361. There is a further interpretation of the divination reading in three other biographies in the same text (see 302, 366, 372), suggesting the popularity of Zhancha divination in Korean Buddhism.
44 *Kanyaku sangoku iji* (Tōkyō: Akashi Shoten, 1997), 362.
45 *Kanyaku sangoku iji* (Tōkyō: Akashi Shoten, 1997), 362.
46 "*Dabing zhong qijian jingshe yuanwen*" 大病中启建净社愿文, *Ouyi dashi quanji*, vol.17, 10383.
47 *Zhancha shan'e yebao jing yishu,* X.21.371.433c5–7.
48 "*Yu shenfu shoufu dun*"与沈甫受甫敦, *Ouyi dashi quanji*, vol.17, 10972.
49 "*Zutang jie tabeitan chanwen*" 祖堂結大悲壇懺文, *Ouyi dashi quanji*, vol.17, 10370–10371.
50 "*Zutang jie tabeitan chanwen.*" *Ouyi dashi quanji*, vol.17, 10371.
51 "*Dabing zhong qijian jingshe yuanwen.*" *Ouyi dashi quanji*, vol.17, 10383.
52 "*Lingfeng ouyi dashi zonglun xushuo*" 灵峰蕅益大师宗论序說, *Ouyi dashi quanji*, vol.17, 10201.
53 "*Zhancha xingfa yuanwen*" 占察行法願文, *Ouyi dashi quanji*, vol.17, 10375.

Primary Texts and Collections

Daoxuan 道宣. *Datang neidian lu* 大唐內典錄, T.55.2149.
———. *Xu gaosengzhuan*, 續高僧傳, T.50.2060.
Fajing 法經. *Zhongjing mulu* 眾經目錄, T.55.2146.
Fei Changfang 費長房. *Lidai sanbao ji* 歷代三寶記, T.49.2034.
Iryŏn 一然. *Samguk yusa* 三国遺事, T.49.2039. And in *Kanyaku sangoku iji* 完訳三国遺事. 1997. Translated by and Sa-yŏp Kim 金思燁, Tōkyō: Akashi Shoten.
Mingquan 明佺. *Dazhou kanding zhongjing mulu* 大周刊定眾經目錄, T.55.2153.
Ouyi Zhixu 蕅益智旭. *Ouyi dashi quanji* 蕅益大師全集. Taipei: Fojiao shuju, 1989.

———. *Zhancha shan'e yebaojing xingfa* 占察善惡業報經行法, X.74.1485.
———. *Zhancha shan'e yebaojing xuanyi* 占察善惡業報經玄義, X.21.370.
———. *Zhancha shan'e yebaojing shu* 占察善惡業報經疏, X.21.371.
Puti deng 菩提燈 (attributed) trans. *Zhancha shan'e yebao jing* 占察善惡業報經, T.17.839.
Sōshō 宗性. *Enryaku sōroku* 延暦僧録. *Nihon kōsōden yōmonshō* 日本高僧伝要文抄, BZ.101.
Zhisheng 智昇. *Kaiyuan shijiao lu* 開元釋教錄, T.55.2154.

Secondary Scholarship

Aramaki Noritoshi 荒牧典俊. 1997. "*Chūgoku bukkyō toha nani ka soshi nishi rai'i no imi suru mono*" 中国仏教とは何か「祖師西来意」の意味するもの. *Chūgoku shakai to bunka* 中国一社会と文化 12:4–40.

Chau, Adam Yuet. 2005. *Miraculous Response: Doing Popular Religion in Contemporary China.*

Chen Ming 陳明. 1999. "'*Zhancha shan'e yebaojing' de liuchuan yanjiu*" 占察善惡業報的流傳研究. *Nanya yanjiu* 南亞研究 1:58–65.

Dean, Kenneth. 2011. "Local Ritual Traditions of Southeast China: A Challenge to Definitions of Religion and Theories of Ritual," *Social Scientific Study of Religion in China: Methodology, Theories, and Findings*, ed. Fenggang Yang and Graeme Lang, Leiden: Brill, 133–165.

Dotson, Brandon, Constance A. Cook, Zhao Lu. 2021. *Dice and Gods on the Silk Road: Chinese Buddhist Dice Divination in Transcultural Context*. Leiden: Brill.

Endo Junichiro 遠藤純一郎. 2000. "'*Sensa zenaku gyōhōkyō' to chigi no zanhō*" 『占察善悪業報経』と智顗の懺法. *Chisan gakuho* 智山学報 49:95–125.

Endō Junyū 遠藤純祐. 2000. "'*Senzatsu zen'aku gōhōkyō' no shinkō*" 「占察善悪業報経」の信仰. *Gendai Mikkyo* 現代密教 13:85–304.

Funayama Tōru 船山徹. 2002. "*Kanyaku to chūgoku sanjutsu no aita—kanbun butten ni tokuyūna keidai o megutte*" 「漢訳」と「中国撰述」の間——漢文仏典に特有な形態をめぐって. *Bukkyo shigaku kenkyū* 仏教史学研究 45(1):1–28.

Guggenmos, Esther-Maria. 2018. "Qian Divination and Its Ritual Adaptations in Chinese Buddhism." *Journal of Chinese Religions* 46(1):43–70.

Ikehira Noriko 池平紀子. 2000. "*Sensatsu zen aku kōhō kyō no seiritsu to denpo ni tsuite*" 『占察善悪業報経』の成立と伝播について, *Tōdai no shūkyō* 唐代の宗教, ed. Yoshikawa Tadao 吉川忠夫. Kyōto: Hōyūshoden.

Kashiwagi Hirō 柏木弘雄. 1981. *Daijō kishinrun no kenkyū* 大乗起信論の研究. Tōkyō: Shunjūsha.

Kuo Li-ying. 1994. "Divination, jeux de hasard et purification dans le bouddhisme chinois: autour d'un sūtra apocryphe chinois, le Zhanchajing." *Bouddhisme et cultures locales: quelques cas de réciproques adaptations*, ed. Fumimasa Fukui and Gérard Fussman. Paris: EFEO, 145–167.

Kyoko Tokuno. 1990. "The Evaluation of Indigenous Scriptures in Chinese Buddhist Bibliographical Catalogues." *Chinese Buddhist Apocrypha*, ed. Robert E. Buswell, Honolulu: University of Hawaii Press, 31–74.

Lai, Whalen. 1990. "The Chan-ch'a ching: Religion and Magic in Medieval China." *Chinese Buddhist Apocrypha*, ed. Robert Buswell. Honolulu: University of Hawai'i Press, 175–206.

Makita Tairyō 牧田諦亮. 1976. *Gikyō kenkyū* 疑経研究. Kyōto: Jinbun Kagaku kenkyūjo.

McGuire, Beverley Foulks. 2014. *Living Karma: The Religious Practice of Ouyi Zhixu*. New York: Columbia University Press.

Mochitsuki Shinkō 望月信亨. 1922. *Daijō kishinrun no kenkyū* 大乘起信論之研究. Tōkyō: Kanao Bunendō.

Moro Shigeki 師茂樹. 2011. "*Sensatsukyō no seiritsu to juyō—naze uranai ga hitsuyō to sareta no ka*" 占察経の成立と受容—なぜ占いが必要とされたのか. *Nihon bukkyō gakkai nenpō* 日本仏教学会年報, 77:135–157.

Primiano, Leonard Norman. 1995. "Vernacular Religion and the Search for Method in Religious Folklife." *Western Folklore (Reflexivity and the Study of Belief)*, 54 (1): 37–56.

———. 2012. "Afterward: Manifestations of the Religious Vernacular: Ambiguity, Power, and Creativity." *Vernacular Religion in Everyday Life*. Routledge, 394–406.

Sakagami Masao 坂上雅翁. 1984. *Nanto bukkyō niokeru sensatsukyō no juō to tenkai* 南都仏教における『占察経』の受容と展開. *Taishō daigaku sōgō bukkyō kenkyūsho nenpō* 大正大学総合研究所年報, 6:1–16.

Teiser, Stephen F. 1995. "Popular Religion." *Journal of Asian Studies,* 54(2):378–395.

Ven, Shengyan 聖嚴. 1975. *Meimatsu chugoku bukkyō no kenkyū tokuni o chushin toshite* 明末中国仏教の研究ー特に智旭を中心として. Tōkyō: Sankibōbusshorin.

Yang Liensheng. 1961. "*Daojiao zhi zipu yu fojiao zhi zipu* 道教自撲與佛教自撲." *Bukkyō shigaku ronshū: Tsukamoto Zenryū shōju* 仏教史学論集: 塚本博士頌寿記念. Kyōto: Jimbun kagaku kenkyūsho Kyōto University, 962–969.

Yoder, Don. 1990. *Discovering American Folklore: Studies in Ethnic, Religious, and Regional Culture*. Ann Arbor: UMI Research Press.

11

SPELLBINDING SKALDS

Music as Ritual in Nordic Neopaganism

Padraic Fitzgerald and Mathias Nordvig

Nordic Neopaganism is, roughly, the revival of various folk beliefs derived from the Scandinavian and Germanic cultural areas in Northern Europe. Nordic Neopaganism is multifaceted and largely vernacular, as scholar Leonard Primiano employs the term (Primiano 44). How adherents live and develop their personal iteration of Nordic Neopaganism differs at the community level and varies even further according to the individual. Recent scholarship defines Nordic Neopaganism as a "non-dogmatic community belief" with no central clerical authority determining the manner of how people believe or practice (Nordvig 5). The non-dogmatic nature of Nordic Neopagan practice allows for ritual creativity, enabling people to personally tailor how they practice and how they live this worldview. In fleshing out their personal ritual practice, adherents make recourse to the vast body of Nordic "lore", including regional popular myths and poetry, Scandinavian history, and Northern European folklore (Nordvig 24). Musically, contemporary Nordic folk musical groups elaborate on this lore and are facets of it themselves; they incorporate this corpus into ritual compositional and personal practices. The music resulting from such practices affects people and puts them in touch with an imagined Nordic past.

In the music scene attached to Nordic Neopaganism, two musical groups are prominently featured: Heilung and Wardruna. Wardruna is a Norwegian band, originally founded by two black metal musicians from the band Gorgoroth, Kristian Espedal (Gaahl), and Einar Selvik. Heilung is a multinational band with a core group in Denmark. The members are from Denmark, Norway, Germany, the Netherlands, and elsewhere in Northern Europe. The Danish-German front-man, Kai Uwe Faust, is a well-known tattoo artist specializing in historical Nordic imagery. The frontwoman is Maria Franz,

DOI: 10.4324/9781003257462-15

a Norwegian singer and Viking Age history re-enactor. Despite being adjacent to heavy metal subculture, Wardruna and Heilung are considered as belonging to the emergent "Dark Nordic Folk" genre (Leivers "The Drum Needed a Blood Sacrifice"). The members and many of their audience self-identify as Nordic Neopagans.

Dark Nordic Folk emerged at the intersection of extreme metal and Nordic folk music, and is characterized by its foreboding and energizing sound. This sound is defined by the use of traditional melodies, instruments such as the lur, drums crafted of hide and wood, and the jaw harp. Additionally, the lyrical content is gleaned from or inspired by pre-Christian Nordic folk culture, emphasizing aspects of gods, spirits, nature, and mythology. With such lyrical content, the songs of Dark Nordic Folk are popular among those identifying with Nordic Neopaganism, and in the case of bands Wardruna and Heilung, the primary performers openly associate with Nordic Neopagan beliefs (Nordvig "Interview with Kai Faust"). In a way, the musicians of both bands carry on the tradition of the skald - those poets, singers, and lore keepers hailing from the Nordic cultural area.

Heilung and Wardruna represent live musical performance as a distinctly Nordic folk oriented, spiritually charged event, which may carry religious import to the audience. Drawing on preserved folk practices and idealized pre-Christian history of Northern Europe, the bands claim to collapse time between the distant past and the present "now" in their performances. Nordic Neopagan-aligned listeners participate in an imagined ancient time, cultivating experiences that realize past Nordic-Germanic concepts and practices in the present. In that way, Nordic Neopagans continually form and reform spiritual identities and experience connectedness with a culture distant in space and time.

If Nordic Neopaganism can be understood as a modern folk belief, a system of ideas and beliefs detached from and running counter to "official" or culturally accepted forms of religion (Yoder 14), then it is possible to perceive the performances of Heilung and Wardruna as vernacular religious ritual, in line with Leonard Primiano's notion of vernacular religion. Below, we will examine the musical experience of Heilung and Wardruna utilizing the definitions of folk and vernacular religion provided by Yoder and Primiano. We will describe a subsection of survey data provided by scholar of anthropological science Ruben Terlouw, himself a previous performer in the band Heilung. These data findings nuance a description of the experience of a Heilung "ritual". Furthermore, we will examine the activities and rituals that bands such as Wardruna and Heilung enact to imbue themselves and their performances with an affective quality. Finally, we will explore the role of music as an affective spiritual medium, establishing that engagement with Nordic folk music can be understood as a vernacular ritual in the space of rapidly growing, global folk religion.

Theory and Method

In his article "Towards a Definition of Folk Religion", folklorist Don Yoder explores the use of the term "folk religion". His definition of folk religion is as follows:

> "folk religion is the 'folk-cultural' dimension of religion or the religious dimension of folk culture. This can include active/creative as well as passive survivalist elements, it also certainly can suggest the element of tension existing between folk and official levels of religion in a complex society."
>
> *(Yoder 14)*

He continues: "Folk religion is the totality of all those views and practices of religion that exist among the people apart from and alongside the strictly theological and liturgical forms of the official religion" (14).

Nordic Neopaganism represents an example of contemporary folk religion. The beliefs we refer to under the umbrella definition of "Nordic Neopaganism" emerged in contemporary form between the 1950s and 1970s. In Iceland, Ásatrúarfélagið[1] was founded in 1972 by a group of practitioners surrounding the farmer and poet Sveinbjörn Beinteinson, who intended to create "a loose organization who believed in the old gods and other deities associated with the old Heathen times." This group has since grown to become a state-recognized religion in Iceland (Strmiska 166). In the USA, the Viking Brotherhood was established in California by Stephen McNallen and Robert Stine, also in the early 1970s (Strmiska 129). Scholar of Neopaganism Michael Strmiska notes that the Viking Brotherhood would change into the Asatru Folk Assembly,[2] one of the many North American Nordic Neopagan organizations to establish a loose hierarchy—based on a perceived Nordic worldview and with a ritual body gleaned from medieval Nordic and English literature—claiming to represent "Scandinavian warrior life" (139). These texts - along with sources such as music and the works of social media personalities - may be considered facets of Nordic Neopagan "lore" (Nordvig 24).

The insistence among practitioners that Nordic Neopaganism is non-dogmatic, without orthodoxy and orthopraxy, in addition to a myriad of local authorities and groups who inform individual praxis, means that Nordic Neopaganism can look different depending on who is practicing it and who is characterizing it. This non-dogmatic atmosphere allows spiritual creativity, leading to many adherents looking toward other religions, other Neopagan spiritualities, and toward indigenous traditions for inspiration. This fluidity of belief fits Yoder's assertion that "the reinterpretations of the official religion are on the folk level" and his claim that folk religion includes passive and active elements such as witchcraft and magic and the engagement with religious visual and sonic arts

(Yoder 15). We propose that Nordic Neopaganism is an example of a contemporary folk religion. Yoder's definition is valuable as a point of departure toward a narrower definition and theory of vernacular religion as presented by Leonard Primiano in his 1995 article "Vernacular Religion and the Search for Method in Religious Folklife". Primiano provides a crucial component to our understanding of Nordic Neopaganism: adherents engage individual and small group beliefs drawn from the body of lore, but ultimately their personal beliefs, outlooks, and private practice will differ from person to person. Primiano emphasizes the individual nature of religious belief and utilizes the term "vernacular" to emphasize that religion, regardless of its form, is a personal endeavor; religion will shift when an individual believer experiences new religious encounters from either within or without their personal belief system and subsequently modifies their personal belief and practice with what they have deemed as beneficial from these encounters.

Primiano explains that:

> "vernacular religious theory involves an interdisciplinary approach to the study of the religious lives of individuals with special attention to the process of religious belief, the verbal, behavioral, and material expressions of religious belief, and the ultimate object of religious belief involving a process of acquisition and formation by way of conscious and unconscious negotiations of and between believers".
>
> *(Primiano 44)*

With vernacular religion, "individual beliefs need not be founded in or based on ideas or practices emanating from a group oriented and structured religious institution" (50). Primiano continues, describing North American iteration of Wiccan Neopaganism: "although they (Wiccans) receive collective materials from sources deemed part of popular culture as well as conventional folklore sources, as solitaries they formulate their religious path on their own" (50). Yoder's definition of folk religion as a belief sitting alongside and in contrast to mainstream belief systems describes Nordic Neopaganism's condition alongside Protestant-influenced Western secularism. Primiano's theory of vernacular religion may be applied to Nordic Neopaganism as well, because individual adherents shape their beliefs and allow their beliefs to be shaped through constructive interaction with other believers, whether they be "everyday" practitioners or those occupying places of spiritual authority, such as prominent figures in the Nordic Neopagan digital community or musicians.

To address Nordic Neopaganism, a widely varied practice, as a vernacular religion akin to folk religion, we suggest that musical groups represent unifying factors for ritual praxis that, in large part, transcend individual and group adherence. While it could be argued that any self-identifying Nordic Neopagan is practicing their own vernacular religion within a folk religion, we can observe on the macro level that Nordic Neopaganism is a contemporary folk religion that critiques ingrained social and religious traditions, which in the case of most practitioners happens to be Western Christianity (Davey 4). Understood as a non-dogmatic folk religion, Nordic Neopaganism privileges adherents with personal creativity in the ritual sphere. As such, an emerging trend in the realm of praxis is the engagement with music as ritual either at a live performance or in solitude (Terlouw "Ancient Resonance").

Self-narration, Sacrality, and Authenticity

In February 2020, Ruben Terlouw, a scholar of archaeology and former member of the band Heilung, submitted his thesis for his Bachelor of Science in archaeology at Saxion University of applied sciences in Enschede, Nederland. Terlouw's project concerned the exploration of audio in a museum setting, analyzing how the use of sound immerses people and enhances their experience of the historical objects on display. These soundscapes, Terlouw argued, must be composed with the aid of historically accurate instruments of the period corresponding to the objects being displayed (Terlouw 18). As a musical group defined as Dark Nordic Folk, Heilung narrate themselves as conveyors and performers of "amplified history". This amplified history is brought to the present through a ritualistic performance utilizing period appropriate instruments, lyricism, and fragments of past ritual practice that can be said to collapse time and space for those open to an affective experience of the pre-Christian Nordic past (Reed "Denmark's Heilung").

Ruben disseminated a survey on Heilung's Facebook page on July 2, 2019 that ultimately garnered 5256 respondents. This survey asked questions largely concerned with what, if any, role Heilung has had in developing personal interest in Northern European history, how frequently respondents visited museums, and how important it is that Heilung utilizes presumed historical garb and instruments in their performances, and if this lends to their perceived authenticity (Terlouw 7). Terlouw left space for respondents to add additional comments.

Ruben was incredibly kind and offered to share the spreadsheet of data from his survey with us. Additionally, he gave us permission to utilize any data trends we noticed. We did not use any data related to the questions Ruben was asking in his survey, rather, we utilized the optional comment section he included as part of his survey. Within, we noticed something interesting. Of the 5256 respondents, 10.05% left comments indicating that the musical experience provided by Heilung imparted the sensation of "being transported to the past", being "put in touch with their roots", and having a distinctly Nordic spiritual awakening. Additionally, 2.6% of respondents elaborated in the comment section that they explicitly identified as Nordic Neopagan and stated that they engaged with Heilung's music in personal spiritual practices. Ruben was kind enough to share his survey spreadsheet with us. While the percentages of respondents who clearly engage the music in a ritualistic manner are relatively low, the presence

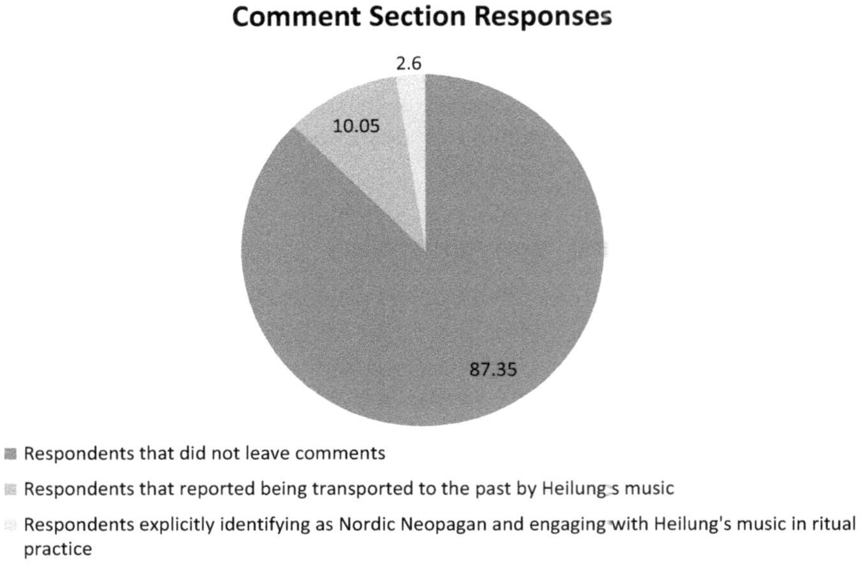

of individuals who offer insight into the religious Nordic Neopagan significance of Heilung's music allows us to theorize that some participants in Heilung's fanbase consider the concerts and music to be, in part, modern Nordic folk ritual. We attended Heilung's sole North American performance of 2021 and observed Nordic Neopagan-aligned bodies in (perceived) historical garb: Thor's hammer pendants, and other signifiers such as particular hairstyles, tattoos, and runic body paint.[3]

Heilung and Wardruna narrate themselves to be culturally and spiritually charged musical groups. This multivalent self-narration is carried out through interviews, videos, and pictures disseminated on social media and engaged by fans. These self-narratives offer a glimpse into the bands' creative praxis and reveal the ritualistic, creative, and performance processes undertaken which reinforces their authenticity as both practitioners and authoritative figures in the Nordic Neopagan sphere and imbues their music with affective power. An aspect of these ritualistic processes is captured in concert recordings, but it is also revealed through written and recorded interviews and posts on social media.

Heilung's members have explained that they utilize musical performance to make past Nordic folk sensibilities real in the present (Reed "Denmark's Heilung"). One way they accomplish this is through utilizing elaborate ritual garb. They evoke themselves as ancient Nordic seers and warriors. Their ritualized creative process, utilization of historically accurate instrumentation, and composed lyrics in both Old Norse and Proto-Germanic transport the audience to a liminal space in which another time is brought to the present. Heilung emphasize that their purpose is to convey reconstructed physical, primordial histories reflective of Nordic Europe. Front-man Kai Uwe Faust, in an interview with Revolver Magazine (Reed "Denmark's Heilung"), states:

> "We try to give a little spark of that emotion: to make people feel how it is to be surrounded by nature, to slaughter their own cattle, to build their own drum, to live from the Earth and feel a part of a universal tribal spirit."

Faust and bandmate Maria Franz grew up with the old folklore and "lived histories"; they both refer to the importance of historical research and reenactments to their current places in life and the art continue to produce (Reed "Denmark's Heilung"). Franz relates a personal tale of the importance of participating in reconstructed history:

> "I didn't feel like I could connect to people around me. But everything changed when I was eleven and I found the Viking reenactment in my hometown. I figured out I could play a drum, I could shoot a bow and arrow, I could make clothes. I felt empowered by that. You make friends and sit around the bonfire with people ten years older than you, exchanging life stories. That's a beautiful place to grow up, and that saved me".
>
> *-(Reed "Denmark's Heilung")-*

Later in the article, Faust shares a similar tale, explaining that he grew up in a very conservative Christian household and felt stifled, going so far as to delve into "Satanic" practice to rebel against his parents. By finding and ultimately identifying with old Germanic shamanistic practice and the associated Norse/Germanic beliefs, he was brought back from an existence punctuated by otherness and sadness (Reed "Denmark's Heilung").

Contemporary Nordic Neopaganism breaks from the dominant Western cultural paradigm through forging relationships with gods in the natural world and through practitioners locating divinity as imminent rather than transcendent. Recognizing divinity's place in the world bolsters Nordic Neopaganism as a religious counter-cultural movement running parallel to secular Christian-influenced Western culture, that dominant culture that enables environmental degradation and the understanding that humans are set apart from nature rather than being of it. Movements emerging within Nordic Neopaganism, namely Nordic Animism, actively discuss and advocate for such a worldview (Rasmussen "Nordic Animism and Academia").

Heilung and Wardruna are groups that self-narrate their creative ritual processes to cement their spiritual authenticity, which carries over to their musical performances that provide a distinctly Nordic Neopagan experience to fans. This self-narrative is carried across social media platforms and in interviews with popular news and culture outlets. Speaking on behalf of Wardruna in an interview with *VICE Magazine*, lead vocalist Einar Selvik narrates that he and his contemporaries actively seek to empower their sound through a consciously ritualistic creative process involving the construction and performance of traditional Nordic instruments, the use of Old Norse as a composition language, the use of traditional melodies, and the use of elements from the natural world such as the ambiance of a flowing river or the sounds of colliding glacial ice cores (Handelman "Wardruna").

In an interview with YouTube Channel *FaceCulture,* Selvik provides a personal narrative describing his involvement with Norwegian history and pre-Christian belief. He states:

> "these things have resonated with me, I learned about them as a child and my father would take me to these places corresponding with the old stories, and then when we began learning about these things in school, they made more sense to me because of being raised around them".
>
> *(Metal Hammer)*

Though Selvik avoids labeling Wardruna's music as explicitly religious, he admits to trance states and professes a "spirituality" surrounding his subject material and how he wants to share it with the world. He elaborates: "I'm not a fan of belief systems that preach, through Wardruna I want to show people what these old practices mean to me, the music can speak to them" (FaceCulture). Wardruna and their songs are described by Selvik as a methodology for spiritual reconstruction: he explains that "this is not about any sort of re-enactment of what was, all we possess of the old ways are fragments; Wardruna to me is about sowing new seeds so that something new and magnificent may grow" (FaceCulture "Interview Wardruna").

Wardruna further reinforce their Nordic character by narrating and sharing the conscious, and occasionally ritualistic, effort of their creative process. From his interview with VICE Magazine, Selvik recalls how during the recording of their song "Isa", named after the runic letter associated with snow and ice, the group worked with the Norwegian national park service to access ice cores from a local glacier to use for percussion (Handelman "Wardruna"). Using glacial cores in such a way gives the phenomenon of ice a sound, and that the cores are old enough to have been around when Nordic folk religion was the norm further enhances the mystique of this compositional choice. Another instance of this engagement with natural forces occurred during the recording process of their song "Laukr", named after the runic letter associated with flowing water. Selvik relayed that he insisted on recording himself delivering the Old Norse lyrics while partially submerged in a river (Leivers "The Drum Needed a Blood Sacrifice").

Both bands' self-narration efforts are strengthened through live performances. While musical performances may be understood as ritual, Heilung explicitly treat theirs as such. The ritualistic nature of their performances are opened and closed with blessing rituals and are punctuated with descriptions of the historical and spiritual qualities of the songs being performed. One such blessing has become a staple of their live rituals; we experienced it at their Red Rocks performance, and it can be seen in a professional recording of one of their concerts on YouTube: "Remember that we are all brothers; all people, beasts, trees and stones and wind. We all descended from the one great being that was always there before people lived and named it, before the first seed sprouted" (Heilung). This recitation along with brief talks and explanations that punctuate the spaces between songs reinforces the narrative and the ritualistic character of their performances. Heilung's legitimacy as perceived spiritual authority figures is further reinforced by their proclivity to invite ritual specialists hailing from first nations and indigenous groups to perform with them. At their 2021 Red Rocks performance, we observed that the band involved medicine specialists hailing from the Plains and Rocky Mountains first nations, who performed during the opening and closing ritual sequences and provided additional percussion at certain points in the performance with their personal drums.

Heilung's inclusion of indigenous spiritual specialists is not localized to just their North American performances. Recounting the first time the group performed in Russia, Heilung's producer Christopher Juul explained to *The Guardian* that news of their arrival brought a handful of Siberian shamans to their show who were invited on stage to join in the performance (Leivers). Juul elaborates that the shaman "just showed up in full gear, drumming along with us. They got it. We cried" (Leivers "The Drum Needed a Blood Sacrifice"). While in certain contexts this could be seen as problematic due to the history of indigenous and first nations' practices being co-opted and exploited by non-indigenous parties, in their social media narrative Heilung are respectful in their inclusion of these ritual specialists in their performances. This engagement with indigenous ritual and medicine specialists legitimizes the group, granting them authority but also reinforcing their authenticity as spiritually inclined figures of authority within the Nordic Neopagan sphere.

Heilung further strengthen their narrative and authenticity by crafting instruments and costumes in accordance with historical records and making use of specific natural materials, and the most notorious among them are human blood and bone. When asked about the use of human bones, Kai Uwe Faust explained that:

> "it adds a ritualistic touch. In Tibetan ritual music, you have a drum made from two human skull caps, you have a flute made from a human thigh bone. In Africa, a lot of instruments are made with human skin. For people from older cultures, it's important for them to have good connections to their ancestors."-
>
> *(Leivers "The Drum Needed a Blood Sacrifice")*

To their credit, members of Heilung have quite literally given a part of themselves to sanctify their chosen instruments. Using their own blood, professionally extracted by a friend of the band who is a nurse, they have ritually blessed the tools of their craft, most notably the large drum they have named "Blod" (blood) that possesses a distinctive red stain from the act (Leivers "The Drum Needed a Blood Sacrifice").

Spiritual Medium and Soundscape

Ritualistic creative efforts, performances, and their self-narration locating the groups within a pre-Christian Nordic spiritual context serve to not only legitimize these bands as Nordic Neopagan authority figures but also to charge their songs with spiritual meaning that affects receptive bodies. The notion of affect, described by Donovan Schaefer as "the flow of forces through bodies outside of, prior to, and underneath language" (Schaefer 4), may serve as a point of departure when exploring music's power in a religious space. Schaefer explains affect as a "thing of the senses" and invites readers to envision a power "outside of a symbol system, something enfolding and exceeding language in the ways it plays across bodies" (Schaefer 23). Scholars of religious studies have noted sound and music's affective capacities and capability to evoke visceral emotions, conceptions, and perceptions in non-traditionally religious spaces. In his piece *Traces of the Spirit*, Robin Sylvan elucidates that sound is a religious medium par excellence because it affects subjects across multiple levels of the sensorium, the sensing elements of human physiology. Music is an ideal medium for the expression of the religious impulse due to its capacity to simultaneously affect subjects at different levels of reality, such as the physical, psychological, and virtual (Sylvan 6). Engaging with the ideas of musicologist Andrew Neher, Sylvan explains that when the body experiences sound, the sound elicits physical reactions and across multiple levels of human physiology. Sylvan discusses Neher's observation that the experience of music causes a "synchronization of cortical rhythms", "rhythms that 'tune' the body and its various subsystems, including circadian rhythms, heartbeat, breathing rate, and muscular activity" (22). This multi-layered corporeal synchronization represents what musicologist Gilbert Rouget identifies as "a nearly universal cross-cultural technique in bringing about trance and possession states" (22). This quality of music to affect the body in such a way reinforces it as a medium for religious experience in a vernacular folk tradition such as Nordic Neopaganism.

The affective capability of music to bring about spiritual experience in a non-traditional setting is further echoed by scholar Owen Coggins in his book-*Mysticism, Ritual, and Religion in Drone Metal.* One of Coggins' more striking elucidations is that of "imagined elsewheres", correlating to Sylvan's level of the virtual (Coggins 84). Imagined elsewhere are culturally informed realms of the imaginary which are experienced when exposed to the rhythms and melodies of specific instruments, culturally and historically specific lyrics, and imagery accompanying these aforementioned factors whether in the form of album art or the regalia of the performers. The music of Wardruna and Heilung operates in a similar fashion, drawing their followers into an idealized Nordic elsewhere with their ritualistic performances enhanced by their ongoing personal narratives and composition choices.

Music, particularly those kinds that are coded as culturally or spiritually charged, sanctifies a space where the said music is experienced. In *The Ethical Soundscape: Cassette Sermons and Islamic Counterpublics*, Charles Hirschkind examines affective soundscapes, or sonic environments, in the Cairene Muslim community. Cairene Muslims actively engage in the construction of "pious" soundscapes by regularly playing recorded sermons from popular imams (Hirschkind 12). By playing these recorded sermons consistently, Cairene Muslims create, and immerse themselves within, an affective soundscape they claim impacts their spiritual lives. Hirschkind argues that this soundscape contributes to the conditioning of an ideal form of piety by creating the sensory conditions for a Muslim ethical lifeworld (16). Engaging these cassette sermons is a technique of self-fashioning predicated on engaged listening, albeit one elaborated in ethical terms and in relation to a theologically Islamic form of reasoning (16). Returning to Heilung and Wardruna, these bands construct soundscapes that convey Nordic cultural symbolism and ideology to receptive individuals who are immersed within such soundscapes. These Nordic soundscapes are empowered by the ongoing narration of these musical groups: their ritualized composition processes and performances undertaken by these groups shared with fans via social media. These processes serve to instill voices and instruments with a perceived ancient power that can collapse time and space for listeners, aid them in making meaning, and occasion spiritual experience.

To Conclude... Vernacular Ritual

As a non-dogmatic system of folk-cultural beliefs, Nordic Neopaganism possesses features correlating to Leonard Primiano's definition of a vernacular religion, a belief system that while potentially influenced from a larger body of outside sources, whether it be an ecclesiastical body or bodies of lore constituted by myths and historical records, is ultimately centered around the individual construction and praxis of a way-of-being-in-the-world (Primiano 50). This allows for personal creativity. Practitioners are validated, drawing from multiple sources to inform their personal practice, whether those sources be long-standing religious traditions or spiritually-flavored elements of popular culture, such as music. Engagement with ritually created and performed Nordic folk music represents an emergent aspect of Nordic Neopagan vernacular ritual, an affective one at that. Due to their ritualistic creative performance efforts and their transparency displaying these efforts, these bands establish themselves as accessible spiritual authorities creating a spiritual medium that affects receptive listeners, inducing states of trance and even experiences of time collapsing in which visions and ideas of the Northern European pre-Christian past are brought to imaginations in the present.

An examination of Ruben Turlouw's data shows that people who identify as Nordic Neopagans or adjacent to Nordic Neopaganism reported using this music in solitary meditative practice or experiencing it live makes them feel drawn to an imagined past. In a growing religion with room for personal creativity such as Nordic Neopaganism, the vernacular ritual engagement with Dark Nordic Folk bands, bands that have narrated themselves as spiritually charged and have demonstrated their capacity to engage historical sources in the ritual creation of their art occupy the space of skalds, Nordic singers learned of lore and legend, in a contemporary setting. As cherishers and keepers of this lore, bands such as Wardruna and Heilung offer their Nordic Neopagan identifying fans a sonic spiritual medium that occasions visions of an idealized Nordic past that actively shapes lives in the present and will no doubt shape a growing religious tradition moving into the future, skalds indeed.

Notes

1 Translates to Asatru Fellowship. Asatru means "Aesir faith" or, faith in the gods.
2 At the time of Strmiska's scholarship, the Asatru Folk Assembly (AFA) and its founder Stephen McNallen were given a wide birth. Today, however, we must acknowledge the AFA as being a problematic upholder of "Volkisch" ideology and must note that they are listed on the SPLC's database of hate groups.
3 The authors attended Heilung's only North American live ritual on October 8, 2021 at the Red Rocks Amphitheater in Morrison, Colorado.

Works Cited

Ben Handelman, "Wardruna Is Sowing New Seeds and Strengthening Old Roots." Last modified October 18, 2016. https://www.vice.com/en/article/qbvjqw/wardruna-is-sowing-new-seeds-and-strengthening-old-roots

Coggins, Owen. *Mysiticsm, Ritual, and Religion in Drone Metal* (London, Bloomsbury Publishing, 2018)

Dannii Leivers. "The Drum Needed a Blood Sacrifice: The Rise of Dark Nordic Folk,." *The Guardian* (London, UK), Feb. 16, 2021.

Davy, Barbara Jane. *Introduction to Pagan Studies* (Lanham, Altamira Press, 2006)

FaceCulture, *Interview Wardruna – Kvitrafn Part 1,* YouTube Video, 4:07. November 11th, 2009, https://www.youtube.com/watch?v=o3XxA9COh8c

Heilung (Heilung) "Dear Listeners, Do You Feel Immersed into Heilung's Music? You Can Help Contributing to Research by Filling in a Survey…,." Facebook, July 2, 2019, https://l.facebook.com/l.php?u=https%3A%2F%2Fsaxion.eu.qualtrics.com%2Fjfe%2Fform%2FSV_3yZ2oWwwinqwxxj&h=AT3jW3EehLcHVxpf-8NPlrcuehc8XpIUMYsXEIG8iUrnznz_-a9Z8u1EXcGyHAwyf2fQXIiFtLfzyxXwMbOGm28aR4dYToHhZVtziXW2h9lEwS83cgnkohORzSwExDP21w&s=1

Heilung, *Heilung | Lifa – Full Show*, YouTube Video, 1:16:40. November 1st, 2017, https://www.youtube.com/watch?v=h1BsKIP4uYM&t=456s

Hirschkind, Charles. *The Ethical Soundscape: Cassette Sermons and Islamic Counterpublics* (New York, Columbia University Press, 2006)

Metal Hammer, *Einar Selvik's Nordic Roots*, YouTube Video, 2:11. February 25th, 2016, https://www.youtube.com/watch?v=IRNTHkfcbns

Nordvig, Mathias. *Asatru for Beginners: A Modern Heathen's Guide to the Ancient Northern Way* (Emeryville: Rockridge Press, 2020)

Primiano, Leonard. "Vernacular Religion and the Search for Method in Religious Folklife" in *Western Folklore* 54, no. 5 (1995, Western States Folklore Society)

Reed, Ryan. "How Denmark's Heilung Are Creating "Amplified History" With Human Bones, Throat Singing." *Revolver Magazine*, February 15, 2018. https://www.revolvermag.com/music/how-denmarks-heilung-are-creating-amplified-history-human-bones-throat-singing.

Ruben Terlouw. "Ancient Resonance: The Sound of Archaeology and the Role of Audio in Museums" (Thesis, Saxion University of Applied Sciences, 2020)

Rune Hjarno Rasmussen, "Nordic Animism and Academia,." YouTube. Dec 1, 2021. Video. 16:45. https://www.youtube.com/watch?v=gtFpiv_gpVk

Schaefer, Donovan. *Religious Affects: Animality, Evolution, and Power* (Durham, Duke University Press, 2015), pg. 23.

Strmiska, Michael. *Modern Paganism in World Cultures* (Santa Barbara, ABC-CLIO, 2005)

Sylvan, Robin. *Traces of the Spirit: The Religious Dimensions of Popular Music* (New York, NYU Press, 2002)

Yoder, Don. *Discovering American Folklife: Studies in Ethnic Religious and Regional Culture.* UMI Research Press 1990.

12

CREMATING THE BODY POLITIC

Mapping the Materiality of the Indo-Caribbean Mortuary Ritual Corpus

Keith E. McNeal

This chapter surveys the history and politics of Indo-Trinidadian mortuary ritual over 150 years of experience in the southern Caribbean. Indentured laborers were compelled to bury their dead upon domicile in the British West Indian colony of Trinidad, and Hindus adapted their mortuary ritual corpus known as *antyeshti samskaar* by condensing and creolizing it in connection with corpse interment. The effort to legalize cremation gathered momentum and triumphed in the late-colonial period, yet pyreside cremation took time to consolidate at the heart of folk Hindu ritual praxis, trumping burial as vernacular orthopraxy only in the last quarter of the twentieth century—well into the postcolonial era, several generations after the legalization of cremation. Indeed, this corpus has been recently revitalized and expanded, now organizing not only most local Hindu response to death but has also become the quintessentially "Indian" way of ritualizing the post-mortem condition more generally, including among Christian Indians as well, generating a novel form of Indo-Caribbean mortuary praxis incorporating Biblical exegesis and Christian sermonizing over a closed casket burned at neo-Hindu cremation sites. These developments can only be understood in relation to the changing political vicissitudes of diaspora, race, and religion in the colony as compared with postcolony, demonstrating the complex multi-dimensional dynamism of "folk" praxis at varied scalar levels.

Mortuary Ritual as Vernacular Religion, Materiality as Method

Most people in the twin-island Republic of Trinidad and Tobago (TT) assume that since open-air pyreside cremation is the most important and iconic method of corpse disposal in the Hindu tradition at large as well as in contemporary Caribbean nations with substantial populations of people of South Asian descent such as Suriname, Guyana, and TT, cremating the body of the deceased on open

DOI: 10.4324/9781003257462-16

pyres at Hindu cremation sites has essentially always been the case. Upon closer investigation, however, this turns out to be a serious anachronism. Indeed, what is interesting when one digs into the history of religious behavior and ritual practice in this context is that there is practically no evidence for anything other than burial for the first hundred years of Indian life in Trinidad. Moreover, even when the fight for the right to cremate on open pyres was fought and won in the mid-twentieth century and became entirely legal in 1953, Hindus did not in fact rush to observe the practice for another thirty years or so, only becoming ascendant in the 1980s and finally fully standard praxis in the 1990s. I survey this history of change and transformation below, but the methodological point I am making from the outset is that it is only by carefully tracking the shape and practice of the Indo-Trinidadian mortuary ritual corpus—its dynamic multi-dimensional materiality—over the longue durée that I have been able to reconstruct a more precise account of the history and politics of lived religion in this instance.[1]

With this strategy in mind—mapping the materiality of the Indo-Trinidadian mortuary ritual corpus over time—I make a corollary argument concerned with the study of folk religiosity. Much critical discussion and debate have been had, and continues to unfold, regarding the analytical status of "folk" as a category for the study of social history and cultural praxis. Because of this category's abiding connotations of orality and non- or pre-literate tradition and behavior among so-called little peoples and traditions of the world, I prefer the concept of *vernacular* here since it emphasizes the everyday and functional without foreclosing on questions of orality, the status of texts, and what counts as official (see Primiano 1995), as well as does not exclude the reality of various social strata—including elites—interacting and interrelating with one another through a shared corpus of praxis. It is difficult to characterize the cultural history surveyed here as "folk" from the very beginning in the Caribbean, given the insertion of indentured Indian laborers into the nineteenth-century colonial-modern capitalist world system, under direct state jurisdiction, surveillance and control, and certainly after the mid-twentieth century, when more privileged Indocentric activists took up the mantle of open pyreside cremation while more grassroots—i.e. proletarian—folks continued to bury their dead. It is only several decades later, in connection with the fraught postcolonial politics of race, nationalism, and diaspora at large that everyday "folk" began to incorporate and practice pyreside cremation in substantial numbers, from the top-down. I map the changing materiality of the Indo-Trinidadian mortuary ritual corpus here understood as a locus of vernacular cultural praxis through which people of Indian descent—and Hindus in particular—have continually navigated and renegotiated their place and identity in the southern Caribbean.

Colonial Indentureship and the Compulsion to Bury

The winds of abolitionism against slavery within the British Empire had begun to finally blow in the late eighteenth century, gaining momentum through the turn of the nineteenth century, with the official slave trade ended in 1807 and then all slaves under colonial British jurisdiction freed between 1834 and 1838. The ex-enslaved of sub-Saharan African descent throughout the British Caribbean territories faced a number of new social, economic, and political challenges. Many newly freed persons moved far from plantation estates—the site of their domination and torture under enslavement by the plantocracy—in order to eke out a new "free" existence elsewhere within the restricted space of Britain's sugar colonies. Others remained within the orbit of the plantation as wage laborers given their lack of material and economic resources post-slavery. Yet they garnered a certain sort of underlying proletarian clout given that Afro-Caribbean peoples were no longer held in bondage and not legally compelled to work, which meant a smaller labor pool for plantation agro-industry and therefore planters were compelled to compete more by offering marginally better wages. Meanwhile, the imperial British government compensated colonial planters for their "losses," as well as engineered new global schemes for continuing capitalist labor exploitation.

In particular, programs of temporary indentured labor servitude were developed in order to recruit, transport, and place persons who—for whatever set of circumstances, often highly downtrodden and impoverished—were "willing" to sign up for typically five-year-long contracts as bonded, unfree laborers on British West Indian sugar plantations between 1838 and 1918. Many indentured laborers who ended up in the colonial nineteenth-century Caribbean hailed from northeast and southeast India as well as southeast China.[2] Not only did far smaller numbers of Chinese indentured laborers reach the shores of British Caribbean colonies, but most did not opt to reindenture themselves after completing their first contracts and relatively rapidly integrated into the wider complex Afro-Euro-Creole society, adopting Christianity and intermarrying with people of African or mixed-African descent. Indentured laborers of South Asian descent, however, arrived in much larger numbers over the seventy-year period of indentureship, and a consequential proportion of them reindentured themselves for a second and sometimes even third contract. Over time, plantation estates in the southern Caribbean British colonies of Trinidad and Guiana became demographically dominated by indentured Indians—a small but significant minority of which were Muslim, with the majority Hindu. Communities of ex-indentured Indians also began forming in circum-plantation contexts and eventually much further afield, slowly yet surely gathering sociocultural momentum in this radically different "New World" context as compared with their ancestral South Asian background. Indentured laborers could not leave the plantations of their own accord and had no economic or political power. Ex-indentured Indians also had no political or economic power, therefore extremely restricted life circumstances and horizons of possibility, but they at least had their "freedom."

It is only within this context that we may understand why subaltern Hindus had to adapt their final rites of passage concerning death and the afterlife in accordance with the highly confining sociopolitical strictures of the colonial nineteenth- and early twentieth-century Caribbean.[3] Though the list varies in South Asia, it is typically said by Caribbean Hindus that the Sanskritic tradition prescribes sixteen rites of passage over the life course, from birth to death, though they understand many to have been unfortunately discarded along the way out of cruel necessity. Many of these rites of passage are multi-dimensional complexes of ritual practice that take place over periods of time, such as the corpus of mortuary ritual dealing with death known as *antyeshti samskaar* in the Indo-Caribbean: the last of the samskaaras. From a theological point of view, cremating the dead is considered the most ideal method of corpse disposal in Hinduism given belief in karma, samsara (the cosmic cycle of death and rebirth), and reincarnation, since the recently departed soul—which is understood to linger around for a period of time post-mortem—has no mortal coil to remain attached to, tempting it to resist moving forward toward full rebirth a year later dictated by a combination of astrological fate and the consequences of past karmic deeds. Cremation on a funerary pyre fully destroys the corpse, reducing it to ash and a few fragments of bone that may be collected and ceremonially scattered back into the bosom of *Dharti Mata*, Mother Earth, by dispensing them in water. Thus Indians being compelled to bury their dead in the Caribbean represents a kind of necessary ritual adaptation to life under imperial domination, for the Christian European political and economic classes that controlled the colonial structures of life favored burial until well into the twentieth century (Laqueur 2015) and looked upon pyreside cremation as "unclean" and evidence of heathen, idolatrous paganism. Even disenfranchised Afro-Caribbean folks of ex-slave descent buried their dead. There was no space or legitimacy whatsoever for cremation in colonial Trinidad, hence Indo-Caribbean Hindus necessarily shifted to burial as method of corpse disposal within their final rites of passage.[4] This was not an issue for Indo-Caribbean Muslims since burial is the dominant tradition in Islam.

From the beginning of indentureship in the Caribbean, both Hindu and Muslim Indians were compelled to bury their dead under makeshift circumstances on or near the plantations where they lived and worked, sometimes on lands already used for slave burials. Given that traditional South Asian Hindus see burial as polluting, it would have been initially even more problematic for them to be forced to be buried alongside people from other religious, cultural, or ethnic groups. Yet they had no choice but to adapt. Canadian Presbyterian missionary John Morton (1916) established one of the first graveyards for Indians on the island, and secured space for Indian Hindu, Muslim, and Christian interment in 1895 at the already established, premier Paradise Cemetery in San Fernando, south Trinidad (see Figures 12.1 and 12.2). Early twentieth-century newspapers contain numerous reports of Indian funerals for which there are no signs of discontent regarding burial. Indeed, a material tradition of increasingly elaborate tomb and crypt construction had emerged, emblematic of newly emergent forms of socioeconomic status among Indo-Trinidadians. For example, an entire entry in the *Port of Spain Gazette* of January 16, 1919 was devoted to lavishly detailed reporting about "an exceedingly pretty family vault" for the late Rampartab

FIGURE 12.1 Some Hindu gravesites in Paradise Cemetery, San Fernando, Trinidad, 2016 (photos by author).

FIGURE 12.2 Some Hindu gravesites in Paradise Cemetery, San Fernando, Trinidad, 2016 (photos by author).

Pandit's progeny and kin in the old Preysal Cemetery in central Trinidad, which due to its hefty construction is still essentially intact to this day (see McNeal 2018:203–205).

Moreover, burial incorporated into the sequence of antyeshti samskaar ritualization as a substitute for cremation was not the only form of change in the mortuary ritual corpus among Hindus of the indentured Caribbean diaspora. Judging from the standardized form of "folk" praxis that emerged by the early twentieth century, and for which there are varying sources of evidence, we can infer a number of other changes, modifications, and transformations in the antyeshti samskaar complex. This ritual corpus was condensed and miniaturized within the highly-constrained sociopolitical context of colonial domination. Meanwhile, the overall set of rites of passage—samskaaras—actually observed in practice revolved around those focused upon birth, youth, marriage, and death. Everyday life was necessarily oriented toward survival in the colony. People of Indian descent wielded no economic or political power and their marriages were not legally recognized, which meant that their children were officially considered "illegitimate" vis-à-vis the colonial state and they could not officially pass down property or wealth to their generational heirs. Hindu marriages were not legalized until 1945, a mere seventeen years before the end of British rule. A small, yet growing minority of Indo-Caribbean converts to Presbyterianism gained formal education and began to pursue limited early avenues of socioeconomic mobility only in the second quarter of the twentieth century.

Two mid-twentieth-century ethnographic studies of Indian life in central and southern Trinidad disclose a standard portrait of activity connected with death (Niehoff and Niehoff 1960; Klass 1961). This includes a sequence of offerings and ritual microactivities immediately after the death; ceremonial procession to the burial site on the day of the funeral; doing *aarti*—offering of lit flame—along the way including the gravesite; token offerings of ghee and brief reading from the *Ramayana* or *Bhagavad Gita* over the burial; planting of a *jhandi*—Hindu prayer flag—at the gravesite; a 10th-day post-mortem ritual shaving—*shraddha*—of men's facial and head hair in the primary family of the deceased by a stream or river by a special ceremonial barber ending the post-mortem period of ritual impurity; and a ritual feast—*bhandaara*—on the tenth or thirteenth day after burial sending the soul officially on its journey and concluding the immediate post-mortem ritual sequence. Ideally, yet less often in practice, another one-year bandhaara would be offered commemorating the dead and honoring the point at which the deceased soul would be reborn into its next reincarnation. Importantly, as compared with later postcolonial iterations of the antyeshti samskaar corpus, both Klass and the Niehoffs hardly mention any officiation by Hindu *pandits* or much about *pinda puja*—offerings of ceremonial rice-flour balls in symbolic relation to cosmic progression of the deceased—as part of the mortuary ritual cycle. And last but certainly not least, Indo-Trinidadians had incorporated the tradition of keeping a multi-night wake immediately after the death leading up to the funeral, as well as the annual observance of cleaning, decorating, and lighting up with candles or oil lamps the graves of the deceased on the eve of (Catholic and Anglican) All Souls Day in early November, from their Afro-Trinidadian neighbors. Thus a century into domicile in the Caribbean, the mortuary ritual corpus had morphed considerably in comparison with its South Asian precedents and cognates.

The Late-Colonial Fight to Legalize Pyreside Cremation

Although Indians began arriving in the colony from 1845 and indentureship came to an end in 1917–1918, it was not until the late 1930s that mortuary ritual surfaced as an overt issue for ethnoreligious assertion in the late-colonial politics of culture. A swelling chorus of political activists and religious leaders both in the Caribbean and from India articulated a vigorous critique of the entire gamut of repression experienced by Indian culture under colonial domination: demanding recognition of Hindu and Muslim marriages, state aid for non-Christian schools, the establishment of a Hindu college, and creation of overarching Hindu and Muslim religious organizations. Agitation for the right to cremate was also among the central demands of this ascendant movement for Indo-Caribbean cultural rights. British imperial authorities were even more incentivized to pay attention and respond after the series of labor protests and riots that unfolded throughout the colonial West Indies in the mid-1930s. A British member of the Indian Civil Service, Mr. J. D. Tyson, visited the Caribbean in order to document the situation and specifically assess the grievances of Indo-Caribbean for presentation to the Moyne Commission, which was investigating the labor disturbances. Tyson's *Report on the Conditions of Indians in Jamaica, British Guiana, and Trinidad* explicitly advocated for granting the right to cremate in line with "the traditional and universal method of disposing of the dead in Hindu India" (1939:76). The issue was subject to considerable conversation and debate by this time.

Symptomatic of the changing times, special permission for a high-profile cremation was granted in 1940 for the funeral of Metharam J. Kirpalani, one of two high-profile Sindhi brothers who had emigrated to the Caribbean in 1927 as aspiring entrepreneurs, establishing various highly successful business ventures in Barbados, Suriname, British Guiana, and Trinidad, were among the first to import and distribute films from the subcontinent, and vocally opposed the racist English-language proficiency restriction in connection with the fight for the universal right to vote. "Metha" Kirpalani died at the age of forty-six of a heart attack and his brother, Murlidhar, petitioned the colonial governor—Sir Hubert Young—for permission to cremate his body through the Kirpalani lawyer, J. Arthur Procope. Permission was granted for the cremation in a win for the Hindu community, yet the advance was paradoxically undermined by the very same token in only being granted space to be conducted in the island's main trash dump east of the capital Port of Spain, known as the La Basse (see Figure 12.3). Thus, the fight continued.

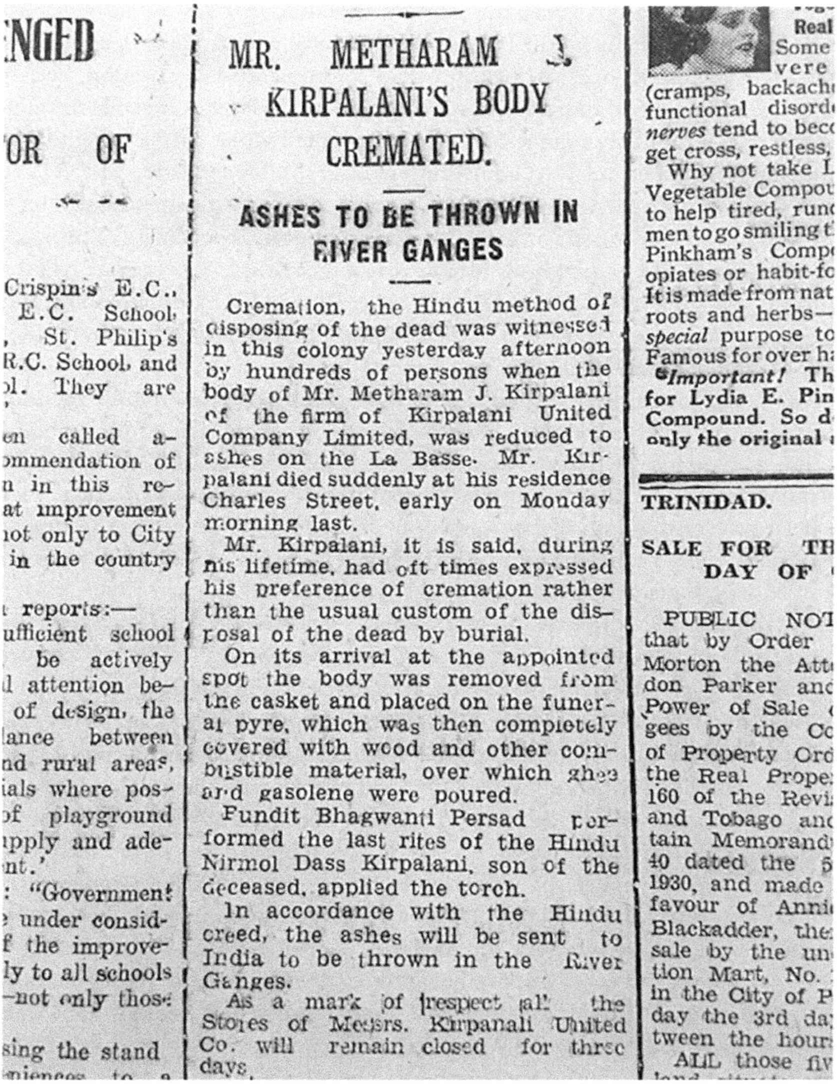

MR. METHARAM J. KIRPALANI'S BODY CREMATED.

ASHES TO BE THROWN IN RIVER GANGES

Cremation, the Hindu method of disposing of the dead was witnessed in this colony yesterday afternoon by hundreds of persons when the body of Mr. Metharam J. Kirpalani of the firm of Kirpalani United Company Limited, was reduced to ashes on the La Basse. Mr. Kirpalani died suddenly at his residence Charles Street, early on Monday morning last.

Mr. Kirpalani, it is said, during his lifetime, had oft times expressed his preference of cremation rather than the usual custom of the disposal of the dead by burial.

On its arrival at the appointed spot the body was removed from the casket and placed on the funeral pyre, which was then completely covered with wood and other combustible material, over which ghee and gasolene were poured.

Pundit Bhagwanti Persad performed the last rites of the Hindu Nirmol Dass Kirpalani, son of the deceased, applied the torch.

In accordance with the Hindu creed, the ashes will be sent to India to be thrown in the River Ganges.

As a mark of respect all the Stores of Messrs. Kirpanali United Co. will remain closed for three days.

FIGURE 12.3 *Port of Spain Gazette*, 1940.

Discussion and debate intensified into the 1940s. Hindu leaders and Indian organizations clamored for the right to cremate in the face of persistent ideological colonial bias against pyreside cremation as unsanitary and offensive. The Hindu community reassented to disposing of cremated ashes only in the sea—not rivers or streams—just as they had a decade before, as Tyson had reported. This was a not insignificant concession given that Hindus traditionally considered the sea, and salt water in particular, to be impure. Legislative Council Member for Eastern Counties as well as then-Minister of Agriculture and Lands—Afro-Trinidadian

Victor Bryan—began to break the political deadlock in 1948 by taking up the cause for cremation on behalf of Indians, not only emphasizing that the West Indies Royal Commission of 1938–1939 had recommended legalization, but also pointing out that open-air pyreside cremation was considered acceptable throughout the rest of the Commonwealth. Bryan sponsored a first draft of the bill that would eventually become the Cremation Act of 1953 after a meeting in 1950 with a Mr. C. B. Mathura—head of what was known as the Cremation Committee—and the respective Ministers of Land, Health, and Local Government. The matter was not simply one of allowing Hindus to observe their "traditional religious customs," but also one of cultural rights: "The demand has existed in one section of our community in the exercise of their fundamental right for a long time, and it is the feeling of Government that this demand should be met" (*Hansard of Trinidad & Tobago*, Cremation Act, 1953, p. 1573). Bryan's bill was supported by the Hon. Ranjit Kumar, another influential businessman who had migrated from India and elected as Council Member for Caroni North in 1950, though he favored the eventual ascendance of "mechanical" crematoria over funerary pyres as a "more modern way of disposal of the dead" (pp. 1575–1580). Three more outspoken advocates—Indo-Trinidadian Council Members the Hon. Chanka Maharaj, the Hon. M. G. Sinanan, and the head of the newly formed Sanatan Dharma Maha Sabha, Bhadase Sagan Maraj—all passionately supported the bill legalizing pyreside cremation, which passed into law on Friday, May 8, 1953. This was the very same session of the colonial Legislative Council that also struck down the 1917 ban on the Afro-Trinbagonian Spiritual "Shouter" Baptist religion.

Yet tellingly, while one might assume that legalization might have precipitated a wave of pyreside cremations within the local Hindu community, this did not in fact happen. A few cremations were conducted intermittently during the period from the 1950s through the 1970s, according to oral testimonies from a handful of elderly folks I have spoken to, but these were exceptional in relation to dominant vernacular practice. By and large, Hindus kept burying their dead. An index of the mid-twentieth-century state of affairs may be seen in the case of Doon Pandit, as he was known, an extra-important figure in the local evolution of Hinduism who was born at the turn of the twentieth century and passed away in 1958 (Singh 2006). Doon Pandit pioneered non-Christian schools for Indian children that gave rise to the wave of mid-twentieth-century school-building efforts taken up by the Sanatan Dharma Maha Sabha (SDMS) after its formation in 1952. He also founded, as well as supported the founding of many temples, and ministered to Afro-Trinbagonians as part of his religious outreach. I mention the extraordinary figure of Doon Pandit here to note that he was buried—*not* cremated—upon his death, five years *after* the political fight for cremation had been won, thereby signifying the persisting vernacular hegemony of burial in Indo-Trinidadian mortuary ritual praxis on the eve of independence from Great Britain in 1962. His tomb was refurbished in the mid-1990s in honor of the sesquicentennial commemorations of "Indian Arrival" in Trinidad (see McNeal 2018:212–213 on Doon Pandit's tomb; Harlan 2013 on the history of Indian Arrival Day).

Postcolonial Revitalization of Pyreside Cremation

The relatively late burial of Doon Pandit affirms that the ascent of pyreside cremation into mortuary orthopraxy is much more recent than typically appreciated. Indian sociologist J. C. Jha investigated Hindu rites of passage during his stint at the University of the West Indies-St. Augustine, Trinidad in the mid-1970s and not only found the local funerary corpus to be "shortened" and "abridged" as compared with South Asian cognates, but also reports that "though there is talk of having a proper crematorium in this island, at the moment many younger Hindus do not like the idea of burning the dead" (1976:50–51). Thus, cremation may have been incipiently growing at the popular level, but was not consolidated at the heart of standard Hindu funerary praxis until the last quarter of the twentieth century, by which point a major sea change in mortuary ritual had taken place. Indeed, by the late 1980s, Trinbagonian anthropologist Kumar Mahabir notes that Hindus "generally cremate their corpses" except for a few members of minority sects, such as Sieunarinis, Kabir Panthis, and Ramanandis (1990:11).

The first legal open-air pyreside cremations took place south of El Socorro along the Caroni River in north-central Trinidad and at "Mosquito Creek" in south-western Trinidad on the bank of the Godineau River where it meets the Gulf of Paria. The Mosquito Creek site then moved up the hill to its own current well-known location in the 1960s and the site of Caroni River cremations moved eastward over time, eventually settling upon its current high-profile location east of the north-south highway in the 1970s. By the time I first visited Trinidad in the late 1990s, cremation was overwhelmingly popular. Something of a prestige hierarchy had developed among the most prominent cremation sites with *Shanti Tiram* ("Shore of Peace")—more commonly known as Mosquito Creek, south of San Fernando in La Romaine—at the top; followed by the Waterloo site next to the *Sewdass Sadhu Hindu Mandir* on the west coast and best known as the "Temple by the Sea" following in status (see Figure 12.4); and the Caroni River site in central-north Trinidad below that (B. Samaroo, pers. comm., 2012); and now flanked by other, newer sites across the island in Felicity, Chaguanas and Mafikin, Mayaro.

The popularity of pyreside cremation not only gained serious momentum in the 1980s and became standard vernacular praxis for corpse disposal among Indo-Trinidadian Hindus in the 1990s, but the entire antyeshti samskaar ritual corpus overall was expanded and embellished in various ways. Counteracting earlier tendencies toward "abridgement," to invoke Jha, several trends in addition to the shift back to pyreside cremation must be emphasized. Firstly, the practice of pinda puja was upregulated throughout the ritual corpus, not only on the twelfth- or thirteenth-day bhandaara after the funeral, but also at the one-year commemorative bhandaara of the death. Moreover, the entire ritual sequence has come under the purview of pandit oversight and officiation, as compared with their relatively less involvement in the antyeshti samskaaras of yesteryear. The significance of this development is thrown into greater relief once we appreciate

FIGURE 12.4 One of the pyre sites at the Waterloo "Temple by the Sea" after a cremation (photo by author, 2014).

that Brahmin pandits in South Asia are not traditionally involved in disposal of the corpse, as it is considered polluting (Knott 1998:21). Indeed, contemporary development of the mortuary ritual corpus is connected to expansive postcolonial revitalization of *all* the samskaaras more generally among Hindus in Trinidad. One pandit told me that people have even begun to ask for prenatal rites unheard of until recently.

Yet cremation is not only now considered Hindu orthopraxy, but has also become the more prototypically "Indian" way of doing things more generally, which helps account for why wakes are anachronistically considered Indian heritage, rather than Afro-Caribbean influences, as reported by Klass and the Niehoffs; many Christian Indians now cremate their dead despite not observing Hindu antyeshti samskaara (Christians cremate with a closed casket, rather than the open one of Hindus); and the sometime claim that even some Muslim Indians now cremate. In other words, cremation has become progressively iconic of a revitalized Indianness in Trinidad and Tobago's era of postcolonial multiculturalism (see Figure 12.5). These developments have inspired further innovations such as hybrid Hindu-Christian funerals, or elements of antyeshti samskaara being performed in funeral homes rather than at the pyreside for whatever circumstantial reasons.

A homogenized form of Hinduism gradually evolved and became dominant over the course of the twentieth century under a neo-traditionalist banner in the Caribbean, consolidating most of its support from conservative rural Hindus (Vertovec 1992). This orthodoxy—operating under the master sign of *Sanatan*

FIGURE 12.5 Main sign at *Shanti Tiram*, on the central-western coast south of San Fernando (2012). Note symbolism signifying both Hindu and Christian "sides" in contemporary Indo-Trinidadian cremation praxis (photo by author).

Dharma, "Eternal Truth"—is identified with North Indian tradition, has become standardized as well as centered upon a limited set of "high" Sanskritic deities, and proctored by a transculturated pandit elite with complex and contentious claims to Brahmin ancestry. Pandits have come to garner expansive authority in all things religious for everyone regardless of ostensible caste background and they manage their flocks akin with parish priests among Catholics and Anglicans. Hinduism may be understood as having become progressively ethnicized under their stewardship in the Caribbean, making being Hindu the authentic way of being Indian (see Van Der Veer and Vertovec 1991). Yet the ascent of a consolidated Hinduism was conditioned by the fact that Christianity retained hegemony as a dominating cultural barometer of status and legitimacy throughout the colony, putting Hindus endlessly on the defensive. Perhaps unsurprisingly given the sociohistorical circumstances, the Indo-Caribbean community internalized values espoused by colonial elites and adopted them as their own terms of reference in an effort to forge a "respectable" Hinduism. This also means that recuperation of the religion has been a complex and uneven process. In the case of mortuary praxis, Indo-Trinidadian Hindus maintained their adopted colonial tradition of burial for quite some time even after the right to cremate the dead had been achieved in the mid-twentieth century. Indeed, it took more than three decades after legalization for cremation to become the most prevalent form of corpse disposal among Hindus in Trinidad, and the reason for this seems clear in retrospect: the postcolonial "Indian Renaissance."

How and why this Indian Renaissance emerged and came to pass is a very complicated topic that cannot be adequately addressed here (see McNeal 2011:Ch. 6 for a fuller discussion). The waning of an earlier era of Afro-creole nationalism after decolonization and transition into the current period of postcolonial multiculturalism was a complex process influenced by many factors. Succinctly put, it involved (a) the political, if not wholly economic or cultural denouement of whiteness with the rise of nationalism and decolonization; (b) the emergence of Black Power in the wake of independence as a form of internal critique connected with wider hemispheric currents concerned with Civil Rights for Afro-Americans; (c) the rise and fall of an oil boom in the 1970s, which wrought unforeseen transformations in economic differentiation, social mobility, and ethnic and religious revitalization across society as a whole; (d) the death of the nation's first Prime Minister, Eric Williams, and subsequent fall of the People's National Movement (PNM) in the wake of the boom; (e) the rise of the National Alliance for Reconstruction (NAR), a coalition of Blacks and Indians headed by A. N. R. Robinson, a Tobagonian, which obtained a plurality of support under a banner of "One Love" from all ethnic groups, religious denominations and social classes, but which soon fractured because of internal racial politics and fierce debate over "culture" and the state; and then, (f) after a one-term return of the PNM to government in the early 1990s the ascent of a more forthrightly Indian-based political party, the United National Congress (UNC), in the mid-1990s. Anthropologist Viranjini Munasinghe (2001) reports that the idea of an Indo-Trinidadian government or prime minister was unthinkable—including among Indians—as late as the 1980s. Yet an Indian-dominated coalition, the United National Congress, came to power in 1995 with Basdeo Panday at the helm as the nation's first Indian Prime Minister. These political developments reflected a series of deeper economic and cultural transformations facilitating the emergence of an Indo-Trinidadian sociocultural renaissance in the last quarter of the twentieth century, based upon a shift from expressing more sectarian and intra-community interests to targeting the formerly uncontested privilege of Afro-Trinbagonian political and cultural power at large.

Hinduism in particular has been embraced as an expression of ethnic revitalization and the assertion of diasporic identity. New wealth earned by Indo-Trinidadians as a result of the oil boom facilitated the construction and maintenance of temples, the sponsoring of multifarious ceremonial and organizational activities, the pursuit of doctrinal or religious knowledge, the proliferation of Bollywood films and Indian radio stations, more active interest in connecting with and traveling to Mother India, a welter of new ritual innovations, and the increasing prominence of Hindu and Indian holidays such as Diwali and Indian Arrival Day. Hinduism has become a privileged vehicle of diasporic identification for a revivifying local Indian ethnicity and this accounts for the expansive elaboration of the entire spectrum of samskaaras in general, as well as antyeshti samskaara in particular—including the ascent of pyreside cremation to a position of orthopraxy within mortuary ritual praxis. The spectacular iconicity of cremation as emblematic of Hinduism along with the theological conceptualization of death and reincarnation upon which it is based have made it a potent locus of postcolonial religious assertion and ethnic revitalization.

Yet it is not only Hindus that have embraced cremation as the primary ritual vehicle for disposing of the corpse, as mentioned above, but also increasing numbers of Indo-Trinidadian Christians as well (Figure 12.5). This is because Hinduism has become ethnicized, as we have seen, and—as a corollary—the ceremonial scope of cremation has been extended beyond the Hindu sphere to include Indianness more generally in connection with the shifting tides of postcolonial multiculturalism. The "otherness" of pyre-based cremation has made it a compelling oppositional symbol of a revitalized postcolonial Indo-Trinidadian ethnicity, not simply the purview of Hindus alone, despite—or perhaps because of—the fact that it stems from the long-term recuperation of Hinduism in the West Indies over the course of the twentieth century. Because Hinduism became racialized as a result of the colonial Caribbean experience, reclaiming a quintessentially "Indian" way of ritualizing the corpse represents recuperation of the body politic at a key life-passage juncture, no matter what one's religious orientation may be.

Coda: Fighting (Again) to Cremate the Body Politic in the Era of #Coronachaos

Now, with the dawning of the latest Coronavirus—COVID-19, aka SARS-2—in early 2020 and ensuing era of #Coronachaos, the local politics of pyreside cremation have taken yet another twist. As a result of public health restrictions incumbent upon the pandemic, civil services such as weddings and funerals were severely restricted in terms of numbers able to attend and tightly regulated in terms of masked protocols and social-distancing early on in order to attempt to dodge the latest zoonotic disease as much as possible. As part of this effort, the Government of the Republic of Trinidad and Tobago under the PNM administration of Afro-Tobagonian Prime Minister Keith Rowley banned the open-air pyreside cremation of people who died from COVID-19. This move not only restricted the ability of Hindus and other Indo-Trinidadians to cremate their dead in open-air pyres in the "traditional" "Indian" way, but also contributed to a clogged backlog of corpses within the limited storage space of the national morgues and funeral homes, thereby doubly exacerbating the pain and difficulties presented by the pandemic.

Whereas things were especially confusing and anxious under emergency conditions earlier on, as the pandemic dragged on, things began to "normalize" with the gradual relaxation of lockdown restrictions and so forth. Yet by the second year of the pandemic, the continuing ban on pyreside cremation of deaths due to COVID-19 took an increasing toll psychologically and logistically. The number of corpses awaiting disposal had by then accumulated dramatically, resulting in extended delays for funerals, burials, and industrial cremations at the small number of mortuary homes and one public crematorium able to undertake them, as well as generating exorbitant storage costs for the families of the deceased. Increasing numbers of Hindus clamored against the prohibition. The irony was not lost on any concerned Hindus involved that outdoor pyreside cremations are obviously ventilated better than indoor funerals and cremations, which had become sanctioned using proper public health protocols. Things came to a head in late July 2021, when the daughter of Silochan Ramsaroop—who died of COVID-19 complications on July 25—was initially given permission to cremate her father's body at the Caroni site, but which was then promptly retracted by the municipal authorities. She mobilized legal support and filed a case suing the government for the right to cremate by open pyre on August 4, 2021. Later that month, thirteen Hindu organizations addressed a formal letter in support of the case, publicly lodging a grievance against the government for this breach of religious-cum-civil rights.

These developments led to a series of negotiations as well as legal maneuvers and counter-maneuvers between the government, litigants, and the prominent Hindu organizations for the remainder of the year. Meanwhile, December 2021 was the single-worst month of the pandemic in TT, which meant further backlog in the national inventory of corpses requiring disposal. The Maha Sabha joined the legal case against the government on December 17, raising the stakes of the game. A month later—in mid-January 2022—the government finally relented, abolishing the ban on pyreside cremations of COVID-positive corpses, a move met with great relief and exaltation by the Indo-Trinidadian community, especially Hindus (see Figures 12.6 and 12.7). The battle for full cultural rights on the part of a minority religious community had been fought and won all over again.

Interestingly, the leading Hindu organizations negotiating the end of the ban received pressure from some prominent Indian politicians to not just consult with the government in sanctioning pyreside cremation but in fact hold out to fight the legal case in order to get more political mileage out of the circumstances—a move which, had it been pursued by the organizations, would have delayed relief for the faithful suffering through extra layers of grief and difficulty in the midst of the pandemic (pers. comm. with someone central to the negotiation, June 2022). The politics of pyreside cremation for lawmakers and officeholders had almost taken its spirituality hostage vis-à-vis the Hindu faithful trying to deal with the challenges of life and death in the midst of #Coronachaos. With the ban lifted, however, Ms. Cindy Ramsaroop-Persad now stands alone awaiting judgment in the case concerning her father, which focuses upon suing for costs and damages related to her father's corpse's long-term storage before having been compelled to have him created in an industrial crematorium, as well as an infringement at that time of her family's rights as citizens of the nation-state of Trinidad and Tobago.

I consider what happened recently during the COVID-19 pandemic not only in order to update the cremation plotline through the still-ongoing era of #Coronachaos, a dramatic and poignant story in its own right, but also in order to make two more additional points about the contemporary disutility of "folk" as an analytical category—or at least the necessity of fully revamping it in light of globalization and the colonial-industrial-modern world system. I took the position at the outset in favor of *vernacular* cultural praxis since it foregrounds the everyday, the routinized, the popular, the proletarian, the unlettered without sidelining the textual, the official, or the complex, messy, contentious dynamics of stratified social relations. I may now extend this further with two final observations regarding the sociohistorical complexity of the case at hand in relation

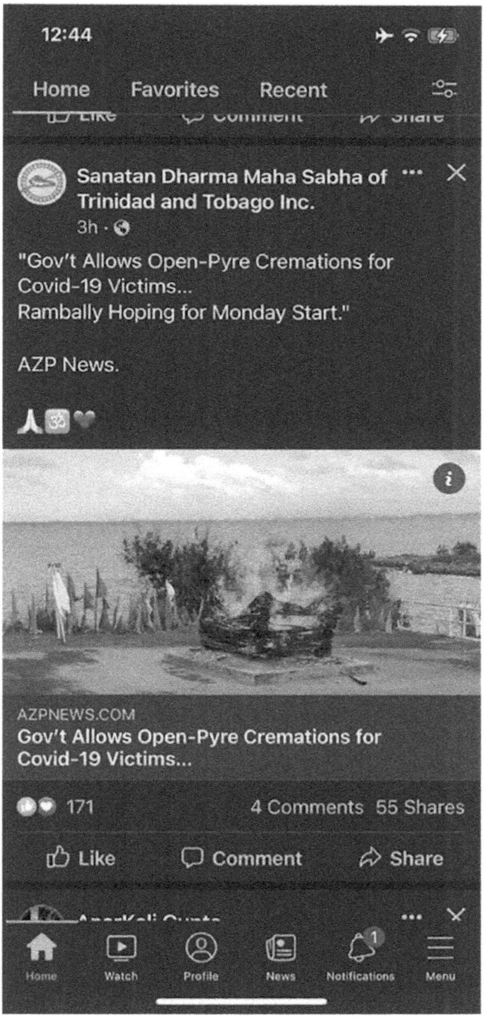

FIGURE 12.6 Screenshots of the Sanatan Dharma Maha Sabha of Trinidad & Tobago's Facebook feed circulating news that the government ban on pyreside cremations of COVID-19 deaths had been lifted in mid-January 2022.

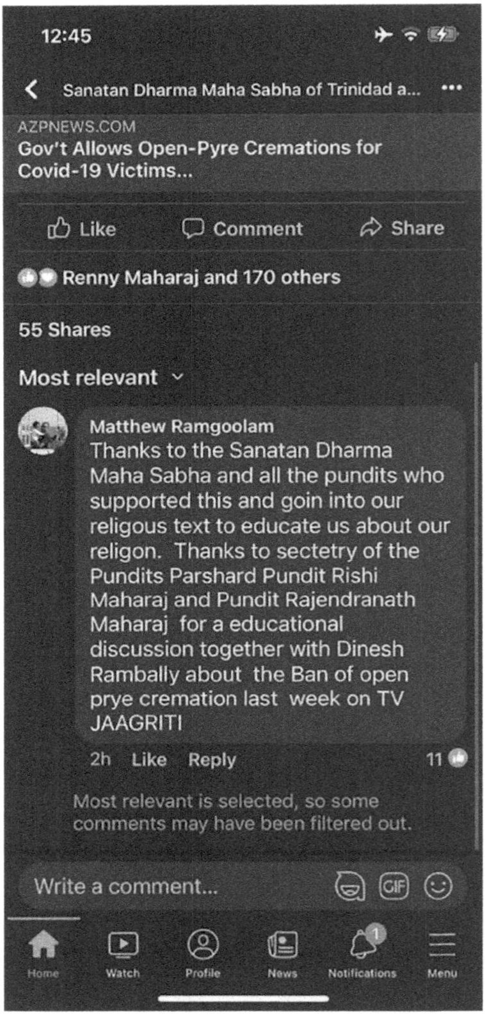

FIGURE 12.7 Screenshots of the Sanatan Dharma Maha Sabha of Trinidad & Tobago's Facebook feed circulating news that the government ban on pyreside cremations of COVID-19 deaths had been lifted in mid-January 2022.

to the analytical category of "folk" religion, which conventionally refers to oral and popular traditions of small-scale societies and the subaltern classes within the industrial world system.

The case of open-pyre cremation in Trinidad has been a legal matter from the beginning and essentially regulated via the colonial-turned-postcolonial state, therefore perennially conditioned in the southern Caribbean by the politics of state recognition and power. Despite being rural agricultural workers, indentured Indians and their descendants during the colonial era were never not captured and directly controlled by state capitalism. If these are "folk," what kind are they? The battle for cremation was largely fought by socially mobile, educated, and transdiasporic political, economic, and religious elites; yet when it was won, the "folk" kept burying. It took more than three decades of generational change for open-air pyreside cremation to subsequently consolidate at the heart of mainstream Hindu mortuary praxis—becoming the central modality of lived religion—yet reached that point largely in relation to the changing postcolonial politics of race, diaspora, nationalism, and culture: from the top-down and outside-in, always mediated by law and the political economy of the state in the Caribbean.

Moreover, the daunting recent experience of death, confusion, and lockdown during the pandemic heightened and dramatized the constitutive intertwined realities of social media, digital culture, and virtualization in the contemporary world, including for the experiences of death and mortuary ritualization in particular. Funerals and cremations had been increasingly photo-documented as well as live-streamed before the era of #Coronachaos, but the pandemic fully reset the parameters of possibility: catapulting mortuary ritualization fully into the realm of the virtual. Once they were allowed again—in TT, first with funerals in churches and mortuary homes with very limited, masked attendees accompanied either by cemetery burial or incineration via industrial ovens in crematoria, and only much later in open pyres at outdoor Hindu cremation sites from January 2022 onward—photographic and videographic documentation, live-streaming online, and sharing on social media and chat platforms like WhatsApp became an utterly essential element in the praxis of mortuary ritual (see Figures 12.8–12.13).

FIGURE 12.8 Screenshot of pandemic-era pyreside cremation of non-COVID-19-related death posted on YouTube: the late Sandra Seepaul, February 2022.

FIGURE 12.9 Screenshot of pandemic-era pyreside cremation of non-COVID-19-related death posted on YouTube: the late Sandra Seepaul, February 2022.

FIGURE 12.10 Screenshot of pandemic-era pyreside cremation of non-COVID-19-related death posted on YouTube: the late Latchmi Rampersad, May 2022.

FIGURE 12.11 Screenshot of pandemic-era pyreside cremation of non-COVID-19-related death posted on YouTube: the late Latchmi Rampersad, May 2022.

FIGURE 12.12 Screenshot of pandemic-era pyreside cremation of non-COVID-19-related death posted on YouTube: the late Latchmi Rampersad, May 2022.

FIGURE 12.13 Screenshot of pandemic-era pyreside cremation of non-COVID-19-related death posted on YouTube: the late Latchmi Rampersad, May 2022.

Things continue to complexify and rehybridize as "post"-pandemic becomes the new normal, but social media and digitalization are here to stay. What are the vicissitudes of "folk" religiosity when online or partly-yet-essentially virtual? The concept of *vernacular* cultural and religious praxis is more salutary here, as it has less conceptual and ideological baggage than "folk" things. Vernacular is everyday praxis, taken-for-granted praxis, habitual praxis even as it may have multiplicitous tentacles, dimensions, inputs, and extensions across contending social strata and mediated registers of discourse. Scholars have already begun mapping the vicissitudes of vernacular culture in Anglophone Caribbean cyberspace (Best 2008a, 2008b). Yet scholarly quibbles aside, what matters is how we define our terms and employ them in documentation and analysis.

Digitalization may be a radically new infrastructure, yet mass mediation is hardly new. We can appreciate the profound reality of modern-industrial mass media well before the turn of the twenty-first century—transnationally, diasporically, historically—in the case at hand. Historian David Arnold (2021:62–67) discloses that pyreside Hindu cremation was traditionally an upper-caste practice, also observed—interestingly—by Sikhs, Jains, and Buddhists in South Asia. Lower-caste Hindus, Dalits, and tribal communities commonly disposed of their dead through burial. Yet with the gathering of late nineteenth- and early twentieth-century forces of early Hindu nationalism in dialectical counterpoint with British imperialism, open-air pyreside cremation became an increasingly central icon of Hindu India from the turn of the early twentieth century, eventually gaining adherents among lower-caste Hindus as well. Arnold writes: "In its new and more emphatically political manifestation, cremation became emblematic of a proud and defiant nationhood, further developing in the years after Independence in 1947 into a powerful expression of India's national identity and its legitimate place in the world" (p. 147). Mahatma Gandhi's cremation in early 1948 was a spectacular national-international-diasporic event with profound global reverberations, violently punctuating the juncture between decolonization and independence. His assassination by a right-wing Hindu nationalist was seen as a revitalizing sacrifice for the faith and nation (as well as diaspora, see Natarajan 2013). Death is not synonymous with obliteration in Hindu cosmology, but embodies rejuvenation, making cremation a kind of micro-cosmogony (Parry 1994).

The global-diasporic impact of Gandhi's cremation was due in no small part to been captured by Henri Cartier-Bresson and Margaret Bourke-White for *Life* magazine (Cookman 1998). Images of the corpse and cremation soon proliferated in the Indian public sphere through the mass production and circulation of cheap lithographic prints (Pinney 2004:138–142). The Mahatma's death embodied self-sacrifice, devotion, and regeneration, and was accordingly sublimated into the project of nation-formation. Again, as Arnold writes, "the growing militancy of Hindu nationalism was directed at increased domination not only over women's bodies, but also the bodies of the dead" (2021:157). These epic global events had profound transnational-diasporic effects. This was the international context for the Legislative Council debates and legislative victories in the early 1950s concerning the legalization of pyreside cremation in 1953 in colonial TT. Events in South Asia had a critical impact upon the unfolding of diasporic colonial politics in ways that further complicate received notions about the "folk" and their cultural praxis.

What I encountered when I first began doing research and living in Trinidad in the late 1990s was the overwhelming dominance of open-air pyreside cremation among Indo-Trinidadian Hindus and many Christians as well. It was standard, non-textual, and practice-based, hence could have been taken as essentially a form of "folk" religious praxis. Yet this corpus of mortuary ritualization reflects the interacting influences of coloniality and post-coloniality, the ongoing ramifications and unintended consequences of historical change, unequal negotiations between state and subject-turned-citizen, dialogue between stratified Indo-Trinidadian socioeconomic classes and among religious faiths, indirect and direct mediation by the law, and the translocal hall-of-mirrors effects and influences of modern global-diasporic mass media now further complicated by digitalization. At the center of everything is the fate of the corpse, which in my view may be seen as the most profound ultimate locus of material culture. Tracking the materiality of the Caribbean Hindu mortuary ritual corpus has enabled a much deeper and more precise sociohistorical view of its sweeping vernacular global genealogy.

Notes

1 Indo-Trinidadian mortuary ritual praxis has been oral and practice-based all along, although there are now two local publications by religious specialists commenting upon and explicating the structure and symbolism of antyeshti samskaar for lay Hindus interested in deeper understanding of the ritual process (see Maharaj, Maharaj and Maharaj 2003; Persad 2016). See Hallam and Hockey (2001) for an extended theorization of death, memory, and material culture within the context of primarily modern Western sociohistorical materials.

2 See Look Lai (1993) for a comparative overview of the historical sociology of the twin indentureship schemes in India and China. The areas of northeast India from which indentured Indians hailed are especially the Bhojpuri Hindi belt in what are today the modern states of Bihar and Uttar Pradesh, with much fewer coming from West Bengal as well as Madhya Pradesh, Haryana, and Rajasthan; folks hailing from southeast India hailed principally from Telugu- and Tamil-speaking regions.

3 A fuller, more detailed, technical examination of the intricate moving history of the Indo-Trinidadian mortuary ritual corpus is available in an earlier paper (McNeal 2018). Here I survey and discuss a synoptic version of this history as a case study for the study of vernacular religion and the methodological utility of focusing upon the materiality of ritual praxis over time and space.

4 I have come across only one instance of cremation by subaltern Indo-Caribbean Hindus in colonial Trinidad: in the 1880s along the banks of the Caroni River on the Frederick Estate, for which its primary observants were arrested and jailed, according to the late prolific lay Trinbagonian historian Angelo Bissessarsingh (2013). Yet he only cites his source for this as "records" indicating that such an event had happened. Otherwise, I have come across no other sources of evidence—either primary sources or in the historiographical literature—reporting cases of open-pyre cremation by Indians during the period of indentureship. Of course, this does not mean that they never happened, but any that transpired were certainly exceptional cases lost to the historical record. Given their spectacular and sensational nature, it seems safe to assume that any instances would have been reported if and when they had been observed to have taken place by the authorities, planters, bureaucrats, or journalists.

References

Arnold, David (2021) *Burning the Dead: Hindu Nationhood and the Global Construction of Indian Tradition*. Berkeley: University of California Press.

Best, Curwen (2008a) Caribbean Cyberculture: Towards an Understanding of Gender, Sexuality, and Identity within the Digital Culture Matrix. In *Constructing Vernacular Culture in the Trans-Caribbean*, ed. H. Henke and K-H. Magister, pp. 377–398. Lanham: Lexington Books.

Best, Curwen (2008b) *The Politics of Caribbean Cyberculture*. New York: Palgrave Macmillan.

Bissessarsingh, Angelo (2013) Back in Times: Hindu Burials of Yesteryear. *Trinidad Guardian* 12 May (Sunday Edition).

Cookman, Claude (1998) Margaret Bourke-White and Henri Cartier-Bresson: Gandhi's Funeral. *History of Photography* 22(1): 199–209.

Hallam, Elizabeth and Jenny Hockey (2001) *Death, Memory, and Material Culture*. Oxford: Berg.

Harlan, Lindsey (2013) Indian Arrival Day: Shifting Boundaries in the Celebration of a National Holiday in Trinidad. In *Lines in Water: Religious Boundaries in South Asia*, ed. E. Kent and T. Kassam, pp. 356–390. Syracuse: Syracuse University Press.

Jha, J. C. (1976) The Hindu Sacraments (Rites de Passage) in Trinidad and Tobago. *Caribbean Quarterly* 22(1): 40–52.

Klass, Morton (1961) *East Indians in Trinidad: A Study of Cultural Persistence*. New York: Columbia University Press.

Knott, Kim (1998) *Hinduism: A Very Short Introduction*. Oxford: Oxford University Press.

Laqueur, Thomas W. (2015) *The Work of the Dead: A Cultural History of Mortal Remains*. Princeton: Princeton University Press.

Look Lai, Walton (1993) *Indentured Labor, Caribbean Sugar: Chinese and Indian Migrants to the British West Indies, 1838–1918*. Baltimore: Johns Hopkins University Press.

Mahabir, Kumar (1990). *Hindu Festivals, Ceremonies, and Rituals in Trinidad*. Trinidad: Chakra Publishing House.

Maharaj, Pandit Munelal, Pandit Randhir Maharaj, and Shrimati Naveeta Maharaj (2003) *Death and the Soul's Journey: Final Rites and Observances, The Journey of the Soul After Death*. Trinidad: Aatmavaani Productions.

McNeal, Keith E. (2011) *Trance and Modernity in the Southern Caribbean: African and Hindu Popular Religions in Trinidad and Tobago*. Gainesville: University Press of Florida.

McNeal, Keith E. (2018) Death and the Problem of Orthopraxy in Caribbean Hinduism: Reconsidering the Politics and Poetics of Indo-Trinidadian Mortuary Ritual. In *Passages and Afterworlds: Anthropological Perspectives on Death in the Caribbean*, ed. M. Forde and Y. Hume, pp. 199–224. Durham: Duke University Press.

Morton, Sarah (1916) *John Morton of Trinidad*. Toronto: Westminster.

Munasinghe, Viranjini (2001) *Callaloo or Tossed Salad? East Indians and the Cultural Politics of Identity in Trinidad*. Ithaca: Cornell University Press.

Natarajan, Nalini (2013) *Atlantic Gandhi: The Mahatma Overseas*. New Delhi: Sage.

Niehoff, Arthur and Juanita Niehoff (1960). *East Indians in the West Indies*. Milwaukee: Milwaukee Public Museum Publications in Anthropology, 6.

Parry, Jonathan (1994) *Death in Benaras*. Cambridge: Cambridge University Press.

Persad, Pandit Hardeo (2016) *What You Need To Know About Hindu Death Ceremonies*. Trindiad: SWAHA Inc.

Pinney, Christopher (2004) *Photos of the Gods: The Printed Image and Political Struggle in India*. London: Reaktion Books.

Primiano, Leonard Norman (1995) Vernacular Religion and the Search for Method in Religious Folklife. *Western Folklore* 54(1): 37–56.

Singh, D. H. (2006) *Doon Pandit: His Life and Times*. Chaguanas: Indian Review Press.

Tyson, J. D. (1939) *Report on the Conditions of Indians in Jamaica, British Guiana, and Trinidad*. Simla: Government of India Press.

Van Der Veer, Peter and Steven Vertovec (1991) Brahmanism Abroad: On Caribbean Hinduism as an Ethnic Religion. *Ethnology* 30(2): 149–166.

Vertovec, Steven (1992) *Hindu Trinidad: Religion, Ethnicity, and Socio-Economic Change*. London: Macmillan.

PART IV

Possession and Exorcism

13

TALKING TO THE OTHER SIDE

Spiritualism as "Vernacular Religion" in Central Ohio

Hugh B. Urban

> I can talk to the other side as easily as I can talk to you. I've always been able to do that. Anybody can learn to communicate with spirits. As a matter of fact, I would say most people do it to some degree.
>
> –Reverend Joseph Mauriello (Interview with the author, 2013)

Beginning in the 1840s, a powerful form of popular religiosity known as Spiritualism spread rapidly across the United States, England, and Europe. Focused primarily on communication with spirits of the dead, Spiritualism evolved as both a philosophical system with a complex metaphysics and a popular form of practice that could be engaged by anyone in the home (Braude 24; Cox 1–21; Gutierrez 3–10; Owen 1–17). While Spiritualism declined as a major religious practice in the twentieth and twenty-first centuries, it is still very much alive and well in most parts of the United States, including my home city of Columbus, Ohio, where at least a dozen Spiritualist churches and a wide variety of mediums are active (Urban, *New Age* 67–89).

This chapter explores the role of Spiritualism in contemporary America, with a special focus on three mediums in central Ohio. These include a Spiritualist reverend who claims to have been able to talk to ghosts since childhood, the head of a Christian Spiritualist church in downtown Columbus, and a medium who channels a variety of beings ranging from the Prophet Muhammad to Vishnu and Quetzalcoatl. From its origins in the nineteenth century in upstate New York, Spiritualism has largely been a "folk" practice, associated as much (if not more) with children, women, African-Americans, and other non-elite groups as with philosophers and intellectuals. Typically practiced in the home through simple technologies such as séances, planchettes, and Ouija boards, Spiritualism has always been and continues to be a popular and "domestic" religion (Braude 24; Urban, *New Age* 67–89).

DOI: 10.4324/9781003257462-18

The research for this chapter is based on a series of interviews conducted with these three mid-western mediums over the last eight years, combined with my attendance at their services and close readings of their various print and online materials. In my analysis of their various practices of spirit communication, I employ Leonard Primiano's key concept of "vernacular religion." As Primiano argues, vernacular religion is not simply another version of the "folk" set in opposition to "official religion;" rather, it problematizes the very idea of an official religion and asks us instead to study "religion as it is lived; as human beings understand, interpret, and practice it" ("Vernacular Religion" 44).[1] The focus here is not on religion as an abstract intellectual system but rather "on the processes and practices of religious belief: their verbal, behavioral, and material expressions" (Bowman and Valk 5). The Spiritualists' "talk with the other side," I argue, is a vernacular practice in a twofold sense – at once a "lived" form of religion and a unique way of *speaking with and about* the divine.

Speaking with the Dead: Rev. Joseph Mauriello and *Ghost Psychology 101*

The roots of Spiritualism can be traced at least as far back as the eighteenth century, particularly to the writings of the enigmatic Swedish philosopher and mystic Emanuel Swedenborg (1688–1772). With his mystical journeys to Heaven and Hell and his detailed conversations with the residents of the spirit world, Swedenborg laid the metaphysical foundations for much of later Spiritualism in Europe, England, and the United States (Swedenborg 11–22). However, as a modern movement, Spiritualism is usually traced to the 1840s and to a small farmhouse in upstate New York. At their home in Hydesville, NY, three sisters named Kate, Margaret, and Leah Fox claimed to have come into contact and learned to communicate with a spirit residing in the farmhouse (allegedly the spirit of a peddler who had been murdered and buried there). When news of the spirit communication got out, thousands came to behold the spectacle, and the Fox sisters became hugely famous, sparking a massively popular movement that spread "like a prairie fire" across the eastern United States (Urban, *New Age,* 67–89; Gutierrez, ed. 1–6).

From its origins in the Fox sisters' humble farmhouse, Spiritualism was a domestic, popular, and largely non-elite movement. While Spiritualism did develop a more complex philosophical framework through the work of authors such as Andrew Jackson Davis (1826–1910; see Davis 18–27), it was, for the most part, a practice that anyone could undertake in their own homes through simple techniques such as séances or the use of a planchette (a small, usually heart-shaped piece of wood on casters used to communicate with spirits and spell out their messages). As Ann Braude notes in her study of women in the Spiritualist movement,

> Spirit circles gathered around parlour tables...The ritual of the séance perfectly suited the domestic environment. It required no participants beyond

> the family, no facilities beyond the home. The introduction of the planchette facilitated the mediumship of untrained family members within the home.
>
> *(24)*

Although Spiritualism probably strikes many readers today as either exotic or anachronistic, it should be understood as a vital part of popular religiosity in the United States over the last two hundred years – "not as a foreign element on America's religious landscape, but rather as a domestic product as American as the Bible belt and as deeply rooted in our national religious longings" (Braude xviii; see Gutierrez, ed. 1–6). In this sense, Spiritualism is also a particularly clear expression of "vernacular religion," as the "power of the individual and communities of individuals to create and re-create their own religion" – not simply through abstract belief systems but through ordinary speech and practice (Primiano, "Afterword" 383–384).

While by no means as widespread as it was at its height in the nineteenth century, this largely non-elite, popular, and "vernacular" form of religious practice has continued in the many Spiritualist churches that we find today, such as the Guiding Light Church in Columbus, Ohio. Located in a humble storefront in a strip mall on the east side of the city, Guiding Light has a small but active and dedicated congregation. Its primary leader is Joseph Mauriello, an ordained Spiritualist reverend who has guided the small church on Morse Road since 1985. "Reverend Joe," as he is known to his congregation, is also an author who has published several books on the subject of mediumship, ghosts, and spirit communication, including *Ghost Psychology 101* and *Only a Thought Away*. A soft-spoken, middle-aged man with an impressive head of thick silver hair, Mauriello also has a very subtle but wicked sense of humor (for example, when I brought a group of Ohio State University [OSU] students with me for a visit one Sunday morning, he greeted our group during his opening remarks and then turned and whispered to his wife, "did you tell them about the human sacrifices?").

I have had a chance to interview Mauriello several times over the last eight years and found him eager to talk about the history of Spiritualism, the nature of spirits, and the practice of mediumship. As he recounted, his mother discovered Spiritualism and became a reverend herself when he was still a small child. However, even before his mother's turn to Spiritualism, Mauriello says that he has been able to communicate with spirits since at least the age of five, having regular interactions with deceased relatives whom he had never met in the flesh:

> I was communicating with spirits my whole life, since before I could talk physically…As a child, communicating with spirits was fantastic. But I didn't know any differently. I had done it all my life. To give an example: my dad's parents and my mom's father had all passed away before I was born, but they were still part of my life. They would show up for special

> events or whatever was going on, and I would talk with them and get to know them.
>
> *(Interview with the author, 2013)*

Mauriello's understanding of spirit communication is very much a kind of "vernacular religion," in Primiano's sense. While he is an ordained reverend and operates a church with a regular weekly service, this is a religion based primarily on the active experience of talking to spiritual beings in daily life. Repeatedly, Mauriello emphasized the sort of "everyday," "lived," and often quite mundane nature of spirit communication. Contact with spirits could be visual or auditory, but it could also be a simple smell or taste: "You hear their words, see their images. And it's not limited to that – I've smelled cookies baking. All the senses can be used by spirits" (Interview with the author, 2013; Interview with the author, 2021). By no means an exotic mystical experience, spirit communication in his view is something that anyone can learn to do, simply by trusting in and developing their natural powers of intuition:

> I've done it every single day of my life. I can talk to the other side as easily as I can talk to you. I've always been able to do that.
>
> Anybody can learn to communicate with spirits. As a matter of fact, I would say most people do it to some degree. They get hunches about a situation, they don't know where it came from; they get a feeling about somebody – like maybe someone is lying to them and not trustworthy, and there's nothing outwardly indicating that, but they just get this sense suddenly "don't trust that person." A lot of that is communication; spirits are trying to let you know: "be aware of that person"
>
> *(Interview with the author, 2013; see Sunday Service)*

Similarly, as he explains in his book *Only a Thought Away*, anyone can learn the basic techniques of talking to deceased loved ones in everyday life and so "make visits with your departed loved ones and spirit guides a daily occurrence" (front cover).

In Mauriello's view, most spirits are beings who are naturally moving on to the afterlife. Many are relatives such as deceased parents or grandparents who return to see us simply "because they're family. They want to visit, share good times with you, share bad times with you, to be there with you." Some, however, are what we call "ghosts" – that is, spirits who "don't accept the fact that they've died" and linger in this realm in a confused state until someone (such as a Spiritualist medium like himself) helps guide them to the other side (Interview with the author, 2013; Sunday Service).

Like virtually all Spiritualists, Mauriello incorporates the practice of spirit communication directly into the lived practice of his church services and into the daily lives and physical experiences of church members. His weekly services at the Guiding Light typically include the following basic elements: a form of spiritual healing in which trained healers lay their hands upon and align the auras and *chakras* (energy centers) of individual congregants; personal spirit messages, in which the reverends give short messages from the spirits directly to each congregant; and (on some occasions) group spirit readings, in which all members of the congregation are invited to meditate and spontaneously describe whatever images or sounds came into their minds so that the reverend can construct a sort of group reading for the entire community (Interview with the author, 2013; Sunday Service).

One of the most striking examples of the lived and vernacular nature of religious practice at Mauriello's church occurred when I brought a group of OSU students to visit his Sunday service in 2005. In the very middle of the service, Mauriello's wife – who was then in training to become a reverend – interrupted everything and announced that there was a spirit in the room at that moment. Mauriello consulted with his wife and mother (also a reverend), and together they determined that it was the spirit of someone who had recently died in a car accident and had come along with some living person in the congregation that day. They then asked if anyone in the room knew someone who had died in a car accident – and, sure enough, one of the students in our group had a friend who had recently been killed in a crash. The three mediums conferred and decided that they needed to help guide the confused spirit safely from this earthly plane and onward to a better place in the spirit world. They invited the entire congregation to meditate and pray together, and, apparently, we all helped usher it along to the other side (Urban, *New Age* 67–68).

Personalized Messages from the Beyond: Reverend Carol Boyd and Christian Spiritualism

While mediums such as Mauriello do not identify as Christian and have little to say about Jesus or the Bible, many other Spiritualists are much more explicitly "Christian" in orientation. Located in a lovely stone historical church in downtown Columbus, the Christian Spiritualist Temple is one of the oldest and largest independent Spiritualist communities in the Midwest. The church traces its origins back to a nineteenth-century gold miner and businessman named Ebenezer Barker, Jr., who is said to have received some surprisingly lucrative stock advice from a Spiritualist medium. In gratitude, he used his subsequent wealth to purchase a Spiritualist church in 1901 (1CSTchurch, "Church History"). Like more or less all Spiritualist communities, the Christian Spiritualist Temple emphasizes gender equality and the importance of women's roles, and is currently led by Reverend Carol Boyd. A thin middle-aged woman with short dark hair and a commanding voice, Reverend Boyd guides a small, largely older, but fiercely dedicated congregation.

According to their website, this particular church distinguishes itself from most other American Spiritualist groups primarily by its more explicitly Christian orientation (though it does not identify with any mainline denominations and incorporates many elements from other religions). While spirit mediumship is essential to the group, so is the use of the Bible and reverence for the person of Jesus Christ:

> Unlike the National Spiritualist Association, we include teachings from the Holy Bible. Using the teachings of Jesus and other Master Teachers as a foundation, we strive to make our beliefs our way of life. We accept each person as an individual example of God's love and power, and help them discover and use their own spiritual gifts. We believe in and use spiritual healing, prophecy, and mediumship.
>
> We know that life is eternal and is, therefore, continuous as shown by the spirit messages we receive.
>
> *(1CSTchurch, "Our Beliefs")*

As Reverend Boyd explained in a sermon, Jesus Christ is the divine energy or power that flows through the entire universe, and Spiritualists are those individuals who know how to channel that energy as a source of enlightenment and healing for both themselves and others:

> Spiritualists got it many, many years ago...Get better from within. Each of us can get better, and that's that personal responsibility part...As Christian spiritualists we celebrate the Christ consciousness, the Christ light that shines and is brilliant in this chapel. It brings us together, it unites us, it supports us, and then we who know and acknowledge it can send it into our communities, into our families, into the hospitals, into the places where there's a need for healing. We're like a conductor of energy.
>
> *(Boyd, "Spiritualist")*

In practice, however, the church's daily activities are a complex mix of more "mainstream" American Christian subjects such as Bible study and what we might consider more alternative or "New Age" sorts of topics, such as discussions of auras, the *chakras*, and how to receive spirit messages. Alongside a monthly "rosary group" (collective recitation of the rosary), the church also offers classes on the key New Age text on spirit channeling, *A Course in Miracles* (1CSTchurch, "Church Services"). The church's understanding of Jesus is also a bit different from that of most other more mainline churches in the United States. While Jesus is a central figure in their teachings, he is largely revered not as the singular, unique Son of God but more as an enlightened "Master" alongside the Buddha, Muhammad, and other enlightened teachers who have appeared throughout human history (Boyd, Interview with the author).

Similarly, its weekly services include both singing of widely known Christian hymns and readings from the Bible, alongside more uniquely Spiritualist practices such as spirit healing and personalized spirit readings. The first of these – spirit healing – is a practice seen throughout most Spiritualist churches today and usually consists of trained healers who lay hands upon and pray over individual members of the congregation. Historically, the Spiritualist practice of healing has roots in older occult ideas of the subtle body; and, in more recent decades, it has also incorporated concepts drawn from Eastern religions, such as *chakras* (subtle energy centers), and more widespread New Age ideas, such as aura alignment (see Samuel and Johnston 1–34; Crow 138–171; Urban, "Subtle Bodies").

The second unique practice – the delivery of personalized spirit messages – usually takes place at the very end of a Sunday service, as the reverend moves around the entire church and offers a short spirit reading for each member of the congregation. The reverend typically closes her eyes and holds each individual's hands for a short time (ranging from a few seconds to a few minutes) before communicating a message from the spirits. For example, one Sunday in October 2014, I brought a small group of students with me. At the end of the service, Reverend Boyd worked her way through the students, holding each of their hands for a very long time. She told one that the spirit of a close relative wanted him to spend more time in the out-of-doors, communing with nature; she told another student that the spirit of a grandmother or aunt wanted her to get in touch with her musical roots and sing. Then when she got to me, she held my hands for about three seconds and informed me that one of my deceased uncles had a very direct message for me: apparently, he wanted me to spend less time reading books and thinking about abstract ideas and instead spend more time interacting with the "real world" (Boyd, Interview with the author). I had to admit that this seemed like a pretty accurate message.

As such, the Christian Spiritualist Temple is a particularly good example of what we might call a kind of "vernacular Christianity" – a living, local articulation of Christianity expressed through the regional dialect of mid-western Spiritualism. The primary emphasis here is not on orthodoxy, dogmatic faith, or theological doctrine; in fact, congregants are told they can believe whatever they want and be welcome in the church. Rather, it is very much an ortho-praxic sort of church, where healing and spirit communication are the primary focus. Surviving as it does in the heart of the mid-western United States, surrounded by largely conservative Evangelical and Catholic denominations, this church clearly speaks a Christian "language" that most mid-westerners will recognize. Yet it also articulates it through the uniquely Spiritualist vernacular language of Masters, spirit guides, mediumship, and healing, that really challenges the very notion of a singular or homogenous Christian discourse today.

"Vishnu Speaks:" Cindy Riggs and Modern Channeling

While Spiritualism reached its height of popularity during the late nineteenth to early twentieth centuries, it also inspired several other related movements that are still flourishing today. One of these is the practice known as "channeling," which is in many ways a modern continuation and re-articulation of the older practice of spirit mediumship. As we see in key figures such as Jane Roberts, JZ

Knight, and others, channelers claim to be able to enter into trance states and "channel" or speak with the voice of particular spiritual entities. For example, Roberts channeled an entity named "Seth," and Knight channels Ramtha, a being from an ancient realm called Lemuria (Melton 1–30; Urban, "Medium is the Message"). Although they use more contemporary language, often drawn from modern science and technology, twenty-first-century channelers have much in continuity with older Spiritualists: like early Spiritualism, channeling tends to be a "domestic" phenomenon, often taking place in the home and in very mundane circumstances; as with Spiritualism, channelers are often female and emphasize the authority of women as having the power to speak with and from the spirits; and like Spiritualism, channeling tends be a kind of "vernacular" religious practice, a means of communicating and interacting with spiritual beings who typically have very practical, pragmatic, this-worldly advice for their audiences (see Urban, *New Age* 220–241; Urban, "Medium is the Message;" Gutierrez, ed. 1–2).

Today, channelers are found not only in more obvious New Age hot spots such as San Francisco or Sedona; they can be found more or less anywhere in the United States, including central Ohio. Cindy Riggs, for example, is a channeler who works out of a small office in Worthington, just north of Columbus. Well-dressed with blond hair and a bright, cheerful smile, she could just as easily be a real estate agent or bank representative as a spirit channeler. As she recounted to me during one interview, she was raised in a "pretty normal Christian (Presbyterian) family," and as an adult, however, went through a period of depression and began to seek out something completely different in order to "just start out fresh." She took a Reiki class, and, after a single attunement, she started spontaneously seeing and hearing things and soon realized she was communicating with beings from another plane of existence:

> I started to get messages in the middle of the night, always at 3:15 am. I was starting to write them down, and I realized that I probably wasn't making that stuff up. So one night I finally said, "who is talking to me?" And he said, "we are light beings, like you." That's when I realized something else really was talking to me.
>
> *(Interview with the author 2013)*

Shortly after this first experience, Riggs recalls, she met her first two spirit guides, who appeared in the form of an Aztec woman and a shape-shifting hawk-man. Eventually, she learned to contact and channel a wide range of beings. Unlike channelers such as Jane Roberts or JZ Knight, who each channel one primary being, Riggs is extremely eclectic and wide-ranging in her communications – what she calls a "Universal Channel" – speaking with "literally thousands" of beings, who include everyone from Jesus and the Prophet Muhammad to the Aztec deity Quetzalcoatl and various Hindu gods and goddesses (Interview with the author, 2013). Indeed, she even "co-authored" a book with the Hindu god,

Vishnu, who one day informed her that they were going to write a text together and appeared each morning at five o'clock, dictating one chapter a day until they were finished (Riggs, *Vishnu Speaks*).

Riggs also describes a unique process by which her spirit communications take place. While many Spiritualist mediums and channelers enter into an unconscious state when they receive messages (for example, Roberts and Knight when they channel Seth and Ramtha; see Urban, "Medium Is the Message"), Riggs claims that she remains fully conscious but chooses to temporarily "step aside" from her body to allow the spirit to enter:

> I know some channelers go completely unconscious, and I do not. I allow the being to come to me wherever they come in. Sometimes they come in my crown or my heart, but usually it's just everywhere now. When they complete the integration, I actually step myself out. But I am conscious. And people who see energy have actually seen me standing over here, beside myself....
>
> I believe that channeling is a skill that can be learned, but I think everyone will do it a little bit differently. My process is going into a trance state, which takes me only second now, waiting to see who wishes to speak to either my group or my client, and allow them to approach me. Then I allow them to merge with me.
>
> *(Interview with the author, 2013; Interview with the author, 2021)*

Just as the kinds of spirits she channels are extremely diverse and eclectic, so too, Riggs' practice with her clients is also extremely wide-ranging. She engages in a striking array of different therapeutic techniques, from basic psychic readings and healings to body-work and hypnosis, from past-life regressions to a special technique that she calls "defragmenting" (Riggs, "Services"). One of her more popular techniques, it turns out, is "remote viewing" – a method she learned from a psychic trained by the CIA in the 1970s – which she uses to great success in finding lost objects for people (Interview with the author 2021). Interestingly enough, Riggs said that the COVID-19 situation had not affected her practice very much during 2020–2021, because she is able to do most of her psychic work just as well remotely via zoom or cell phone as in-person (except for a few techniques such as hypnosis and past-life regression, where physical presence is more helpful, though not absolutely essential; Interview with the author, 2021).

Most of her clients, she says, are seeking something that traditional religious institutions and conventional medicine do not offer; her basic aim is simply a practical goal of helping people "get to happy" – understood physically, spiritually, and emotionally – in their everyday life:

> I help people get to happy. So I am helping to remove things that may be blocking them or remove things that may be interfering with their energy. That could be a spirit attaching, or it could be a pattern of belief that they

> have created throughout their lifetime. We use some hypnosis; I do a lot of energy body working; and I do sessions I call defragmenting, because they're kind of like a soul retrieval session. But it could incorporate any of tools that I use. So it could be some psychic reading, it might be some channeling, it might be some energy work. I also do past life readings and past life clearings. I can do a past life regression, where I would put you under hypnosis and you could maybe see you own past life....
>
> Most are seeking something. They're seeking some kind of spiritual understanding for themselves that's not traditional religion. Or they're looking for something that traditional medicine has not helped them with.
>
> *(Interview with the author, 2013; Interview with the author 2021)*

It is worth noting that most of Riggs' clients – about 75% by her estimate – are women (Interview with the author 2013). Again, this is in continuity with the older tradition of Spiritualism going back to the nineteenth century, which also had a strong affinity with women and the domestic sphere, as an alternative to the largely male-dominated institutional religious sphere (Braude 1–9, 192–201; Owen 1–40).

At the same time, however, it is worth noting that Riggs is also a businesswoman, whose many channeling services come at a certain cost. Unlike Mauriello and Boyd, who both lead non-profit religious organizations and only ask for donations, Riggs operates more like a private therapist with set fees for each particular service on offer. Her basic rates for in-person consultations are $45 for a 15-minute session, $75 for a 30-minute session, and so on up to $337 for a 3-hour intensive session. She also offers phone consultations at a discounted price as well as other group services, such as "LoveLight Connection Sessions" for couples at $125 for 60 minutes (Riggs, "Fees"). As such, Riggs is also a clear example of what scholars such as Kimberly Lau have called "New Age capitalism," or the ways in which spiritual practices such as channeling, aura readings, Reiki, the use of crystals, and so on tend to become commodified and absorbed amidst a thriving new kind of spiritual marketplace (Lau 1–20; see also Carrette and King 1–29). Like most New Age channelers, Riggs is also quite fluent in the very American "vernacular language" of advertising, marketing, and consumer capitalism.

In sum, Riggs' form of channeling is a particularly striking example of vernacular religion in Primiano's sense, as "the art of individual interpretation and negotiation of any number of religious sources" ("Afterword" 384). Riggs is drawing upon, reworking, and re-interpreting a huge number of religious sources, ranging from early Spiritualist traditions to Christianity and Islam, to Aztec, Hindu, Buddhist, and other traditions. And she is also drawing upon and re-configuring a wide range of spiritual and psychological techniques, ranging from Reiki and hypnosis to past-life regression. Finally, she is also re-translating all of these into her own sort of mid-western vernacular dialectic that seems to communicate quite well with suburban audiences in regions such as Worthington and Ohio.

Conclusions: Spirit Communication and the Double Valence of "Vernacular Religion"

To conclude, I would just like to make some broader comparative comments on the phenomenon of spirit communication and its implications for the study of folk and lived religion. While I have only examined three mediums from my small region of central Ohio, I do think they reveal some larger insights into the idea of "vernacular religion," as authors such as Primiano, Bowman, and Valk have used the phrase. Most importantly, I think these spirit mediums reveal a sort of double valence or dual aspect in the idea of vernacular religion. The first aspect is more or less what Primiano means when he talks about "religion as it is lived; as human beings understand, interpret, and practice it." Vernacular religion in this sense is not simply another iteration of the "folk" set in opposition to the "official" religion; more importantly, it challenges the very idea that there is an "official religion" at all and asks us always to think about religion in its lived, everyday forms, the ways in which religion is inevitably the product of interpretations and negotiations of multiple resources by ordinary religious actors (Primiano, "Afterword" 383–384). Spiritualism and Channeling, I think, are perfect examples of this sort of vernacular challenge to the very idea of an "official" religion. While they are often rooted in "mainstream" belief systems such as Christianity, these spirit mediums also complicate that "official" religion with a wide range of popular practices drawn from nineteenth-century occultism, psychology, Eastern religions, and New Age spirituality (see also Bender 1–55).

In a second and perhaps more interesting sense, however, these spirit mediums also represent a unique sort of "vernacular religion" as a very specific way of *speaking about*, *with*, and *from* the divine. As a living practice, spirit mediumship is first and foremost a technique for communicating with unseen realms and translating the knowledge gained to a local, human, and contemporary audience. For example, when Reverend Mauriello speaks with ghosts in his small storefront church, he is also translating Spiritualist ideas drawn from the nineteenth century into a new local idiom in central Ohio. When Reverend Boyd communicates personal spirit messages to her congregants, she is also translating fairly esoteric Spiritualist ideas into a kind of hybrid "New Age-Christian dialect" for twenty-first-century residents of a mid-western city. And when Cindy Riggs channels Vishnu, she is translating this ancient Indian deity (or at least a contemporary American imagining of an ancient Indian deity) into the vernacular language of New Age spirituality and the dialect of middle-class suburban women in central Ohio. In each case, we find a unique form of religious speech that takes place largely outside of more established religious institutions and yet allows ordinary individuals to hear from, interact with, and talk back to the spirit world in their daily lives. This is what we might call a kind of "*vernacular vernacular religion*," which doubly disrupts the idea that there is any sort of "official religion" and instead reveals the remarkable diversity of religious life in all its manifold, weird, and wondrous articulations.

Note

1 Vernacular religion "highlights the power of the individual and communities of individuals to create and re-create their own religion . . .Vernacular religion is not the dichotomous or dialectical partner of 'institutional' religious forms. Vernacular religion. . . shifts the way one studies religion with the people being the focus of study and not 'religion' or 'belief' as abstractions. Religious traditions, and the institutions which can be related to them, therefore, have vernacular religion as their foundation. . . Vernacular religious theory understands religion as the art of individual interpretation and negotiation of any number of religious sources" (Primiano, "Afterword" 383–384).

In this chapter, I am also influenced by Robert Orsi's notion of "lived religion" (Orsi, *Between Heaven and Earth*; Orsi, *Madonna of 115th Street*) and Courtney Bender's discussion of spirituality (*New Metaphysicals*).

Works Cited

1CSTchurch. "Church History." *1CSTChurch.org*, 2021, https://www.1cstchurch.org/church-history. Accessed 24 July, 2021.

———. "Church Services." *1CSTChurch.org*, 2021, https://www.1cstchurch.org/church-services. Accessed 24 July, 2021.

———. "Our Beliefs." *1CSTChurch.org*, 2021, https://www.1cstchurch.org/our-beliefs. Accessed 24 July, 2021.

Bender, Courtney. *The New Metaphysicals: Spirituality and the American Religious Imagination*. Chicago, IL: University of Chicago Press, 2010.

Bowman, Marion and Ülo Valk, editors. *Vernacular Religion in Everyday Life*. New York: Routledge 2014.

Boyd, Carol. Interview with the author. October 15, 2014.

———. "Spiritualist." *1CSTChurch.org*, 2021, https://www.1cstchurch.org/sermons/. Accessed 24 July, 2021.

Braude, Anne. *Radical Spirits: Spiritualism and Women's Rights in Nineteenth Century America*. Bloomington: Indiana University Press, 2001.

Carrette, Jeremy and Richard King. *Selling Spirituality: The Silent Takeover of Religion*. New York: Routledge, 2004.

Cox, Robert S. *Body and Spirit: A Sympathetic History of American Spiritualism*. Charlottesville, VA: University of Virginia Press, 2003.

Crow, John L. *Occult Bodies: The Corporal Construction of the Theosophical Society, 1875–1935*. PhD Dissertation, Florida State University, 2017.

Davis, Andrew Jackson. *The Harmonial Philosophy*. Whitefish, MT: Kessinger Publishing, 2010.

Gutierrez, Cathy. *Plato's Ghost: Spiritualism in the American Renaissance*. New York: Oxford University Press, 2009.

Gutierrez, Cathy, ed. *Handbook of Spiritualism and Channeling*. Leiden: Brill, 2020.

Lau, Kimberly J. *New Age Capitalism: Making Money East of Eden*. Philadelphia: University of Pennsylvania Press, 2000.

Mauriello, Joseph. *(Your Departed Loved Ones and Spirit Guides are) Only a Thought Away*. Bloomington, IN: iUniverse, 2005.

———. *Ghost Psychology 101*. Plantation, FL: Llumina Press, 2008.

———. Interview with the author, Columbus, Ohio, June 18, 2013.

———. Interview with the author, Columbus, Ohio, August 2, 2021.

———. Sunday Service, Columbus, Ohio, August 1, 2021.
Melton, J. Gordon. *Finding Enlightenment: Ramtha's School of Ancient Wisdom.* Hillsboro, OR: Beyond Words Pub., 1998.
Orsi, Robert. *Between Heaven and Earth.* Princeton: Princeton University Press, 2004.
———. *The Madonna of 115th Street: Community in Italian Harlem, 1880–1950.* New Haven, CT: Yale University Press, 2010.
Owen, Alex. *The Darkened Room: Women, Power, and Spiritualism in Late Victorian England.* Chicago: University of Chicago Press, 2004.
Primiano, Leonard. "Vernacular Religion and the Search for Method in Religious Folklore." *Journal of Western Folklore,* vol. 54, no. 1, 1995, pp. 37–56.
———. "Afterword." *Vernacular Religion in Everyday Life,* edited by Marion Bowman and Ülo Valk. New York: Routledge 2014, pp.382–394
Riggs, Cindy. *Vishnu Speaks: Messages of Enlightenment from the Ancient Deity.* CreateSpace Independent Publishing Platform, 2012.
———. Interview with the author, Worthington, Ohio, 10 June, 2013.
———. "Home." *CindyRiggs.org,* 2021, https://cindyriggs.com/. Accessed 24 July, 2021.
———. "Services." *CindyRiggs*.org, 2021, https://cindyriggs.com/services/. Accessed 24 July, 2021.
———. "Fees." *CindyRiggs.org,* 2021, https://cindyriggs.com/fees/. Accessed 24 July, 2021.
———. Interview with the author, Columbus, Ohio, 5 August, 2021.
Samuel, Geoffrey and Jay Johnston, eds. *Religion and the Subtle Body in Asia and the West.* New York: Routledge, 2013.
Swedenborg, Emanuel. *Heaven and Hell.* New York: Swedenborg Foundation, 1976.
Urban, Hugh B. *New Age, Neopagan, and New Religious Movements: Alternative Spirituality in Modern America.* Berkeley, CA: University of California Press, 2015.
———. "The Medium is the Message in the Spacious Present: Television, Channeling, and the New Age." *Handbook of Spiritualism and Channeling,* edited by Cathy Gutierrez. Leiden: Brill, 2020, pp. 317–339.
———. "Subtle Bodies: Cartographies of the Soul from India to 'the West.'" *Hermaion,* vol. 6, 2022, pp. 29–49.

14

BECOMING A GOD

Spirit Possession Practices at a South Indian Temple

Julie Edelstein

In late December 2016, I sat in Madurai city's Pandi Koyil temple with several women who were employed there as sweepers, listening to them warn me about walking alone. Among them was Sushila,[1] a woman in her 50s who worked cleaning the temple and managing the animals slated for sacrifice to the main deity, Pandi Muneesvarar. A *kāval teyvam* ("guardian deity"), Pandi Muneesvarar is a regional protector god with a penchant for possessing his devotees. He is worshipped by people from a variety of caste and religious backgrounds in Madurai, Tamil Nadu, India. Seated that day, Sushila and the others cautioned me about dangers lurking in the shadows around the temple precincts. They knew that I walked, often alone, between the bus stop and the temple, separated by a long, lonely dirt path where stray dogs roamed. Ghosts and rapists might also populate those out-of-the-way places, they warned. I should be very careful. Wasn't I afraid? When my research assistant Hemalatha[2] suggested that surely Pandi would protect me, Sushila interjected. She raised her right arm as if wielding an *aruvaḷ*, a curved blade associated with *kāval teyvam*, insisting I would be safe. Sushila proclaimed, "If anyone tries to rape you, you yourself will become Pandi Muni and kill that person."

What does it mean for me, a western researcher, to become a god? Sushila's comment makes sense in the context of Pandi Koyil. Here practices of spirit possession catalyze a transformation wherein the deity enters a devotee's body and that person becomes, temporarily, the god himself. Possession experiences are common in South India, South Asia more broadly, and in diverse cultural formations worldwide, yet possession is extremely difficult to categorize. Defined broadly by anthropologist Janice Boddy, possession "refers to the hold exerted over a human being by external forces or entities more powerful than she" (407). Taking on a diversity of forms and meanings, possession phenomena in Tamil Nadu, as elsewhere in South Asia, are regular facets of lived religious practice.

DOI: 10.4324/9781003257462-19

Sanskritist and historian Frederick M. Smith argues that possession is the most fundamental, widespread, and enduring religious practice of South Asia (597). Although there are many kinds of South Asian possession phenomena, the primary type found at Pandi Koyil is what Smith identifies as "oracular possession," positive possession caused by a god or goddess that is revered and often welcomed rather than managed through exorcism.

Sushila's comment about me turning into a god suggests prominent traits evident in possession practices: intimacy, immediacy, and fluidity. Possession challenges assumptions that humans are discrete, bounded entities with fixed identities, behaviors, and capacities. Instead, possession phenomena offer an alternative worldview emphasizing the fluidity of selfhood, the permeability of human beings, and the transformational potential of ritual practice. Possession is an embodied practice effecting both the possessed and those who interact with the possessed. Folklorist Leonard Primiano's framework of "vernacular religion" is a useful scholarly approach to possession practices because of his focus on verbal and behavioral expressions of religiosity (44). At Pandi Koyil, the altered behaviors of the possessed, including bodily movements and verbal utterances, are entry points to interpret possession as lived religious practice. Although it is challenging to define and interpret possession, I argue that at Pandi Koyil, possession is fundamentally about relationships. Two primary kinds of relationship are present in possession practices: (1) the relationship between the deity and the possessed, and (2) the relationship between the deity and the larger community. Possession at Pandi Koyil is an ambivalent interaction between beings, a relationship marked by intimacy and danger, the erotic and the fearsome. This ambivalence is apparent in the mixed reactions possession elicits from those who experience or witness it. Possession is sometimes welcomed, but not always. The ambivalence of possession is also evident in its troubling of institutionalized hierarchies. The intervention of a priest is unnecessary to mediate possession which often happens spontaneously to people without ritual training or authority. As folklorist Dan Yoder points out, "folk religion exists in a complex society in relation to and in tension with the organized religion(s) of that society" (76). So it is at Pandi Koyil where, for example, I have seen possessed teenage girls attract larger crowds of devotees seeking guidance and blessings than the sanctioned priests attending the inner sanctum are able.

This chapter is based on ethnographic field research conducted in Madurai between 2016 and 2019. In 2016–2017, I spent one month conducting research for my Master's thesis.[3] During this time, I spent most days at Pandi Koyil, engaged in participant observation research and conducting informal interviews with temple employees and attendees. I worked with an assistant, Hemalatha, a woman in her early 20s, who helped translating between Tamil and English.[4] I returned to Madurai in June 2017–May 2018 for Tamil language training. During this time, I attended Pandi Koyil twice a week, without a research assistant. In June–August 2019, I conducted preliminary dissertation research at Pandi Koyil.[5] During this period, I attended the temple most days and conducted informal interviews without a research assistant.

Pandi Koyil and Possession: An Introduction

Located in the South Indian city of Madurai, affectionately dubbed "the Temple City" because of its many Hindu temples, the Pandi Koyil temple has an infamous reputation. Although Pandi Koyil is neither very old (it was founded just five generations ago), nor does it boast an elaborate architectural magnificence (such as displayed by the Meenakshi Temple nearby), there is a special aura to Pandi Koyil that radiates from its location on the outskirts of the old city; once the area was home to paddy fields and wasteland, but now it is the site of encroaching urban development. The temple's main deity is Pandi Muneesvarar (hereafter, Pandi): an imposing figure of black stone, seated in a cross-legged position in the inner sanctum, sporting a prominent mustache, draped in garlands of roses and limes. Pandi is a *kāval teyvam* who protects a specified jurisdiction and its inhabitants. Like other guardian deities, Pandi is exceptionally powerful, though ambivalent, and he is linked to a specific site framed by local mythologies and specific practices. Pandi's popularity has increased in the last decade, and the small shrine that was once a thatched-roof hut has expanded into a large temple complex at the center of a vibrant marketplace.

Devotees of many religious backgrounds including Hindu, Muslim, and Christian come to Pandi Koyil in search of bodily healing and fertility, and also to find jobs and gain protection for newly purchased vehicles. These practical requests underscore the vernacular, everyday relevance of Pandi in the lives of those who worship him. Devotees often fulfill ritual vows to Pandi: piercing of the ears, hair tonsure, cooking offerings of *poṅkal* (sweetened rice), or sacrificing a goat or chicken. A couple may come to Pandi Koyil after their marriage if they are having difficulty conceiving. They may promise Pandi that if the wife gets pregnant, they will come back after delivery, offer an animal in sacrifice, and honor the deity by naming their child after him and shaving its head in his temple. Such offerings are nodes in a web of reciprocal exchanges flowing back and forth between deity and devotee. These exchanges establish bonds of intimacy and ensure the continuity of relational attachments. Such acts are common throughout the lived religious practices of the region. In their edited volume on religious vows in South Asia, Selva Raj and William Harman argue that for many in South Asia, vows "constitute the core-and sometimes even the entirety-of how the nonprofessionally religious . . . participate in their tradition" (6). Raj and Harman describe the relationships between humans and deities that are forged and sustained through vow-making as ones of "personal obligation, commitment, and indebtedness" (8). Most of the vows made at Pandi Koyil fall into what Raj and Harman categorize as "mundane" vows, those "concerned with achieving the good life in society, and with materialism, stability, and order" as opposed to "soteriological vows . . . concerned with each individual's ultimate spiritual achievement" (250). Such vows are no less important because they deal with the here and now; at Pandi Koyil, those are the most pressing concerns and Pandi is famous for satisfying his devotees' requests.

I interpret possession as one type of exchange relationship occurring between deity and devotee. Like other deities associated with Hinduism, Pandi accepts offerings from his worshippers and reciprocates by giving blessings, including granting desired wishes and infusing ritual substances with healing potencies, such as *tirunīṟu* (sacred ash) and *cāmi cōṟu* ("god rice," sanctified foodstuffs) distributed by priests at his temple. Ongoing relationships of mutuality are solidified and reaffirmed through the multiple exchanges of substance and desires flowing between the god and devotees. In this environment of ritual exchange, possession is another practice that underscores the intimate relationship between Pandi and his devotees.

Scholars examining possession in South Asia make a categorical distinction between types of possession experiences. Beneficent possessions caused by the agency of a god or goddess, described as oracular possession, are contrasted with malignant, disease-producing possessions caused by the infiltration of a ghost or other harmful spirit (Wadley 235–236; Smith 597). Yet, even oracular possession can be agonistic: "Possession is always to some extent disruptive and almost always in some sense violent" (Smith 597). Anthropologist Ann Gold highlights the overlap between categories of possession in her work on religion in a Rajasthani village, claiming that divine versus malignant possessions are not exclusive categories, for one kind of experience may morph into the other over time (35). This fuzzy categorization of possession certainly characterizes Pandi Koyil. While Pandi is worshipped as a god, a powerful, beneficent being, he is a deeply ambivalent figure. While possession by Pandi is seen as a blessing indicating the devotee's purity and close relationship with the deity, it is simultaneously understood to be troublesome. For instance, familial and marital problems often follow after a devotee gets possessed. This polysemy in interpretations reveals that possession cannot be reduced to a binary typology; it is not merely beneficent or malignant.

Possession by Pandi takes place on any day of the week, at any time. On Fridays and Sundays, when the temple is busiest, the number of possessions dramatically increases, and the activity around possessed individuals intensifies. Pandi primarily possesses women. Many scholars have theorized the greater involvement of women in possession practices (Keller; Ong), postulating women's lesser social status as a reason they may find comfort in and seek solutions to problems through the power and authority they achieve while possessed. At Pandi Koyil, gender imbalance in possession practices is understood to be a matter of relationship preference: Pandi is said to be especially fond of beautiful young girls, and his possession of them is seen as an expression of this erotic attachment.

Many possessed devotees utter prophecies, and people come to the temple to seek advice from those who speak with the voice of god, for these possessed humans are regarded to be the deity himself during possession experiences. Accordingly, supplicants who approach possessed devotees address them using respectful terms for Pandi – such as *ayyā* ("sir"), *appā* ("father"), or *cāmi* ("god") – regardless of their gender, age, or status when not possessed. The possessed also refer to themselves as Pandi, using first-person pronouns, referring to "my temple" and even requesting offerings to be given "to me." Those who are barred from roles of authority in daily life – such as young women or individuals from communities considered low in caste hierarchy – take on a drastically altered persona, set of behaviors, bodily comportment, and status when they are possessed by Pandi: these are all indications of the transformation that possession initiates.

Unlike the English word "possession" which refers primarily to ownership, and, by extension, to the takeover of a person by a spirit being, the Tamil words translated by the term possession have a different semantic range; many terms highlight movement and spatial relationships between entities. The term *cāmi aṭittal* ("god dancing") is one of the most common Tamil expressions for possession. This phrase captures the characteristic motion of the possessed person who exhibits patterned movements, including rhythmic stepping, jumping, or swaying, often with arms raised above the head. Other common phrases for possession include saying that the deity or spirit "came" (*vantatu/vantācchu*) and "went" (*pōṉatu/pōcchu*); the onset of possession is the spirit's coming, and its departure is the end of the possession episode. Similarly, the spirit entity is often described as "descending/getting down" (*iraṅkutal*) onto the body of the possessed person. A spirit may also be described as "grabbing/plucking" (*piṭikkiratu*) the person it possesses. This last term is used to refer to the initial instance of possession when a deity selects a devotee for the first time; it is also used for negative spirits who afflict those they possess. This range of vocabulary is used across Tamil-speaking communities to indicate possession experiences (Bloomer 127–133).

Possession as Bodily Transformation and Relational Intimacy

When Sushila stated that I would become Pandi and kill any aggressors who attempted to assault me, she implied the potential of a transformation in which a young, small, foreign woman could transmogrify into a ferocious, knife-wielding god, capable of slaying an attacker. What does it mean to become a god? What does it mean for a human woman to become a male god? What kinds of assumptions do such comments reveal about the nature of being and becoming? Anthropologist Kalpana Ram comments on the bodily transformation that accompanies possession in Tamil Nadu. Ram explains that "possession represents at once a break with a woman's ordinary *naṭamuṟai* [comportment] and a behavior that assumes its drama only against the invisible backdrop of that ordinary, day-to-day discipline" (236). The activities of possession diverge from the normal behavior of the non-possessed, and these changes are especially striking exhibited by women.

Possessions at Pandi Koyil are marked by any of the following actions: running, jumping, screaming, maniacal laughter, heavy breathing, belching, stretching the arms above the head with clasped fingers, sticking out and biting the tongue, rolling eyes, pushing, shoving, or hitting, verbally berating social superiors, and allowing the hair and garments to become loose in a manner that shirks local modesty standards. At Pandi Koyil, possessed women sometimes smoke cigars and drink alcohol: Pandi is fond of these indulgences, but they are strictly forbidden to women and discouraged for men in public. In December 2016, a temple regular named Pandiyammal explained to me that authentic possessions could be distinguished from faked possessions by considering the intensity of possession symptoms. In her early twenties, Pandiyammal spent most days during my 2016–2017 field research at Pandi Koyil with her baby, sitting with the temple sweepers. Pandiyammal's husband had become a priest at Pandi Koyil by the time of my second research period in 2019. Pandiyammal explained to me the more extreme, or *payaṅkaramāka* ("ferocious") the bodily movements displayed, the more likely this possession was truly Pandi, and not a charlatan faking to make money. In January 2017, Sushila commented while watching a possessed woman rapidly smoke an entire cigar, "She is Pandi's favorite because cigars are Pandi's favorite and this woman is able to smoke a whole cigar." For Sushila, the physical feat of quickly smoking an entire cigar was an indication of this woman's intimacy with Pandi because her capacities and proclivities transformed to being his capacities and proclivities during possession. The change in a person's behavior inaugurated by the onset of possession is regarded as the presence of god, shown on the body. Kristin Bloomer, whose ethnographic work focuses on Tamil Christian possession practices, explains the possessed "are generally understood to *be* that deity as long as they show the signs of possession" (8). The bodies of the possessed are divinized through possession; they are temporarily transformed into the bodies of gods, with divine capacities and qualities. This enables them to be worshipped, not merely as representatives of god, but as Pandi himself.

Possession is an imminent religious practice. The deity does not exist in some far-away realm; instead, they are present, tangible, and capable of interacting with devotees in real time. Possession creates a link between the human and the divine immediately, not in the afterlife or a future birth, but today, in the temple, right now. Possession phenomena at Pandi Koyil are correlated with verbal ritual practices, *kuṟi collutal* ("saying of prophecy/interpreting of signs") and *aruḷ vākku* ("statements of grace/benediction"). The ability to speak as god and offer prophecies is an authenticating sign that Pandi has entered a person's body. In June 2019, I witnessed a woman in her early 20s undergo an intense possession episode, screaming loudly. When her screaming subsided, she began prophesying and attracted a small crowd of devotees. A middle-aged woman standing nearby pointed to the young woman prophesying and described that this was a genuine, *uṇmaiyāṇa* ("truthful"), possession, contrasting it to those which are *cumma*, "just play/waste/not serious." She underlined the presence of Pandi in the prophesying woman, stating "*cāmi irukku* ('it is god')" and "*aruḷ iraṅkiyācchu* ('divine grace has descended')." In instances such as this, words spoken by a possessed person *are* the voice of the deity who is present in the possessed. Possessed individuals give advice, effect bodily cures, solve domestic disputes, and prescribe ritual actions – acting as Pandi himself. Speaking as Pandi invests the possessed devotee with authority, even if such power is temporary. This transformation of status is recognized socially, while it is manifested bodily. Anthropologist Diane Mines describes the enmeshment of Tamil possession practices and social power. Commenting on the religious practices of Dalits (those formerly referred to as "untouchables"), Mines writes, "Possession can make the powerless powerful. It can make the small grow large in power and strength. It can give voice to the voiceless" (19).

It is common for devotees at the temple to bow and touch the feet of the possessed, a gesture of humble respect generally reserved for social superiors or divine beings. In June 2019, I saw a teenage girl possessed by Pandi; she attracted a large crowd because her possession was deemed exceptionally potent. Onlookers wrapped her head in a turban like that worn by Pandi, showcasing her ritual prominence and authority as she stood in the temple, receiving devotees whom she blessed with her hands, answering their questions with prophetic utterances. The devotees who approached her, even older men, bowed and touched her feet in reverence, gestures that would typically never occur if the girl was not transformed into a deity. This temporary augmentation of the girl's status was possible in part because possession is deemed the result of a close bond between deity and worshipper, indicative of the purity of heart and depth of devotion of the possessed and the favor of the deity. In January 2017, Dhanalakshmi, an older woman belonging to the Pandi Koyil priests' family, explained this concept by stating Pandi does not discriminate based on caste. She told me Pandi will possess people of any caste, "even Kuravars," who she went on to describe in a derogatory manner as "those who don't bathe."[6] She also stated Pandi possesses children, making them dance "so beautifully" because they are the most innocent of all.

People often told me that Pandi selects certain devotees for a special relationship when they are very young. Although he may not possess them until years later, his initial selection establishes an intimate connection that intensifies after possession experiences begin. A Muslim woman who reported possession by Pandi told me in January 2017 that she doesn't want to come to Pandi Koyil, but that Pandi makes her come because "pāṇṭi eṉ uṭampil irukkiṟār ('Pandi is inside my body')." She also explained that Pandi chooses young girls he thinks are beautiful. A temple sweeper named Selvi joined our conversation to confirm. Selvi said Pandi selected her as a young girl, but that he possessed her for the first time after her marriage when she was twenty-two. Sushila also joined in, relating a story about a foreign woman she once saw at Pandi Koyil. Sushila said this foreigner had visited Pandi Koyil as a child with her parents, during which time Pandi had taken a liking to her. Now as an adult, the foreign woman had returned to the temple with her husband. Sushila said this made Pandi jealous, causing him to lay claims on the woman by possessing her now for the first time as an adult.

While possession marks a level of special intimacy between devotee and deity, this closeness bears deep ambivalence. Pandi demands commitment from those he selects to possess. In December 2016, Fatima, a woman in her mid-40s, described being punished by Pandi for failing to visit his temple often enough. Because she had not visited for some time, Pandi compelled her to come to his temple in a terrifying dream where he threatened to kill her two daughters-in-law and have her blamed if she did not come to worship him. The force of Pandi's warning was enough to draw Fatima back to his temple, even though she was Muslim and struggled with the fact that worship of Pandi did not fit within Islamic religious prescription. Although Pandi Koyil is generally considered a Hindu temple, Muslims and Christians occasionally worship there as well. Fatima attended Pandi Koyil years ago with a Hindu college friend. Seeing this friend's possession made an impression on Fatima, although she stopped attending the temple when she became "more serious" about practicing Islam. A chilling warning from Pandi was necessary to bring her back to worship. This story highlights the *payaṅkaramāna* ("frightful/terrible/ferocious") nature for which Pandi is famed.

Pandi is also described as *poṟāmai* ("jealous"). Pandi's jealousy manifests primarily in the context of intimate relationships he forms with female devotees. Erotic attachments between deities and their human worshippers are a common theme in South Asian religiosity, and at Pandi Koyil, erotic themes pervade possession practices. In January 2017, Dhanalakshmi elaborated on Pandi's jealousy and how it impacts marriage. She explained, when Pandi possesses a woman, "He will think, 'This is my girl,'" and become jealous when she gets married, worrying her husband will take her away from him. Dhanalakshmi emphasized if Pandi possesses a woman after marriage, "she won't be able to live with her husband," indicating that the marriage will undergo difficulties. She said she has witnessed many possessed women "throw away" their *tāli*s (marriage necklace worn by Tamil women). A month earlier, I observed such a scene where a possessed woman, seemingly unable to bear her *tāli*, tore at it and attempted to remove it. Examples from Bloomer's ethnographic work further emphasize Pandi's sexual jealousy. Bloomer relates the story of a Tamil Christian informant chosen by Pandi at a young age because of her beauty and possessed by him for the first time on her wedding night. The jealous god intervened to prevent the consummation of the wedding by possessing the bride and making her refuse sex with her husband (Bloomer 156–158). A possession by Pandi during such a moment displays the deity's claim over a devotee, a claim that cannot be trumped by a marital relationship.

While these examples focus on Pandi's controlling behavior over his worshippers, many stories emphasize an individual devotee's ability to control the god through that same intimate relationship. Sushila related in January 2017 that Pandi had possessed her only once because she struck a deal with him and requested he never possess her again. Sushila explained that she did not want to get possessed, because possession would interfere with her duties as wife and mother. She was also nervous her family might stop her from going to Pandi Koyil if she got possessed. Pandi agreed to her request. Nevertheless, Sushila's relationship with Pandi contained agonistic elements, including nightmares in which Pandi chased her and compelled her to be physically intimate with him against her will. Both uncontrollable possession episodes and negotiated relationships of possession reveal the intimacy that binds Pandi to his closest devotees, even if such intimacy is accompanied by strife.

Possession reveals an intimate relationship between Pandi and his individual devotees. Possession also indicates a triangular intimacy between the possessed, non-possessed devotees seeking succor, and the deity. By interacting with the possessed, devotees access Pandi directly through speech and touch. The possessed person is not regarded only as a medium who channels or carries messages from a divine source; they *are* the god in that moment. The words spoken by the possessed are Pandi's utterances; their bodies are his body, conferring blessings or cures, empowered to pronounce judgments or make demands. Communication occurs without intercession by priests or sanctioned ritual specialists. This is one of the key features that distinguishes Pandi Koyil as a site of folk religiosity. Yoder's definition of folk religion describes it as practices "apart from and alongside the strictly theological and liturgical forms of the official religion" (80). Possession at Pandi Koyil takes place at a temple with hierarchical power structures including a lineage-based priesthood. But anyone can become possessed, empowered to speak using the words of the deity they have temporarily become, posing an alternative to priestly authority. Pandi Koyil priests, the representatives of the official, sanctioned religion of Pandi Koyil rarely, if ever, become possessed; I only saw it in the case of the temple's main female leader Rajathiammal during festival days. Perhaps because ritual authority is distributed beyond the priesthood through possession, complicating the temple's social hierarchy, there are frequent contestations of the authenticity of certain possessions wherein observers will comment on whether a specific possession is true or false, genuine or an act. Possession is often a form of garnering power. For example, the possessed are capable of effecting change in the world through the instructions regarding ritual performance they give to supplicants. The possessed are also treated with heightened levels of respect, evidenced through the words and gestures of those around them. Those who listen to the prophecies of the possessed sometimes offer money or gifts in exchange for the religious guidance the possessed provide. Due to this power conferred by possession, there are high stakes of engaging in possession practices and not all devotees agree on who is invested with genuine authority. It is no small thing to become a god.

Possession and Erotic Danger

"Erotic danger" often characterize the intimacy that unfolds at Pandi Koyil, and that danger arises broadly in discourses about possession in Tamil society. Focusing on elements of erotic danger in possession illustrates the ambivalence of possession experiences. There is simultaneously closeness in erotic encounters between Pandi and his devotee but also danger and fear accompanies this closeness.

Possession in Tamil society has long been linked to erotic themes, especially in literature. References to possession are present in Tamil texts across historical periods, dating back to the earliest extant Tamil literature, the classical Caṅgam corpus. In Tamil poetry, possession is used as a literary device alluding to a love affair. The Caṅgam-era *Aiṅkuṟunūṟu* anthology includes the following poem by Orampokiyar, wherein the heroine's girl-friend addresses the heroine's foster-mother:

> If you think, mother,/she's tormented by that goddess/of sweet-water places,/why then/is she growing so thin/that her ornaments come loose,/her soft arms grow sallow?/It's all for that man/from the riverside/where the crabs' feet/make designs/on the cool wet sands.
>
> *(Ramanujan 99)*

The narrator references her friend's strange behavior causing the heroine's foster-mother to wonder about its source. The implication is that the foster-mother assumes the heroine is possessed – tormented by a goddess. But the girl-friend knows the true cause of the heroine's mysterious condition, namely she suffers from lovesickness for a human man. This metaphoric use of possession reveals that as early as the Caṅgam period possession behavior was meaningfully compared to that of people undergoing intense emotional states like romantic love and the pain of frustrated desires. This metaphoric use of possession to indicate romantic love is present in later Tamil literature as well, including medieval devotional poetry and its commentary. Poem V.6 from Nammalvar's *Tiruvāymoḻi* describes a girl repeatedly claiming to be the god Krishna (Clooney, "Land and Sea," 239). Commentaries on this poem by the 13th-century Vaishnava theologian Nanciyar contain explanations almost identical to the scene represented in Orampokiyar's poem: a girl-friend of the heroine reveals that the strange behavior of her friend is not caused by possession, as feared by her family, but instead by the heroine's passion for her lover Krishna whom the heroine sees as human, although he is actually a god (Clooney, "Nanciyar," 1).

Literary connections between eroticism and possession resemble lived practices of possession at Pandi Koyil. Dhanalakshmi explained that Pandi both attracts and is attracted to beautiful girls; she used the word *īrppu* ("attraction, allure") to describe this bond. Sushila elaborated on this point, explaining in January 2017 that Pandi chooses who to possess based on how much he likes them. When I asked Sushila why mostly women and not men get possessed, she said Pandi is attracted to beautiful women and girls, and he comes to them for that reason. Pandi's jealousy seeing his chosen devotees engaging in sexual contact with their new husbands represents another instance of Pandi's erotic connection to those he possesses. Pandi's eroticism is further recognizable in his famous power to bestow the gift of offspring (Goslinga 6). Pandi Koyil is filled with wooden models of baby cradles and torn bits of sari fabric tied around limes and affixed to trees, fences, and metal posts. These are the remnants of fertility rituals devotees perform as offerings to Pandi in the hopes of getting a child. Many devotees attribute the miraculous birth of children after infertility to Pandi's potency. Erotic encounters between the god and his female devotees, whether occurring in dreams or during possession experiences, seem to be the source of divine impregnation. Bloomer describes Pandi as "the bachelor god believed to impregnate virgins and newlyweds" (156).

Despite the beneficent power of Pandi's erotic energy, there is a fearsomeness, a danger, that accompanies this power. Many informants emphasized that families hope their unmarried daughters will not get possessed, for it would be difficult to secure husbands if the girls were known to be possession prone. It seems that the challenge in finding marriage partners for girls who have been possessed is linked to Pandi having first laid an intimate claim on those he enters. One woman insisted in December 2016 that in previous times, pre-pubescent girls were not allowed at Pandi Koyil for fear the erotically charged deity would forcibly possess the girls he so desires. I do not know if it was a practice to exclude unmarried girls from the temple precincts at any point, but the perception that this occurred underscores the erotic danger of possession.

While possession is revered since it demonstrates the purity of the devotee's love for god and his reciprocal granting of *aruḷ* ("grace"), it may also be painful, exhausting, or disturbing. Possession is not merely a blessing or an experience of divine benediction, but it is a direct encounter with the power of a deity, who, in the case of Pandi, has fearsome qualities. The erotic is not just dangerous because of social sanctions against premarital or extra-marital relations, such as those that possession suggests, but it is dangerous because Pandi himself may inflict sexual violence, forcibly possessing unsuspecting women. Sushila related a number of her dreams in which Pandi appeared in different guises, attempting to coerce her into an intimacy that she refused. In one dream that Sushila had when pregnant, she felt a man come near and attempt to touch her. It was Pandi, appearing as a man dressed in white. Pandi held a baby boy and offered the child to Sushila in exchange for her "coming" to him, but she refused to obey his demand. When I pressed her further, Sushila elaborated with a euphemism, saying that Pandi was asking her to come to him "in the way that a woman comes to a man in a film." Sushila used the verb *varutal* ("to come/coming") to describe sexual intimacy between film actors. This same word is regularly used to describe possession experiences, when the deity "comes" to the devotee. Similar dreams from Sushila included scenes of Pandi appearing as a traumatic person from her childhood or in the form of men chasing her; the dream figure always urged her to come to him, and she always refused. These graphic dreams occurred during the period in Sushila's life when Pandi possessed her for the first and only time. Sushila's refusal of Pandi's aggressive, erotic demands in her dreams parallels, her request that he not enter her through possession.

Conclusion: Toward a Relational Interpretation of Possession

Along with introducing possession at Pandi Koyil, I aim to move toward a non-reductive interpretation of possession that highlights relationships among people and between people and deities. Despite the theoretical models anthropologists have put forward to explain possession, the quantity and diversity of the phenomena resist classification. I take inspiration from the anthropologist of Brazilian Condomblé Mattijs van de Port who emphasizes "the inadequacy of our conceptual categories" (190) to explain possession phenomena, and also Smith who cautions "it is highly inadvisable to essentialize the phenomenon of possession" (597). I aim to interpret possession alongside the explanations offered by people at Pandi Koyil for whom this practice is significant. For them, possession is the temporary transformation of a human being into a deity worthy of worship and capable of divine speech and altered capacities.

Possession, then, is a type of relationship, an instance of intimacy to the point of overlapping identity between deity and worshipper. Other kinds of relationships are also created and sustained through possession when community members interact with those empowered by the divine while possessed. Anthropologist Karin Kapadia writes in connection to Tamil possession rituals, "possession is not a solitary experience: it needs a social context to stimulate and create it and to celebrate it" (196). The community aspect so crucial to possession hearkens back to Yoder's theories of folk religion that highlight the circulation of religious ideas and meanings among a group of people, adapting and reinterpreting the official, sanctioned religion. Yoder writes of folk religion, "the little community puts in its ingredient of self-expression, adds its own local coloration, to universally accepted official-religious forms" (80). Possession at Pandi Koyil exists within a larger cultural context in which there is literary precedence for possession experience. But Pandi's devotees do not reference scriptural or ecclesiastic authority when describing possession which is instead regarded as a direct, unmediated experience available to anyone Pandi chooses to possess.

As the stories above demonstrate, the relational ties established through possession are ambivalent; they are not easily categorized as benevolent or malignant. Pandi's is a power that is intimate and erotic, yet overbearing and dangerous. Possession experiences instantiate that power in the bodies, the movements, and the utterances of people who have, even if only for a short period of time, become a god.

Notes

1 Names of research participants are pseudonyms unless otherwise noted. Sushila, my primary interlocutor, passed away in November 2021. I use her real name here.
2 Hemalatha's real name, used with permission.
3 Research supported by a Syracuse University grant.
4 Tamil is the primary language spoken in Madurai and the main language of the research participants I worked with. All non-English terms in this chapter are transliterations of Tamil words.

5 Research supported by a Harvard University grant.
6 Kuravars are discriminated against as extremely low on the caste hierarchy. I interpret Dhanalakshmi's emphasizing Pandi's willingness to posses "even Kuravars" as a way of highlighting the equalizing power of devotion to him.

Works Cited

Bloomer, Kristin C. *Possessed by the Virgin: Hinduism, Roman Catholicism, and Marian Possession in South India*. New York: Oxford University Press, 2018.

Boddy, Janice. "Spirit Possession Revisited: Beyond Instrumentality." *Annual Review of Anthropology* 23, no. 1 (1994): 407–434.

Clooney, Francis X. "'I Created Land and Sea': A Tamil Case of God-Consciousness and Its Śrīvaiṣṅava Interpretation." *Numen* 35, no. 2 (Dec. 1988 : 238–259.

Clooney, Francis X., trans. *Nañcīyar on Tiruvāymoḻi IV.6, V.6, and VII.9.* N.D.

Goslinga, Gillian. "The Ethnography of a South Indian God: Virgin Birth, Spirit Possession, and the Prose of the Modern World." PhD diss., University of California, Santa Cruz, 2006.

Kapadia, Karin. "Pierced by Love: Tamil Possession, Gender and Caste." In *Invented Identities: The Interplay of Gender, Religion, and Politics in India* edited by Julia Leslie and Mary McGee, 181–202. New Delhi: Oxford University Press, 2000.

Keller, Mary. *The Hammer and the Flute: Women, Power, and Spirit Possession*. Baltimore: Johns Hopkins University Press, 2005.

Mines, Diane P. *Fierce Gods: Inequality, Ritual, and the Politics of Dignity in a South Indian Village*. Bloomington: Indiana University Press, 2005.

Ong, Aihwa. *Spirits of Resistance and Capitalist Discipline: Factory Women in Malaysia*. Albany: State University of New York Press, 1987.

Primiano, Leonard Norman. "Vernacular Religion and the Search for Method in Religious Folklife." *Western Folklore* 54, no. 1 (1995): 37–56.

Raj, Selva J., and William P. Harman, eds. *Dealing with Deities: The Ritual Vow in South Asia*. Albany: State University of New York Press, 2006.

Ram, Kalpana. *Fertile Disorder: Spirit Possession and Its Provocation of the Modern*. Honolulu: University of Hawaii Press, 2013.

Ramanujan, A. K, trans. *Poems of Love and War: From the Eight Anthologies and the Ten Long Poems of Classical Tamil*. New York: Columbia University Press, 2011.

Smith, Frederick M. *The Self Possessed: Deity and Spirit Possession in South Asian Literature and Civilization*. New York: Columbia University Press, 2006.

Van de Port, Mattijs. *Ecstatic Encounters: Bahian Candomblé and the Quest for the Really Real*. Amsterdam: University of Amsterdam Press, 2011.

Wadley, Susan S. "The Spirit 'Rides' or the Spirit 'Comes': Possession in a North Indian Village." In *The Realm of the Extra-Human: Agents and Audiences*, edited by Agehananda Bharati, 233–251. The Hague: Mouton Publishers, 1976.

Yoder, Dan. "Toward A Definition of Folk Religion." In *Genres of Folklife*, 67–84. Ann Arbor: UMI Research Press, 1990.

15

POST-CHRISTIANITY AND ESOTERICISM

A Study of a Satanic Exorcist

William Chavez

Introduction

Imagine an exorcism that didn't result in a contest of screams and physicality, instead fostering a ritual partnership between recipient and practitioner. Imagine an exorcist who delivers individuals – mostly around his own age (25–40) across the United States – from repeat occurrences of sleepwalks, black outs, strange dreams, poltergeists, and magical attacks (Bilé 2021c). Imagine a syncretic collection of "spiritual technologies" used in ritual performance, namely Palo Santo, (black) sage, frankincense and myrrh, salt water, ceremonial daggers, oils, written pacts, ritual bells, and sigils drawn on paper or the floor (Bilé 2021e; Bilé 2021c). Finally, imagine the worship of an explicitly violent form of divinity: a "living force" that is at once "visceral and dramatic," "instinctual and primeval," "experienced through immersive engagement" (Bilé 2020, 146–148).

As this magic-working devotee explains, this "god of violence," the "Violent Divine," called Viaios (βίαιος) ("Vee-eye-ohs"), is "ever-present and immanent; he precedes – and serves as the source of – wrath, rage, hatred, and above all, action itself." Indeed, the essence of Viaios, the "spirit of violence," "pervades, pierces, and encapsulates the totality of our world and beyond" (Bilé 2020, 145) for action is fundamental to revolution, a catalyst for "beginning": "a disruption of the current order to create something or render it anew" (145fn.1). This "violent divine persona" (147) essentially develops the "spirit of man" (145) through practices of both "internal" and "external viatheosis" (149) – that is, transformative violence via divine union.

> [In practice] one might endeavor to bring form to divine violence by invoking the iconography of a multitude of gods, goddesses, spirits, and principalities; of "war," "weaponry," "wrathfulness," "destruction,"

DOI: 10.4324/9781003257462-20

> "vengeance," "courage," and "conflict." Worshipped as Týr, Nergal, Ares, Abaddon, Lilith, Set, Satan, and Sekhmet. Most certainly, these divinities' iconography resoundingly express elements of cosmic, spiritual, and divine violence. The warrior, the maiden, the murderer, the horned, and the serpentine – all of these are vehicles through which an aspect of divine violence may be expressed. (147)

"There is no wading in the waters of the Violent Divine," this practitioner continues, "only total submersion and flooding of one's body and spirit. On the precipice of drowning, evolution is achieved" (149). Thus, the pursuit of "external viatheosis" is "most immediately achieved through acts of controlled self-inflicted physical injury, such as bloodletting, self-scarification, hook or body suspension, recreational acupuncture (or 'needle play'), or other forms of body modification/alteration." Such transgressive acts are then deployed within the exorcism rituals of a magical practitioner and Esoteric Satanist named Shea Bilé – sole subject of this chapter.

I aggregate a variety of research and scholarship to contextualize Bilé as a modern religious practitioner. The main sections below examine his relationship with popular media and entertainment, the cultic milieu and metaphysical traditions that inform his practice, and the stakes and implications of the transgressive ritual acts introduced above. As such, his significance to the study of American religion concerns his reflection of complex modes of Christian supersession – that is, how his individual creation of religious practice (that is, contemporary folk religion) still operates within the bounds of modern Christianity.

Methodology

What can we learn from the individual instantiations of a single religiosity and/or ritual practice? This question becomes an issue of methodology for we must first engage which specific analytic tools are useful when rendering Bilé's information significant. Does Bilé represent a "folk," a larger cultural movement? Furthermore, why is this question more complicated given its twenty-first-century context?

Studies of American religious populism tend to favor highly mediatized individuals, especially those commanding large audiences, mainstream social capital, and/or institutional/financial backing. In contrast, my study of Shea Bilé (b. 1985) is most comparable to the research of David Hall (1989) and Paul E. Johnson and Sean Wilentz (1994) concerning the figures of Samuel Sewall (1652–1730) and Robert Matthews (1788–1841). In the former, Hall (1989) reconstructs the folk-level religiosity of colonial-era Americans using autobiographical materials, like diary entries. Samuel Sewall's diary, itself reflecting the broader, more elusive beliefs and attitudes of provincial New England, functions like a personal almanac and dream journal, which Hall uses to reconstruct the magic worldviews of Puritan laity. A common analytic maneuver, for historians and others, is to use a folk figure like Sewall (his words, beliefs, and solitary actions) to represent the *margins* of (religious) society: how a common Puritan in Boston exists in conversation with more notable Puritan ministers, authors, and pamphlet-makers like Increase and Cotton Mather and how such a commoner, nevertheless, constructs his own complex form of religiosity divorced from traditional Puritanism.

In the latter example, Johnson and Wilentz (1994) use a journeyman carpenter turned prophetic preacher as the basis for "a story of sex and salvation in 19th-century America" (as the book's eventual subtitle markets). Robert Matthews was a disgruntled religious outsider who spiraled into apocalypticism following his rejection of membership to a middle-class Presbyterian church (Johnson 1991, 846). Under the name of the "Prophet Matthias," this marginal figure converted a number of wealthy Christians into a politically reactive cult, opposing free-market capitalism and bourgeois evangelicalism. Contrary to the idealized historical narrative that such populist religious leaders were warmly welcomed by a radically democratic American public (as if eager to reward ambition and competition in the spirit of egalitarianism), Matthias and others like him rose to challenge the same kind of institutions that drove him into obscurity. This "Second Great Awakening," itself an interpretive fiction, functioned not as a democratization of American Christianity (that is, a support of lively experimentation with popular religious forms of discourse and organization) but rather functioned as a transformation in Christian leadership and technique. Preaching was merely transformed into a "democratic and democratizing art" (Johnson 1991, 843–844). New institutions were established, positioning new authorized leaders in power, especially those, on the one hand, in favor of entrepreneurial individualism and, on the other, supported by the early nineteenth-century revolution in print culture.

Matthews, a representative of folk religiosity in New York, is not just a *marginal* figure. He became *marginalized* as a fanatic or charlatan, especially once his enemies began publicizing the sex scandals of his commune via the New York penny-press (Johnson and Wilentz 1994, 10–11). In general, religious enthusiasm in this era did not represent a path for upward social mobility. Studies of obscure figures like Sewall and Matthews call into question the contributions of historical and/or anthropological scholarship. Neither figure is highlighted as a vehicle or agent of immediate change; their significance to the study of American religion stems primarily from their reflection of social and historical processes, both at the time and today.

Though Sewall and Matthews were socially well positioned as White, male, Christians, their practices reflect a personalized deviation. I, thereby, challenge the academy to consider Shea Bilé as their contemporary analog. My analysis does not require him to wield considerable social influence, popularity, and/or institutional authority before contributing to the field of religious studies; he need only to intersect multiple analytic narrative threads. Consider the following admission from Bilé taken from one of our interviews:

> Given some of the ways that I practice my craft, it can feel pretty lonely. But I think that's one of the paths of religiosity in the modern world. Especially in the West, anyone who lives a religious life is going to have a solitary component. But even though I may feel alone at times, I know I'm not alone in that journey.
>
> *(Bilé 2021e)*

Bilé positions himself as a modern religious practitioner and, as such, sees solitude as a recurrent theme of such a condition. Though *modernity* is a loaded term signifying the global capitalist market, the political ascendancy of Europe and North America, technological and scientific advancements, and more, for the purposes of this chapter, I direct this conversation to the development of secularism (or post-secularism) and the Western religious turn toward the self. Bilé's instantiation of practice, though individual, represents an intersection of larger religious movements like Satanism, Western Esotericism, New Age, and other alternative spiritualities but also several other phenomena related to the conditions of modern religiosity, including antiauthoritarian ideologies, privatized spiritualities, non-Christian re-enchantment, religious experimentation and eclecticism, and more. Though all these pertain to Bilé's individual experience, this chapter focuses on three conditions in particular: popular mediatization, self-orientation, and transgressive expression.

More than Sewall and Matthews, Shea Bilé represents a story about Christianity supplanting itself; his complex Satanic practice ultimately stems from a post-Christian framework. This chapter entertains the question: "What do Christians do once they no longer want to be Christian?" To be clear, that which supersedes the other I don't interpret as either improved or superior, nor that those traditional manifestations of Christianity are either dying out or require revision to survive. I signal only that we have much to learn from the experimental and fringe side of American vernacular religion and the historical socio-religious dynamics that complicate its study.

Representative of Sensationalist Media

The relationship between Western exorcism practice and popular media is a microcosm of the modern response to religion. The use of exorcism by popular news outlets to generate public interest, excitement, or scorn in "premodern" depictions of religious practice has a history spanning several decades (Cuneo 1998). The popular entertainment industry cultivates the moniker of "exorcist" into a brand for which to effectively market dark supernatural content. Yet Shea Bilé embraced the brand reluctantly (Bilé 2021d). In 2016, he was approached by a friend and executive producer of *60 Second Docs*, an online docuseries profiling "the world's most interesting characters" (60 Second Docs 2022). This friend sought to profile an "exorcist," one different than the likes of Fr. Gary Thomas or Rev. Bob Larson (Chavez 2021). "I eventually accepted the label," Bilé says, "because I had the opportunity to present a very unique idea to a larger audience: that Satanists and occultists can do exorcisms" (Bilé 2021e). Following the release of this profile, *Vice News* reached out soon thereafter, demonstrating the efficacy of this marketing gimmick. Bilé became branded with an additional alterity, arguably one more sensational than "Satanist."

"'Exorcist' is such a stigmatized, loaded term," Bilé reflects (Bilé 2021e). "It conjures silly trappings." The first, most obvious for biblical audiences, stems from Mark 3:22–27: the presumption that exorcism, by its very nature, evokes a strict sense of cosmic dualism. "How can Satan cast out Satan?" Yet Bilé is not quite "in league with Satan," as many would assume. His practice is aimed neither at the construction of Satan's Kingdom nor the deconstruction of Christendom. As Jason Bunch (2018) writes for *Vice*, "[This] only seems at odds because of our popular but limited understanding of the subject. We think Satan is on the side as the demons, and angels are on the side of the exorcist."

Bilé challenges this assumption of hierarchy; that all spirits directly answer to Satan (Bilé 2021c). "Lucifer has domain," he clarifies, especially as Bilé regularly calls upon such deities for spiritual assistance. "Empower me Lord to cast this out," he says in ritual. "I petition your assistance in this matter." "Thank you for the blessings of which I'm ready to receive." He invokes a Satanic name as a summoning of strength or will – rhetorically similar to the glorifications of God found within traditional Christian liturgy. Within this dynamic, Lucifer is summoned not as taskmaster but spiritual facilitator. Satan gets involved because Bilé is a devotee, not because Satan is responsible for the problems that unfold. Though this divinity's power is awesome – capable of influencing renegade malefic spirits – Satan is not immediately associated with spirit hordes harassing humankind on a daily basis.

Accordingly, Bilé's vernacular ritual tactics deviate from the traditional forms of Western exorcism. "I do consider myself an exorcist without controversy, especially within the traditional magic sense of the word in that I *conjure* and *control* spirits" (Bilé 2021c). Bilé intentionally interacts with spirits, in either a neutral or a positive manner, to recruit or befriend, for the purpose of the ritual task at hand but also his own spirituality (Bilé 2021b). "Most of my work is a collaboration with 'demons': establishing a relationship, giving offerings, and the like." This is then the second "silly trapping" of accepting the brand of "exorcist": a practitioner need not battle or antagonize every spirit encountered. Spirits, like angels, operate amorally (Bilé 2021a). Though many can manifest as dangerous, this exorcist frames their nature as malefic but not malicious.

Despite these "trappings" of theology, themselves the result of a religious milieu reified through popular media and other institutional forces, Bilé accepts the "exorcist" brand "in order for Satanists to have a seat at the table," to demonstrate an alternative approach to practice and spirituality (Bilé 2021c). As hinted above, he's been treated as a clickbait-worthy subject ever since his media debut. A "Satanic Exorcist" native to California is quite a find for an entertainment talent scout. Thus, it is interesting to hear about the media productions Bilé rejected – chief among them *To Tell the Truth*. Originally a celebrity panel show from the 1950s where panelists attempt to match the unusual occupation or experience to one of three mystery contestants following a general description and series of interrogations. This television program has been renewed at least once every decade since its debut; the current iteration released in 2016. Should Bilé have accepted the offer to appear as a contestant, it wouldn't mark the first time this program sensationalized the "exorcist" brand. In 1972 William Peter Blatty, author of *The Exorcist* (1971), and two imposters appeared on the show, fielding questions regarding their knowledge of the Jesuit order and Catholic ritual procedure along with their personal beliefs and observations regarding related phenomena.

Why would Shea Bilé turn down an opportunity to reach to wider audience? First, "it would be fucking obvious that I was the real one," he laughs, based on his physical appearance (Bilé 2021c). Second, he found the "silliness" of a game-show off-putting. "I want the practice to be taken seriously," he says, envisioning an episode where his "I am an exorcist" blurb is read alongside "I live in a boat" and "I am an 80-yr-old gamer." "I don't want to be treated as an oddity [or] joke," Bilé affirms.

How then was Bilé profiled for *60 Second Doc* or *Vice*? Did either attempt to reduce him to a socio-religious anomaly for the purpose of reifying mainstream American religion? The *60 Second Doc* begins with the hands of another practitioner sticking pins into Bilé's eyebrows – "external viatheosis." Bilé, through both voiceover and subtitles, introduces himself as an "occultist [and] exorcist," as the camera cuts to various shots of the "spiritual technologies" mentioned earlier. After seeing photos of both Bilé and his Christian "medium" mother in younger form, the footage cuts to an adult Bilé watching a ritual pact burn while pierced by the ceremonial dagger in his hand and blood dripping down his face (the result of the punctures to his brow). Prior to this ritual's conclusion, Bilé is shown sticking pins into the arms of the other practitioner (the recipient of the exorcism). She, a young Black woman, is the author of the written pact; shown briefly dictating its message before handing it to Bilé for immolation.

There is no mention of the "Satanist" label at any point in the *60 Second Doc* or in the brief Q&A available in the YouTube description. Instead, Bilé associates himself with "the 'darker' aspects of occult practice": The Left-Hand Path. "A fundamental aspect to this practice," he continues, "is to abandon and liberate yourself of commonly accepted social norms and fears, fears that would debilitate and weaken you as an empowered individual" (60 Second Doc 2016). The Left-Hand Path, as Kennet Granholm (2016, 87) observes, is a category of antinomian practice and spirituality, primarily used as an emic term within the Dragon Rouge, a magic order of Western Esotericism that, like its older tantric inspiration, attempts to transcend the boundaries of "black" and "white" magic and "good" and "evil" paradigms. Though Bilé fancies himself a Satanist, he takes pride in his practice of magical workings – a skill not always emphasized within Modern Satanism.

The *Vice* profile includes both realities: categorizing Bilé in the headline as an "Occult Exorcist" then later as a "Theistic Satanist" following his differentiation from the Australian "Eclectic Witch" also interviewed (Bunch 2018). The article also further sensationalizes the Satanic-Catholic conflict in its headline: "These Occult Exorcists Say the Catholic Church Makes Demons Worse." For Bilé, this is the result of not recognizing the power that the recipient of the exorcism truly wields: the power of the individual. He sees "the average Catholic exorcist as a novice, but thinks they succeed because sometimes exorcism requires less effort than you think," the *Vice* story reads.

> You merely need to point at something, acknowledge it, and command it. It just takes intention and power of assertion of your will. So even [by] not understanding what demons actually are, [exorcisms] are accidentally successful.

In our interviews, Bilé elaborates in the following manner:

> Most exorcists would like to think that they're the sole distributors of a liberating circumstance. But I think, in most instances, the person is doing more than the exorcist. Such exorcisms are successful by accident because the participation framework of the recipient isn't stated. [. . .] But that's where the magic happens, so to speak. That's where the emotion comes; that's where the power comes. (Bilé 2021c)

As the *60 Second Doc* illustrates, most of Bilé's magical exorcism practice resolves around his instruction to the recipient, a fellow practitioner and peer, to take control of the situation, to learn the art of *self-exorcism*. Though "there is a set ceremonial structure," he invites magical workers to improvise – as opposed to adopting a series of formulaic responses – whenever cleansing spirits. Ritual preparation must be individualized, he says, according to each case and person. Following ritual completion, though there's a liberation achieved from whatever immediate concern, a "follow-up and maintenance" is required of the recipient (a topic discussed below).

While the *Vice* profile is more an opinion piece, a significant portion narrates Bilé's early contact with the realm of the supernatural, i.e., his encounter with a spiritual presence via astral projection and, years later, his first exorcism performed at the age of sixteen. As Bilé tells Bunch (2018):

> Growing up there were spirits that attacked me, but I didn't have the tools to protect myself. I was the victim of these things. This exorcism was the first time I fought back.

Bilé elaborates that, as a child, he frequented a haunted house belonging to his grandmother; a house marked with the death and suffering of multiple relatives (Bilé 2021b). Such a traumatic family history allowed Bilé to understand the often-parasitic nature of restless spirits. "They feed off of fear and emotional experience," he tells me; "gain access to your thoughts and memories, use them to facilitate a particular reaction from you."

Tied to this generational trauma, Shea Bilé often visits the house in the form of visionary dreams and via the astral plane. "During the projection," he tells Bunch (2018), "I went to my grandmother's and in the backyard, I see this gigantic seven-to-eight-foot black shade of static, knife-like energy, and it started chasing me. I immediately just ran back into my body." Soon thereafter, Bilé officially moved into his grandmother's house, where he and others grew to accept a variety of paranormal activity – e.g., lights turning off and on, sounds of footsteps moving, and an ephemeral discoloration in the air (Bilé 2021b). As Bunch (2018) narrates, this continued until one night when all the lights failed, including the circuit breakers: "Bilé had enough [and in] frustration. . . grabbed one of the lights and yelled, 'In the name of Satan I command you to stop, in the name of Satan I command [that] this stops immediately.'" The lights were restored and with them brought the appearance of a moth – which Bilé interprets as a signifier of spiritual phenomena. As an epilogue to this Satanic exorcist origin-story, Bunch adds that weeks later, "Bilé and a friend would conduct a much larger, full-blown exorcism to challenge the spirit once and for all," setting the former "on a path where exorcisms would become a regular part of his [spiritual] practice."

The two online profiles illustrate, first, the material culture Bilé engages as a practitioner, namely his ritual construction for a standard exorcism; second, the self-narration of his spiritual journey and the impact of his early supernatural encounters; and, third, the nuances of his status as an occult exorcist, challenging much of the hegemonic Christian doctrine and theology that permeate the subject. The profiles are presented "in good faith," he cites – on his terms, using his voice, and not as the target of someone else's joke (Bilé 2021c). To return to the entertainment productions he declined:

> A talent scout approached me about a competition reality show. It would have judges. Like *Dancing with the Stars* but with exorcism. . . and that's fucking absurd. So that one was an aggressive denial.

The above pitch, along with this section more generally, illustrates the popular mediatization of a single religious subject, himself marketed with the "occultist," "Satanist," and "exorcist" brands. The relationship between Western exorcism practice and popular media reflects contemporary tendencies to sensationalize religious content for the purpose of (1) reifying the division between "modern" and "premodern" phenomena; (2) deriving interest and/or entertainment from social competition (a staple of reality television, especially); (3) educating and, possibly, re-enchanting certain sectors of the American religious market, such as those in search of personally tailored spiritualities; and (4) embracing the visual doxa of various countercultural movements, expressing autonomy and difference via a challenge to traditional institutions and the hegemonic boundaries they impose.

Representative of Self-religion

As Michael Cuneo (1998, 459) writes of American exorcism, "[w]ith its promises of therapeutic well-being and rapid-fire emotional gratification, [the practice] is oddly at home in the shopping mall culture, the purchase-of-happiness culture, of turn-of-the-century American." Though Bilé never charges for his services (and disapproves of those that do), his magical exorcism practice is still "oddly at home" within America's spiritual marketplace due to his worship of the individual spirit and promotion of personal growth and care. As Bilé says in his *60 Second Doc*:

> [A]n exorcism is obviously a personal experience. I'm very against the idea [of the] exorcist sav[ing] you. You can only save yourself. People need to liberate themselves. I merely facilitate them and give them the tools to do so. (60 Second Docs 2016)

This excerpt signifies an authenticity of belief (positioning Bilé firmly within a Christian-centric framework where sincerity and conviction are valued) but also a prioritization of the self. This section examines the self-orientating "spirit" that dominates contemporary religious discourse and practice in the West – simultaneously revealing the "folk" that Bilé represents and the complications that arise when one tries to study them.

As Bilé jokes: "In a room of ten Satanists, you'll have ten religions" (Bilé 2021d). For his specific practice of Modern Satanism, Bilé employs a liberal approach to divinity, labeling himself something akin to an "omnitheist": he believes all gods could exist and symbols can, indeed, gain metaphysical properties through the power of individual devotion. As Kate Bowler (2013, 14) writes, such metaphysical worldviews render the material world into a product of the mind's projection, with people sharing in God's power to create by means of thought itself. Such religious traditions provide powerful vehicles for American individualism (e.g., New Thought, prosperity gospels, and self-help literature) – with effects still observed today in Shea Bilé's practice of magical exorcism.

Bilé tells Bunch (2018):

> [My exorcisms are not] a passive, 'I'm your savior' [kind of ritual] – ultimately you have to be your own savior in this situation. At the end there is healing and empowerment, resulting in peace for the person, and all this takes place in. . . ritualistic fashion.

As Bilé elaborates:

> The act of expulsion that an exorcist does is available to everybody. It's not some weird practice you have to do [or] training you go through from some school. The dressings of it, practices surrounding it, or the methods, they, in the end, don't necessarily matter. [T]he exorcist understands how to approach the situation; they understand what to look for and how to facilitate the exorcism that person participates in. I can't do a fucking exorcism on someone who is not willing to do one on themselves. It's absolutely useless. I need to impart on them how to be their own exorcist (Bilé 2021c).

As Cathy Albanese (2007, 12–13) observes, this self-religious practice is not as "esoteric" as many would assume. Esoteric Satanism is open to the public, "accessible and ubiquitous" like the egalitarian "spirit" of its traditional Christian roots. This section demonstrates how Bilé's prioritization of the self, metaphysical worldviews, and, even, his non-Christian magical sensibilities are, nevertheless, shaped by a Christian-centric framework – which Bilé acknowledges.

BILÉ: [E]xorcism [is like] rehab but you have to maintain sobriety after. We can take you in to detox but you have to develop a sober lifestyle.

CHAVEZ: If you were evangelical, the "sober lifestyle" would translate into accepting "Jesus in your heart," being "born-again," to "stop sinning" or "dealing with the occult and/or non-Christian religions."

BILÉ: I believe. . . you have a quite natural ability [to expel spirits] so long as you have a firm footing, spiritually speaking. Conviction. . . in one's self. [. . .] Once you understand and you become assured of your personal spiritual power and you conduct your life in such a way that you facilitate this resistance – you facilitate this emboldening – that then continues what the exorcism started. It maintains the "spirit" of the exorcism – "spirit" in the sense of a qualifier.

CHAVEZ:Is that a life-changing spirit? How do they keep up the good fight after they see you?

BILÉ: By understanding what behaviors allowed them to be vulnerable.

CHAVEZ: In terms of personal growth?

BILÉ: Sure. There's a self-religious component to it. [Exorcism] is a holistic concept, a prosperity component of spiritual health that discusses loving one's self. Becoming aligned with one's abilities, capacities, capabilities. Stop hating [or belittling] one's self. [I]n my mind, exorcisms are all tied to that. It all comes together. You do not have someone who is willing to undergo an exorcism that cannot name other things. . . in their life that are problematic. This is a broad, wide-ranging experience. And so, my exorcism practice takes into account these various components of their life.

CHAVEZ: Would you be comfortable using the term "conversion"?

BILÉ: "Conversion" or "revival." [I accept these terms.] I would say, personally, I was "born-again" and I say that with everything associated except the Christian component. Thus, I want those exorcised to undergo a revival; to be born-again into themselves (Bilé 2021c).

Bilé represents the cultural shifts of self-religious, self-help, and metaphysical thinking. He seats himself at a table set by American Evangelicals, playfully embracing Christian discourse as a form of resistance (discussed more in the section below), an effort to expand categories of thought so that Satanists and others can be recognized and included in public conversations about religion. This impetus to conjure specific self-religious sensibilities – i.e., "empowerment, self-realization, actualization, assertion or development" (Petersen 2016, 3) – largely results in a culture of modern religious practitioners so individualized that it dissolves the need for community.

In his magical exorcism practice, Bilé collaborates with few fellow Satanists, working mostly with nondenominational New Age practitioners, some Christians, and atheists (Bilé 2021c). Instead of bringing them in union with a community, Bilé works to bring them in commune with an authentic self (Bilé 2021d). This chapter is an exercise in narrating macro-level social and historical forces – specifically that of alternative spiritualities and modern forms of religious re-enchantment in the West – for the purpose of delineating the bounds of our academic paradigms. Though he feels isolated and singular, I argue that Shea Bilé represents a modern religious "folk" unified in being disunified ("unchurched") but also one that utilizes a host of self-religious mechanisms that itself stems from a post-Christological framework.

Representative of Transgressive Expression

For this final section, I seek to complement the following argument from Jesper Aagaard Petersen (2016, 3) regarding Modern Satanism's status as a Christian sect:

> The self-project is a project of non-conformity. But this element of non-conformity and de-conditioning is *not* tied to Christianity alone; it is a general opposition to all traditional and modern institutions of authority. Christianity is understood as the prime example of a totalitarian, oppressive moral force – other enemies are capitalist society's dictum of consumerism and passive entertainment; "liberal" society's "universal" human rights and bland equality; puritanical morals of sexual repression; the welfare state; and the blind obedience and irrationality of the herd in all religions. Satan is the adversary or ultimate rebel and is thus symbolically a stance one takes in the pursuit of self-interest and self-development. All in all, the Satan of Satanism is heavily detraditionalized and, while nominally tied to Christianity, cannot be understood in a strictly Christian sense.

> Thus modern Satanism is *not* a Christian sect, inverted Christianity or a Christian hermeneutics.

It is a mistake to assume that such "totalitarian, oppressive moral forces" operate independent from the Christian hegemonies that produce them. But this final section opposes another segment of Petersen's claim. I approach the modern instantiation of Bilé's Satanic practice as evidence of a post-Christian religious complex, one that ultimately (ironically and not) reifies Evangelical Christianity as a paradigmatic category of conception. As Evangelical Christians dominate political discourse in the United States (Harding 2000), they influence the cultural associations used to evaluate religious phenomena – that is, what constitutes "good" religion versus "bad." Modern Satanism, in its mission to troll and resist the hegemony of Christian discourse, models itself not just in opposition to global Christianity but in the form of what has traditionally been labeled as "bad religion": big institutions, scary iconography, body rituals, clerical clothing, and the like. As Bilé observes: "Fascination with goats and orgies, all of these things became an instruction manual for Modern Satanists as they began to find themselves" (Bilé 2021e).

How useful then is this category of "post-Christian" to the study of Modern Satanism? Consider first its political wing in the form of The Satanic Temple (TST). Their primary tactics include spectacles of guerilla theater and "poison pill" legal strategies aimed at challenging Christian supremacy in public life (Laycock 2020, 139) – a theatrical enforcement of secularism. Such performance art and legal action "attempt to leverage the discourse of evil" (147) in order to disrupt mainstream cultural and political conversations, maintain the principle of religious neutrality, and/or troll, shock, and outrage the dominant religious faction. Even their lesser known tactics of serving a local community through philanthropy – blood drives, "adopt a highway" agreements, and public programs like "Menstratin' with Satan" (152–153) – are themselves attempts to "out-Christian" Christians. Many TST demonstrations take inspiration from the political activism, militant reactionism, and moral sensationalism of conservative Christians, especially the public spectacles of Catholics, anti-abortion activists, and those affiliated with the Westboro Baptist Church. The iconography and ritual constructions of TST demonstrations at once mock and invert various elements of Christian practice but filtered through the discourse of "bad religion" – i.e., (black) mass celebrations, gay conversions via Mormon baptisms for the dead, prolife fetishization of dead babies, and more (35, 161). In this way, such Satanic practice unironically traffics in symbols and discourse related to violence, sex, morbidity, ritual abuse conspiracies, and more while ironically reifying a select group of religious "others" as fringe.

TST represents not only an atheistic or "rationalistic" (Petersen 2016, 7) instantiation of Modern Satanism but a popularly mediatized and, therefore, exaggerated practice of transgressive and legalistic demonstrations, in which only a few chapters thereof directly participate or engage (Laycock 2020, 150). As an

Esoteric and Theistic Satanist, Shea Bilé feels mostly removed from the creation of such political drama, though he is still interested in the personal transgressive journey of his imagined community.

BILÉ: Throughout its history, Satanism seeks to find a sacred inversion.

CHAVEZ: Is your personal practice of Satanism shaped by this tradition of weaponized irreverence?

BILÉ: I think there's something to be said that, maybe, earlier on in a practice [such inversion is healthy]. For me I first started to identify as a Satanist as age thirteen. So a lot of that opposition and antinomianism was more frequent in the earlier years. A disgust with Christianity. I burned a few bibles in my day. Defiled a few bibles too. (That is a form of sexuality I never knew I had.) And I think there's room for that and it makes sense! There's this emancipation; there's a process of liberation that Satanism offers. When we break the law, it helps us to understand where our boundaries are. And it gives us a sense of freedom; we have to test our freedom. And it makes perfect sense that you have this reactionary form of Satanism but as I've gotten older, I've softened that idea. I now view many religionists as brothers. I often feel that I have a lot in common with Christians or Jews or Mormons or Muslims. Given my time dedicated to devotional practice, it's not too hard for me to compare myself to them. If I were to fast or engage in ritual that takes weeks to prepare. It would be remiss of me to not find connection to other religious people.

I was mad when I saw people in my community celebrating the burning of Notre Dame. I was very disappointed because now I look to it as a symbol of European history and wisdom and a contribution to Western art, aesthetics and architecture. I am disappointed that people are filled with such wrath. I actually wrote in a [Facebook] post. . . I hardly ever comment on politics nowadays – because it's become very religious. But in my post, I said, "If we are unable to identify who our enemies are, we have already lost the war." I no longer believe the Christians are my enemy. I think that's a really tired argument. It's not as simple as "those that practice other religions."
And yet, I must be honest. On the other side, I still engage in blood ritual, body suspension and hooks and cutting and self-mutilation and things like that. Antinomian ritual and transgressive ritual. I would like to say, "This is what is meaningful to me. This carries power. Blood and pain are powerful vehicles or mediums for expression." Maybe that's true but I would be lying if I were to completely discount the element of transgression that feeds that for me. Could I say that it's 100% my *connection* to this transgressive expression? Maybe. But there's a good part of me that knows "This is unsafe." "This is kvlt!" K-V-L-T, as they say in black metal. It's pure! It's underground. I want to see those Satanic Temple kids do that. There's this authenticity to it. Antinomianism gives you a sense of the laws you should

break and Satanism still pulls us to break them. This is valid. And in regards to our Satanic Temple brothers and sisters, they're still doing that fight too; finding which buttons to push (Bilé 2021e).

Bilé views bodily transgression as both a liberatory and sacrilegious vehicle of expression. He, unlike other contemporary esoterics, isn't interested in the rehabilitation of Satanic practice. Self-inflicted ritual violence, according to Bilé (2020), is transformative. "Once one plunges into the depths of their own terror," he writes, "and communes with the deepest recesses of Viaios, the liberation of the spirit is attained, and the box of Pandora will contain all the gifts of the world" (153).

Bilé's individual creation of religion is not widespread. He possesses few friends and religious collaborators willing to dedicate so many hours of ritual experimentation spent in the wilderness (Bilé 2021e).

BILÉ: Satanists are few when it comes down to who joins into these types of practice. I've been fortunate to have one or two very serious ritual partners over the years. And I consider that a significant amount. Satanism is a solitary religion for many people and we still are very few and far between. When it comes to *religious* Satanists – not "I'm going to go to the protest at six o'clock on Sunday" Satanists – those who participate in ritual and worship, this is a very small number of people.

CHAVEZ: Is that for lack of trying? I don't believe that you proselytize, but are you in search of a larger community? Or are you content with the smaller inner circle?

BILÉ: I've had a couple of orders, or more like groups, at the university. When I was at San Francisco, I created an "occult student union" but that was more for me to share my knowledge with young bucks. Younger kids that needed a sympathetic ear. And what other than a devil worshipper to be sympathetic? And I did the same when I was at KU Leuven in Belgium. I repeated the same project. And that was more for me to teach; to give kids a gateway to. . . sin. (Just kidding.) A gateway to express themselves religiously in the occult in what level they felt comfortable doing it. That's fulfilling for me. Other than that, I have a very particular approach to my religiosity; my religious practice. And there are just very, very few who are not only interested in the same kind of path but who would also execute it in a way that I feel is in alignment. So, I guess I have a level of specificity that makes me genuinely uninterested in group religious practice.

This excerpt reveals the complications of associating Bilé with a modern religious "folk." "Satanism," perhaps more than other forms of Western Esotericism and post-Christian iterations, "is a solitary religion" due in large part to this practice of transgressive expression. Yet we analyze this particular religious complex in order to comment on modern Christianity and its various cultural modes of supersession.

At levels of individual and culture, this chapter narrates at once the function and positioning of various subgroups and traditions that shape and are shaped by the post-Christian framework. In the case of Bilé, traces of Christian rhetoric surface within his performance of religiosity, ironically and not. He exists in clear conversation with the dominant set of Protestant sensibilities, namely the authenticity of belief, power of personal conviction and mindful projection, individual relationships with the divine, and publicly accessible and ubiquitous teachings. He also exhibits the broader conditions of modern religiosity – that is, antiauthoritarian ideologies, privatized spiritualities, non-Christian re-enchantment, and religious experimentation and eclecticism – themselves the fruit of a post-Christian complex of behavior. I argue that Bilé's relationship to popular media intersects larger narratives of sensationalized religious content; his self-religious orientation intersects the larger cultic milieu and metaphysical imagination of Western culture; and, finally, his individual Satanic practice constitutes an experimental and fringe byproduct of a dominant Christian system that demonizes magical workings and derides bodily transgression.

What then is the closest Bilé has felt to achieving a spiritual union, even if from afar, with a community of similarly practicing Satanists? He answers:

> *Vice* put out a few video-articles on Satanic groups in Latin America. And I am really attracted to that kind of Latin folk magic/Santería/devil worship, where particular places in Latin America are beginning to worship the Devil and it's this growing movement! They take things a bit further with animal sacrifice and doing things with cutting [than I'm used to]. I think there's a church dedicated to a being they call "Little Devil." *Angelito Negro*. I think he's supposed to be the brother of Satan. And they're there cutting their backs open and that is crazy inspiring! I respect it at a high level because you're not seeing that a lot in the United States or even in Europe. It's in Latin America that you're seeing this really visceral practice that I'm very attracted to; where they're not afraid to do animal sacrifice or afraid of believing in it so much that they're crying. They get in this religious rapture and they live that life. I'm very drawn to that. Just like I'm drawn to the cult of Santa Muerte. I had a practice of Santa Muerte for a few years because I am drawn to the visceral culture or spirit (Bilé 2021e).

In both contexts (Angelito Negro and Santa Muerte), Bilé cites the physicality of cult performance as the impetus of admiration (Bilé 2021b). Yet, because he respects the social dynamics involved (his positionality as a White man and potential issues of cultural appropriation), Bilé simply draws a spiritual inspiration from the "external viatheosis" displayed within such cultural customs. Additionally, this Satanic devotee admires their cultural "attempts to leverage the discourse of evil," at once celebrating a practice of freedom and nonconformity but also cultural heterodoxy.

Returning to the claims of Jesper Aagaard Petersen, I argue that scholars would do well to consider such modern Satanic practices as instantiations of a "Christian sect," a form of "inverted Christianity," and/or a set of "Christian hermeneutics." It becomes clear that this performance of antinomianism and transgressive expression belongs to a larger cultural conversation that Protestant Christianity has with itself, a form of internal communication. Modern Satanism looks to the discourse of "bad religion" for its construction of a *religious boogeyman*, purposely trafficking symbols and practices related to violence, sex, morbidity, cult conspiracies, and more in pursuit of a sacred inversion. Such antithetical constructions ironically reify a select group of religious "others" historically marginalized as "fringe" – i.e., Catholics, Mormons, Christian fundamentalists, and the like. Modern Satanism functions as a cultural response to the political activism, militant reactionism, and moral sensationalism of conservative Christians; "rehabilitating" the Satanic mythos of Christian tradition in order to support the self-serving attitudes and sensibilities of modern religiosity while simultaneously negotiating the "trappings" of a Christian theological milieu.

Conclusion

This chapter is made possible by Shea Bilé's sense of self-awareness and introspection.

CHAVEZ: How singular do you feel as a Satanic practitioner? Are there others like you? If the answer is no, that they are practicing in their own individual ways, then what unites you and them as "Satanists"?

BILÉ: I see Satanism as a family. I extend olive branches wherever possible. I see (even though I disagree with quite a bit of it) the Order of Nine Angles; and I do see Dragon Rouge; and I do see The Satanic Temple; and I do see the Church of Satan; and I do see the Temple of Set, all of these, as part of a family. Even though, many of them do not see each other as such. I make jabs at The Satanic Temple, but it's out of fun. They're my cousins, and it's fine to rough up your cousin from time to time. Their practices are certainly not mine but they are part of the family (Bilé 2021e).

The "folk" that Bilé represents extends beyond the immediate branches of Modern Satanism. He represents the *margins* of religious society, yet this baptized Catholic from Long Beach, California, raised by a New Age medium mother, exists as a result of the same modern cultural conditions that lead many Western subjects to enter either stages of religious disenchantment, non-Christian re-enchantment, or forms of religious experimentation; a convergent yet unchurched collective. The "folk" he represents are not unified through collective practice or large-scale organizational efforts. As such, individualized vernacular practices like Bilé's are vulnerable to being co-opted by the cultural mainstream and trivialized by mass media, which Bilé works hard to avoid. At the time of writing, he recently completed filming a Satanic ritual performed in the dried river bed of the Mojave Desert, to be included in a ten-part docuseries on occult religion – coming soon to Apple TV+. In the episode on Satanism, Bilé's ritual practice will feature alongside interviews with the former leader of the Church of Satan, Blanche Barton. This popular mediatization of a religious subject discursively marked with alterity – wearing the "occultist," "Satanist," and "exorcist" brands – at once sensationalizes ritual practice as *exotic* while, in line with Bilé's interests, contributes to the formation of popular worldviews and, in so doing, influences what people accept as plausible.

Shea Bilé, a "Satanist who does exorcisms" (Bilé 2021e), ironically celebrates the post-Christian ideology of self-made optimism. Through individual ambition, his vernacular religious practice creates a "disruption of the current order," an opportunity for a new "beginning." Like Satan, Bilé is a religious outsider but former member of the dominant religious faction of the West. Through him, we narrate the major historical and cultural shifts that continue to alter the Western religious landscape. His Satanic/magical exorcism practice teaches us more about modern religious syncretism, as Cuneo (1998, 465) says of modern exorcism in general, "[d]rawing its inspiration from traditional religious symbolism, pop-culture iconography, and current notions of psycho-spiritual healing."

Following this discussion, I designate the category of "post-Christian" to refer a wide array of practices, including Western Esotericism and other forms of re-enchantment but also movements of secularism, American civil religion, what has been called the "Gospel of Disney," and the "unchurched"/"spiritual but not religious" movement. A future study could examine how this post-Christian framework, indeed, applies to Americans and other Westerners that are (1) currently unchurched or perhaps loose converts to a non-Christian form of religious practice or spirituality; (2) nevertheless, beholden to Protestant Christian ideals (the products of a Christian socio-political system) such as the privatization of spirituality, prioritization of religious individualism (beliefs and convictions included), and distrust of traditional institutions, theocratic leadership, and archaic rituals; and (3) prejudice toward most forms of religious fundamentalism with the exception of Neo-Nationalism, patriotism, and other forms of political tribalism. In doing so, we could study Christendom the same way others study the Islamicate.

Works Cited

60 Second Docs. Indigenous Media, 2017, https://www.60secdocs.com/. Accessed 27 Apr. 2022.

60 Second Docs. "I'm an Exorcist//60 Second Docs," YouTube, 20 Oct. 2016, https://www.youtube.com/watch?v=PwaRXBjK30k. Accessed 27 Apr. 2022.

Albanese, Catherine L. *A Republic of Mind and Spirit: A Cultural History of American Metaphysical Religion*. New Haven: Yale UP, 2007.

Bilé, Shea. "In the Hands of the Violent Divine: Magickal Acts of Devotional Violence." *Pillars: Seeds of Ares*, vol. 2, no. 2, edited by G. McCaughry and Evan Davies, Montréal: Anathema Publishing, 2020, pp. 145–153.

———. Personal Interview. 4 Apr. 2021.

———. Personal Interview. 11 May 2021

———. Personal Interview. 24 Jun. 2021.

———. Personal Interview. 26 Jul. 2021.

———. Personal Interview. 29 Nov. 2021

Bowler, Kate. *Blessed: A History of the American Prosperity Gospel*. New York: Oxford UP, 2013.

Bunch, Jason. "These Occult Exorcists Say the Catholic Church Makes Demons Worse," *Vice*, 15 Jun. 2018, https://www.vice.com/en/article/4354zp/these-occult-exorcists-say-the-catholic-church-makes-demons-worse. Accessed 27 Apr. 2022.

Chavez, William S. "Modern Practice, Archaic Ritual: Catholic Exorcism in America." *Religions*, vol. 12, no. 811, 2021, pp. 1–27.

Cuneo, Michael W. "Of Demons and Hollywood: Exorcism in American Culture." *Studies in Religion*, vol. 27, no. 4, 1998, pp. 455–465.

Granholm, Kennet. "Embracing Others than Satan: The Multiple Princes of Darkness in the Left-Hand Path Milieu." *Contemporary Religious Satanism: A Critical Anthology*, edited by Jesper Aagaard Petersen, 2009, New York: Routledge, 2016, pp. 85–101.

Hall, David D. *Worlds of Wonder, Days of Judgment: Popular Religious Belief in Early New England*. New York: Alfred A. Knopf, 1989.

Harding, Susan Friend. *The Book of Jerry Falwell: Fundamentalist Language and Politics*. Princeton: Princeton UP, 2000.

Johnson, Paul E. "Democracy, Patriarchy, and American Revivals, 1780–1830." *Journal of Social History*, vol. 24, no. 4, 1991, pp. 843–850.

Johnson, Paul E. and Sean Wilentz. *The Kingdom of Matthias*. New York: Oxford UP, 1994.

Petersen, Jesper Aagaard. "Introduction: Embracing Satan." *Contemporary Religious Satanism: A Critical Anthology*, edited by Jesper Aagaard Petersen, 2009, New York: Routledge, 2016, pp. 1–24.

16

CONTROLLING THE LORE

A Survey of UFO Folklore in the United States

Diana Walsh Pasulka

Scholars within the fields of religious studies, folklore studies, and anthropology observe and study tensions between doctrinal or orthodox religions and expressions of popular or devotional religious forms—so-called folk or vernacular religion (Primiano 382). An example of this tension is found in Catholic religion and scholarship in the form of private and public revelation. Private revelation is expressed by practitioners who have alleged to have seen, for example, the Virgin Mary (i.e., Marian Apparitions). Public revelation, on the other hand, is believed to have been revealed in the Christian Old and New Testaments (Walsh Pasulka, *Heaven Can Wait*, 124–128). The difference between these two types of revelations is that one is optional and the other is required belief. Private revelation is optional, whereas Catholics are obligated to believe in public revelation. This framing places private revelation in a marginal relationship to public revelation. Similarly, folk or popular religious expressions are defined by their marginal or "outsider" status. It is ironic that private revelation, within Catholic tradition, is very popular and informs most religious practices, even more so than public revelation. For example, Catholics are seldom familiar with their own Church's sanctioned, obligatory beliefs and dogmas. The private revelations alleged to have been given by the Virgin Mary to three children in Fatima, Portugal, in 1917, for example, are known by almost all Catholics, whereas the dogma of Purgatory, a belief that all Catholics are expected to hold, is almost universally unknown by contemporary Catholics.

This example, in particular, sheds light on how a popular form of testimonial devotion, the lore Catholic folk religion, or Catholic folklore, is identified as marginal and secondary to public revelation, yet is much more popular and forms an important epistemology for Catholic practices. Similarly, the new and fast developing religiosity of the UFO, or the Unidentified Flying Object, reveals a pattern where vernacular or non-sanctioned lore informs the beliefs and practices

DOI: 10.4324/9781003257462-21

of most people regarding UFOs. Given the prodigious efforts of the US military to marginalize civilian and popular UFO folklore and sanction a military-inspired narrative, one would assume that the official state version would be the most accepted narrative. This, however, is not the case. The popular or vernacular narrative, which includes fictional accounts, forms the basis for what most Americans believe about UFOs.

Several factors align belief in UFOs with traditional religions. UFO religions such as Raelism and the Nation of Islam are defined as New Religious Movements, and within these and other UFO religions, the UFO event is interpreted as transcendent (Finley 2012). Little scholarly attention has been paid to UFO folklore and its management by the US government. This is in stark contrast to populist or civilian accounts of interest in this topic, both in fiction and in nonfiction. Attention to the tension between sanctioned belief in UFOs and popular ideas about UFOs is almost non-existent in academic discussions of the topic, whereas communities of people who believe in UFOs are acutely aware of this tension and share it with each other in various popular forms, including nonfiction and fiction, videos, photographs, and other media (Denzler, I). The popular 1990s television series *The X-Files* is based on this tension, as its premise is that the US government is managing the perception of UFOs. It is significant that a survey by National Geographic found that people reported that if there was an invasion by extraterrestrials, it would most resemble a season of *The X-Files* (Walsh Pasulka, *American Cosmic*, 127). The almost complete silence by academics regarding this easily documented relationship might be explained by scholars' reticence to engage with what the US government and universities have identified as stigmatized knowledge or conspiracy theory (Dehaven-Smith, Chapter 3). Dr. John Mack of Harvard University, for example, was investigated by his university for engaging in such scholarship. However, an honest and thorough examination of UFO folklore is not possible without such an examination.

To further complicate the issue of the study of UFO folklore, the US government, through its military branch, The Pentagon, published a report in June 2021, acknowledging the existence of UFOs, which they renamed UAPs, or unidentified aerial phenomenon. Although the unclassified report did not definitively state that UAPs were of extraterrestrial origin, credible public figures like NASA administrator Bill Nelson went on national television to report on his assessment of the classified report. He said that he did not think that humans are alone in the universe (Brufke 2021). This is a remarkable shift in the tradition of popular belief in UFOs in that the institution that had debunked and denied their existence shifted its focus to seemingly align its official assessment with popular belief (Walsh Pasulka, *Religious Dispatches*). This essay examines the history of the tension between institutional revelation of UFOs and private or citizens revelation—here termed "The peoples' UFO"—and discusses tactics and strategies used by each community to control or manage UFO folklore.

In the case of the UFO "mytheme" or religiosity, there are two competing and identifiable narrative streams (Levi-Straus). One narrative stream is that the US government is attempting to centralize UFO belief and practices, while many UFO experiencers and their communities post images, videos, and reports of experiences that counter what they perceive to be this "official" narrative. Another narrative stream is that the government is finally ready to disclose the presence of extraterrestrial life to the American public, and this is being done through no less than the cultural authorities of Harvard University (through Dr. Ave Loeb's The Galileo Project) and the Pentagon (Pentagon Report). Factions of believers have aligned into different camps with respect to these two divergent positions. Currently, the decentralized nature of the internet gives voice and agency to those who oppose government positions and has created the conditions for a pluralism of perspectives that can fall under the categories of the peoples' UFO narrative—comprised of civilian content—against a military version of the UFO—comprised of content that features military personnel and is disseminated by major media sources like *The New York Times.* Is the portrayal of the issue of competing UFO narratives really so simplistic as suggesting there is a government metanarrative posited against a peoples' narrative of UFO events? Surprisingly the evidence suggests that, *yes*, this is indeed what has been the case.

UFO Influencers

There are several historical origin points associated with the rise in belief and practices about UFOs in the United States. Social scientists and scholars of humanities generally place the origin of the beliefs and practices surrounding the UFO in the 1940s, coeval with the beginning of the cold war between the United States and Russia. Other scholars point out that evidence for the belief in extraterrestrial life and aerial phenomenon are found in historical documents and have been around as long as human beings have had written and oral culture (Mueler and Consolmagno, Introduction; Atalay, Lempert, Shorter, and Tallbear 2021). With respect to intentional social influence about UFOs, the 1940s stands out as the time period when influencers—those who influence public opinion about UFOs—became a clearly identified presence. Although UFOs as unidentified aerial phenomena have been present in religious and esoteric texts and discourse for more than a thousand years, the presence of intentional influencers appeared on the US scene with two very public and now iconic UFO sightings.

Two UFO-related events happened within months of each other in the 1940s and catapulted the term "flying saucer" into public consciousness; soon thereafter, the image of the flying saucer became a fixture within the North American social imagination. Coeval with these events was the rise of the UFO influencer. The first event was the sighting of an anomalous aerial object by pilot Kenneth Arnold. Arnold flew his plane over Mt. Rainer in Washington state, and during his flight, he saw nine silvery bright objects that he estimated were traveling at approximately 2700 km/hour. At first, he thought he had happened upon a new kind of stealth aircraft, but he later realized that the objects displayed movements beyond any known technology. News of his sightings spread fast through the news media of the era, including in *The Chicago Sun*, which dubbed the objects flying saucers (*Chicago Sun*).

The second event happened approximately one month after Arnold's sighting. In the town of Roswell, New Mexico, farmer W. Mac Brazel found something that appeared to be a broken mash-up of metal and mesh netting. Brazel announced his discovery, and soon personnel from the Roswell Army Air Field came to assess the debris. They described the debris as coming from a crashed flying disc, and they issued this information in a press release. News of a crashed flying saucer instigated a national public reaction of fear and wonder. Soon after, the same group of Air Force personnel retracted the statement and called the debris a fallen weather balloon (Saler, Ziegler, Moore). This second news release focused even more attention on the incident. Regardless of what the debris was, this marks one of the first known cases where the public perception of a UFO event was managed by influencers—in this case Air Force personnel. The coverage not only inspired distrust in perpetrators of an "official story," because there appeared to be conflicting reports from authorities, but it also motivated religious reactions throughout the United States. Religious responses to the Arnold sighting as well as the Roswell incident added impetus to a burgeoning development of Christian and non-Christian apocalypticism focused on the UFO (Cusack, 340–350).

The Roswell incident, which constitutes overt management of the public perception of UFOs, is an example of the first generation of UFO influencers. Other official explanations of the Roswell event followed and further confused the situation, casting suspicion on any explanation related to the debris. A later, official (by the Air Force) iteration of the Roswell story explained the discrepancy with the first publicly released knowledge to be motivated by the need to cover up an *actual* classified mission called Project Mogul. It is claimed that Project Mogul's goal was to create technology that utilized microphones and aerial technologies like balloons to identify signals from Russia or non-allies. In the 1990s, several books and reports of government investigations were released to support this view of the Roswell incident (Saler, Ziegler, Moore). This 1990s version of the story stated that the first and second press releases in the 1940s were to cover up an actual classified program in the interests of national security. Perhaps this recounting was true, but by this time, any official story seemed likely to change given time, and the ongoing shifting of the official narrative solidified a culture of suspicion and distrust that the government would be a credible source for information about UFOs. How could the public believe the third release of official information did not constitute yet another attempt at perception management? There was no way to know. By this point, the US government version about the Roswell incident had changed at least three times, making conclusions about the incident impossible. Regardless of the truth of any story associated with these two iconic incidents, the point is that the public's perceptions were actively managed, and the events in the 1940s were the first chronicled large-scale social influence effort regrading UFOs.

Whereas the first generation of UFO influence seems haphazard and even clumsy, the second generation of UFO influencers were organized if not sophisticated. There is a distinction between influencers and researchers. Influencers are agenda driven, and their goal is to influence the perception of an event; researchers identify evidence to understand the nature of an event. After the UFO sightings of the 1940s, there was a concerted effort by the US government to organize the public perception of UFOs. This effort constitutes a second generation of UFO influencers. The government employed disinformation agents to "debunk" UFO sightings. This came to light when the government declassified documents related to the program known as Project Bluebook in 1969.

Project Bluebook was a study organized by the US Air Force. It began in 1952 and ended in 1969. One goal of the program was to study data related to UFO sightings to determine if there was a national threat posed by unidentified aerial phenomenon. Among its other goals was the development of a campaign to manage the US public's perception of UFOs. This was suggested by members of The Robertson Panel headed by Dr. Howard Percy Robertson. His panel's stated position in 1953 was that it would be necessary to adopt an official strategy of "debunking" witness testimonies regarding UFO sightings to discourage civilians and military personnel from reporting UFOs. The panel stated that reports of sightings were so numerous that they prevented military personnel from doing the work of national security. They also suggested that specific members of the program should work with media influencers like Walt Disney and producers of documentaries. In the latter case, it was suggested that documentaries would be able to focus on a popular sighting and then provide an answer that reduced the UFO sighting to natural causes, such as the famous and now cliché phrase "swamp gas" used by Professor Allen Hynek, an astronomer and the scientific consultant for Project Bluebook, to explain a series of UFO sightings in Michigan in 1966. A UFO flap is defined as a series of sightings of UFOs that happen within a short time period over a small or specific geographical location. Hynek's job was to be the official debunker of UFO sightings during Project Bluebook.

An examination of one of the more popular UFO sightings debunked by Dr. Hynek, the 1966 UFO flap in Michigan, provides insights into how UFO experiencers—those who have seen UFOs—resist the appropriation of their narratives by influencers, in this case the US Air Force. This early case sheds light on how oral traditions appear within public media spaces to give voice to counternarratives that challenge and destabilize government-curated influencer narratives.

In 1966, there was a UFO flap in southeastern Michigan. Aerial phenomena were witnessed by multiple people over a period of days and reported to Michigan resident Gerald Ford, who was later to become the president of the United States. The phenomenon, described as aerial vehicles with multiple lights that also emitted whistling bullet sounds, was terrifying to Michigan residents. Members of local police forces were dispatched to investigate the events, and they also reported that the phenomenon was strange and inexplicable. Dr. Harry Willnus investigated the events at the time and obtained police reports and other primary source material of the flap.

> Over a period of some weeks UFOs were widely reported by the public and police in southeastern Michigan. Things came to a head on March 20 and 21, 1966, in Dexter and Hillsdale, Michigan. On the night of March 20, Frank Manor and his son saw a strange object from their farm house in a nearby swamp. Police and a number of locals gathered to watch a football shaped craft with multi-colored lights that appeared to be having trouble in lifting off. The object would rise in the air to about 500 feet then, "come down making a lot of noise."

Dr. Willnus also reported that the Air Force sent Dr. Hynek to investigate the scene. At that time, Dr. Hynek's official role was to debunk the claims of people who saw UFOs. This is exactly what he did in Michigan. However, it was apparent that Dr. Hynek's debunking did not succeed, and the Michigan case became famous as the "swamp gas" case that revealed the Air Forces' clumsy attempts to discredit witness testimonies. Dr. Willnus was a witness to these developments.

> Dr. Hynek arrived on the scene several days later to investigate with instructions to release a statement about the cause of the sightings. Press coverage intensified. I was teaching high school at that time not far from the some of the reported UFO sightings. I recall an impromptu faculty meeting regarding a curriculum matter was called for after school. One of the staff promptly stood up and remarked, "You better get this meeting over real quick because it gets dark early. I've got a long drive home and I'm not hanging around here very long with this UFO stuff going on." Many area residents were fearful.
>
> I interviewed Washtenaw County Sheriff Doug Harvey about the Dexter event. Harvey related how he had taken Hynek to the Mannor farm where the professor sloshed about in the swamp and inspected the site. Harvey noted that they returned to the Sheriff's office and Hynek admitted he had no idea what people had witnessed. "That's when the phone call came in," Harvey said. "What call?" I asked. Harvey said the dispatcher stepped into the room and told Hynek he had a call from Washington. Minutes later Hynek returned mumbling, "its swamp gas, its swamp gas they saw." Over the years a number of stories have been put forward regarding just where Dr. Hynek had picked up on the swamp gas phenomenon. After interviewing Sheriff Harvey I'm convinced Hynek was directed from Washington as to what explanation he might offer up.[1]

It is important to note that the efforts of Project Bluebook to discredit witnesses of UFO events were successful, and that the Michigan case was the exception that proved the rule and opened a space for a public rejection the government's narrative. There were so many witnesses that it was impossible to control the narrative of the Michigan flap. Willnus goes on to describe the ways in which public spaces of information such as news media and word of mouth formed a counternarrative of mockery that undermined Hynek's claims.

> The next day newspaper stories reported that swamp or marsh gas was the real culprit. The story was met with laughter, ridicule, and derisiveness and Hynek would leave Michigan as quickly as he could. Soon political cartoons appeared in papers across the country which poked fun at Hynek and swamp gas as being the culprit in the Michigan sightings.
>
> *(Strickler)*

The groundswell of mockery was soon coupled with cultural authority. Gerald Ford was a member of the US House of Representatives, representing the people of Michigan from 1949 until 1973. As Michigan's government representative, he fielded questions and concerns from witnesses, and he believed they were reliable. He called for a Congressional Hearing. In a letter to his constituency, he wrote,

> Last week Michigan aroused excitement in Washington, instead of the other way around. People here showed keen interest in the unidentified flying objects (UFOs) reported sighted in the Hillsdale and Ann Arbor areas. At week's end, the Air Force explained away the UFO's as a product of college-student pranks, swamp gas, the rising crescent moon, and the planet Venus. But the Air Force has been explaining away UFO's for years, and I don't believe the American people are generally satisfied with its statements.
>
> *(Gerald Ford Presidential Library)*

Congressman Ford's cultural and political authority lent credibility to the discourse of suspicion that flooded the media after Hynek's visit to Michigan. Significantly, Ford positioned himself as a representative of the people. In 1966, a peoples' narrative of UFOs, which was already suspicious of government authority, was authorized *by* government authority. In 1969, Project Bluebook was officially terminated. The Air Force washed its hands of the study of UFOs, and supposedly of the program that intended to influence the public's perception of UFOs.

Post-Project Bluebook UFO Influencers

The Michigan UFO flap was just one instance where public suspicion of official statements by Allen Hynek drove the narrative that there was a government cover-up of UFO events. This narrative was correct—the Air Force did misinform the public about UFO events through agents like Dr. Allen Hynek. The venues that spread this lore included media like newspapers, magazines, and news radio programs as well as an oral tradition that fed these venues and was fed by them (Denzler).

By the 1980s, there were thriving communities of self-identified experiencers, people who felt they were in contact with extraterrestrials or had a life-changing experience after seeing a UFO. Against the curated and intentionally manipulated media generated by military-affiliated UFO influencers, experiencers rallied around media personalities who bolstered their stories and presented them to a wider public. Author Whitley Strieber wrote a bestselling nonfiction book, *Communion*, about his own experiences, and Harvard researcher John Mack's psychiatric work with experiencer patients revealed that they were completely normal and had no pathologies. If Air Force influencers were to shape the perspectives of members of these communities, or shape how the general population would view them, they needed different tactics than they had previously employed.

Richard Doty is the most infamous and known of the post-Project Bluebook influencers. He deployed (presumably) different tactics than Allen Hynek. Doty, a former and possibly current intelligence officer with the US Air Force Office of Special Investigations, claims that in the 1980s, he was tasked with spreading disinformation about UFOs and even placing false and misleading information on a computer owned by a veteran of World War II, Paul Bennewitz (Bishop). Doty's work marks a shift in how UFO folklore is shaped by government actors. The framework that defined the Project Bluebook era was characterized by the work of Allen Hynek. Hynek used his cultural authority to create a sanctioned version of the UFO narrative in an attempt to shape the people's version of the UFO. The work of Doty provides valuable insight into the interplay between a powerful institution's attempt to shape folklore, and a community's response to that. As will be revealed, the opacity that is intrinsic to the "Doty Narrative" is intentional and provides both an opportunity and a challenge for scholars of folklore. One goal of the contemporary study of folklore is to identify vectors of power and social discipline, and to identify ways in which marginal communities resist these. The Doty Narrative provides an opportunity to identify the vehicles of these vectors of power, that is, the means by which UFO folklore is created and distributed through an institution of power in an attempt to manage its meanings.

Scholar of American Studies, Timothy Melley, provides a helpful lens through which to analyze Doty's influence. He identifies fiction and the use of nonfiction media such as news editorials as the means through which the powerful institution of the Central Intelligence Agency manages the social sphere. Melley calls this use of fiction and news media (which is assumed to be nonfiction) "the covert sphere."

> This is not to say that the discourses of "fact" have no place in the covert sphere. But in its precincts they are more likely to take on fictional

> qualities—a reliance on anonymous sources, speculation, invention, and confabulation. Daniel Ellsberg, who in 1971 leaked the top secret Pentagon Papers to the New York Times, describes how his top secret clearance made him "really look down on the New York Times readers." Once granted access to "whole libraries of hidden information," Ellsberg began to see the New York Times as "fantasies basically" and read it "just to see what the rubes and the yokels are thinking." From inside the secret archive of the security state, in other words, the most serious institutions of the public sphere seemed vehicles of fiction.
>
> *(Melley, 16)*

Doty worked within the covert sphere. He used people and communities to spread disinformation about UFOs. He also targeted individual media personalities, like journalist Linda Molton Howe, who were cultivated as "assets" to spread UFO disinformation. When these tactics were finally exposed by the work of researchers like Greg Bishop, the anti-government narrative about UFO secrecy was in full swing. The case of Paul Bennewitz contributed to the folklore that the US government took liberties with its own citizens in its goal of promoting UFO disinformation. Bennewitz, an electrical engineer, lived near Kirtland Air Force Base, in New Mexico, and believed in UFOs. He was also a vulnerable target because he appeared to suffer from delusional paranoia. His proximity to the Air Force Base allowed him to carefully watch its aerial activities throughout the day and night. He possessed a unique combination of characteristics: a belief in UFOs and a vulnerable mental state. This combination of traits became the perfect vehicle for the spread of Doty's messages. Doty, who allegedly was armed with a psychological profile of Bennewitz provided by the Air Force, teamed up with other agents to exploit Bennewitz's vulnerabilities and to spread disinformation.

Doty stated that he secretly placed information on Bennewitz's computer—false information that indicated the Air Force was aware of an imminent UFO invasion. This, of course, was not true, and Bennewitz's belief in this information became a factor that compelled his family to institutionalize him. Why did Doty do this? Were his actions intended to discredit any witness who would come forward with a UFO sighting or story? Was Bennewitz being used as a poster child for the cliché of the tin foil hat wearing UFO believer? Doty also targeted media personality and journalist Linda Molton Howe. Howe was a well-known personality in communities who were interested in accounts of cattle mutilations. Doty approached her and offered to take her to a restricted Air Force base to show her documents that related to UFOs. She agreed to this and publicized her experience. By targeting vulnerable individuals like Bennewitz and media influencers like Howe, who both publicized their experiences, Doty swayed public opinion about UFOs.

Doty's employment status, agenda, and actions have been shrouded in mystery and obfuscation. Perhaps the unnamed program in which he has publicly stated he was involved, like Project Bluebook, was a program created to spread disinformation about UFOs, but different from Bluebook in that it was created to spread confusion. It is impossible to know whether Doty's actions were sanctioned by the Air Force. The Air Force has not released any information about the program or Doty's involvement in it. Yet that has not stopped Doty's public confessions of his work as an Air Force agent of disinformation. To clarify, the truth of Doty's claims is not what is most important to the study of UFO folklore. What *is* important is that the "Doty Narrative" came to play such an important role in the ongoing narrative of UFO secrecy, the US government's part in that secrecy, and the attempts by civilians to separate fact from fiction. The Doty Narrative is such a quagmire of confusion that historical reproduction of events is impossible. If Doty's job was to seed disinformation and to lead civilians off of the path of the truth of UFOs, he was more than successful. Another effect was that people who might have studied the topic academically were repulsed. A prominent scholar who was interested in the religious aspect of UFOs chose not to study the topic because "the whole government secrecy thing makes it impossible for me to say anything substantive about the topic" (personal correspondence, 2015). If nothing else, the post-Project Bluebook era of UFO folklore emphasized the ethical obligations of the press and the status of government transparency. It also revealed a new strategy of managing the UFO narrative. Doty, and presumably others who are not known, was at the center of an impenetrable cell of individuals, some of who were unwittingly cultivated as assets such as Howe and Bennewitz, and some of whom were purposely working with Doty. Some of the stories that leaked from this cell were true, such as Howe going on to an Air Force base to view documents, and some were false. Threads of truth mixed with lies formed this cell of disinformation which was The Doty Narrative.

A New Era of Digital Influence

The technological shift that engulfed society from the 1990s onward is definitive in that *everything* changed within countries wealthy enough to own and utilize digital technology. The shift to digital infrastructures changed how members of these countries work, eat, procure lodging, communicate, engage with family, vote, obtain education, and practice religion. The COVID-19 pandemic that began in 2019 and 2020 intensified the move to online environments. Digital infrastructures created new forms of UFO influence. They also created new ways for UFO experiencers to counter official government narratives about UFOs.

Two features of online environments—the shift in the perception of time, and the creation of platforms that connect large populations—provide the conditions for a potentially democratic and autonomous peoples' UFO narrative, at least throughout the 1990s and early 2000s. Digital timeframes in which information is shared almost instantaneously among many people, were not in place for the first three generations of government UFO influencers. A linear timeframe benefited and allowed influencers like Hynek to maintain a government narrative because information was slow to move through communities and populations. When Hynek went to UFO sighting locations, his assessments reached local news and for the most part never attracted national attention. These conditions helped Hynek control the UFO folklore. It was only due to the sheer number of people involved in the Michigan UFO flap that this model was challenged, and the addition of Gerald Ford's interest helped it achieve national attention.

In addition to the shift to a digital timeframe that links millions of people instantaneously, another important feature of digital platforms is that users can, nowadays, upload their own images of UFOs and provide their own interpretations of these events. These are shared immediately with other users and experiencers. This has generated new interpretative frameworks for UFOs that challenge media representations that portray extraterrestrials as little green people or generally anthropomorphic beings. Along with images that appear to be orbs or light, experiencers share their accompanying interpretations. Users of Twitter, reacting to photos of one user's photos, posted a link to a YouTube video that offers animated visuals of "Biblically Accurate Angels," or angels as described in the Hebrew Bible and the Christian New Testament. Users were aligning orbs and UFOs with angels in the Jewish tradition (Walsh Pasulka https://www.youtube.com/watch?v=8sROESLRudM).

Another way in which digital infrastructures allow for the people's version of the UFO to flourish is that it opens a space that is potentially free from impinging market constraints and government interference. In the past, media contents like television shows, commercials, and music videos were determined by media production companies. Production companies would choose which content was valuable and worthy of being seen, heard, and watched. Digital environments have the potential to skirt these constraints. An example of this is revealed by the experience of a colleague who is a life-long UFO experiencer. He created a documentary about a UFO sighting in Ruwa, Zimbabwe (author's personal correspondence, 2022). In 1994, a UFO was alleged to have landed outside of a school in Ruwa. Many of the children who attended the school saw the UFO and its inhabitants, while the children were at recess. The incident caused a sensation; John Mack went to Ruwa to interview the witnesses. Over many years, my colleague created the documentary about the incident, using footage from Mack's interviews interspersed with present-day interviews with the now-adult experiencers. While my colleague was trying to get his documentary released and signed by production companies, he was met with resistance. In an email to me and several other colleagues, he said that companies were interested in his documentary and offered him a lot of money for it under the condition that he include two specific people in the documentary as experts. These experts are a former contractor with the military and a former intelligence administrator who is involved the dissemination of information about UFOs. These placements would have framed the RUWA story within the narrative of the US military. The director was adamantly opposed to the addition of these men in his production because they had nothing to do with the original sighting. Ultimately, he was able to release the documentary on his own terms. Internet streaming services allowed him to release his work unfettered by unwanted and uninvited influence.

Fiction plays a central role in UFO folklore. Experiencers state that their experiences of extraterrestrials are real and not metaphoric or fictional, yet their accounts are testimonial and not backed by quantitative evidence. Additionally, an objective, corporal extraterrestrial has yet to be produced by any community or individual, making fiction the primary way to imagine what one might look like. Fictional narratives, therefore, fill in the imaginative gap and support the belief in UFOs and extraterrestrials. Fiction provides a lexicon of images that includes a variety of flying saucers, entities, and space-fauna, and these prompt individuals who view unknown aerial phenomenon to use these imagistic categories as reference points. Additionally, digital entertainment media, such as video games, films, videos, memes, and documentaries, utilize fiction in ways that erase the distinction between fact and fiction (Walsh Pasulka, *The Fairy Tale Is True*; Zacks). This makes fiction, as Melley suggests, important in the covert sphere and a site where the meaning of UFO folklore is presented and contested.

> Intelligence officials who curate these institutions clearly recognize the crucial role of fiction in the work of the state. Fiction "reveals" covert action in a form dismissible as fantasy, melodrama, mere entertainment. It satisfies the public desire to know the work of the state while also pretending not to know what the state does in the public's name.
>
> *(Melley, p. 27)*

Within UFO folklore fiction is often presented as fact, or there is the strong suggestion that even though the account is officially presented as fiction, the author insinuates that one should receive it as factual. This is the case with *Alien Interview*, which has a wide circulation within digital environments related to UFOs. *Alien Interview* is a text edited by Lawrence R. Spencer, who claims that it was provided to him by an Army Air Force Nurse who telepathically interviewed an alien kept by the government after the alleged 1947 UFO crash in Roswell, New Mexico. Lawrence makes no official claim regarding the objective truth of the interview but suggests that it is true. The text has been translated into twelve languages and has become an authoritative account for many experiencer communities who cite it in chat groups, on social media, and ask about it during podcast interviews with experts. This is a case where cultural authority is ascribed to fictional content.

The narrative of the *Alien Interview* is an alien—an extra-biological entity or an EBE (a term the author claims is used by the Air Force)—is a non-corporal entity that inhabits a created biological proxy, the EBE. It will eventually leave its "body", but it first wants to impart important information to a nurse who has figured out that she can communicate with the alien via telepathy. The alien describes the history of human beings on Earth, how there are other alien species, and that some humans and aliens have agreed to enslave most humans and much of human history is based on created memories and humans have amnesia about their true identities. Humans are immortal beings who are not aware of these facts. The dominant motif throughout *Alien Interview* is anti-government. Given the history of the Air Force managing the public perception of UFOs through influencers, the popularity of *Alien Interview* is not surprising. Although the appropriation of *Alien Interview* as a credible source of information about UFOs might be alarming, it is well documented that digital hoaxes and fiction such as the *Star Wars* franchise inform many contemporary religiosities and inspire widespread belief in UFOs (Walsh Pasulka; Cusack). *Alien Interview*, skirting the line between fiction and alleged fact, is an example of how the covert sphere is utilized as a site where creators can contest a government-sponsored UFO narrative.

Conclusion

UFO folklore has been deeply intertwined with the military from the 1940s. Due to secrecy surrounding the UFO, it has been difficult and at times impossible to separate the military's management of the folklore from a people's UFO narrative. However, it is possible to identify a consistent tension between the two narratives, especially when one attends to the once stigmatized knowledge about military intervention and propagation of UFO disinformation. With the shift to digital environments, what will the future hold for UFO folklore?

It is important to recall that the proto-internet, ARPANET, emerged from a military program. Therefore, an analysis of the military's use of technology platforms will help to forecast how social influence might be used by future UFO influencers. Former Marine Sergeant and squad leader Jose Herrera is working on programs of intervention for mental health and what he describes as a situation of meta-war with respect to internet platforms, mostly involving social media. He outlines the addictive qualities of platforms as well as the ways in which they specifically target individuals to spread a specific narrative. Artificial Intelligence algorithms play into this process, sometimes with unintended effects. Social media influence instigates and compels human behavior. Of the contemporary situation, Herrara notes,

> The influencer of today is in a parasitic relationship with artificial neural networks. At first glance, narrative-centric posts, comments, and shares, by design, draw in users through dopaminergic means. Still, the rate of constancy in information transfer and the process of narration through a billionth user framework eventually turn the relationship into a toxic one. *(Herrera)*

Herrera's goal is to help civilian users mitigate disinformation and the pernicious effects intentionally created by users who have political and social agendas. As an agent of the military Herrera understands, like Melley, how unwitting civilians are caught in webs of disinformation and believe information that is not accurate. UFO influencers like Hynek and Doty have been active participants in debunking and spreading disinformation which takes the form of folklore. Herrera's and Melley's work reveal these entanglements and suggest that users must become sophisticated in their use of media as they are now targets of disinformation within these new environments.

Note

1 Found at this website: Interview with Dr. Harry Willnus published by Lon Stickler, 50th Anniversary: Swamp Gas & Dr. J. Allen Hynek, March 16: (2016).

Works Cited

Atalay, Sonya, Lempert, William, Delgado Shorter, David, and TallBear, Kim. "Indigenous Studies Working Group Statement." *American Indian Culture and Research Journal,* vol. 45, no. 1, 2021, 9–18.

Biblically Accurate Angels. Anonymous. https://www.youtube.com/watch?v=8sROESLRudM, accessed November 2, 2021.

Bishop, Greg. *Project Beta: The Story of Paul Bennewitz, National Security, and the Creation of a Modern UFO Myth.* Gallery Books, February 8, 2005.

Brufke, Juliegrace. "NASA Administrator Bill Nelson Says We Are Not Alone in the Universe." *NY Post.* June 28, 2021. https://nypost.com/2021/06/28/nasas-bill-nelson-believes-we-are-not-alone-in-the-universe/, accessed September 10, 2022.

Consolmagno, Guy; Mueler, Paul. *Would You Baptize an Extraterrestrial?: .... and Other Questions from the Astronomers' In-box at the Vatican Observatory.* Image, 2014.

Cusack, Carol. "Apocalypse in Early UFO and Alien-Based Religions: Christian and Theosophical Themes." Erik Tonning and Matthew Feldman (eds), *Modernism, Christianity and Apocalypse.* Brill, 2015, 340–354.

Dehaven-Smith. *Conspiracy Theory in America.* Austin: University of Texas Press, 2014.

Denzler, Brenda, *The Lure of the Edge: Scientific Passions, the Lure of Belief, and the Search for UFOs.* University of California Press, 2003.

Finley, Stephen. "The Meaning of Mother in Louis Farrakhan's "Mother Wheel": Race, Gender, and Sexuality in the Cosmology of the Nation of Islam's UFO." *Journal of the American Academy of Religion.* June 2012. Vol. 80, No. 2, pp. 434–465.

Gerald Ford Presidential Library. Box D6, folder "Ford Press Releases – Column for 5th District Weeklies, 1966" of the Ford Congressional Papers: Press Secretary and Speech File. https://www.theblackvault.com/documentarchive/gerald-ford-pushes-congressional-ufo-hearings-1966/, accessed August 2, 2022.

Herrera, J.A. "The Emergence of the Invisible Vector," unpublished manuscript, May 10, 2022.

Levi-Strauss, Claude. "The Structural Study of Myth", *Structural Anthropology,* 1963: 206–231.

Melley, Timothy. *The Covert Sphere.* Ithaca: Cornell University Press, Kindle Edition, 2013.

Official United States Air Force Website. "Unidentified Flying Objects and Air Force Project Bluebook." https://www.af.mil/About-Us/Fact-Sheets/Display/Article/104590/unidentified-flying-objects-and-air-force-project-blue-book/, accessed September 10, 2022.

Pagels, Elaine, *The Gnostic Gospels*. Vintage; September 19, 1989.

Pasulka, D. W. *American Cosmic: UFOs, Religion, and Technology*. New York: Oxford University Press, 2019.

———. *Heaven Can Wait: Purgatory in Catholic Popular and Devotional Culture*. New York: Oxford University Press, 2012.

———. "With Release of Pentagon Report, UFO Narrative Belief System Is Suddenly Supported by Military Witness Testimonies." *Religious Dispatches*. 2021. https://religiondispatches.org/with-release-of-pentagon-report-ufo-narrative-belief-system-is-suddenly-supported-by-military-witness-testimonies/, accessed September 10. 2022.

Pentagon Report, "Preliminary Assessment: Unidentified Aerial Phenomena," https://www.dni.gov/files/ODNI/documents/assessments/Prelimary-Assessment-UAP-20210625.pdf, accessed June 25, 2021.

Primiano, Leonard. "Vernacular Religion and the Search for Method in Religious Folklore." *Journal of Western Folklore,* vol.54, no.1, 1995, pp.37–56.

Spencer, Lawrence. *Alien Interview*. November 7, 2021. https://alieninterview.org/, accessed September 10, 2022.

Strickler, Lon. "50th Anniversary: Swamp Gas and Dr. J. Allen Hynek," March 18, 2016. https://www.phantomsandmonsters.com/2016/03/50th-anniversary-swamp-gas-dr-j-allen.html, accessed September 10, 2022.

"Supersonic Flying Saucers Sighted by Idaho Pilot." *The Chicago Sun,* June 26, 1947.

UFO Crash at Roswell: The Genesis of a Modern Myth, Benson Saler, Charles A. Ziegler, and Charles B. Moore. New York: Smithsonian Institution Press, 1997.

Wineburg, Sam; McGrew, Sarah; Breakstone, Joel; Ortega, Teresa. "Evaluating Information: The Cornerstone of Civic Online Reasoning," *Stanford Study on Assessing Fact from Fiction*. https://purl.stanford.edu/fv751yt5934, accessed October 29, 2017.

Watson, Nigel. "UFOs and the Cold War", May 1, 2015. https://www.thehistorypress.co.uk/articles/ufos-and-the-cold-war/, accessed September 10, 2022.

Zacks, Jeffrey. *Flicker: Your Brain on Movies*. New York: Oxford University Press, 2014.

PART V

Health, Healing, and Lifestyle

17

INDIGENOUS REVITALIZATION, ROCK MUSIC, AND THE HOLY SPIRIT

The Religious Logic of Healing at Lake Junaluska

Jason E. Purvis

Introduction

The air was heavy with a damp mist in the mountains of western North Carolina on this June morning of 2015. As I crossed the threshold into the dining hall at the Terrace Hotel, there was a buzz among "Sing to the Mountain" conference attendees. However, to my surprise, the collective stir was not about swirl of mouth-watering odors given off by the eggs, bacon, or waffles on offer. Rather, these people believed that they had come into intimate contact with the Holy Spirit during a Christian rock concert the previous night. Band members, community leaders, conference speakers, and conference attendees discussed their collective revelatory experience with a high level of enthusiasm. Band and audience members alike acknowledged the profound spiritual experience of the previous night and several agreed that it was a sign of the Creator's (God's) stamp of approval, foreshadowing miraculous things to come.

Two bands had taken the stage the previous evening. The well-known and widely traveled Indigenous Christian rock band "Broken Walls" opened and "Lilly among Thorns," a lesser-known, decidedly heavier, thrash metal Christian band closed. The concert was perceived to be extremely powerful and had purportedly received the sanction of the Holy Spirit who, according to several individuals, had been felt moving throughout the concert hall and touching the many souls in attendance. This collective effervescence (and agreement) was clearly a sign that the healing power of Christ had made itself present. More importantly, participants believed that God would surely perform His divine charge, carry out its prophesied mission, and heal Indigenous communities throughout North America, ending the cycles of domestic violence, substance abuse, and suicide.

DOI: 10.4324/9781003257462-23

This was the scene during the "Sing to the Mountain" Native American Conference (SMNAC) held on the grounds of Lake Junaluska retreat center in western North Carolina in July 2015. Indigenous and non-Indigenous evangelicals converged on this space to explore the role that God/Christ would play in the empowerment and healing of native communities across the North American continent. More specifically, the conference was dedicated to the necessity of spiritual healing among Indigenous youth and the need for theological answers to the problems of domestic violence, substance abuse, and suicide. The weekend retreat consisted of several events; including formal presentations, musical performances, ritual demonstrations, and (as is typical of Indigenous-led events across North America) a weekend powwow. As I participated in and observed the weekends various events, the religious logic – the connective strands of discourse and practice that bound the various aspects of the conference together into a framework of meaning – became increasingly clear. Put together, the events urged attendees toward a particular set of actions and dispositions that could result in individual and collective spiritual healing.

In the following, I will demonstrate how the form and content of the SMNAC consisted of a "lived religious logic of healing." This logic was embedded in and emerged out of three key components of the conference: "contextualized" ceremonies, presentations, and a charismatic rock concert. The events – planned and organized by Indigenous evangelicals Jonathan Maracle, Bill Pagaran, and Leonard "Casey" Church – combined to, in my estimation, produce a prescribed set of dispositions and outcomes.

The first and most crucial step is that one must achieve the core of evangelical religiosity, which is to accept Christ as one's personal savior. Without this prerequisite disposition, the following steps cannot bear fruit. This sentiment is arguably fundamental to the evangelical worldview. The second step is to revitalize and emphasize one's Indigenous heritage within the context of one's devotion to Christ. This step is decidedly more complicated as it requires careful consideration, and it is a process of determining which aspects of Indigenous cosmology, belief, and practice can be "redeemed through Christ" and which aspects come to be understood as irredeemable and ultimately discarded. For Indigenous Christians in particular, the second step is of vital importance. Discarding the ethnocentric assumptions embedded in American Protestantism allows one to express Indigeneity fully within the context of evangelical Christianity. For non-Indigenous Christians, this means – at a minimum – tolerating Indigenous methods, perhaps even embracing them in one's own style of worship. Non-Indigenous Christians are also encouraged to become advocates for Indigenous communities as these communities attempt to decolonize theology. Once steps one and two have been achieved, Indigenous evangelical/charismatic practices can be made "contextualized" (understood from the emic perspective as having been "redeemed through Christ") and, thus, can now be empowered to illicit the work of the Holy Spirit. The Indigenous (or non-Indigenous advocate) Evangelical self, then, becomes fully realized and capable of engaging properly in "contextualized" practices (combinatory practices that incorporate both Christian and "traditional" Indigenous forms), rendering the body an appropriate vessel for the healing powers of the Holy Spirit.

For analytical purposes, "healing" in the context of these "contextualized" set of practices will be understood a "lived religious logic of healing" that allows adopters (or compels them) to engage in a delicate bifurcation between decolonization and Christianization, pushing back against the perceived ethnocentrism of mainstream evangelical belief and practice while simultaneously limiting and constraining Indigeneity in specific ways. In other words, healing was presented as a "lived" religious idiom that offered both resistance and discipline.[1]

The Setting: Lake Junaluska's Cultural Significance

Lake Junaluska resort and retreat center was founded in 1913 as a center for Methodist revivalism. According to the website, it remains "steeped in the Wesleyan tradition" and has maintained its dedication the Wesleyan theological worldview due to its ongoing association with United Methodist Church. The centerpiece of the compound is the event hall named after George R. Stuart, a Methodist minister who, after experiencing revivalism at a lake retreat center in upstate New York, convinced the Southern Assembly to purchase 1,200 acres in the South for similar purposes. According to a hundred-year anniversary tribute, Stuart Auditorium was erected to inspire missionaries from the Methodist Episcopal Church "to conference and worship, to fellowship and celebrate." It would provide a hub for missionary fervor, design, and deployment.[2]

The cultural heritage and Indigenous connections at Lake Junaluska are significant. The lake and compound are named after Chief Junaluska (c. 1775 – October 20, 1868), the leader of the Eastern band of Cherokee Natives who lived in and around western North Carolina. Junaluska was instrumental in organizing the Eastern Cherokee against the Red Stick faction of Creek Indians which constituted a resistance movement against Euro-American settler's encroachment upon native lands. Junaluska is said to have fought alongside Andrew Jackson in the battle of Horseshoe Bend during the War of 1812 and purportedly saved Jackson's life during this battle. After the war and in anticipation of Jackson's Indian Policy of Indian Removal, Junaluska urged Jackson to relent, allowing the Cherokee to remain in their ancestral lands. Junaluska's request had fallen on resolute ears, however, and Indian Removal commenced as originally planned, displacing Eastern Band Cherokee, and many other native peoples, from their homes. Popular legend says that after this monumental disappointment, Junaluska expressed regret for having rescued Jackson from certain death.[3]

Conducting the SMNAC at Lake Junaluska, therefore, was anything but arbitrary, nor simply a matter of convenience. The Methodist revivalist compound around Lake Junaluska is a site of contestation. It is a place whose name represents cooperation, where newly minted US citizens and the Cherokee led by Chief Junaluska agreed to combine forces and thwart English, the military invasion threatening both community's claims of sovereignty. However, its name is also representative of disagreement; Junaluska's conflict with Andrew Jackson and his policies of demographic displacement and cultural genocide. Ultimately, Jackson succeeded, displacing Junaluska's people in 1830. Returning to this site to "sing to the mountain," therefore, is nothing short of a performative reconquest of the space, which is a way for Indigenous evangelicals (as well as their non-Indigenous supporters) to simultaneously enact the practices of resistance and conformity.

Concerning Christian (Western) Imperialism

My aim in this piece is not to use Christianity as a foil for Indigenous authenticity. Doing so would constitute a privileged ethnographic position that has befallen countless scholars of Indigenous Studies and Christian History alike. This is why the "lived religion" approach is so effective. As Robert Orsi make clear in their careful articulation of the "lived religion" research program, lived religions are those that straddle the fence; they "emphasizes dissent [from], subversion [of] and resistance [to]" the dominant or "orthodox" claims concerning belief and practice. Yet, lived religions also entail repression, "the inevitability of discipline," a conviction to mold one's moods and motivations according to a set of divinely ordained principles.[4] As Indigenous theologians, presenters, and performers transgress mainstream, dominant forms of evangelical thought and practice in the name of Indigenous empowerment, they also draw a line in the sand; they stake a claim and determine which forms of Indigenous belief and practice to include among those "redeemed through Christ." Worshiping the Indigenous pantheon of spiritual entities beyond the Father, Son, and Holy Spirit, therefore, is considered by many Indigenous evangelicals to be inappropriate.

For many Indigenous evangelicals, in other words, Indigenous traditions have immense potential to bring people into closer alignment with Biblical truth. Conversely, Indigenous traditions also have immense potential to lead people astray. To suggest that Indigenous evangelicals are guilty of a self-inflicted re-packaging of Christian imperialism, however, would be arrogantly condescending at best and harmfully devaluing of their difficult work at worst. These negotiations are simply what religious actors do; they make carefully negotiated (and at times, hasty) decisions concerning belief and practice that involve both inclusion and exclusion, reconciliation and discord. Issuing charges about the "re-packaging of imperialism" is too easy. We should focus, rather, on the "lived religious idioms," i.e., the beliefs, practices, strategies, and networked relationships that make these attempted negotiations and theological ambiguities bearable.

Contextualized Pipe (Sunrise) Ceremony

The contextualization movement has a long and complicated history, the details of which cannot be fully rendered as part of this chapter. In short form, however, the movement began as a solidified theological and political movement in the late nineties. Members (both Indigenous and non-Indigenous, theologians and lay-practitioners alike) promotes grassroots, from-the-bottom-up processes of Christianization among Indigenous communities that allow Indigenous actors to retain cultural forms (rituals, ceremonies, beliefs, cosmological frameworks, norms, and values) and understand and make use of them as fully "Christian."

Sunrise Pipe Ceremony is a staple of Dr. Leonard "Casey" Church's contextualized ministry. He conducts Sunrise Ceremony every morning at every event to which he contributes. Dr. Church is a member of the Potawatomi or Anishinaabe people of the Great Lakes region. According to Church, the version of Sunrise Ceremony he carries with him and teaches to others, was passed on to him, in large part, by the *Midewiwin* (a secretive society of spiritual specialists among the Indigenous communities of the New England, Great Lakes, and Eastern Plains region of the US and Canada), who, over the course of many generations, had adapted their traditions to the colonial moment, incorporating aspects of Christianity (to varying degrees) along the way.[5] Dr. Church describes his version of the ceremony as derived from those generational teachings. His intention is to bring them into productive tension with the modern mainstream evangelical milieu.

While at the Native American Conference at Lake Junaluska, Dr. Church conducted Sunrise Ceremony in the early morning hours, usually around 6 am. The event is simultaneously instructional and spiritually significant, and Dr. Church works hard to provide detailed descriptions of the various aspects of the ceremony as he also conducts it for his intended purpose – as a form of Christian prayer. His aim is to demonstrate for his audience the specific methods (with accompanying theological justifications) through which this Indigenous ritual is "redeemed through Christ."

The first phase of the ritual involves the passing out of tobacco. Each person is allowed to take a pinch of tobacco from Dr. Church as he moves around the circle explaining its significance. For the Nishnaabeg, tobacco, or "Sema," is traditionally associated with the east, the color yellow, and with spring. Tobacco is considered a medicine related to renewal, containing the power to entice or invite powerful spirits to ritual or ceremonial space. The precise spirit invoked depends on the problem facing the community, but typically the ceremony was a daily form of expressing gratitude to the Creator for the life-giving and life-sustaining gifts bestowed upon humans for their sustenance and survival.[6] For Dr. Church's contextualized version of Sunrise Ceremony, on the other hand, the tobacco has the power to instead enlist only the Holy Spirit as an emanation of Christ, rather than spirits of various types, for the purposes of hearing individual and collective prayers. So, the "Christianized" ceremony as a whole is an expression of gratitude to God the Father for life and Christ's sacrifice. This re-direction or reorientation is how Dr. Church and like-minded Indigenous evangelicals achieve the status "redeemed through Christ."

After moving around the circle, distributing tobacco, Dr. Church asks participants to pray over their pinch of tobacco and hold onto it. As individual participants prayed over their tobacco, Dr. Church prepared phase two of the ceremony. From his bundle, he pulls out his sacred pipe, more tobacco, and a lighter, all the while praying over the various devices and explaining in further detail to his participants the differences between pre-Christian Indigenous methods and contextualized forms that have been "redeemed through Christ." Dr. Church kneels on the ground working carefully with the pipe and praying. He loads the pipe bowl with the tobacco. Standing up, he explains that he will now light the tobacco and begin the crucial phase of the ceremony.

Dr. Church then raises the sacred pipe to the east, where the powers of creation first emerge each day. He says a prayer in Anishinaabe, brings the pipe to his lips, tokes the pipe, and blows the smoke eastward. He does the same in the three remaining directions: south, west, and north in sequence. Dr. Church then explained that in pre-Christian Indigenous traditions, prayers to the four directions would have been in the service of various distinct spirits (often associated with non-human animal species) each with specific powers to help humans sustain themselves and maintain creative balance. However, for contextualized Sunrise Ceremony, praying in the four directions has a different purpose; to function as a conduit, channeling the individual prayers of the participants from their pinches of tobacco and enlisting Christ and the Holy Spirit to send those prayers in all directions, permeating God's creation, increasing the potential for those prayers to be heard and answered. After praying participants are then asked to sprinkle the tobacco into the grass. Doing this, as Dr. Church describes, re-integrates the tobacco with the Holy Spirit's powers of creation and enlists those powers in the dispersion and distribution of prayer power.

Indigenous Revitalization and Christian Self-Actualization

The core feature of SMNAC was the conference papers, cultural demonstrations, and theological conversations. There were two primary concerns articulated in a variety of ways by a series of presenters. First was the issue of how one can and/or should expresses their Indigenous heritage within the context of also being Christian. Some presentations, therefore, offered varying perspectives from Indigenous people (Potawatomi, Inuit, Native Hawaiian, and African Indigenous, to name a few) detailing precise strategies and theological justifications for doing so. The second concern emerged out of the various speeches and performances as a patterned theological discourse suggesting that once Indigenous peoples are able to recover their Indigenous identity within the context of Christianity, they can then utilize the healing power of Jesus Christ and the Holy Spirit to repair the socio-economic, cultural, and psychological damage wrought by colonialism in America. Consequently, the sicknesses of suicide, substance abuse, domestic abuse, and self-loathing can be healed. What is more, through individual self-realization through Christ on a wider scale, entire communities can be revitalized and brought back into harmony with creation (hence, the

Indigenous evangelical impulse to spread the "Good News" and bring other Indigenous people into the fold).

Bill Pagaran (a Tlingit from Palmer, Alaska and drummer of Broken Walls) detailed the psychological trauma plaguing his own community. From tragically high suicide rates to rampant substance abuse, Pagaran made clear that Indigenous communities continue to deal with the effects of colonization even in the twenty-first century. The lasting conditions of colonialism are catalysts for the underlying psychological traumas that lead to substance abuse, domestic violence, and suicide. In his presentation, Pagaran highlighted examples of US and Canadian governmental abuses perpetrated against Indigenous communities: such as land expropriation, the boarding school system, and forced migration or removal. Much like socio-economic disenfranchisement, Pagaran averred, theological ethnocentrism existed in concert with these political and socio-economic policies. Ethnocentrism in the context of Christian theology barred (and continues to bar) Indigenous Christians from worshipping Christ in the context of their own cultures, creating a barrier between Indigenous Christians from intimacy with Christ. Worse yet, he argued, this dynamic often convinces Indigenous people to discard their Indigenous heritage as they engage in assimilative practices in an effort to become increasingly "Christian." According to Pagaran and other speakers during the conference, these assumptions are precisely what led to the various genocidal policies of the colonial and US governments perpetrated against Indigenous communities across North America. These, in turn, have led to the tragic prevalence of substance abuse, domestic violence, and suicide among Indigenous communities (especially among the younger generations).[7]

Pagaran's propositions are part of a broader, emergent evangelical and charismatic movement. The notion that Indigenous ways of life are actually more in line with Biblical truth and that Indigenous individual identity must be recovered to establish that personal connection to Christ has become a popular rallying cry for proponents of contextualization.[8] From smaller conferences like the *Native American Conference: Sing to the Mountain* in *Lake Junaluska* to larger, more globally oriented symposiums sponsored by groups like *NAIITS: An Indigenous Learning Community* (which are often held annually at Universities and Seminaries across North America), Indigenous revitalization and identity recovery has become a necessary condition for many Indigenous evangelicals. For Indigenous evangelicals, identity recovery functions like a second "born-again" experience. From their perspective, God, Christ, and the Holy Spirit were present in North America prior to European migration. The Indigenous cultures that existed throughout North America prior to the introduction of European Christianities are, they demand, part of creation and a reflection of Providential history and, therefore, divinely sanctioned. In the same way that European Christianity required theological and ceremonial "fine-tuning" to make sure that heresies were cut out from the "orthodox" program, so too, they aver, must contextualized Indigenous forms become increasingly "fine-tuned."

Evangelical "Christ intimacy" is combined with the language of Indigenous revitalization. Indigenous revitalization is, by most accounts, a fundamentally collective experience, requiring the individual to become re-integrated into the cultural and social matrix of their Indigenous heritage. For some Indigenous evangelicals, however, one must first come into intimate relationship with Christ before the broader and more communal processes can take hold.

Music, Indigenous Dance, the Holy Spirit, and Healing

Once the conference sessions were complete (sometime around 9:00 pm EST), the atmosphere shifted considerably. The contemplative tone of the auditorium, which had lasted most of the day – brought on by the presentations, bible studies, and workshops – transitioned into one of celebration. A well-known and widely traveled Indigenous Christian rock band, "Broken Walls," performed a lengthy set late into the night. Their performance and lyrical arrangements embodied the religious logic of the weekend's conference.

Broken Walls performed several of their more popular tracks, including "Rise up Mighty Warrior" and "Ride the Wind." Broken Walls were accompanied by several powwow dancers who danced fervently and with conviction on and off the stage. The band itself is a reflection of the contemporary Indigenous Christian contextualization movement. At the time that this research was conducted, the band consists of three members, John Maracle, Bill Pagaran, and Chris DeLorenzi. The band was originally conceived by Maracle. During a conference in Ottawa, Ontario in 1995, he realized that the metaphorical walls separating the Euro-settler population and Indigenous communities needed to be broken. Consequently, he wrote a song titled "broken walls," a title that eventually also became the band's name.[9]

The atmosphere was thoroughly charismatic as the dancer's bells and rattles (standard for powwow regalia) became integrated into the beat and rhythm of the music. The lyrics of "Rise Up Mighty Warrior" address many of the concerns of the weekend's papers and presentations. The song begins by placing the colonial experience of Indigenous people into the context of the gospels and, more specifically, Jesus' message of love and forgiveness. The song urges its Indigenous listeners to discard the resentment caused by colonial dispossession of land. According to the song, the Indigenous evangelical warrior is one who, like Jesus, forgives his transgressors and combats further transgressions with love.[10] Linking the suffering of Jesus at the moment of his crucifixion to the suffering of Indigenous peoples at the hands of colonial agents and governments is clear here. The song then emphasizes Jesus' role as resister, revolutionary, and nonconformist. Conversely, the song also calls upon Indigenous people to overcome their "bitterness" and "shame." These are the psychological dispositions, so the song implies, that lead to destructive behavior. The song suggests that these dispositions can be overcome by further emphasizing Jesus as "forgiver," highlighting his willingness to forgive his assailants. Forgiveness, so the lyrics suggest, is a necessary condition prior to any further act of reconciliation. Through Jesus, Indigenous people can come to forgive the settler population, healing the psycho-social conditions of "bitterness" and "shame." What is more, God the Creator (of the Abrahamic tradition) is the singular source of the healing power of forgiveness that will facilitate this vital process. "The mighty [evangelical] warrior," therefore, arms her/him/their self with radical forgiveness and takes on full responsibility for the processes of reconciliation. In making use Christian values to overcome the colonial culpability of Christian agents and institutions, the song exemplifies the bifurcation between resistance and discipline.

"Rise Up Mighty Warrior" also includes allusions to land, culture, and identity. The catalysts of psychological trauma – the transgressions perpetrated by the settler population – are brought into stark relief. Verses speak of deceptions of the past that were deployed in an effort to take from Indigenous people vital aspects of their life-ways, alluding to the loss of land and cultural integrity. The deceptions of the Indigenous past are references to the consequences of European missionary work among Indigenous communities, the resultant loss of land, as well as the Indian boarding school system of the nineteenth and twentieth centuries (all talking points throughout the weekend's presentations and papers). The song again cautions its Indigenous listeners, however, casting the warrior as one who, in becoming caught up in the power of the "Holy Spirit" has the ability to overcome resentment, channel that energy into love rather than violent reprisal.[11]

References to the various mechanisms through which Indigenous children were taught – by both Catholic and Protestant missionaries and educators – that their traditions and cultural frameworks were at best "uncivilized," inherently "savage," and at worst "demonic" had defined many of the conversations leading up to the concert.[12] This, as the song also suggests, is what leads directly to the "bitterness" and "shame" – two psychological dispositions often associated with the propensity for drug abuse, alcoholism, domestic abuse, and suicide.

Warrior culture also plays heavily in the song "Ride the Wind." As the lyrics suggest, the Holy Spirit (which is referred to generically as "spirit") is a force that must be embraced by the warrior. The song opens with the chorus, which is repeated six times and is accompanied by Indigenous drumming. It speaks of the warrior being lifted up, carried by, and integrated with the wind of the "Holy Spirit." As the Indigenous drumming continues, the song transitions into verses explaining the nature of the connection between the Spirit and the warrior individual.

Wind is recast in the song. Indeed, Indigenous communities throughout North America believed (and continue to believe) that wind was (is) an important part of the cosmos, representing variously (and depending on specific cultural context) the powers of creation, the breath of the Creator, or an agential cosmic entity acting upon humanity in a variety of ways. Pre-contact and contemporary traditionalist understandings of wind are often associated with specific spiritual entities/powers that are fundamental parts of each of the four cardinal directions. For Maracle and the songs of Broken Walls, the significance of wind is retained but understood as the Holy Spirit with the ability to move throughout the landscape, intervene in human affairs, and produce otherwise impossible outcomes.

Combining drumming and traditional Indigenous singing in the background, the song admonishes the "words of man" and advocates, instead, for reliance on the Holy Spirit and the purity of God's words. The song uses the analogy of David's battle with Goliath, suggesting that in ignoring the "words of man" and giving himself over to the purity of the "words of God," David himself became engulfed by the Holy Spirit and – having done so – was able to defeat his foe, Goliath. Without the usual instruments of war (i.e., a sword, shield, or armor), David defeats his enemy by trusting the word of God and the promise God he would intervene on his behalf. In the end, David topples Goliath by hurling a single stone. Thus, as the lyrics of "Ride the Wind" unfold, the Indigenous warrior is recast, rendering them an agent of God's "word" rather than an agent of resentment and/or violent retaliation. Here again, the Indigenous warrior is reigned in, redirected toward the evangelical emphasis on forgiveness. According to the song, the enemy that must be felled is the overwhelming compulsion toward resentment. According to the theological interpretations of the songwriters, the typical instruments of war, resentment and violent retaliation, not only run contrary to God's word, but also constitute the psychological catalysts for domestic violence, substance abuse, and suicide.[13]

Audience members were anything but passive during the performance. Many (if not most) in attendance periodically entered into, what I refer to as, "holiness" or "charismatic posture" – standing hands raised, eyes closed, mouths in prayer. These postures are common among charismatic evangelical Christians and are markers of one's conviction that they are embroiled in in-the-moment connections with the Holy Spirit. These postures demonstrate for charismatic individuals and their fellow believers that regular and ongoing contact with the swirl of "Holy Ghost power" is possible and that power of the Holy Spirit now permeates the space in question – in this case, the Stuart Auditorium at Lake Junaluska. As it permeates the space, the "Holy Spirit" has the potential to constitute several outcomes, not least of which is physical and psychological healing.

The music, lyrics, and charismatic accompaniments pulled the historical reality of Indigenous colonial experience and its multi-generational affective consequences into the charismatic moment. The contents of the conference presentations, contextualized rituals, and the musical performances were threaded together in a bubbling up of musical, lyrical, and bodily effervescence. Bodies, which in the typical charismatic fashion become conduits and/or vessels for the Holy Spirit, also become vessels of healing with the potential to not only cure the traumas in the individual, but also carry healing power to afflicted communities more broadly.

Conclusion

The cultural contextualization of Christianity is nothing new. Christianity has adapted to cultural context where and whenever it has crossed borders or traversed vast oceans. Indigenous peoples across the Americas, in similar and typical fashion, have been contextualizing Christianities to their ways of life and cosmological frameworks since European migration and first contact. Conferences such as the SMNAC are a continuation of that long, ongoing, colonial (now neo-colonial) set of processes.[14] As "lived" experiences to their very core, religions always and everywhere have conformed to and also altered the cultures with which they have intermingled.

The "contextualized" forms of Christianity, such as the examples described throughout this chapter, are fundamentally "Lived" or "Folk." They are "folk" because they constitute local, rural, grassroots modes of religiosity, most often emerging with a certain degree of spontaneity in an attempt to pragmatically solve the most pressing problems faced by an individual or group of people. They are "lived" because they constitute religiosities that transgress the designs dictated by those who own and/or control the modes of theological production. In other words, contextualized forms incorporate, emphasize, and even favor "unorthodox" beliefs and practices that cut across, strategically re-arrange, and push back against institutional, authoritative, or "orthodox" forms of religiosity.

These "lived religious phenomena" are not purely the creation of and carried out by non-elites or beyond the scope of the centers of power. As I have demonstrated, the authority and legitimizing power of figures like Dr. Church blends together with the needs and desires of non-authoritative, lay-practitioners as both enter into dispositions of urgency. Rather, they are "lived" because the desired outcomes are focused on solutions to immediate, day-to-day, life-or-death concerns and those concerns might necessitate creativity and innovation, dynamics that can often clash with institutional authority. Healing the mental and psychological damage stemming from generations of cultural and socio-economic oppression; healing the generational trauma that has been and continues to be passed down as a consequence of the Indian boarding school system; and healing the fragmented selves that come with being Christian and also Indigenous; these are the life-or-death, basic-survival, quality-of-life, right-here-right-now concerns that define what Robert Orsi meant as he described the simultaneity that is fundamental to religion-in-practice.

The religious idioms of "healing" promulgated during SMNAC, likewise, made "desire and imagination possible at the same time that they [constricted] and [disciplined] desire and imagination."[15] For healing to occur, individuals and communities needed to combine Indigenous revitalization with Christ's perceived redemptive power. Christianity is the singularly appropriate path toward Indigenous self-realization. The presenters and performers repeatedly argued that one's Indigenous identity must emerge and be recovered within the confines of the Christian faith. The presentations, rituals, and other events entailed explicit theological checks, warning against full slippage into Indigenous "traditionalism." Emphasis on a multiplicity of powerful spirit entities or the abilities of medicine men and women to make use of these powers for a variety of pragmatic purposes are strongly prohibited. All forms of cultural expression (powwow dancing, singing, drumming, smudging, etc.), according to theologians at SMNAC, must adhere to the fundamentals of evangelical Christian.

The contextualized evangelical forms at SMNAC (i.e., Sunrise Ceremony, paper presentations, and rock concert) are also examples of resistance because they challenge the mainstream evangelical network by offering alternative ritual forms that diverge from "evangelical orthodoxy." The disciplinary process of redeeming Indigenous ritual forms and cultural perspectives through Christ, on the other hand, limits and constrains which aspects of Indigeneity are "appropriate" for a Christian lifestyle. Simultaneous acceptance and calculated skepticism of Indigenous traditionalism was, therefore, part of the SMNAC (and continues to be a part of the broader contextualization movement). The lived religious logic of healing that was embedded in and emerged from the events at SMNAC constituted a prescriptive blueprint that urged its prospective adopters to internalize and enact a delicate bifurcation between resistance and conformity.

Notes

1 The fieldwork for this chapter was conducted between 2013 and 2018. My attendance at the SMNAC was part of an attempt to reach and interview Dr. Leonard "Casey" Church concerning his involvement and work with NAIITS: An Indigenous Learning Community. I spent the three days of the conference as a participant observer, taking notes, taking part in ceremonies, listening to presentations, and interacting with organizers and attendees.

2 "Our Story," Lake Junaluska [https://lakejunaluska.com/about-us/our-story/], accessed 4-26-19.

3 The narrative paraphrased here can be found on a plaque posted on the statue of Chief Junaluska that has been placed in front of the Stuart Auditorium on the grounds of Lake Junaluska Resort and Retreat Center.

4 Orsi, Robert. 1997. "Everyday Miracles," *Lived Religion in America: Toward a History of Practice*. Princeton, NJ: Princeton University Press, p. 9.

5 For more on the significance of the *Midewinini* ("medicine man")/Midewikwe ("medicine woman") and their role in the Indigenous cosmological worldview and spirituality of the New England, Great Lakes, and Eastern Plains regions, see Michael Angel's *Preserving the Sacred: Historical Perspectives on the Ojibwe Midewiwin*, published in 2002.

6 Angel, Michael. 2002. *Preserving the Sacred: Historical Perspectives on the Ojibwe Midewiwin*, Winnipeg, MT: University of Manitoba Press.

7 For more on the prevalence (and causes) of alcoholism, domestic violence, and suicide among North American Indigenous communities, see U.S. Department of Health and Human Services, Office of Minority Health. (2018). Profile: American Indian/Alaska Native [https://minorityhealth.hhs.gov/omh/browse.aspx?lvl=3&lvlid=62].

8 Indigenous cultural revitalization as a thoroughly individualized, "come-to-Christ," "born-again" experience has been and continues to be prevalent and pervasive during these gatherings. In my various informal conversations and formal interviews, I have found that this constitutes a second "born-again" experience.

9 "About Broken Walls," Broken Walls.com, [http://brokenwalls.com/about-broken-walls/], accessed 12-3-2022.

10 Readers are encouraged to listen to the songs by visiting the Broken Walls official website. Links to the songs analyzed as part of this research project can be found on "Songs" page of the Broken Walls website. "Rise up Mighty Warrior," Broken Walls, [http://brokenwalls.com/media/songs/], accessed 10-24-2021.

11 Readers are encouraged to listen to the songs by visiting the Broken Walls official website. Links to the songs analyzed as part of this research project can be found on "Songs" page of the Broken Walls website. "Rise up Mighty Warrior," Broken Walls, [http://brokenwalls.com/media/songs/], accessed 10-24-2021.
12 For more on the Indian boarding schools of the nineteenth and twentieth centuries, see Jacqueline Fear-Segal's *White Man's Club: Schools, Race, and the Struggles of Indian Inculturation* (2009); Fear-Segal and Rose's *Carlisle Indian Industrial School: Indigenous Histories, Memories, and Reclamations* (2018); and Adama Fortunate Eagle (ed. Laurence Hauptman) *Pipestone: My Life in an Indian Boarding School* (2010).
13 The analogy of David and Goliath in the verses of "Ride the Wind" is based on a popularized reading of the biblical passage that emphasizes the words of God over those of man. Readers are encouraged to listen to the songs by visiting the Broken Walls official website. Links to the songs analyzed as part of this research project can be found on "Songs" page of the Broken Walls website "Ride the Wind," Broken Walls, [http://brokenwalls.com/media/songs/], accessed 10-24-2021.
14 For more on the contemporary contextualization movement, see my previous work titled *A 'Circle in a Rectangle': Native Evangelicals, Trans-Indigenous Networks, and the Negotiation between Legitimation and Evasion*.
15 Orsi, Robert. 1997. "Everyday Miracles," *Lived Religions in America: Toward a History of Practice*. Princeton, NJ: Princeton University Press, p. 16.

Bibliography

Alexander, Corky. 2012. *Native American Pentecost: Praxis, Contextualization, Transformation*. Cleveland, TN: Cherohala Press.

Church, Leonard "Casey" (NAIITS Board Member, Director of Wiconi), interview with Jason E. Purvis, Lake Junaluska, NC, 6-27-2015.

Church, Casey. 2014. "Creating Native American Expression of Christian Faith: More than the Looks on their Faces," presented at the 2014 NAIITS annual symposium. Newberg, OR: George Fox University.

De Certeau, Michel. 1984. *The Practice of Everyday Life*. Berkeley: University of California Press.

Fear-Segal, Jacqueline. 2007. *White Man's Club: Schools, Race, and the Struggle of Indian Acculturation*. Lincoln: University of Nebraska Press.

Glick-Schiller, Nina. 2005. "Transnational Social Fields and Imperialism: Bringing a Theory of Power to Transnational Studies," *Anthropological Theory*, 5: 439.

Hall, David D. et al. 1997. *Lived Religion in America: Toward a History of Practice*. Princeton, NJ: Princeton University Press.

Hiebert, Paul G. 2009. *The Gospel in Human Contexts: Anthropological Explorations for Contemporary Missions*. Grand Rapids, MI: Baker Academic Publishing.

LeBlanc, Terry. 2011. "NAIITS: Contextual Mission, Indigenous Context." *Missiology: An International Review*, XXXIX (1): 87–100.

Martin, Joel W. and Mark A. Nicholas. 2010. *Native Americans, Christianity, and the Reshaping of the American Religious Landscape*. Chapel Hill: University of North Carolina Press.

McNally, Michael. 2000. "The Practice of Native American Christianity." *Church History*, 69 (4): 834–859.

———. 1997. "The Uses of Ojibwe Hymn-Singing at White Earth: Toward a History of Practice." In *Lived Religion in America: Toward a Theory of Practice*, ed. David D. Hall. 1st ed. Princeton, NJ: Princeton University Press, 133–159.

Nagel, Joane. 1996. *American Indian Ethnic Renewal: Red Power and the Resurgence of Identity and Culture*. New York: Oxford University Press.

Primiano, Leonard Norman. 1995. "Vernacular Religion and the Search for Method in Folklife." *Western Folklore*, 54 (1): 37–56.

Smith, Andrea. 2008. *Native Americans and the Christian Right: The Gendered Politics of Unlikely Alliances*. Durham, NC: Duke University Press.

———. 2010. "Decolonization in Unexpected Places: Native Evangelicalism and the Rearticulation of Mission." *American Quarterly*, 62/3 (Sept): 569–590.

Sweeney, Douglas A. 2005. *The American Evangelical Story: An History of the Movement*. Grand Rapids, MI: Baker Academic.

Treat, James, ed. 1996. *Native and Christian: Indigenous Voices on Religious Identity in the United States and Canada*. New York: Routledge.

———. 2003. *Around the Sacred Fire: Native Religious Activism in the Red Power Era: A Narrative Map of the Indian Ecumenical Conference*. 1st ed. Basingstoke: Palgrave Macmillan.

Twiss, Richard. 2000. *One Church Many Tribes: Following Jesus the Way God Made You*. Ventura, CA: Regal Publishing.

———. 2015. *Rescuing the Gospel from the Cowboys: A Native American Expression of the Jesus Way*. Downers Grove, IL: InterVarsity Press.

Woodley, Randy. 2001. *Living in Color: Embracing God's Passion for Ethnic Diversity*. Downers Grove, IL: InterVarsity Press.

———. 2012. *Shalom and the Community of Creation*. Grand Rapids, MI: Wm. B. Eerdman's Publishing.

Yoder, Don. 1990. "Toward a Definition of Folk Religion." *Discovering American Folklife: Studies in Ethnic, Religious, and Regional Culture*. Ed. Don Yoder. Ann Arbor, MI: UMI Research Press, pp. 67–83.

18

THE TRIPLE GODDESS

Examining Maiden, Mother, Crone in Wiccan-Witchcraft Traditions

Jason Mankey

Wiccan-Witchcraft is a modern religious and magical system that first rose to prominence in England during the early 1950s, largely due to the efforts of a retired English civil servant named Gerald Gardner (1884–1964). By the end of the 1960s, Wiccan-Witchcraft groups (often known as covens) could be found throughout the United Kingdom, Canada, Australia, and the United States. Gardner, and many who came after him, claimed that Wicca-Witchcraft was "the old religion," in that it predated Christianity and could be connected to ancient forms of shamanism: neither claim is true in a literal sense. (Cunningham 4)

Gardner's Wiccan-Witchcraft was originally an initiatory tradition to participate in Wiccan-Witchcraft one had to be initiated by other Wiccan-Witches. Upon receiving initiation, new adherents were given a small collection of rituals and magical information with the condition it be kept secret, or "oath bound." For approximately the first twenty years of Wiccan-Witchcraft's existence, such limitations resulted in a mostly uniform style of practice and belief, but that orthodoxy was not to last. By the early 1970s, "do it yourself" books on Wiccan-Witchcraft complete with ritual liturgy began to appear in general bookstores, and on spinner-racks at supermarkets.

The "do it yourself books" on Wiccan-Witchcraft resulted in a wide variety of "creative phenomena" and "reinterpretations or expressions" (Yoder 1990: 82) in folk religion: religion in which authority is decentralized, scripture is lose and evolves, that is localized among people, among folk. Wicca-Witchcraft continues anddepartsfromwhatwasproposedbyGeraldGardnerandhisearlyfollowers.Books developed and circulated new forms of practice and belief in Wicca-Witchcraft without a dominant authoritative voice; what was lived and experienced by individuals and groups of practitioners itself became authoritative. Gardner was no longer the founder and arbiter of Wicca-Witchcraft, for the craft was placed

DOI: 10.4324/9781003257462-24

under the care and authority of those folk who interpreted, wrote about, and practiced the religion. Describing the theology of Wiccan-Witchcraft can be a vexing task for a religious scholar and also for Wiccan practitioners. Depending on the individual, Wiccans can and will identify as polytheists, duo-theists, atheists, Neo-Platonists, monotheists, etc. Some Wiccans look at deities, such as goddesses and gods, as metaphors for the natural world, while others insist their deities are real and active entities. Central to the practice of most Wiccans is the acknowledgment of a Great Goddess and a Horned God in ritual. Gardner (and many after him) claimed these figures were of ancient origin, from "the morning of the world" and of "immeasurable antiquity before Egypt and Babylon . . . ." (Gardner "Meaning of Witchcraft" 21) In the years after Gardner's death, the Great Goddess of antiquity, who appeared in his published works *Witchcraft Today* (1954) and *The Meaning of Witchcraft* (1959), would become more than just one goddess, and she would become "The Triple Goddess" one being who is also Maiden, Mother, and Crone (henceforth referred to as MMC).

MMC as a concept in Wiccan-Witchcraft derives from two sources: books and other practitioners. The first source is literary, and Wiccan-Witchcraft has been heavily influenced by books since its founding in the early 1950s. With very few periodicals, in-person gatherings, and easy access to other practitioners, books were one of the primary transmitters of Witchcraft practices. The second source is practitioners themselves, who have continually reinterpreted and added to the idea of MMC. This chapter examines how practitioners have changed MMC of their own volition, most often ignoring precedent and established practices within the tradition of Wiccan-Witchcraft.

The aspect of folk religion that applies most to MMC is the "folk-cultural dimension of religion." (Yoder 1990: 45) The application and usage of MMC in Wiccan-Witchcraft represents an active creative phenomenon, with practitioners shaping the concept of MMC to suit their own needs. Absent from the original liturgical aspects of Wiccan-Witchcraft and the transmitters of those ideas, today's Wiccan-Witchcraft practitioners have both created new modes of expression with the MMC model, and have freely discarded parts of MMC that no longer serve their needs or fit into their personal beliefs. This expresses the dynamism inherent to folk religions, especially lived folk religion and the folk who live them out.

This chapter uses the term "Wiccan-Witchcraft" for the religious ideas of Gerald Gardner and his followers, but such usage is not universal among practitioners or scholars. "Wiccan-Witchcraft" is often shortened to simply "Wicca," ignoring the fact that Gardner and his early adherents self-identified as Witches and labeled their practice Witchcraft. In recent years, the term "Wicca" has become anathema to many practitioners, resulting in many moving away from the word, despite using ritual techniques and language taken directly from Gardner. Because of these varying preferences I have chosen to use the term "Wiccan-Witchcraft" in this chapter to describe the practices of those influenced both directly and indirectly by the Witchcraft of Gerald Gardner.

I discovered Wiccan-Witchcraft and became a practitioner as an adult in the Summer of 1994, due in large part to stumbling across the book *Celtic Magic* by author D.J. Conway (Llewellyn Publications, 1990). Conway's book is more a "Wicca 101" primer than a book about Celtic magical practices. Conway weaves a fanciful tale linking various Celtic deities to the archetypal (and apparently culturally universal) Maiden-Mother-Crone. Conway's Celts worshipped a "White Moon Goddess", and while the Celts petitioned individual goddesses, they also knew that "all goddesses are one goddess," at least according to Conway. (Conway "Celtic Magick" 43–44) "The Triple Goddess, or triple aspects of the Goddess, was well known to the Celts" and that various goddesses written about in both Welsh and Irish myth are representatives of the MMC, she argues. (Conway "Celtic Magic" 43–44) Much of this chapter is a critique of arguments presented by Conway and others who have articulated similar ideas. That critique is accompanied by a survey of how those arguments have been reinterpreted, discarded, and used by Wiccan-Witches.

Conway's ideas about the Triple Goddess were not isolated. Nearly all the books I read as a young person that were contemporary to *Celtic Magic* told much the same story. The Triple Goddess was *the* original goddess, present at the dawn of humanity, and her forms as the MMC could be linked to the waxing (Maiden), full (Mother), and waning (Crone) moon. The Triple Goddess was to be representative of all women: the MMC story being an allegory for menstruation, sexual awakening, and the ability to bear children.

Modern Origins

While the inclusion of MMC in Modern Witchcraft is the result of speculative history and occultist-written fiction published during the first half of the twentieth century, the first mention of something approaching the MMC model appeared in academia. Writing in 1903, classicist Jane Harrison (1850–1928) wrote that the Great Earth Mother, believed by Harrison to be humanity's first deity, had three forms. Harrison names two of these forms: Maiden and Mother, and he gives them dominion over life and death, respectively. (Hutton 38) Harrison never names her third aspect.

Harrison was correct that in many traditions goddesses assumed three forms. The Greek goddess Hekate was frequently pictured as three-formed, the custom originating from three masks hung in her honor at the meeting of three pathways. (Burkert 171) Near the end of pagan Rome, poets and scholars sometimes wrote about a disparate goddess in triplicate, and, on occasion, linked them to the waxing, full, and waning moon, but such impulses are not reflected in ritual activity. (Hutton 38) Goddesses were not limited to triple forms either, in order to illustrate their various aspects goddesses like Aphrodite were depicted as seven (or more) deities. (Rosenzweig, Illustration 13) In none of these instances, however, were the goddesses written about or depicted or described to be MMC.

Over the last one hundred years, fiction has played a large role in the development of MMC. Most often, the works of fiction that have influenced Wiccan-Witches have been written by practitioners of magical rites and/or individuals sympathetic to traditional pagan deities. Fiction provides an opportunity for writers to present ideas that might not fit within the defined parameters of a specific religious tradition or engage in idealized rituals and practices not possible in personal practice. One of the most influential fiction authors was the English magician Dion Fortune (born Violet Firth, 1890–1946). For the majority of her adult life, Fortune practiced ceremonial magic, in a style heavily influenced by the Hermetic Order of the Golden Dawn, an occult group founded in 1887.

Fortune did not identify as a Witch (and her work predates Wiccan-Witchcraft), but her 1938 novel *The Sea Priestess* has influenced many Modern Witches. The identity of an author, or lack of identity of the author as an insider, does not disqualify the author from influencing Witches. In *The Sea Priestess*, Fortune never mentions MMC by name, but she writes about the "Great Mother" inhabiting many forms in a variety of distinct goddesses:

> "The daughter of the Great Mother is Persephone, Queen of Hades, ruler of the kingdoms of sleep and death . . . . Likewise she is Aphrodite . . . for it is decreed that none shall understand the one without the other." (222)
> Later Fortune brings together even more goddesses:
>
> "Hera in heaven, on earth, Persephone;
> Levanah of the tides, and Hecate.
> Diana of the Moon, Star of the Sea
> Isis unveiled . . . .!"
>
> *(225)*

Combining her goddesses into one universal figure, Fortune paved the way for various disparate goddesses to be grouped into a greater whole, regardless of myth and history.

The most influential figure in the emergence of the MMC figure was English poet and novelist Robert Graves (1895–1985). Graves' pseudo-historical work *The White Goddess: A Historical Grammar of Poetic Myth* (1948) has been an influence on Wiccan-Witches since shortly after its publication. Graves wrote about magical practices and the pre-Christian past with sympathy and longing and that made his work appealing to a large number of Wiccan-Witches, especially in an era with few books sympathetic to such ideas. Summarizing *The White Goddess* is a near impossible task, the book explores a variety of different of topics, but much of the work concerns the worship of a universal "White Goddess," thought by Graves to be the inspiration of most great poets. The work itself is a deluge of goddess names, dates, and references to various Greek, Celtic, and Middle Eastern myths (sometimes wildly taken out of context). Historian Ronald Hutton has described *The White Goddess* as "not merely a diatribe against the modern world but against modern poets." (200) Graves' primary concern was never history but poetry, and yet Graves' work feels scholarly because of the sheer amount of referenced information contained (which was a selling point to many, no doubt).

Graves' prose ideas on what would become MMC read like the poetry he was known for, transforming his White Goddess figure into both a historical character and an inspirational deity. Graves compares his Goddess to the seasons, a motif we will see again:

> As the New Moon or Spring she was girl; as the Full Moon or Summer she was a woman; as the Old Moon or Winter she was Hag.
>
> *(386)*

Graves links his White Goddess to the moon, giving his three-form goddess dominion over various aspects of life:

> The New Moon is the white goddess of birth and growth; the Full Moon, the red goddess of love and battle; the Old Moon, the black goddess of death and divination . . .

By making his "Mother" figure a goddess of "love and battle," Graves unknowingly anticipates the recent trend of adding a fourth aspect to the MMC model, the "Warrior" which is discussed below. Graves' work reads as if it were designed to be slipped into the rituals of the Wiccan-Witch, and in my own practice, I have said things similar to: "white raiser, red reaper, and dark winnower of grain." (70)

Writing just over ten years later in *The Meaning of Witchcraft* (1959), Gerald Gardner would mention the "triple goddess" in a variety of contexts. Writing about the religion of the Celtic-Gauls, Gardner alludes to the MMC model: "the Great Mother in triple form (the Virgin, the Bride, and the Hag)." (79) In other parts of *The Meaning of Witchcraft*, Gardner's triple goddess bares no resemblance to the MMC model. When sharing Arthurian myth, Gardner's triple goddess becomes the "Three Queens" said to have taken the body of King Arthur to the Isle of Avalon. (133) Elsewhere, he writes of a "triple moon goddess" capable of appearing as "Three Mothers." (75)

By the early 1970s, both conventional and specialty publishers began releasing books written by practitioners of Wiccan-Witchcraft and aimed at a general market. Most of those works had almost nothing to say about MMC. Influential writers during this period such as Raymond Buckland (1934–2017), Paul Huson (1942–present), Doreen Valiente (1922–1999), and Lady Sheba (born Jessie Wicker Bell, 1920–2002) mention a Great or Mother Goddess, but they never describe a being in triplicate referred to as MMC. Works of this period sporadically mention springtime maidens but never with never with the conciseness of the MMC model suggested by Graves. Why is this publication history important? Because Wiccan-Witchcraft is primarily a religious path propagated by books. Authors have generally been the community's most well-known commodity, and with no churches and little in the way of national (let alone global) institutions, books became the primary transmitters of Wiccan-Witchcraft beginning in the late 1960s. Such non-institutional control of a religious narrative is a hallmark of folk religion.

Most writers of the 1960s and 1970s had little enthusiasm for the MMC model, but that would change by the end of the 1970s. In her seminal work, *The Spiral Dance: A Rebirth of the Religion of the Great Goddess*, San Francisco Witch Starhawk (born Miriam Stamos, 1951–present) cemented the place of Maiden-Mother-Crone in Modern Witchcraft. Blending ideas from Gardner's Witchcraft, second-wave feminism, and American home-grown Witchcraft[1] [most notably the "Anderson Feri Tradition" begun by Victor (1917–2001) and Cora Anderson (1944–2008)], Starhawk was implicit about Witchcraft's Great Goddess being a figure in triplicate. Starhawk writes that the Moon Goddess has three aspects: "As She waxes, She is the Maiden; full, She is the Mother, as She wanes, She is the Crone." (78), spaces that had once been bereft of the MMC began to feature this version of Wiccan-Witchcraft's Goddess.

Two of Wiccan-Witchcraft's most prolific writers during the 1970s and 1980s were Stewart (1916–2000) and Janet Farrar (1950–present). Initiated into the Alexandrian tradition of Wiccan-Witchcraft (an offshoot of Gardner's original initiatory tradition), the couple's early books omit the MMC model in their conception of the Goddess. Beginning in their 1984 book *The Witches Way*, MMC emerges as a central component of Wiccan-Witchcraft practice, and the MMC model becomes a primary vehicle for understanding the self:

> Every woman, and every Goddess-form, contains all three-both cyclically and simultaneously. No woman who fails to grasp it can understand herself; and without grasping it, no one can understand the Goddess.
>
> *("Witches Bible" 72)*

Though they link their MMC directly to the menstrual cycle of women, the Farrars also suggest that the MMC represents certain personal qualities that can be found in women regardless of age. The Maiden represents "enchantment, inception, expansion," while the Mother suggests "ripeness, fulfillment, stability," and the Crone "wisdom, retrenchment, repose." ("Witches Bible" 71–72) A MMC model no longer reliant on age allowed female practitioners of Wiccan-Witchcraft to see themselves in every aspect of the Triple Goddess. In my personal practice, I have seen nineteen-year-old women identify as Crones and forty-year-old women identify as Maidens.

The prominence of MMC continued in Witchcraft-related books. Scott Cunningham's (1956–1993) *Wicca: A Guide for the Solitary Practitioner* (1989) locates the MMC as the natural starting place for understanding the Goddess: "As the Wicca know Her, She is often of three aspects: the Maiden, the Mother and the Crone." (Cunningham 11) Writing just a year later in *To Ride a Silver Broomstick: Next Generation Witchcraft*, author Silver Ravenwolf (born Jenine Trayer,

1956–present) makes "The Triple Goddess" and the triad of "Maiden, Mother and Crone" integral to the practice of Witchcraft. (48)

By 1994, the MMC model had become such an established part of Witchcraft communities that entire books were being dedicated to the subject. 1994's *Maiden, Mother, Crone: The Myth and Reality of the Triple Goddess* (Deanna "D. J." Conway 1939–2019) weaves numerous goddesses as like threads through an archetypal quilt of MMC archetypes, sometimes erroneously. In a pre-internet age with limited access to quality resources, such misattributions were not only a part of Wiccan-Witchcraft books but a part of the Wiccan-Witchcraft world in general. It's also possible that the practice of being able to take creative liberties with history of any myth were a feature of Wiccan-Witchcraft and not an uninformed accident. Both creative liberties and misattributions can be crucial to the development of folk religions.

Personal Folk Religion of the Maiden, Mother, Crone

I started my practice of Wiccan-Witchcraft in 1994. By 1997, I was personally leading rituals in a local community of Wiccan-Witches located in East Lansing Michigan and affiliated with a student group at Michigan State University. Most of the rites took place on the sabbats, the "holy days" of Witchcraft, that occur on the solstices and equinoxes of every year, and also on the "cross quarter days" (October 31/Samhain, February 2/Imbolc, May 1/Beltane, August 1/Lughnasa) that are approximately located between the solstices and equinoxes. Since the time of Gerald Gardner, Witchcraft rituals have focused on a reborn "God" at the Winter Solstice, a figure who grows old and is eventually slain (or dies) in the Autumn to renew the fertility of the Earth. In his first Witchcraft book (*Witchcraft Today*, 1954), Gardner writes of this deity in the context of a Yule (Winter Solstice) rite:

> Queen of the Moon . . . Bring to us the Child of Promise!
> It is the great mother who
> Giveth birth to him. It is the Lord of Life who is born again.
>
> *(Gardner 21)*

The trope of the dying and resurrecting Wiccan-Witchcraft god was borrowed from James Frazer (1854–1941), best articulated in his multi-volume work *The Golden Bough*, but Frazer never employed a similar pattern for goddess figures.

By 1997, in my practice I felt like it "just made sense" for the Goddess of the Witches to follow a similar pattern as the God. I was not alone in this inclination. In my experiences with other Wiccan-Witches at the time, many of our rites revolved around an aging Goddess and God. A survey of the most popular published sources from the time (beginning with Starhawk into the present) does not show a depiction of what many of us were doing. It's also worth noting that the oldest initiatory branches of Wiccan-Witchcraft had no material suggesting an aging, dying, and continually reborn goddess.[2] Writers like Scott Cunningham suggested various periods of growth—his book *Wicca* has a marriage ceremony for Goddess and God on May first—but the entire year is not mapped out on a cycle of ceremonies for Gods and Goddesses. (134)

Despite its absence from the books that shaped my early practice of Wiccan-Witchcraft, a triple goddess who tied directly into the change of the seasons felt like a natural progression of the MMC, and without that concept my own rites would have felt incomplete to me.

Despite its absence from the books that shaped my early practice of Wiccan-Witchcraft, I made the decision early on to link MMC with the change of the seasons and plan out my ritual year accordingly. I was not alone in this either, many practitioners in my local community had similar ideas. We had made our own interpretation, expressed in rituals, of the materials we were given, and in our interpretation the MMC was directly connected to the turn of the seasons. This resulted in a large degree of personal self-expression in the rites I was leading) in my community. Left to our own devices, we chose to construct our own MMC mythology.

Among my fellow practitioners in Michigan, we constructed a ritual calendar where the Maiden goddess during the Winter at the celebration of Imbolc (February 1) as an older adolescent, and from there she matured into a young woman at Ostara (Spring Equinox) before transforming from Maiden to Mother at Beltane (May 1). This often included a "sexual awakening" at Beltane, the transformation from Maiden to Mother involving sexual activity. At the Summer Solstice, the Mother goddess steps completely into her power, and by Lughnasa (August 1), her powers of fertility have resulted in a bountiful harvest. The Fall Equinox begins the transition from Mother to Crone, with the Goddess becoming the Crone at Samhain (October 31). I found that many Wiccan-Witches in other communities outside of mine built their rituals around similar ideas.

Given the focus on sex at Beltane, it was natural that the Maiden goddess become pregnant on the first of May, and this became a common ritual trope in our community. She would then give birth to her child at the Winter Solstice. No one seemed to care that even a casual glance at this idea meant that the Crone (past childbearing age) was giving birth at the Winter Solstice. Unlike the God who most often sacrificed himself in the Goddess/God seasonal narratives, the Goddess never "dies," and she simply returns as a Maiden sometime after the Winter Solstice; there is no explanation given.

The idea of a Crone goddess giving birth to a child sounds nonsensical, but Witchcraft rituals have long been elastic, allowing ritual writers wide berths to tell whatever stories they wish to tell. Wiccan-Witches outside organized traditions have long written their own rites. Those rituals include reflections centered on the local climate and regional folklore. Adapting religious practices to fit a particular climate or social environment is another factor in the creation of a folk religion. As a transplant from Michigan to California's Silicon Valley, my previously written rituals focused on imminent colder weather and made no sense in my new state. This is a not uncommon problem. Wiccan-Witchcraft, with its focus on seasonal devotion, can easily vary from region to region. Folk religions, in general, are not just about the folk involved but the locality and context for practices; new religious practice arise from new locations and established religious practices are adapted to locations.

MMC cosmology has experienced a great deal of criticism in recent years because it is not inclusive of all women, and, furthermore, it links life stages of women exclusively to the idea of "childbirth", and childbirth is not a universal female experience. That said, many Wiccan-Witches who have sought to distance themselves from MMC still use parts of the myth in rituals because it provides a clear and easily understood ritual narrative.

Finding a Crone: The Transformation of Hekate

The MMC is not merely a part of Wiccan-Witchcraft but can be found throughout western culture, even pop culture. On the Netflix program *The Chilling Adventures of Sabrina*, the character Aunt Zelda summons the goddess Hekate as the Triple Goddess using the Maiden-Mother-Crone model:

> We call on you now Maiden, in your unbounded potential. We call on you Mother in all your divine power. We call on you Crone, in your arcane wisdom . . . the powers that have been denied us imbue us with them Hekate and we shall pray to you morning, moon, and night. And we shall live to honor thy three faces, thy three forms . . .

Greek and Roman images of Hekate depict the goddess in triplicate, a reference to her role as a cross-roads deity, for when coming upon a crossroad, the traveler is presented with three different paths, Hekate as a triple goddess was representative of these three different roads. None of these depictions of Hekate suggest that the goddess is of three different ages. This begs the question where does the idea of Hekate as MMC come from?

The first instance of Hekate as a Crone can be found in the writings of the English occultist Aleister Crowley (1875–1947), who wrote that "Hekate is the crone, the woman past all hope of motherhood . . ." in his 1929 novel *Moonchild*. (Crowley 187) Crowley also turns Hekate into a "thing altogether of Hell, barren, hideous, and malicious, the queen of death and evil witchcraft . . ." an idea that, understandably, did not become popular in Witchcraft circles. (Crowley 188) Considering how much of Crowley's conception of Hekate has been ignored by Modern Witches, it seems likely that the second major writer to consider Hekate a crone goddess was much more influential.

In *The White Goddess*, Robert Graves contextualizes the idea of the Triple Goddess as MMC, and in his 1957 work, *The Greek Myths*, he begins conflating the goddesses Persephone (Kore), Demeter, and Hekate as one goddess with three names:

> Core, Persephone, and Hecate were clearly the Goddess Triad as Maiden, Nymph, and Crone . . . . Core stands for the green corn, Persephone for the ripe ear, and Hecate for the harvested corn . . . But Demeter was the goddess' general title . . .
>
> *("Demeter's Nature and Deeds")*

While Hekate features in some versions of the Persephone/Demeter mythology, she always appears in a supporting role, and the goddess is never described as an older woman. Demeter and Persephone are separate beings in such stories as well, conflating Demeter, Persephone, and Hekate has a certain poetic elegance, but that conflation is unsupported by classical mythology and art.

Books on Witchcraft became more plentiful in the 1980s and 1990s, and Hekate, as part of MMC, featured prominently. The writers involved in such projects extensively refer to both mythology and archeology in their works yet continually cast Hekate in the MMC role. Janet and Stewart Farrar's *The Witches' Goddess* (1987) consults a wide range of primary sources on matters of mythology and archeology, but they still cast Hekate as a crone goddess when convenient. In a ritual to the goddess, these authors mention Hekate's "three aspects"—"young (the Maid), mature (the Mother), and old and wise (the Crone)"—comprising the nature of Hekate as a triple goddess. (126) A list of goddesses in Silver Ravenwolf's *To Ride a Silver Broomstick* doesn't even allow Hekate three aspects; she is simply "Moon Goddess as in Crone or Dark Mother." (51)

Author Demetra George (1946–present), in 1992's *Mysteries of the Dark Moon: The Healing Power of the Dark Goddess*, casts Hekate in a variety of roles. Alongside "Persephone the daughter, Demeter the mother," Hekate transforms into a grandmother, an idea with no basis in Greek mythology. (140–141) With the goddesses Hebe and Hera (maiden and wife), Hekate is cast as the widow, despite never marrying in most Greek mythology. (141) Perhaps influenced by Graves, George also presented Hekate as the crone in a model, with Artemis as a virgin and Persephone as a nymph. (140)

Writing a few years later, D.J. Conway's *Maiden, Mother, Crone* (1994) combines the MMC model with Graves' idea of Demeter having a triple nature. There is no ambiguity here, and Conway writes about "Demeter's trinity with Kore-Persephone and Hecate." (54) In books containing "deity correspondences," Hekate is often reduced to one of many crone goddesses, an indication that the transformation was complete in the popular imagination of Witches . . . up to a point. (Broch and Macler 129)

Over the last fifteen years, Hekate has become one of the most popular goddesses in Modern Witchcraft circles. There are dozens of books aimed at popular audiences focused on this one particular deity, and many Modern Witches self-identify as "Hekatean Witches," signaling their devotion specifically, and sometimes exclusively, to Hekate. (Gwyn, hekatenawitchcraft, modwitchofthewest, melaninhuntress) The amount of attention paid to Hekate has led to re-evaluating the goddess, with many writers now actively pushing against the idea of Hekate as a crone. But the idea of Hekate as a Crone might never be overcome, the first listing in a Google search of the words "Hekate Triple Goddess" brings up an article calling Hekate "Maiden, Mother, and Crone." Art featuring Hekate as an older figure remains popular among Witches, as do illustrations featuring Hekate as one part of a triple goddess in the MMC model.

Whether or not the idea of Hekate as a crone goddess will survive the scrutiny applied to the idea remains an open question. Adherents of Hekate such as Sorita d'Este (1974–present) whose 2009 work *Hekate: Liminal Rites* (with author David Rankine 1979–present) was one of the first books aimed at the Witchcraft community that was dedicated solely to the goddess; this book both bristles at and seems to accept the transformation of Hekate into a crone. Writing in 2017, d'Este argues that the classical Hekate is best understood as a maiden and a mother (based on appearance), but these deities are capable of revealing themselves in "new manifestations." (159–162)

Since the publication of Ronald Hutton's scholarly survey of Wiccan-Witch history in *Triumph of the Moon* (1999), Wiccan-Witch literature has become increasingly studious. Many books now feature extensive footnotes citing academic sources. Hekate-focused authors such as d'Este have focused on Hekate as she was worshipped by both the Greeks and Romans, foregoing the addition of "Crone" to her mythos. It will be fascinating to see if these more scholarly approaches to Hekate result in a re-evaluation of the goddess, or perhaps Hekate will stay an example of the MMC in the popular imagination of Wiccan-Witches. As in most cases involving folk religion, just how the figure of Hekate will be interpreted going forward will vary from practitioner to practitioner, with the influences of books, teachers, and personal gnosis playing large roles in the process.

Maiden, Mother, Crone . . . Backlash and Forward

The Modern Wiccan-Witchcraft community is sprawling and decentralized; most efforts to record a wide range of opinions on various Witchcraft topics (such as Maiden, Mother, Crone) generally meet little success. In 2018, a Pew Research Center survey estimated that in the United States alone, there were 1.5 million Witches, Wiccans, and Pagans. (Zilber) By way of comparison, a major effort to survey Witches on a wide range of issues begun by individuals in the Witch community met with only 16,000 responses. (witchwithme) Gathering information and perspectives from Wiccan-Witches can be a challenging task, though it is much easier today in the age of social media.

As a popular author on the subject of Wiccan-Witchcraft, I have a large social media following. My reach is especially strong on Facebook, and on March 29,

2022, I asked my Facebook followers: "Maiden-Mother-Crone, thoughts positive, negative, or neutral?"(Mankey) Those eight words resulted in several days of online discussion, and as of July 6, 2023, 453 individual comments. As the privacy settings on my post were set to "public," comments on my question were open to anyone. The majority of respondents, as of this writing, identified as women, by a nearly four to one margin (169 to 72). With one cited exception, all of the following comments on MMC come from the discussion hosted on my Facebook page. Direct comments from practitioners on MMC felt like the fastest way to look at the ongoing evolution (and in this case devolution) of MMC as folk religion.

Many Wiccan-Witches, especially female ones, believe that ideas behind MMC are too concerned with when a woman does or does not menstruate and her ability to procreate. Many Witches believe the MMC bases a woman's worth "entirely on fertility/reproduction," and does not take into account "how diverse the female experience really is." (LaVoie) Some respondents believe that MMC "reduces a woman to her utility to man and a patriarchal, hierarchical society," and that this results is an exclusion of many "in the Pagan community and in society at large." (Lynx)

In recent years, the greater Witchcraft community has become much more greatly concerned with issues of inclusion, and there are many who find the idea of MMC especially limiting to individuals in the LGBTQ+ community. Many Witches believe that MMC actively "ignores NB (non-binary), trans and queer folk," (Greenhood) and has too much focus on "binary gender ideas," which, by extension, excludes "non-binary and sometimes even trans people. (sic)" (Gabbert) Many believe that the idea of MMC excludes those not interested in or incapable of having children. Female Witches who have chosen not to have children find they are "unable to relate" to the concept because of its perceived focus on childbirth. (Gillis)

The focus on menstruation found in many explanations of MMC has made some Witches feel that the idea "reduces goddesses, and by extension women, to reproductive value" (Gabbert) or "patriarchal utility." (Anthoinette) One respondent wrote that MMC "focuses too much on women as 'breeders,' marking reproductive rites of Passage and discounts other markers or miles (sic) stones . . ." (Sherman) For those who have chosen not to have children, they have found that the MMC "doesn't fit in my frame of reference as a person with lived experience." (Zakroff)

As early as the late 1990s, many Witches were actively adding a fourth element to the MMC concept; the most common additions being "the Warrior" and "the Queen." Such additions were thought of as additional stages between Maiden and Mother, and Mother and Crone, respectively. Additions to the MMC idea are looked at by practitioners as corrections and fixes to a model that is not truly representative.

The Warrior is most often representative of a young woman in early adulthood, but not yet ready for motherhood (or simply a woman who does not desire to be a mother). One respondent wrote about the Queen in her tradition:

> This is a stage of full possession of power . . . .We have 4 seasons for the wheel of the year, and see the moon cycle as waxing, full, waning, and new. It makes sense to us to have 4 life cycle representations.
>
> *(Veach)*

The idea that a fourth stage should be included in MMC models, to mirror the four stages of the moon cycle, was/is a frequent theme in Wiccan-Witch communities, online and in person.

My respondent who commented on the Queen addition to MMC indicated that my question about the place of MMC in Contemporary Witchcraft had caused her coven to re-evaluate their use of MMC and that they ultimately chose less gender-focused terms:

> after discussing this with my coven, we thought apprentice, nurturer/protector, adept, and elder were the terms we liked best as neutral terminology.
>
> *(Veach)*

Other alternatives to Crone include "Enchantress" (Wirsching) and "Matriarch." (Miller)

Group evaluation is not uncommon in Wiccan-Witchcraft circles. Without a central authority, groups and individuals are free to adapt religious ideas at will, or within the parameters of a group. While books remain influential sources, both social media and long-form writings (such as blogs or online magazine articles) often encourage a re-evaluation of ideas. A social media question influencing coven practice can be seen as an example of dynamic folk religion that does not take recourse to scriptural or clerical authorities.

For some groups adding a fourth category was not enough, and at least one Witchcraft tradition incorporates an eight-fold goddess: "Girl-Child, Maiden, Woman-Grown, Mother, Warrior, Queen, Crone, Hag;" this adds Girl-Child and Woman-Grown to the already popular terms Hag, Warrior, and Queen. (Ballard) Perhaps the most surprising suggestion was simply changing Maiden, Mother, Crone to "Maiden, *Middle,* Crone" which allows for a lot of leeway during that long middle phase. (Scalice)

It should not be a surprise that a religious tradition heavily influenced by literary fiction might encourage creativity among its members. Terms such as "middle" and "Girl-Child" may not yet be a part of regular Wiccan-Witch discourse, but it's possible that they will be in the future. When soliciting responses on the idea of MMC, I was continually surprised that most individuals had no problem with adding to or subtracting from the MMC model. Instead of disdain, new ideas are most often with acceptance or quiet disinterest, further suggesting that authority is not only decentralized but is circulates rather freely.

There are Witches who single out the positive connotations of recognizing older women as crones, and croning ceremonies are a part of many Witchcraft traditions. One respondent writes:

> I've participated in a community croning ritual and it was a beautiful celebration of her status as one of the wisest and most experienced among us. But she chose to view it that way, and not all who identify as women feel the same. I will say it sucks that "sage" and "crone" have polarized connotations in society at large.
>
> *(Diamond)*

One Witch wrote that she loves "the idea of one day being a Crone, with the dignity and mystery that the title bequeaths." (Manson) Another added that MMC "has the advantage of not being derogatory towards aging." (Werger)

In my personal experience, the Wiccan-Witchcraft community's public face has most often been liberal and progressive. There are most certainly conservative Wiccan-Witches, but the public faces of the movement are overwhelming left of center. Since the 1970s, gays and lesbians have been an active and public part of Wiccan-Witchcraft, whether as members of covens/traditions or individuals starting their own groups. The push for inclusion and acceptance of trans-individuals in the Wiccan-Witchcraft community feels like an extension of early liberal impulses. The acceptance of trans-individuals in Wiccan-Witchcraft is reflective of just how quickly ideas can be disseminated and accepted in the broader Wiccan-Witchcraft community, and, in this case, rapid changes are made to decades-long standing ideas about deities.

Many Wiccan-Witches find inspiration and beauty in nature (Wicca is sometimes described as a "nature religion"). Proponents of MMC argue that the trifold goddess has value because it can be related to nature and the cycles of the moon. One wrote that MMC was positive "in its relation to lunar energy and phases," but "Limiting in its capacity to capture all that is female." (Miller)

Despite a growing number of voices lamenting the MMC model, there are still many Witches who hold onto it. Those who find value in MMC do so for internal reasons. One respondent wrote that MMC is "a helpful mirror in understanding aspects of myself." (Kresch) Others see the "phases of life if a woman chooses to give birth," (McGuiness) one respondent linked the model to the "story of the wheel . . . . (the) cycle of life and rebirth." (Davis-Summerhayes) Mentions of death and rebirth (many Witches believe in reincarnation) in MMC mythology can lead to greater "Acceptance of the Cycles of, Life, Death, and Rebirth" for one commenter. (O'Leary) For at least one respondent, MMC helped illustrate "that every stage of life really did have positive aspects." (Burt)

In my own experiences, it often feels like there are two different groups in the Wiccan-Witchcraft community. Out in front are the writers, teachers, and influencers, and these individuals advocate loudly for social change within Wiccan-Witchcraft. The second group might be considered the "rank and file"

Wiccan-Witches, and adherents generally concerned only with their own practice or that of their small group. In my own experience, I'm much more likely to hear about dislike of MMC within my peer groups: other authors and social influencers. At Witch-gatherings with a wider-ranging audience in attendance, I'm more likely to see MMC imagery in vending and ritual spaces, and hear the idea being talked about positively. This dichotomy helps explain the acceptance of MMC in some Wiccan-Witch spaces, and its exclusion in others.

Another factor in the acceptance or disapproval of MMC may be the very age of the idea, and the age of the materials that have influenced individual Wiccan-Witches. For an individual who has spent the last forty years with MMC, it might feel like a dereliction of religious priorities to no longer engage with the concept. Many of today's current Wiccan-Witchcraft bestsellers are the same titles that were the best sellers thirty years ago. Since those materials reference MMC, many newer Wiccan-Witches who have been influenced by those materials choose to continue to honor the idea of MMC as one goddess in three beings.

For scholars of religion, the various disagreements about MMC, along with the various changes many Wiccan-Witches have given to the MMC model, provide real time examples of a dynamic spiritual tradition embracing change. Adherents of Wiccan-Witchcraft are adjusting their ideas about MMC on social media platforms, in public spaces, and in contemporary books. That these various ideas are often being refined and reinterpreted by individuals and smaller communities is illustrative of folk religion that is characterized by variation, evolution, and innovation while also unifying communities under a common, though diverse, identity.

Even those who object to the MMC model readily admit it will most likely be a part of Modern Witchcraft into at least the immediate future. One respondent wrote:

> A lot of women find worth in it but I find it quite limiting and from a craft perspective, it plays no part in what I do. I rather it just quietly disappeared but I suspect it will be hanging round like a bad smell when my daughter is my age.
>
> *(Sanchez)*

Despite the disapproval of some, it feels likely that MMC will continue to be a part of Wiccan-Witchcraft practices, but that understandings and interpretations of the model will continue to change and evolve.

Notes

1 Lacking access to previously initiated Wiccan-Witches, many individuals started their own religious witchcraft traditions. These were most often influenced by figures such as Fortune, Gardner, and Graves but still possessed unique ritual structures and influences. They innovated.

2 Traditions such as Gardnerian and Alexandrian Witchcraft require oaths of secrecy from initiates, and initiates are not allowed to share rituals. However, as an initiate of the Gardnerian tradition, I feel comfortable telling you that MMC is not a part of the rites.

Works Cited

Anthoinette, Anneliese. "Maiden-Mother-Crone, Thoughts Positive, Negative, or Neutral?" *Facebook*, 29 March 2022, www.facebook.com/jmankey/posts/pfbid02YHHMNvZrgdhitev6BUHUHJ6AcMCMuGcgeGL4eTHJozh8xG2CGQftz2G6XrfVjAMSl, Accessed 6 April 2022.

Broch, Janice, and Macler, Veronica. *Seasonal Dance: How to Celebrate the Pagan Year.* York Beach, Me: Samuel Weiser, Inc. 1993.

Burkert, Walter. *Greek Religion: Archaic and Classical.* Translated by John Raffan. Oxford: Wiley-Blackwell, 1991.

Burt, Kelly. "Maiden-Mother-Crone, Thoughts Positive, Negative, or Neutral?" *Facebook*, 29 March 2022, www.facebook.com/jmankey/posts/pfbid02YHHMNvZrgdhitev6BUHUHJ6AcMCMuGcgeGL4eTHJozh8xG2CGQftz2G6XrfVjAMSl, Accessed 6 April 2022.

Ballard, Byron. Personal correspondence. 30 March 2022. "Chapter Twenty-Four: The Hare Moon." *The Chilling Adventures of Sabrina*, written by Donna Thorland, directed by Viet Nguyne, Warner Brothers Television, 2020.

Crowley, Aleister. *Moonchild.* 1929. Reprint. Boston: Samuel Weiser, Inc. 1975.

Cunningham, Scott. *Wicca: A Guide for the Solitary Practitioner.* St. Paul: Llewellyn Publications, 1988.

Davis-Summerhays, Grace. "Maiden-Mother-Crone, Thoughts Positive, Negative, or Neutral?" *Facebook*, 29 March 2022, www.facebook.com/jmankey/posts/pfbid02YHHMNvZrgdhitev6BUHUHJ6AcMCMuGcgeGL4eTHJozh8xG2CGQftz2G6XrfVjAMSl, Accessed 6 April 2022.

d'Este, Sorita, *Circle for Hekate, Volume 1: History & Mythology.* London: Avalonia Books, 2013.

Diamond, Mary. "Maiden-Mother-Crone, Thoughts Positive, Negative, or Neutral?" *Facebook*, 29 March 2022, www.facebook.com/jmankey/posts/pfbid02YHHMNvZrgdhitev6BUHUHJ6AcMCMuGcgeGL4eTHJozh8xG2CGQftz2G6XrfVjAMSl, Accessed 6 April 2022.

Farrar, Janet, and Stewart. *A Witches' Bible: The Complete Witches' Handbook.* London: Phoenix Publishing, 1996. [Originally released in two volumes as *Eight Sabbats for Witches* (1981) and *The Witches' Way* (1984).]

———. *The Witches' Goddess.* London: Phoenix Publishing, 1987.

Fortune, Dion. *The Sea Priestess.* 1938. Reprint. York Beach: Samuel Weiser, Inc, 1978.

Gabbert, Emily. "Maiden-Mother-Crone, Thoughts Positive, Negative, or Neutral?" *Facebook*, 29 March 2022, www.facebook.com/jmankey/posts/pfbid02YHHMNvZrgdhitev6BUHUHJ6AcMCMuGcgeGL4eTHJozh8xG2CGQftz2G6XrfVjAMSl, Accessed 6 April 2022.

Gardner, Gerald. *The Meaning of Witchcraft.* 1959. Reprint. Magickal Childe Pub., New York, 1991.

———. *Witchcraft Today.* 1954. Reprint. Thame: I-H-O Books, 1999.

George, Demetra. *Mysteries of the Dark Moon: The Healing Power of the Dark Goddess.* San Francisco: Harper Collins, 1992.

Gillis, Jennifer Deveaux. "Maiden-Mother-Crone, Thoughts Positive, Negative, or Neutral?" *Facebook*, 29 March 2022, www.facebook.com/jmankey/posts/pfbid02YHHMNvZrgdhitev6BUHUHJ6AcMCMuGcgeGL4eTHJozh8xG2CGQftz2G6XrfVjAMSl, Accessed 6 April 2022.

Graves, Robert. *The Greek Myths: Volume One*. London: Penguins Books 1954.

———*The White Goddess: A Historical Grammar of Poetic Myth*. 1948. Reprint. New York: Farrar, Straus, and Giroux, 2001.

Greenhood, Lizzy. "Maiden-Mother-Crone, Thoughts Positive, Negative, or Neutral?" *Facebook*, 29 March 2022, www.facebook.com/jmankey/posts/pfbid02YHHMNvZrgdhitev6BUHUHJ6AcMCMuGcgeGL4eTHJozh8xG2CGQftz2G6XrfVjAMSl, Accessed 6 April 2022.

Gwyn. "Yes. Hecate Is a Real Deity But More Than a Crone." Three Pagans and a Cat, *Patheos*, 13 Jan. 2020, https://www.patheos.com/blogs/3pagansandacat/2020/01/yes-hecate-is-a-real-deity-more-than-crone/. Accessed 29 March 2022.

Hutton, Ronald. *The Triumph of the Moon: A History of Modern Pagan Witchcraft* (Second Edition). New York: Oxford University Press, 2019.

Kresch, Laura. "Maiden-Mother-Crone, Thoughts Positive, Negative, or Neutral?" *Facebook*, 29 March 2022, www.facebook.com/jmankey/posts/pfbid02YHHMNvZrgdhitev6BUHUHJ6AcMCMuGcgeGL4eTHJozh8xG2CGQftz2G6XrfVjAMSl, Accessed 6 April 2022.

Lavoie, Laura. "Maiden-Mother-Crone, Thoughts Positive, Negative, or Neutral?" *Facebook*, 29 March 2022, ww.facebook.com/jmankey/posts/pfbid02YHHMNvZrgdhitev6BUHUHJ6AcMCMuGcgeGL4eTHJozh8xG2CGQftz2G6XrfVjAMSl, Accessed 6 April 2022.

Lynx, Jo. "Maiden-Mother-Crone, Thoughts Positive, Negative, or Neutral?" *Facebook*, 29 March 2022, www.facebook.com/jmankey/posts/pfbid02YHHMNvZrgdhitev6BUHUHJ6AcMCMuGcgeGL4eTHJozh8xG2CGQftz2G6XrfVjAMSl, Accessed 6 April 2022.

Mankey, Jason. "Maiden-Mother-Crone, Thoughts Positive, Negative, or Neutral?" *Facebook*, 29 March 2022, www.facebook.com/jmankey/posts/pfbid02YHHMNvZrgdhitev6BUHUHJ6AcMCMuGcgeGL4eTHJozh8xG2CGQftz2G6XrfVjAMSl, Accessed 6 April 2022.

Manson, Megan. "Maiden-Mother-Crone, Thoughts Positive, Negative, or Neutral?" *Facebook*, 29 March 2022, www.facebook.com/jmankey/posts/pfbid02YHHMNvZrgdhitev6BUHUHJ6AcMCMuGcgeGL4eTHJozh8xG2CGQftz2G6XrfVjAMSl, Accessed 6 April 2022.

McGuiness, Colleen. "Maiden-Mother-Crone, Thoughts Positive, Negative, or Neutral?" *Facebook*, 29 March 2022, www.facebook.com/jmankey/posts/pfbid02YHHMNvZrgdhitev6BUHUHJ6AcMCMuGcgeGL4eTHJozh8xG2CGQftz2G6XrfVjAMSl, Accessed 6 April 2022.

Melanin Huntress. "What Is Hekatean Witchcraft." *Melanin Huntress, Tumblr*, 26 Nov 2020, https://melaninhuntress.tumblr.com/post/635838228612644864/what-is-hekatean-witchcraft, 30 March 2022.

Miller, Jen. "Maiden-Mother-Crone, Thoughts Positive, Negative, or Neutral?" *Facebook*, 29 March 2022, www.facebook.com/jmankey/posts/pfbid02YHHMNvZrgdhitev6BUHUHJ6AcMCMuGcgeGL4eTHJozh8xG2CGQftz2G6XrfVjAMSl, Accessed 6 April 2022.

Modern Witch of the West. "Modern Hekatean Witchcraft-Lesson 1." *Modern Witch of the West, WordPress*, 28 Sept. 2019, https://modwitchofthewest.wordpress.com/2019/09/28/modern-hekatean-witchcraft-lesson-1/, Accessed 29 March 2022.

O'Leary, Stacia. "Maiden-Mother-Crone, Thoughts Positive, Negative, or Neutral?" *Facebook*, 29 March 2022, www.facebook.com/jmankey/posts/pfbid02YHHMNvZrgdhitev6BUHUHJ6AcMCMuGcgeGL4eTHJozh8xG2CGQftz2G6XrfVjAMSl, Accessed 6 April 2022.

RavenWolf, Silver. *To Ride a Silver Broomstick*. St. Paul: Llewellyn Publications, 1993.

Rosenbriar, Meg, Dean, Louisa, and O'Regan, Christie. "2020 Census Reults: Presented by Witch with Me." *Witch With* Me, https://witchwithme.com/census-2020-results/ Accessed 6 April 2022.

Rosenzweig, Rachel. *Worshipping Aphrodite: Art and Cult in Classical Athens.* Ann Arbor: University of Michigan Press, 2004.

Sanchez, Tara. "Maiden-Mother-Crone, Thoughts Positive, Negative, or Neutral?" *Facebook*, 29 March 2022, www.facebook.com/jmankey/posts/pfbid02YHHMNvZrgdhitev6BUHUHJ6AcMCMuGcgeGL4eTHJozh8xG2CGQftz2G6XrfVjAMSl, Accessed 6 April 2022.

Scalice, Misty. "Maiden-Mother-Crone, Thoughts Positive, Negative, or Neutral?" *Facebook*, 29 March 2022, www.facebook.com/jmankey/posts/pfbid02YHHMNvZrgdhitev6BUHUHJ6AcMCMuGcgeGL4eTHJozh8xG2CGQftz2G6XrfVjAMSl, 6 Accessed 6 April 2022.

Sherman, Laurie. "Maiden-Mother-Crone, Thoughts Positive, Negative, or Neutral?" *Facebook*, 29 March 2022, www.facebook.com/jmankey/posts/pfbid02YHHMNvZrgdhitev6BUHUHJ6AcMCMuGcgeGL4eTHJozh8xG2CGQftz2G6XrfVjAMSl, Accessed 6 April 2022.

Starhawk. *The Spiral Dance.* San Francisco: Harper and Row, 1979.

Werger, Nellie. "Maiden-Mother-Crone, Thoughts Positive, Negative, or Neutral?" *Facebook*, 29 March 2022, www.facebook.com/jmankey/posts/pfbid02YHHMNvZrgdhitev6BUHUHJ6AcMCMuGcgeGL4eTHJozh8xG2CGQftz2G6XrfVjAMSl, Accessed 6 April 2022.

Wirsching, Thea. "Maiden-Mother-Crone, Thoughts Positive, Negative, or Neutral?" *Facebook*, 29 March 2022, www.facebook.com/jmankey/posts/pfbid02YHHMNvZrgdhitev6BUHUHJ6AcMCMuGcgeGL4eTHJozh8xG2CGQftz2G6XrfVjAMSl, Accessed 6 April 2022.

Zakroff, Laura Tempest. "Maiden-Mother-Crone, Thoughts Positive, Negative, or Neutral?" *Facebook*, 29 March 2022, www.facebook.com/jmankey/posts/pfbid02YHHMNvZrgdhitev6BUHUHJ6AcMCMuGcgeGL4eTHJozh8xG2CGQftz2G6XrfVjAMSl, Accessed 6 April 2022.

Yoder, Dan. *Discovering American Folklife: Studies in Ethnic, Religious, and Regional Culture.* Ann Arbor: UMI Press, 1990.

Zilber, Ariel. "Witches Now Outnumber Presbyterians in America as Number of Pagans Soar to 1.5 MILLION - and Millennials' Love of Yoga and Star Signs Is to Blame." *Dailymail*, 19, Nov. 3029, https://www.dailymail.co.uk/news/article-6404733/Number-Americans-practice-witchcraft-estimated-high-1-5-MILLION.html, Accessed 29 March 2022.

19

LIFESTYLE BRANDS THAT ROCK YOUR SOUL

Wellness Culture as Folk Religion in North America

Anya Foxen

How seriously should one take the "soul" in SoulCycle, a popular brand of indoor cycling ("spin") classes? More or less seriously than the exhortation by CorePower Yoga, the popular yoga studio chain, that its classes are "soul-rocking"? What about the statements of Renaissance Neo-platonist Marsilio Ficino, who tells us that in order to nourish our souls, we should "exercise by keeping constantly in motion and make various circular movements like those of the heavenly bodies" (Ficino 373)? This chapter positions wellness practices—especially those focused on physical fitness, such as modern postural yoga or spin—and the larger cultural contexts (which we might call "wellness culture") where such practices thrive within a history of complex intersections between religion, health, and self-cultivation. Even more specifically, we'll focus on how today these practices enable and are in turn enabled by the phenomenon of the "lifestyle brand," which has come to serve as a powerful organizing principle among the growing demographic identifying as "spiritual but not religious" (SBNR), a term to which I'll return shortly. As a loose network of concepts and practices, enacted by individual and communities outside the formal confines of religious institutions, wellness culture thus serves as a modern form of folk religion that approaches the ideal of spiritual salvation as a practical and lived reality.

The intersection of religion and health (whether as active healing or more expansive notions of wellness) has been well documented by scholars of Western spirituality. A brief survey follows, ranging from the broad to the more specific. Wouter Hanegraaff, in his study of New Age religion, argues that such traditions place a core emphasis on healing, which they indelibly link to a larger agenda of "personal growth," resulting in a vision of religious salvation where the "aim is not the elimination of suffering, but the promotion of *health*" (46). By this, Hanegraaff means "Health in the sense of radical 'well-being,' which is the

DOI: 10.4324/9781003257462-25

proper aim of healing as well as of personal growth" (47). And though healing has, across time and place, been intimately tied with religious concerns, Hanegraaff stresses that in the New Age context, especially, it is often "all but impossible to draw the line and decide whether a given practice or technique is religious or therapeutic in nature" (46). Catherine Albanese includes this same conception of healing as salvation among the identifying features she assembles under her rubric of American metaphysical religions (15). And, finally, to highlight this intersection of the religious and the therapeutic in a more specific context, Holly Folk positions the American history of chiropractic as a form of "alternative medicine" amidst parallel themes of vitalism (a basic belief in a spiritual life force) and populism, noting that "the persistence of these [vitalist] ideas into the modern age points to an enduring uncertainty about how to demarcate the natural from the supernatural, and the sacred from the profane" (2).

My goal is to pick up and extend Folk's argument regarding chiropractic, reformulating her set of parallel themes as a triangulation of folk practice, spirituality, and health. Through practices enacted by individuals outside the structures of institutions or formal doctrines (the "folk"), wellness culture emerges as a way of cultivating health as a form of self-cultivation that ultimately carries religious significance. Wellness culture exists on a continuum with modern "alternative medicine," extreme versions of which might reject mainstream allopathic medicine altogether. However, using a wider lens reveals that wellness practices crop up in a variety of spaces where they may be used as alternatives as well as complements to other methods of getting and staying well. Going beyond simply remedial understandings of medicine, wellness practices are often predicated on the possibility of becoming optimally well or even "better than well," whether that's meant physically, mentally, or spiritually. In other words, the stronger meaning of wellness is salvific. In the context of wellness culture, then, the basic act of exercising takes on religious value.

Though healing and therefore wellness culture may certainly crop up in a broader religious framework or formal institution, on the cultural landscape of modern North America, it is often linked with the more structurally diffuse framework of spirituality. Scholars of "religion" have a long history of trying and failing to conclusively define the term "religion." The term "spirituality" proves no less slippery. Recently, this latter term has gained traction in its application to the "spiritual but not religious" (SBNR) demographic, which, as of 2017, accounted for 27% of the population in the United States (Lipka and Gecewicz). Robert Fuller and William Parsons have summarized this demographic's distinguishing features as follows:

> Those who profess to being SBNR also tend to valorize individualism, free creative choice and expression, egalitarianism, progressivism, a psychological/therapeutic approach to spiritual growth, and a seeker/quester/consumer mentality. They are more apt to see humans as basically good (hence rejecting the stronger claims of "original sin"); are more liable to

> devalue a traditional community in favor of participating in multiple, diverse, yet entangled institutional forms (think the local Jung institute, the local Zen center, and, yes, even the Catholic mass); are on the whole pantheistic/monistic in outlook, affirm a liberative ethic, and are more likely to endorse the possibility of reincarnation.
>
> *(1–2)*

Fuller and Parsons readily admit such a sketch fails to capture the group's true diversity, a move which, in my view, is neither possible nor desirable when it comes to individual practitioners. Let me state, however, that when I say "spirituality" in the context of this chapter, I do actually mean something fairly specific when it comes to ideology (close to, but not precisely the same as, the constellations designated by Hanegraaff's use of "New Age" and Albanese's use of "metaphysical"). Though Western spirituality tends to absorb and subsume a number of translated concepts from other cultures, it nevertheless has its own specific history and broad set of logics. Drawing on my previous work in *Inhaling Spirit* (2020), I suggest we can treat "spirituality" as a type of Western (in this chapter, specifically North American) religion that is centered on three basic assumptions about the world: monism, correspondence, and harmony for benefit of body and soul. In other words, everything is one, all is connected, and, if there is such a thing as salvation, it rests in our ability to realize our place in this order so that we too become connected and whole.

There is a lot more detail we could add to this picture, but such detail would quickly take us into the realms of philosophy, if not theology. But this level of detail is not crucial. Spiritual people rarely sit down to outline their metaphysical assumptions, but they seem to know spirituality when they see it. This, in particular, is the appeal of the wellness "lifestyle brand." A brand, broadly understood as the constellation of identifying markers—a name, a symbol, a motto, and so on that work to create a coherent and recognizable identity for some (usually commercial) entity—makes circumscribed and tangible something that is otherwise diffuse and unarticulated. This is also where the turn to what scholars have historically termed "folk" or "vernacular" religion can prove most useful. In advancing these categories, foundational scholars of the field like Don Yoder and Leonard Norman Primiano have struggled with how to locate such lived religion (which they still far too frequently reduce to *belief*) outside of formal institutions. Examining the "organizing" work performed by brands, not only in terms of concepts but also concrete behaviors and ways of forming and negotiating identity (both individual and communal), provides insights into ways that religion is structured by institutions not normally considered "religious" by either practitioners or scholars.

To be sure, not every lifestyle brand is spiritual, and not every instance of spirituality involves branding. But, the two phenomena share enough overlap to be combined into a useful lens. A lifestyle brand is a brand that positions itself to offer not only a product (let's say, an array of goods or services) but also an experience, even an identity (Jain, *Peace, Love, Yoga* 19; Featherstone 81). Lifestyle brands speak to the aspirational values of their target demographic, creating a sense of community and shared purpose. As one marketing agency has framed it, the ideal lifestyle brand is something one joins rather than simply buys, inviting its audience to be part of the experience even when they are not actively purchasing anything. The brand is an active participant in this imagined community—it offers its customers a space to experience their common culture and champions the causes they care about (Saltwater). In other words, an optimally successful lifestyle brand has more than a little in common with a church.

By speaking the language of spirituality and mimicking its goals, a wellness-oriented lifestyle brand positions itself as a vehicle for not only self-care but also self-realization in a way that transcends the actual parameters of the product. Wellness lifestyle brands use an implicit set of metaphysical assumptions to marshal the therapeutic and communal aspects of fitness. To be well is to be an integrated self, in a like-minded community, in harmony with the world. On every level, connection emerges as a salvific ideal. The lifestyle brand succeeds by positioning itself as instrumental in helping you live your best—that is, your most connected and whole—life.

In practice, wellness brands rely on strategies that stack the personal therapeutic, communitarian, and ethical dimensions of what it means to "buy into" the brand. Wellness is articulated, on an individual level, as self-care that leads to self-perfection. However, what wellness looks like tends to reflect the specific priorities of the brand's target demographic and speaks to its ideals, both physical and social. This dimension, which helps the brand attract its adherents, also allows the brand to take on the qualities of a participatory community. For instance, the brand may sponsor events or highlight causes that reflect the community's social attitudes and ethical commitments. With this in mind, let us turn to three examples to highlight how such phenomena manifest, and indeed have manifested for well over a century.

Balancing Mind and Body in CorePower Yoga

Yoga is an easy target when it comes to the intersection of lifestyle, wellness, and spirituality given its history within the religious traditions of South Asia. However, what we today refer to as "yoga" (globally, but certainly in North America) is ultimately the product of a complex cultural fusion. As scholars of South Asian yoga traditions have demonstrated, "wellness" oriented concerns are by no means a purely modern element (Birch). But, as I have argued in *Inhaling Spirit*, today's mainstream postural yoga practice draws heavily not only on Indian but also on Western traditions of spirituality and physical culture. This blended background is a crucial lens for our first case study: CorePower Yoga.

Founded in Colorado in 2002, the CorePower brand has expanded across the United States, and, as of 2019, encompasses 200 studios in twenty-three different states. Trevor Tice, tech entrepreneur and one of the company's co-founders, once expressed a goal of turning the brand into the "Starbucks [coffee] of yoga"—an accessible nationwide chain that customers would identify as the gold standard of the industry. CorePower teachers are trained to eschew practices like chanting that crop up in smaller studios and are typical in certain lineage-affiliated styles, like Iyengar or Ashtanga Yoga. They are discouraged from using Sanskrit, even when it comes to the names of poses. On the one hand, such policies might be seen as stripping yoga's South Asian roots from the practice—this is certainly true, especially given that the brand insists on marketing itself as "yoga" while making no reference to South Asia. On the other hand, it is also a move that brings the practice in line with its history as an outgrowth of spiritualized North American fitness.

CorePower's yoga is no more grounded in Hinduism than it is in Christianity (which is to say, not much). However, this does not mean that it is not "religious" in character. Instead, CorePower draws on the modern North American repertoire of spirituality. Its classes are "soul-rocking" and "transformational," encouraging practitioners to "discover the magic that happens when physical meets mindful. The power of practice is yours—wherever you are" ("CorePower Yoga"). CorePower's style of yoga is famously vigorous. Most of the chain's classes take place in a heated room, with temperatures sometimes reaching above ninety degrees Fahrenheit, and some involving the use of weights. As such, the physical intensity of the practice is generally assumed and taken for granted. However, like more traditionally organized (that is, non-corporate) studios, CorePower doubles down on the holistic nature of its classes as not just "exercise" but "wellness." Quoting one of the chain's teachers, an image on CorePower's Instagram account declares: "I love yoga because it is my only hour to stop, become mindful of my movement, and let my breath become the soundtrack to my movement" ("Feel the rhythm. . ."). The focus is not on attaining a particular physical result. In fact, CorePower's branding seems to intentionally avoid any references to weight loss. Instead, the focus is consistently on the experience of the class—the breath, the sweat, and above all the sense of presence. "Feel the rhythm in your soul," the accompanying caption reads.

Though every CorePower studio is more or less the same, every teacher and every class is a bit different. In addition to standardized principles for how to scaffold the physical components of the class—that is, the actual physical poses that comprise the session's sequence—teachers are encouraged to "theme" on a chosen topic. This might be something as simple as gratitude, curiosity, or stillness. Or, as evidenced by one teacher, whose class I attended at my local studio in September of 2021, it might build an anecdote about a friend's non-violent removal of cockroaches from her New York apartment (which involved carrying the roaches down several flights of stairs and a distance of some blocks) into an extended metaphor for mindfully eliminating impatience, judgment, and other negative thoughts and emotions from one's experience of the practice. One teacher may speak explicitly to finding one's "inner divinity," while another will encourage the class to take their practice into their day, going forth "purified, peaceful, and present." In either case, the therapeutic is spiritual. Self-care is salvation.

CorePower's Instagram account is littered with inspirational phrases, written out in bubbly block letters and freestyling loopy scripts. These are superimposed onto photos of pastel Post-It notes, splashed across the brand's signature creamsicle-orange background, or hand-drawn on sandwich boards positioned invitingly outside studios. "Inhale peace, exhale all the rest," says one post ("Release anything. . ."); "Positive mind, positive vibes, positive life," declares another ("A little positivity. . ."); and "Recharge yourself as often as your phone," advises a third ("Would you leave. . .").

Some posts are more directly calibrated to mirror the community's aesthetic by issuing cheeky pronouncements like: "Everything in moderation, except avocados and yoga" ("Truth. . ."), or "I run on coffee, crystals, and yoga" ("Ready to take on. . ."). Such mirroring is cultural, but it is also ideological, especially as it seeks to foreground the ethical commitments, social stances, and values of the community members. For instance, following the murder of multiple Asian women by a gunman targeting Asian-owned businesses in Atlanta in March of 2021, CorePower's Instagram account posted a somber block of white-on-black text calling to "Stop AAPI [Asian American and Pacific Islander] hate" ("Together we stand. . ."). Likewise, in June of 2020, following the murder of George Floyd at the hands of Minneapolis police and the subsequent nationwide protests, CorePower made several posts in honor of Juneteenth (June 19, a day commemorating the emancipation of enslaved people in the United States) and in support of the Black Lives Matter (BLM) movement ("Today we recognize. . ."). Notably, no such content appeared a year later in June of 2021, when the company's non-brand-specific posts were chiefly dedicated to celebrating LQBTQ Pride month.

CorePower's messaging suggests the brand's target demographic neatly overlaps with the general sensibilities of the SBNR. Its focus is therapeutic, its outlook is optimistic, its politics are nominally progressive. However, a sample of attendees across even a handful of CorePower classes quickly reveals that wellness culture captures a specific subset of the SBNR demographic—it leans feminine. This is borne out by the general demographics of yoga practitioners, 72% of whom identify as women according to a 2016 study ("Yoga in America Study"), as compared to 53% women among SBNR individuals as a whole (Lipka and Gecewicz).

Aspiring and Respiring to Poise in Delsarte Gymnastics

One might assume wellness brands are a modern phenomenon. This is true, with the caveat that they are as old as modernity itself. The general template of the modern is fairly well established by the nineteenth century. Of course, projecting the concept of the lifestyle brand back to Victorian times requires a bit of qualification. Typically, when we talk about brands, we are referring to the proprietary identity of a specific commercial entity. However, for this case study, I suggest we consider the eponymous label of "Delsarte," which I will describe below, as a sort of "public domain" brand—a designation that can be applied to physical practices, classes, manuals, and even related material goods that evoke a common set of ideas.

Delsarte practice inherited its name from a system of dramatic expression and oratory codified by a French composer and musical instructor named François Alexandre Nicolas Chéri Delsarte (1811–1871). During his time studying at the prestigious Paris Conservatory, Delsarte became frustrated that the training of its students in the performance arts seemed not to be following any set of systematic aesthetic principles; as such, he developed his own. Ironically, very few of the practices that turned Delsarte into a household name were part of his original system, which was designed specifically for artists, actors, and orators. Of Delsarte's system, perhaps only the following can be safely said: it is a theory of aesthetics governing bodily movement that, in its highest form, becomes a sort of body language for the soul.

Elaborated into a system of exercises by later innovators, "Delsarte" became a style of physical culture grounded in subtle shifts of weight and articulated spiraling gestures. Even when it became calisthenics, it remained a system of bodily expression. The thread running through every Delsarte manual relied on the assumption that every part of the body carries a specific meaning, and every movement is a communication. Delsarte—practiced in flowing Greek-style tunics and sometimes drawing upon sequences of poses that imitated the dynamic postures of Greek statues (a practice literally called "statue posing")—was decidedly Neo-Classical in its aesthetics. However, some of the most popular manuals, such as Genevieve Stebbins' *Dynamic Breathing and Harmonic Gymnastics* (1892), dispensed with the more formal poses of Greek statuary and instead relied on less aesthetically complex and more dynamic sequences of poses from contemporary systems of popular calisthenics. Stebbins' instructions featured routines coupling breath and bodily movement that would not look out of place in a modern yoga class.

Like today's yoga brands, the aspect of wellness foregrounded by Delsarte was the elimination of stress and the cultivation of a composed and harmonious body and mind. CorePower's messaging appeals to balance and power. Delsarte language called this poise and vitality. Both promise calm and relaxation, above all else. Delsarteans were explicit in positioning their exercises as part of a holistic framework meant to cultivate an ideal lifestyle. For instance, Stebbins, who achieved fame as a major innovator of the Delsarte system, ultimately framed her physical exercises as one element of a larger "psycho-physical culture." This was

> a completely rounded system for the development of body, brain and soul; a system of training which shall bring this grand trinity of the human

> microcosm into one continuous, interacting unison, so that nothing shall be useless, nothing thoughtless, and, consequently, nothing that is vital wasted.
>
> *(Stebbins 57)*

For Stebbins, the ultimate goal of such practices was spiritual but pragmatic. She saw herself teaching

> the art of being able to always express the true self; to elevate the soul to its highest aspiration and the mind to express its highest possible plane of thought; and last, but not least, to concentrate the whole vital energy at a moment's notice to any portion of the body for the immediate execution of the behests of the will . . . the art of graceful dynamic presentation of self under all possible circumstances, and an increase of life by increasing the capacity for the reception, storage and utilization of the vital power.
>
> *(Stebbins 70)*

Such elaborations of Delsartean culture maintained that one's full potential could not be realized until one learned to breathe, exercise, eat, bathe, and dress correctly. Like today's wellness practices, Delsarte is a method for living one's best life.

The Delsarte "brand" extended beyond simply designating a style of physical exercise. Today there are "yoga pants," but in the late nineteenth century, women donned "Delsarte corsets" (Ruyter xvii). Delsarte's emphasis on the naturally healthy body and especially on the practice of deep breathing was reflected in its Neo-Classical aesthetics—the ideal of beauty and health lived in the soft waists and free chests of Classical female nudes. A Delsarte corset rejected the overdramatic hourglass shape of contemporary fashion, aiming instead to preserve this "healthier" and more "natural" form. But this advocacy of unconstrained waistlines and sensible clothing was also deeply intertwined with social ideologies of dress reform and other contemporary progressive movements such as women's education and suffrage. It's hardly surprising that Delsarte demographics were as highly gendered as those of today's wellness culture. Between 1870 and 1900, over 400 active American teachers and performers identified as Delsarteans or expressed a significant debt to the system, 85% of whom were women (Ruyter 57–58). The Delsarte teacher Emily Bishop noted that her classes were composed of women of all ages, with only "an occasional gentleman" (vii).

Notably, by the early 1900s, the Delsarte trend had begun to morph in a way that prefigures the modern popularity of yoga. Neo-Classicism gave way to Orientalism, which meant that Greek robes turned into imitation-kimonos, and statue posing became "Oriental Dance." The dancing girls of the East—often referred to as "Nautch Girls" in an echo of India, but commonly dressed up in fashions evoking everything from the Middle East to East Asia—replaced the Classical Greek nudes as ideals of feminine beauty and fitness. It's important to note, though, that even as the aesthetics changed, the actual physical practices and their goals remained largely the same. Inspired by the stardom of Ruth St. Denis, society ladies in New York took to declaring: "We shall mold our hands until they are wedge-shaped, dye our fingertips with henna, and hire a Nautch Girl to teach us Delsarte" (Kendall 54).

Finally, in addition to speaking to the concerns and preferred aesthetics of its (largely white and female) demographic, Delsarte culture intertwined with larger social movements and agendas. Delsartean manuals, following a basic pattern that goes at least as far back as Plato, divided up the human body into three parts, each tied to a specific metaphysical meaning. For them, the lower torso was connected to one's natural animal impulses, the chest to one's moral core (the part most closely tied to the soul), and the head to one's intellectual capacities. Under this rubric, the balanced poise, strong slender core, and deep breathing prized by Delsartean manuals were articulated as—pun intended—moral imperatives above all else. Cultivating the kind of ideal body promoted by Delsarte practice meant that one was also cultivating an ideal self, positioned to engage in social activism. As Carrica Le Favre put it when describing a basic standing and breathing exercise:

> These two exercises lift not only your thoughts to a high attitude, but your physical conditions as well. These are the ones above all others, that I devised and recommend for temperance work and, indeed, all moral reform. It is equally fine for mental expansion and high bodily culture. It is the greatest health-giving exercise I can offer.
>
> *(75)*

It's also worth pointing out that though mainstream Delsarte culture appears to be the exclusive province of upper- and middle-class white women, this is due to an active erasure of Black practitioners, rather than Black practitioners' actual absence. As Carrie Streeter has made clear, Black women also turned to Delsarte practice not only as a form of personal empowerment but also as a tool to support their community building and activism.

Spinning Up Soul in SoulCycle and Peloton

Both modern yoga practitioners and nineteenth-century advocates of Delsarte often buttress the spiritual accolades of their practice by appealing to ancient tradition and universalist principles of sacred dance, aesthetics, and the precise metaphysics of controlled breath and geometric movement. (Though, it's important to note that CorePower, which aims to maintain a broad appeal that tiptoes around problematic exoticism, does not make these arguments. Being called "yoga" seems to be enough.) However, such appeals are not integral to the potential of exercise to become religious, as evidenced by the spiritual dimensions of something like spin cycling. When it comes to spiritualizing the physical, what one does can matter much less than how and why one does it. Thus, a lifestyle brand like SoulCycle can draw on the folk logics of North American spirituality by signaling spiritual ideals through key terms and aesthetics familiar to its target demographic without ever explicitly referencing any kind of conceptual framework or tradition.

As its name would suggest, the "spiritual" valence of the SoulCycle brand, founded in New York in 2006, is something the company cultivates intentionally. Classes take place in a darkened, candle-lit room and are set to pulsing music. According to the company's self-description:

> SoulCycle instructors guide riders through an inspirational, meditative fitness experience designed to benefit the body, mind and soul . . . During the class, the instructor leads the rider on an emotional journey that runs parallel to the physical workout. We believe the combination of the physical, musical and emotional aspects of the ride leaves riders inspired and connected to both the brand and the community. Based on the impact we've had on our riders' physical and mental well-being, we believe SoulCycle is more than a business, it's a movement.
>
> *("SoulCycle Inc. Form S-1")*

Riders are encouraged to "inhale intention" and "exhale expectation" as they push themselves to their limits. "People come to us for the workout, but they stay for the breakthroughs they have on the bike," says former Chief Executive Officer Melanie Whelan in a promotional video. The same video flashes a series of descriptors: "a movement, a motivator, a community, a connection, a tribe" ("Find your SOUL"). Everywhere, one sees the language of soul, love, community, connection, transformation, and freedom. The brand touts itself as transforming both bodies and lives. There is no reliable demographic data on practitioners of SoulCycle, or spin in general, but anecdotal evidence suggests that the tribe is largely female.

Like CorePower, SoulCycle cultivates a specific aesthetic aimed at representing an aspirational lifestyle. This speaks to the individual practitioner, but also to that practitioner's larger set of cultural priorities and values. For example, one SoulCycle instructor describes her LGBTQ Pride playlist, saying

> I want to create an experience that is safe and fun and challenging and is so much more than a physical workout . . . I always want to offer a message of compassion and create an experience that feels safe and celebratory—specifically for members of the queer community and allies alike.
>
> *(Chan)*

However, even a company that does not start out with spiritual intentions may acquire such intentions as it sets itself up to grow into a lifestyle brand. Here, we might look at Peloton, which was founded in 2012 as a company that made and sold stationary bicycles that could be used alongside a subscription to replicate a spin class in the comfort of one's own home. Unlike SoulCycle, Peloton's IPO documentation only declares: "We believe physical activity is fundamental to a healthy and happy life. Our ambition is to empower people to improve their lives through fitness" ("Peloton Interactive Inc. Form S-1"). There is nary a whiff of spiritual language to be found.

And yet, as Peloton's popularity has grown, it has come to rely on many of the same tools as SoulCycle in building its brand, from the emphasis on music and communal experience, to building up the images of star-instructors who can support riders on their journeys. In the summer of 2021, Peloton's blog (which also contains standard "lifestyle" features like healthy recipes, featuring lots of avocado) announced the company's "All for One" virtual music festival, inviting its users to "be part of the collective frequency of the weekend." The branding for the event was a scattershot of harmonial spiritual terminology, declaring:

> Every day, whether it's an average Tuesday or the day of your Century Ride, our passion and effort reverberates off the collective energy of the Peloton community—and it amplifies. From July 1–3, we're harnessing that energy and packing it into an epic three-day celebration of music, movement and one another. We'll unite to create one force, one frequency—felt across the globe.
>
> *("All For One Music Festival")*

Real Religion? Which Folk? And the Difficulties of Neoliberalism

This is all well and good, but is it "religion"? Since its initial publication in 2004, Jeremy Carrette and Richard King's *Selling Spirituality* has become a foundational condemnation of commercial spirituality, bemoaning the "silent takeover of 'the religious' by contemporary capitalist ideologies by means of the increasingly popular discourse of 'spirituality'" (2). However, Andrea Jain, explicitly refuting Carrette and King, has identified the problematic ways that creating such an "opposition between capitalist commodification and religion amounts to an assessment of what counts as real religion" (*Selling Yoga* 100), painting a reductive vision of spiritual practices that stands at odds with the actual views and experiences of those who engage in them. In a later work, Jain affirms that we should regard commercialized spirituality "not as a takeover or replacement of religion or as an alternative to religion, but as a modern manifestation of religion" (*Peace, Love, Yoga* 26). Karlyn Crowley has further pointed out that the very same features—especially individualism and consumerism—that have led scholars of religion to condemn modern spirituality as a dangerous breakdown of "traditional" religious values, serve as avenues of empowerment for those who practice it. Citing the preponderance of women in New Age circles, Crowley argues that a worldview based on the sacralization of the self is bound to appeal to those whose selves have been historically denied. Purchasing power, in general, maybe a source of empowerment for those who have historically lacked a sense of self-determination. This is all the more so when individuals who have been marginalized in the context of religious institutions suddenly find that they can literally buy their way into a religious ritual (34–52). And so, reading between the lines, one begins to suspect that dismissals of spirituality as not sufficiently "serious" on the grounds that it is commercial are also buttressed by the implicit understanding that it's popular (that is, "folk") and often gendered feminine. The fact that, as Crowley points out, most of these women are white further highlights the role of the complex ways that markers of privilege and oppression shift when religion becomes a marketplace.

The scholarly conversations on commercial spirituality have thus mirrored those on folk religion. Both have been juxtaposed, sometimes unfavorably, to "real" religion. Both have been attributed to actors who fall outside the sphere of "official" or institutional religious doctrine and practice. Indeed, drawing the two together under a single rubric can help us enhance our understanding of both. Treating commercial spirituality as folk religion affords us a lens for taking such spirituality seriously. It also allows us to expand the range of how we talk about folk religion, especially with regards to deeply problematic historical tendencies that treat it as the province of the poor, the unsophisticated, the marginalized, and the otherwise "other."

Relatedly, to say that we should not dismiss consumerist spirituality does not imply that we should not thoughtfully critique it. Recent scholarship provides compelling examples of what this critique might look like. In her book *Peace, Love, Yoga*, Jain treats consumers of modern yoga brands as earnest ethical and spiritual actors, even as she identifies their consumption as "gestural subversion" that ultimately serves to reinforce the very systems of environmental degradation and social injustice that it purports to oppose. Similarly, in her work *White Utopias*, Amanda Lucia advances transformational festivals as sites of genuine community and spiritual seeking, even as she lays bare their pervasive reliance on exoticism and appropriation. But we might also ask why we are tempted to cringe at pastel witch kits from the modern cosmetics retailer Sephora but not at bejeweled crosses or decorated bibles from the European Renaissance. As though feudalism is somehow more conducive to authentic spirituality than capitalism.

In particular, scholars like Jain and Lucia, alongside others such as Farah Godrej and Sophia Rose Arjana, have taken to pointing out the neoliberal logic of modern spirituality. Expanding the term's scope beyond its purely economic applications, such studies have identified neoliberalism as an ideology of radical individualism in which "nothing imposes an obligation, and everything, including one's own mind, body, and emotional state is a resource, a force to be excited, an opportunity to be developed, exploited, or leveraged for advantage in a world of competitive actors" (Binkley 4). Neoliberal individuals are supremely free, in the sense that they are utterly autonomous—self-governing, self-cultivating, and self-helping. Neoliberalism is capitalism writ large: every individual becomes the entrepreneurial manager of their own existence.

In such a context, physical fitness practices like yoga or spin are only one aspect of a broader regimen of "self-care" in which the notion of wellness becomes associated with proper (because "healthy") behaviors of exercise, eating, stress-management, grooming choices, and so on (Godrej 785–786). However, it's important to note that wellness culture's ethic of individual choice in the spirit of self-optimization is not only physical, but it's also metaphysical. It's no coincidence that staples of the "self-help" genre like holistic wellness and positive thinking were a major feature of the pop spiritual movements of the nineteenth century, loosely grouped under the label of "New Thought." In fact, New Thought was rather old insofar as its ideological scaffolding was formed from notions of harmonial correspondence (for example, "like attracts like") that can be traced all the way back to the ancient Greek world—the same logic on which we saw the Renaissance mage Ficino calling when he suggested that bodily movement could activate the subtle links between our souls and the essence of celestial bodies. However, at the dawn of the Gilded Age, industrialization drastically transformed the social and economic landscape on which these ideas operated. If we are to talk about lifestyle brand consuming spirituality as a kind of folk religion, then we have to acknowledge that it assumes a very specific kind of folk—the consumerist middle class—that rises to demographic prominence during the nineteenth century. Practitioners of Delsarte, not surprisingly, are representatives of precisely this social block.

Thus, we may well wish to critique the ethics of neoliberalism, but such a critique does not negate its potential to serve as a locus of authentic religious phenomena. All that we call "religious" is and has always been intimately and inextricably entangled with the human lives that form the basic building blocks of every tradition and institution. Lived religion thus exists on a continuum: the individual (their beliefs, but perhaps even more importantly their acts and experiences); a community, whether actual or imagined; social, political, and economic institutions; and the more ineffable cultural framework of shared concepts and values that reinforces and is reinforced by all of these. In this sense, as Primiano has argued, the distinction between "official" and "folk" religion is an utterly empty binary (45). Religious elites are only another demographic of folk. Religious institutions are only another kind of institution, one among the many that necessarily structure our ways of participating in society.

Today, wellness-oriented communities are becoming increasingly more visible while more "traditional" religious institutions decline. But wellness culture is not simply a surrogate for religion. Rather, it has long been a staple of religion's practical and popular dimensions. The power of lifestyle brands lies in their particular ability, as neoliberal cultural formations, to marshal individual striving into a community of aspiration. However, the "product" being sold by brands like CorePower and SoulCycle is also fundamentally grounded in the experience of the individual practitioner—it is a kind of therapeutic pop mysticism—a gateway to being your best self and living your best life, here and now.

Works Cited

Albanese, Catherine L. *A Republic of Mind and Spirit: A Cultural History of American Metaphysical Religion*. Yale University Press, 2007.

"All For One Music Festival." *Peloton | The Output*, 29 June 2021, https://blog.onepeloton.com/all-for-one-music-festival/.

Arjana, Sophia Rose. *Buying Buddha, Selling Rumi: Orientalism and the Mystical Marketplace*. Oneworld Academic, 2020.

Binkley, Sam. *Happiness as Enterprise: An Essay on Neoliberal Life*. State University of New York Press, 2014.

Birch, Jason. "Premodern Yoga Traditions and Ayurveda: Preliminary Remarks on Shared Terminology, Theory, and Praxis." *History of Science in South Asia*, vol. 6, 2018, pp. 1–83.

Bishop, Emily M. *Americanized Delsarte Culture*. Emily M. Bishop 1892.

Carrette, Jeremy R., and Richard King. *Capitalist Spirituality: The Silent Takeover of Religion*. Routledge, 2004.

Chan, Tim. "For SoulCycle, Pride Pedals on Even After June." *RollingStone*, 30 June 2021, https://www.rollingstone.com/product-recommendations/lifestyle/soulcycle-home-bike-review-1187847/.

"CorePower Yoga | Live Your Power (Home Page)." *CorePower Yoga*, https://www.corepoweryoga.com/. Accessed 24 Aug. 2020.

CorePower Yoga. @corepoweryoga. "A little positivity. . ." *Instagram*, 13 September 2019, https://www.instagram.com/p/B2XSe8PFhDD/.

CorePower Yoga. @corepoweryoga. "Feel the rhythm. . ." *Instagram*, 5 April 2018, https://www.instagram.com/p/BhNJPH_FOzk/.

CorePower Yoga. @corepoweryoga. "Ready to take on. . ." *Instagram*, 17 June 2019, http://www.instagram.com/p/By0bMM9lS3m/.

CorePower Yoga. @corepoweryoga. "Release anything. . ." *Instagram*, 6 December 2017, https://www.instagram.com/p/BcYY6JWFost/.

CorePower Yoga. @corepoweryoga. "Today we recognize. . ." *Instagram*, 19 June 2020, https://www.instagram.com/p/CBnh6KBFAyN/.

CorePower Yoga. @corepoweryoga. "Together we stand. . ." *Instagram*, 17 March 2021, https://www.instagram.com/p/CMijP6ZgKrG/.

CorePower Yoga. @corepoweryoga. "Truth. . ." *Instagram*, 1 August 2019, https://www.instagram.com/p/B0oryYTFq_o/.

CorePower Yoga. @corepoweryoga. "Would you leave. . ." *Instagram*, 19 August 2019, https://www.instagram.com/p/B1XCFUDlj0D/.

Featherstone, Mike. *Consumer Culture and Postmodernism*. 2nd ed., Sage, 2007.

Ficino, Marsilio. *Three Books on Life*. Translated by Carol V. Kaske and John R. Clark, Center for Medieval and Early Renaissance Studies, 1989.

"Find your SOUL." YouTube, uploaded by SOULCYCLE, 2 November 2016, https://www.youtube.com/watch?v=CJncd6VYJe8.

Folk, Holly. *The Religion of Chiropractic: Populist Healing from the American Heartland*. The University of North Carolina Press, 2017.

Foxen, Anya P. *Inhaling Spirit: Harmonialism, Orientalism, and the Western Roots of Modern Yoga*. Oxford University Press, 2020.

Fuller, Robert C., and William B. Parsons. "Spiritual but Not Religious: A Brief Introduction." *Being Spiritual but Not Religious Past, Present, Future(s)* edited by William B. Parsons, Routledge, 2018, pp. 15–29.

Godrej, Farah. "The Neoliberal Yogi and the Politics of Yoga." *Political Theory Political Theory*, vol. 45, no. 6, 2017, pp. 772–800.
Hanegraaff, Wouter J. *New Age Religion and Western Culture: Esotericism in the Mirror of Secular Thought*. Brill, 1996.
Jain, Andrea R. *Peace, Love, Yoga: The Politics of Global Spirituality*. Oxford University Press, 2020.
———. *Selling Yoga: From Counterculture to Pop Culture*. Oxford University Press, 2014.
Kendall, Elizabeth. *Where She Danced: The Birth of American Art-Dance*. University of California Press, 1984.
Le Favre, Carrica. *Delsartean Physical Culture With Principles of the Universal Formula*. Fowler and Wells, 1891.
Lipka, Michael, and Claire Gecewicz. "More Americans Now Say They're Spiritual but Not Religious." *Pew Research Center*, 6 Sept. 2017, https://www.pewresearch.org/fact-tank/2017/09/06/more-americans-now-say-theyre-spiritual-but-not-religious/.
Lucia, Amanda J. *White Utopias: The Religious Exoticism of Transformational Festivals*. University of California Press, 2020.
"Peloton Interactive Inc. Form S-1 Registration Statement under the Securities Act of 1933." *EDGAR*. Securities and Exchange Commission, 2015, https://www.sec.gov/Archives/edgar/data/1639825/000119312519230923/d738839ds1.htm.
Primiano, Leonard Norman. "Vernacular Religion and the Search for Method in Religious Folklife." *Western Folklore*, vol. 54, no. 1, 1995, pp. 37–56.
Ruyter, Nancy Lee Chalfa. *The Cultivation of Body and Mind in Nineteenth-Century American Delsartism*. Greenwood Press, 1999.
"SoulCycle Inc. Form S-1 Registration Statement under the Securities Act of 1933." *EDGAR*. Securities and Exchange Commission, 2015, https://www.sec.gov/Archives/edgar/data/1644874/000119312515270469/d844646ds1.htm.
Stebbins, Genevieve. *Dynamic Breathing and Harmonic Gymnastics: A Complete System of Psychical, Aesthetic and Physical Culture*. Edgar S. Werner, 1892.
Streeter, Carrie. "Breathing Power and Poise: Black Women's Movements for Self-Expression and Health, 1880s–1900s." *Australasian Journal of American Studies*, vol. 39, no. 1, 2020, pp. 5–46.
Yoder, Don. *Discovering American Folklife: Studies in Ethnic, Religious, and Regional Culture*. UMI Research Center, 1990.

INDEX

Note: *Italic* page numbers refer to figures and page numbers followed by "n" denote endnotes.

Abrahamic faith 64–74; belief in magic 69; exorcism 73–74; and folk religion 64–74; followers of 64–74; formal Islam 68–69; harmful spirit 73–74; Jinn and Minor Angels 69–73; saints and sainthood 67–68; sects in Islam 68; supernatural entities other than God 68–69; *thawabit* of Sunni Islam 66–67; upper and nether 69; white/light/*nûrani*/ and black/ sorcery/*shaytani* 69
Ācārya Tulsi of Śvetāmbara Terapanth tradition 41
accepted absence/negotiated presence 44–45
activism, narrative 129–130
Advanced Research Projects Agency Network (ARPANET) 287
African religions 15; Indigenous 13, 127, 137, 139n3; traditional 127
African religious beliefs 126–127
Agastya (Vedic rishi) 161, 165–169, *167,* 173
aggressive magic rites 11
akarsana (attracting) 10
al-Azhar 66
Albanese, Catherine L. 15, 266, 326–327
Alien Interview 286–287
Amarmuni Sampraday 37, 41, 47
American Christianity 259
American Institute of Indian Studies 31n7
American Jain communities 39
American religions 15, 259; and Christian supersession 258; Indigenous 15; mainstream 262
Ammerman, Nancy Tatum 15, 19
ancestors 4, 92, 101, 126–127, 129, 131, 132–138, 139n5, 140n13
ancestral beliefs in *sangoma* narratives 130–132
ancestral marriage 131–132, 140n10, 140n14
ancestral wife 131
Ancient Greece 11
Anderson, Cora 312
anthropology 6, 43, 275
anti-sacred forces 85
antyeshti samskaar 204, 207, 209, 213–214, 216, 226n1
anxieties 3, 182, 184
Appalachian spirit 9
Apple TV+ 273
Āranyakaparvan 109n2
Arjana, Sophia Rose 336
Arnold, David 224–225
Arnold, Kenneth 277–278
Asatru Folk Assembly (AFA) 193, 202n2
Asian American and Pacific Islander (AAPI) 330
Asian Religions 8, 10
Authenticated Hadith 66–67

authenticity: Nordic Neopaganism 195–200; and sacrality 195–200; and self-narration 195–200

Bālājī temple 3–4, 6
balancing mind/body in CorePower yoga 328–330
Bardo Thödrol (Bar do thos grol) 52; *see also Tibetan Book of the Dead*
Bardo Thodrol literature 57
Batuk (Little Boy) Bhairava in Kamācchā 120–121
Belgium 43, 46n3
beliefs 15, 19, 69; African religious 126–127; diversity of 44; in magic 69; orthodox 1
Bengali religion/culture 20
Bengali ritual performance 19–30
Bennewitz, Paul 282–284
Bhagavad Gita 5, 209
Bhairava 13, 113–122; the deified dead 116–118; and Hanumān in Deurā village 116–118
Bhandu Triputi 40
Bhatt, Mayur 31n5
bhattārakas 41
Bhujangabhushan's Paścim Uday Pa¯l a¯ 23–28
bhūta ('spirits') 4
Bile, Shea 258, 260–273
bīr bābās: official 118–120; vernacular 118–120
Bishop, Greg 283
Bissessarsingh, Angelo 226n4
Black Lives Matter (BLM) movement 330
black/sorcery/*shaytani* 69
Blatty, William Peter: *The Exorcist* 262
bliss *(ananda)* 4, 12, 29, 173–174
Bloomer, Kristin 249, 251, 254
Boddy, Janice 244
bodhisattvas 51, 52, 107
bodily transformation 248–252
body politic 204–225
Boulnois, Jean 107
Bowler, Kate 265
Boyd, Carol 235–237, 240; and Christian Spiritualism 235–237
brahman 4
brahmanical Buddhism 50, 59
brahmins 91, 98
Braude, Ann 232
"breaking through" into performance 31n14
Briggs, Charles 23
British Empire 205
Broken Walls 293, 300–301, 304n9, 304n10, 305n11, 305n13
Bryan, Victor 212
Buckland, Raymond 311
Buddha 22, 35, 49, 51, 52, 53, 105, 106, 180, 182, 183, 184, 186
Buddhism 2, 59, 61; Amitābha's Pure Land 179; authentic 12; East Asian 180, 184; elite 49, 62n9; folk 49–61; Himalayan 61n2; inauthentic 12; Indian 56; institutional 49, 62n10; Korean 188n43; lived and popular 50; Mahāyāna 62n3; naturalistic 52; normative 49, 52–53, 59–60; of ordinary people 60–61; shamanic 53; Sri Lankan 123n1; true 104; Vajrayāna 62n3
Buddhist(s): apocrypha 179; Asian 53; catalogs 180, 185; cultures 50; *Dhammapada* 98; elite 50, 59, 61; Himalayan 52–54, 58, 60; iconography 105; institutions 50, 53, 60; magic 53; modernist 50; monastics 50, 61; philosophy or meditation 61; precepts 178–186; scriptures 51, 53; societies 50; sūtras 180; tales 105; Tantra 62n9; teachings 57; texts 50, 53, 180; values 57–58
Budshishiyya 148, 150, 151, 155, 157
Bunch, Jason 261

Chandanaji (Acharya Shri) 45
Cakravarti, Ghanaram 21
Calvinist 11
Calvinist Christianity 8
cardinal sins 71
Cariter-Bresson, Henri 225
Carrette, Jeremy: *Selling Spirituality* 335
Casey, Leonard 294, 297
Catholic religion 275
Celtic deities 309
Celtic Magic (Conway) 309
Central Ohio: Carol Boyd and Christian Spiritualism 235–237; Cindy Riggs and modern channeling 237–240; double valence of vernacular religion 241; Joseph Mauriello and *Ghost Psychology 101* 232–235; personalized messages from beyond 235–237; speaking with the dead 232–235; spirit communication 241; spiritualism as vernacular religion in 231–241; "Vishnu Speaks" 237–240
chaityavāsin movement 38
channeling, modern 237–240
charisma 15, 40

"charismatic posture" 302
Chavez, William 14
The Chicago Sun 278
Chief Junaluska 295–296, 304n3
The Chilling Adventures of Sabrina 315
Chinese folk religion 2
Chitrabhanu 39–40, 44–45
Christian (Western) imperialism 296
Christianity 2, 9, 65–66, 139n3, 241; and Afro-Euro-Creole society 206; American 259; anti-Christianity 14; Calvinist 8; and CorePower's yoga 329; cultural contextualization of 302–303; European 137, 299; Evangelical 14, 268, 294; global 268; inverted 270; modern 258, 270; post-Christianity 14–15; in postcolonial Africa 13; Protestant 272; traditional manifestations of 260; vernacular 237; Western 195
Christians 4, 9, 13–15, 20, 69, 75, 93, 127, 128, 135, 137, 140, 192, 195, 197–198, 200–204, 207, 210–215
Christian self-actualization 298–300
Christian spiritualism 235–237
Christian Spiritualist Temple 237
Christian theology 4, 137, 299
city of pilgrims: convergences and synergies 102–108; local place and translocal space in 89–108; Varanasi 89–102
Classical Hinduism 5
Cohen, Richard 194
colonial indentureship, and compulsion to bury 205–210
colonialism 128, 298, 299
Comparing Religions: Coming To Terms (Kripal) 15
computer-mediated communication technologies 42–44
consciousness *(chit)* 4, 15; human 2, 15, 55
Contributions to Indian Sociology 123n1
Conway, D.J. 309, 316; *Celtic Magic* 309
Coomaraswamy, Ananda K. 19
CorePower yoga: balancing mind and body in 328–330; Instagram account 330
#Coronachaos: cremate body politic in 217–225
corrective rape 128
Cort, John E. 43–44; 'Models of and for the Study of the Jains' 43
Council of Senior Ulama 70, 77n20
COVID-19 pandemic 217–224, *219–220, 222–224,* 239, 284
Crone, finding 315–317
"Crossroad Goddess" (Caura Devī) 94, 101
Crowley, Aleister: *Moonchild* 315
Crowley, Karlyn 335–336
cult institutions 65–66
culture(s) 1; Bengali 20; buddhists 50; folk 9, 64, 192–193; human 2; wellness 325–337
Cuneo, Michael 265
Cunningham, Scott: *Wicca: A Guide for the Solitary Practitioner* 312, 314

Dalits 224, 250
dance: Indigenous 300–302; and songs 70; worship through 70
Dark Nordic Folk 191, 195, 202
Davis, Andrew Jackson 232
dead, speaking with 232–235
"The Dead Speak: A Case Study from the Tiwa Tribe Highlighting the Hybrid World of Śākta Tantra in Assam" (Borkataky-Varma) 4
deified dead 113–122
deified humans 84
deities 4, 23–24, 27, 92, 104; Celtic 309; folk 116; forest 105; guardian 246; of the Hindu pantheon 22; humans and 246; local Tamil 166; neighborhood 13; and Pandi Koyil 246–247; planetary 160; possession phenomena 4; Sanskritic 215; Tibet's autochthonous 56; traditional pagan 310; tree 105–108; and Wiccans 308
Delhi Sultanate 92
delog 49, 50, 52–61
DeLorenzi, Chris 300
Delsarte, Francois Alexandre Nicolas Cheri 331–333, 337
Delsarte gymnastics 330–333; aspiring to poise in 330–333; respiring to poise in 330–333
demonic 301; beings 69; traditional healing as 127–128
Denis, Ruth 333
d'Este, Sorita: *Hekate: Liminal Rites* 317
Deurā village 115–119, 121
Devanagari scripts 163, 169
devās 7
devīs 7
Dhammapada 98, 101
Dharmamangal 21, 28, 30n4
dhikr 66–67, 70–72
dichotomies 19–20
Digambara Jainism 41
digital bridges, constructing 42
digital influence 284–287
digital media 37, 42, 46n3

disbelievers/unbelievers 68
Discovering American Folklife: Studies in Ethnic, Religious, and Regional Culture (Yoder) 12
diversity 7, 29–30; of belief 44; gender 129, 137–138; sexual 129, 137–138; of Sufism 148
divination: emerging of Zhancha divination 181–182; observing Buddhist precepts by 178–186; Ouyi and *Zhanchajing* 182–186; overview 178–179; Zhancha 181–182; *Zhanchajing,* a text of divination 179–181
Doty, Richard 282–284, 288
Dundes, Alan 29
Dynamic Breathing and Harmonic Gymnastics (Stebbins) 331

ecclesiastical 66n4; authority 12; body or bodies 201; institution 64; religions 2–3; traditions 12
Edelstein, Julie 14
Egyptian political system 65
elites 49, 50, 59, 61, 62n9
Ellsberg, Daniel 283
The Encyclopedia of Religion 12, 51
epic texts 6; *Mahabharatas* 6; *Ramayanas* 6
Epprecht, Marc 130
erotic danger, and possession 252–254
esotericism: methodology 258–260; overview 257–258; post-Christianity and 257–273; self-religion 265–267; sensationalist media 260–265; transgressive expression 267–272
Eternal Truth 215
ethnocentrism 295, 299
ethnographic 2, 6, 21, 35, 46n 3, 106, 209, 245, 249, 251, 296
European: Christianity 137, 299; colonial influences 5; cultural studies 2; folklore 191
Evangelical Christianity 14, 268, 294
Evangelical Christ intimacy 300
existence 4; divination's mode of 186; free 206; *jinn* 69; of Satan and Jinn 71; Wiccan-Witchcraft's 307
exorcism 4, 6, 13–14, 73–74, 245, 257–258, 260–267; expulsion of a harmful spirit 73–74
The Exorcist (Blatty) 262
expulsion of harmful spirit 73–74

Facebook 122, 195, 317–318
fakelore 2
"family resemblances" 20
Farrar, Janet: *The Witches' Goddess* 316; *The Witches Way* 312
Farrar, Stewart: *The Witches' Goddess* 316; *The Witches Way* 312
fatwas 64, 67–68, 70, 71, 75n10, 76n18
Favre, Carrica Le 333
Ficino, Marsilio 325, 337
Fitzgerald, Padraic 9, 13
folk 1, 49–51, 53, 55–61, 335–337; -belief practice system 83–85; Islam 12, 74, 145–148, 158, 159; religiosity 147, 149, 205, 224, 252, 259; religious practices 9
folk Buddhism 49–61; Buddhism of ordinary people 60–61; impure and inauthentic 55–58; magic and miracles 51–53; marginal and low status 58–60; overview 49–51; questionable and unreliable 53–55
folk-classical divide 19–30
folk culture 9, 64, 192–193
folk deities 116
folk Hinduism 5–6, 10
folk horror films 9
folk Islam: in Morocco 145–148; or vernacular Islam: 74
folklore 2–3, 6–7, 9, 29, 174, 191, 194, 197, 275, 276, 282–288
folk religion 1–3, 9–13, 17, 29, 30, 34, 53, 55, 63–67, 69–79, 83, 113–115, 117, 126, 127, 137, 147, 155, 186, 192–195, 198, 220, 245, 252, 255, 258, 275, 306–321, 325, 336; *see also Specific religions*
folk religiosities: authorizing 145–159; performing 145–159
Ford, Gerald 279, 281, 285
Ford Foundation 31n7
forest deities 105
formal Islam 68–69
former mendicants 40
Fortnight of the Fathers 104
Fortune, Dione 8, 310, 321n1; *The Sea Priestess* 310
Fourfold Jain community 35–36
Foxen, Anya 14
Franz, Maria 191, 197
Frazer, James: *The Golden Bough* 313
Fuller, C.J. 43–44
Fuller, Robert 326–327
fundamentalists 67, 70, 272

Gallows, Goddamn 9
Ganges River 94, 114, 167
Gardner, Gerald 307–308, 311–313, 321n1; *The Meaning of Witchcraft* 308, 311; *Witchcraft Today* 308

Gay and Lesbian Archives 129
gender 1, 12, 14–15, 126–140, 235, 247, 318, 319; diversity 129, 137–138; in *sangoma* narratives 130–132; and sexuality 15
Gender DynamiX 136, 140n12
George, Demetra: *Mysteries of the Dark Moon: The Healing Power of the Dark Goddess* 316
German *volk* 1
Ghost Psychology 101 (Mauriello) 232–235
global spiritual guides, gurus as 41
God: and formal Islam 68–69; and supernatural entities other than 68–69
Godrej, Farah 336
Gold, Ann 247
The Golden Bough (Frazer) 313
Gordon, David 12
Grand Shaikh al-Tayyib 68
Graves, Robert 310–311, 315–316, 321n1; *The Greek Myths* 315; *The White Goddess: A Historical Grammar of Poetic Myth* 310, 315–316
Great Earth Mother 309
The Greek Myths (Graves) 315
guardian deities 246
gurus as global spiritual guides 41
Gutschow, Niels 91, 92

Haberman, David 109n19, 110n25
Hall, David D. 15, 258
Hanegraaff, Wouter J 325–327
Hanumān (Hindu god) 113–122
Harman, William 246
harmful spirit, expulsion of 73–74
harmonious relationships 4
Harner, Michael: *Way of the Shaman* 8
Harrison, Jane 309
Harvey, Doug 280
Haskett, Christian 93
healing 300–302
Heilung 13, 191–192, 195–202
Hekate, transformation of 315–317
"Hekatean Witches" 317
Hekate: Liminal Rites (d'Este and Rankine) 317
hereditary pilgrimage priests (*pandās*) 92
Herrera, Jose 287–288
heteronormativity 128, 130, 138
heterosexual marriage 140n14
hijrah 67
Himalayan Buddhists 52–54, 58, 60
Hinduism 5–6, 7, 10, 14, 24, 29, 43, 92, 98, 101, 102, 104, 106, 108, 113, 114, 115, 117, 119, 121, 172
Hindus 89, 90, 91, 92; cultural performances 19; orthopraxy 214; practices 6; scripture 7; traditions 4, 5; values 5; voices 7
historical erasure 62n9
historical religions 1
Holy Spirit 127, 293–304
homosexuality, transgender 132–135
Howe, Linda Molton 283–284
Hsuan Tsang 109n3
human consciousness 2, 15, 55
human cultures 2
Huson, Paul 311
Hutton, Ronald 310; *Triumph of the Moon* 317
Hymes, Dell 31n13
Hynek, Alan 279–282, 285, 288, 288n1

iconography 105–108, 118–120
Idol Worshipping 67
independent mendicants 40
Indian diaspora 20
Indian Renaissance 215–216
Indic religions 19–30
Indigenous 13–15, 20, 29, 57, 59, 65, 104, 107, 121, 126, 127, 130–133, 135–140, 178, 181, 187, 189, 193, 199, 273, 288, 293–298, 300–306; African religions 13, 127, 137, 139n3; dance 300–302; languages 126; revitalization 293–304
individual travelling monks 39–41; gurus as global spiritual guides 41; independent and former mendicants 40; institutionalized mendicant travel 40–41; settlers and visitors 39–40; and Western Orders 40–41
Indo-Caribbean mortuary ritual corpus 204–225
Indological model 5
Indological scholarship 5
Indo-Trinidadian: Christians 217, 225; community 218; ethnicity 217; Hindus 13, 213, 215, 225; mortuary rituals 204–205, 226n1, 226n3; sociocultural renaissance 216
infidels 69, 70
infinity *(ananta)* 4
innovations 1, 3, 10; illegitimate 146, 148, 151; modern renunciation 12; ritual 29, 216
in-person encounters 42, 43
institutionalized mendicant travel 40–41
International Mahavir Jain Mission (IMJM) 39
intimacy, relational 248–252
inverted Christianity 270

Islam 2, 12, 65, 90, 128, 139n3, 146–148, 159, 240, 251; defined 65; formal 68–69, 71, 74; formal orthodox 70; as *munzal*-faith 65; radical 13; sects in 68; Sunni 64, 66–67, 74
Islamic 67; countries 74; fundamentalism 71; institutions 67
IX International Congress of Anthropological and Ethnological Sciences, Chicago, Illinois 82

Jackson, Andrew 295–296
Jain: authority 12; charismatic leaders 12; communities 35, 40; initiation ceremonies 40; mendicant community 35; monastic and lay lifestyles 35; monastic lineages 41; philosophy and yoga 40; religious practice 42, 44, 45
Jain, Andrea R. 335–336; *Peace, Love, Yoga* 336
Jain Associations in North America (JAINA) 39
Jain diaspora 37; accepted absence/negotiated presence 44–45; community 40; constructing digital bridges 42; Fourfold Jain Community 35–36; individual travelling monks 39–41; mendicant encounters in 37–38; mendicants in 38–39; revising tropes of disconnection in 35–45; studying *sadhu* who came for lunch 43–44; two-tiered applied ethics 35–36
Jainism 12, 15, 35–36, 39, 43–44; ethical imperative 36
Jain Meditation International Center 39
Jain monastic 35
Jataka tales 51, 105
Jesus 9, 127, 135, 136, 138, 266, 298, 300, 301
Jha, J. C. 213
Jhaveri, Rakesh 41
Jinn, harnessing 69–73
Johnson, Paul E. 258–259
Judaism 65–66
Jug Face 9

Kakar, Sudhir 4
Kal Bhairav 118, 120, 122
Kali Mahal Preservation and Development Association 98
Kapadia, Karin 255
Karkariyya 148–151, 155
Karom, Frank 12
King, Richard 335
Kirpalani, Metharam J. 210
Kirshenblatt-Gimblett, Barbara 19
Knight, J.Z. 238
knowledge *(jnana)* 4
Koran 66–67, 69–71
Kothari, Nalinbhai 41
Kripal, Jeffrey: *Comparing Religions: Coming To Terms* 15
Krishna 27, 253
Krodhana 120–121
Kumar, Ranjit 212
Kumar, Satish 40
Kumar, Sushil 39–40, 45

Lady Sheba 311
Lake Junaluska: Christian (Western) imperialism 296; Christian self-actualization 298–300; contextualized Pipe (Sunrise) Ceremony 296–298; cultural significance 295–296; healing 300–302; Holy Spirit 300–302; Indigenous dance 300–302; Indigenous revitalization 298–300; music 300–302; religious logic of healing at 293–304
Larson, Bob 261
Lau, Kimberly 240
Leach, Edmund R. 30n1
The Left-Hand Path 262
legitimacy 64, 66
Levi-Strauss, Claude 30n1
LGBTIQ 126–135, 137–139
LGBTIQ+ *sangomas* (traditional healers): ancestral beliefs in *sangoma* narratives 130–132; narrative activism 129–130; overview 126–127; from secrecy to visibility 129–130; sexuality/gender in *sangoma* narratives 130–132; in South Africa 126–138; in South African society 127–129; "transgender homosexuality" 132–135
LGBTQ+ community 318
lifestyle brands 325–337
The Little Community (Redfield) 123n1
lived religion 3, 13, 15–16, 19, 116, 121, 205, 221, 241, 242n1, 296, 327, 337
living Hinduism: in Varanasi, North India 113–122; vernacular, official, and folk registers of 113–122
Lokesh Muniji (Acharya Shri Dr.) 45
lore, controlling 275–288
Lucia, Amanda J.: *White Utopias* 336
Lutgendorf, Philip 31n15

Mack, John 276, 282, 285
magic 7–8, 10–11, 50, 52; belief in 69; and folk Buddhism 51–53; upper and nether

69; white/light/*nûrani*/ and black/ sorcery/*shaytani* 69
magical intent 51
magical procedures 69
magic rites/ritual 11; performers of 65; sources 10
Mahabharata 22, 89
mahalla 92, 93, 94, 98
Mahāmāyūrīvidyārā-jñī-sūtra 107
Maharaj, Chanka 212
mahasamasan 123n 4
Mahatma Gandhi 40, 46n11, 225
mahatmyams 89, 91, 93, 105, 107
Maiden, Mother, Crone 317–321; personal folk religion of 313–315
Maiden, Mother, Crone: The Myth and Reality of the Triple Goddess (Conway) 313, 316–321, 322n2
Majallt al-Azhar 74n4
Mandelbaum, David Goodman 30n1
mangalkabya 20
Mankey, Jason 14
Maracle, John 300
Maracle, Jonathan 294
Maraj, Bhadase Sagan 212
marana (murder) 10
mashayikh-healers 73
Mashyakhat al-Azhar 74n4
maswim 146, 148, 151, 152, 155
materiality as method 204–205
Mathura region 100, 106, 107
Mathura, C. B. 212
Matthews, Robert 258–260
Mauriello, Joseph 231–235, 240; *Ghost Psychology 101* 232–235; *Only a Thought Away* 233–234
mawlid 146, 148, 150, 151, 155
McNallen, Stephen 193
McNeal, Keith E. 13
The Meaning of Witchcraft (Gardner) 308, 311
Mecca 67, 75n6
mechanical associations within the supernatural 85
Medieval Bengali literature 20
Medieval Europe 11
Medina 67
Mehandipur Bālājī Temple 6
Melley, Timothy 282, 286, 288
mendicants: encounters in Jain diaspora 37–38; former 40; history and typology of 38–39; independent 40; in Jain diaspora 38–39
mendicant travel 40–41
method, materiality as 204–205
Midsommar 9
mild supernatural illness 71
Milton, Singer 19
Mines, Diane 250
Mingxiang ji 56
minor angels 69–73
miracles 60, 67, 75n8; and folk Buddhism 51–53
mistaken dichotomies 19
'Models of and for the Study of the Jains' (Cort) 43
modern channeling 237–240
modern Christianity 258, 270
modernist 56; Buddhists 50; Cambodian monks 59; monks 56
modern Satanism 14
modern witchcraft 309
Modi, Narendra 115, 117, 123n9
mohana (bewildering) 10
monastic leaders 12
monks: individual travelling 39–41; modernist 56
Moonchild (Crowley) 315
Morocco: Folk Islam in 145–148; Sufi festivals in 148–158; Sufi festivals in contemporary 145–159; Sufism in 145–148
mortuary ritual 204, 205, 207, 209, 210, 212–214, 216, 221, 225–227; as vernacular religion 204–205
Moslem Brotherhood 68
Munasinghe, Viranjini 216
music 300–302; as ritual 191–202; as ritual in Nordic Neopaganism 191–202
musical performances 2
Muslims 68, 69, 90, 98, 145, 146, 152, 153, 155, 201, 206, 207, 210, 214, 246, 250, 251
Mysteries of the Dark Moon: The Healing Power of the Dark Goddess (George) 316
mythology 6; classical 316; Greek 316; Hindu 7; Indic religious 22; MMC 314, 320; Persephone/Demeter 316; pre-modern 14; Purānic 123n3; Śaiva 108; Tamil vernacular 168; yogic 165

NAIITS: An Indigenous Learning Community 299, 304n1
Narada (Brahman) 27
Narayanan, Vasudha 6
narrative activism: importance of 129–130; secrecy to visibility 129–130
National Alliance for Reconstruction (NAR) 216
National Spiritualist Association 236
Nation of Islam 276

Native American Conference: Sing to the Mountain, Lake Junaluska 299
Native Americans 294, 297, 299
neighborhood deities 13
Nelson, Bill 276
neoliberalism 335–337; difficulties of 335–337
The New York Times 277
Nkabinde, Nkunzi 126, 128–135, 137, 140n9
Nordic Neopaganism 2, 13, 191–195, 197, 200, 201, 202; as modern folk belief 192; music as ritual in 191–202; overview 191–192; self-narration, sacrality, and authenticity 195–200; spiritual medium and soundscape 200–201; theory and method 193–195; vernacular ritual 201–202
Nordvig, Mathias 13
North America 37, 40; wellness culture as folk religion in 325–337
North Americans 2, 39
North India 94, 96, 104, 106, 113, 161, 165

Ohio State University (OSU) 233, 235
Only a Thought Away (Mauriello) 233–234
oral literary criticism 29
oral traditions 6, 29, 127, 279
Orsi, Robert 15, 242, 296, 303, 304n4, 305n14
orthodox 9, 49, 51
orthodox belief 1
orthodoxy 11, 29, 43, 44, 59
orthopraxy 1, 11, 19, 29, 59, 192, 204, 214, 216
Ouyi Zhixu 179, 182–186; and *Zhanchajing* 182–186

Pacification Goddess 94
pagan deities 310
Pagaran, Bill 294, 299–300
Pandi Koyil temple (Madurai) 14, 244–255; and deities 246–247; and possession 246–248; possession and erotic danger 252–254; possession as bodily transformation 248–252; relational interpretation of possession 255; relational intimacy 248–252; spirit possession practices at 244–255
Paris Conservatory 331
Parsons, William 326–327
Pattanaik, Devdutt 7
Peace, Love, Yoga (Jain) 336
pedagogical experiments 5
pedagogy 14–15
Peloton, spinning up soul in 333–335
People's National Movement (PNM) 216–217
personal folk religion of MMC 313–315
personalized messages 235–237
Petersen, Jesper Aagaard 267, 272
philosophy 7, 10, 39–41, 52, 59, 61, 166, 327
physiological death 58
Pieper, Jan 109n9
pilgrimage 75n6, 89, 90, 91
Pipe (Sunrise) Ceremony: contextualized 296–298; Lake Junaluska 296–298
planetary deities 160
Port, Mattijs van de 255
possessing spirits: *zar* appeasing 70–73
possession: as bodily transformation 248–252; and erotic danger 252–254; Pandi Koyil and 246–248; relational interpretation of 255; and relational intimacy 248–252
post-Christianity and esotericism 257–273
postcolonial revitalization of pyreside cremation 213–217
post-project bluebook UFO influencers 281–284
practical religion 30n1
Primiano, Leonard Norman 1, 12, 19, 44, 104, 113, 115, 174, 179, 191, 192, 194, 232, 234, 240–241, 245, 327, 337
Prinsep, James 92, 93, 94
Procope, J. Arthur 210
Project Bluebook 279, 281, 282, 284
Prophet Muhammad 66–67
Protestant Christianity 272
Protestants 3, 194, 271–273, 301
psychic self-defense 8
Pure Land 179, 180, 183, 185, 186
purusa/purusottama 4
Purvis, Jason E. 9, 14
pyreside cremation 210–212; late-colonial fight to legalize 210–212; postcolonial revitalization of 213–217

Raelism 276
Raj, Selva 246
Ram, Kalpana 248
Ramayana 7, 209
Ramsaroop, Cindy 218
Ramsaroop, Silochan 218
Rankine, David: *Hekate: Liminal Rites* 317
Ravenwolf, Silver: *To Ride a Silver Broomstick:Next Generation Witchcraft* 312, 316
real religion 335–337

Redfield, Robert 3, 19; *The Little Community* 123n1
relational interpretation of possession 255
relational intimacy and possession 248–252
Religion Matters: An Introduction to the World's Religions (Prothero) 15
religions 2, 64, 65; among folk-belief practice system 83–85; aspects of 15; Bengali 20; codes 15; communities 15; creeds 15; cultuses 15; orthopraxy 19; Tamil vernacular 162–163, 167, 174; *see also specific religions*
religious: conflicts 3; engagements 1; institutions 69, 70; literacy 15; literature 67; logic of healing at Lake Junaluska 293–304; practices 2; worldview 6
Religious Studies 2, 6, 7, 10
religose volkskunde 2
Renaissance 215, 216, 225, 336, 337
Report on the Conditions of Indians in Jamaica, British Guiana, and Trinidad (Tyson) 210
Republic of Trinidad and Tobago (TT) 204
Research Foundation Flanders (FWO) 46n1
Richards, Peter 8
Ricoeur, Paul 29
"Ride the Wind" 300–302, 305n13
Riggs, Cindy 238–241; and modern channeling 237–240
"Rise up Mighty Warrior" 300–301, 304n10, 305n11
rituals 4, 10, 66, 70, 92; music as 191–202; sacrilegious 70–73; vernacular 201–202
Robert, Paul 54
Roberts, Jane 237–238
Robertson, Howard Percy 279
Robinson, A. N. R. 216
Robinson, Sandra 21
rock music 293–304
Rowley, Keith 217

Sabhapati Swami 13, 160, 161, 163, 164, 166–168, 170, 172–174; vernacular religious ritual in literature of 160–174
sacrality: and authenticity 195–200; Nordic Neopaganism 195–200; and self-narration 195–200
sacrilegious ritual 70–73
sādhūs 35–45
saints/sainthood: Abrahamic faith 67–68
Śakta Tantra 4
same-sex sexuality 13
Sanatan Dharma Maha Sabha (SDMS) 212
Sanford, Whitney 107
sangomas 15, 126–140; ancestral beliefs in 130–132; gender in 130–132; sexuality in 130–132
Sanskrit 4, 93, 108n 1, 122, 123n 10, 162, 163, 166, 169, 170, 172, 173, 174n 1, 179
Sanskritic deities 215
Sanskritization 22, 123n10, 170
Sanskrit languages 10
santi-pusti (tranquilizing-increase) 10
Satan 9, 68, 69, 71, 258, 261, 264, 267, 268, 271–274
Satanic exorcist 2, 257–273
Satanic/Satanism 14, 128, 197, 257, 260–264, 265–274
The Satanic Temple (TST) 268
satī sthālas 123n4
Scandinavian warrior life 193
Schneider, Rachel C. 13, 15
Schopen, Gregory 53
"scriptural allusions" 23
scriptural sources 12
The Sea Priestess (Fortune) 310
Second Great Awakening 259
secrecy and visibility 129–130
secretive practices 6
sects in Islam 68
self-actualization 298–300
self-narration: and authenticity 195–200; Nordic Neopaganism 195–200; and sacrality 195–200
self-reflecting 8
self-religion 265–267
Selling Spirituality (Carrette) 335
sensationalist media 260–265
settlers, individual travelling monks 39–40
Sewall, Samuel 258–260
sexual diversity 129, 137–138
sexuality 1, 12, 13, 15, 126–130, 132–140, 269, 288; in *sangoma* narratives 130–132
sexual orientation 128, 132, 133, 136
sexual rights 128, 134
al-Shafiᶜi, Mohammad ibn Idris 69
Shah, Natubhai: *Western Order of Jainism* 41
"shamanic" Buddhism 50
El-Shamy, Hasan 12
Sherpa shamans 59
Shevetambara Terapanth tradition 41
Shree Raj Saubhag 41, 46n11
Shri Chandanaji Maharaj 41
Shri Chandana Vidyapeeth (SCVP) 37
Shri Charukeerthi Bhattaraka Swamiji *(digambara bhattāraka)* 45
Shrimad Rajchandra Mission Dharampur 41
Shri Rakeshbhai 45

Shri Vishvanath-ji ki Galli 93, 94
Shunya Puran 31n5
Sikhism 15
Sinanan, M. G. 212
Singer, Milton 19
Singh, Rana P. B. 91
"Sing to the Mountain" Native American Conference (SMNAC) 294–295, 298, 303–304, 304n1
Siva 4, 89, 90, 92, 106, 107, 108, 161, 163, 172, 173
60 Second Doc 260, 262–263, 265
Skanda Purana 89, 114, 116, 122
Smith, Frederick M. 245
Smith, J. Z. 32n16
song: and dance 70; worship through 70
soul 325–337
SoulCycle: spinning up soul in 333–335
South Africa 13, 126, 127, 130, 131, 132, 135, 137, 138, 139; LGBTIQ+ *sangomas* (traditional healers) in 126–138
South Asia 7, 11, 35–36, 38, 41, 42, 43, 44, 89, 98, 105, 107, 145, 160, 161, 165, 170
South Asian religions 8, 10, 104, 108, 113
South Asian Studies 19
South India 14, 162, 166, 172, 197, 245
South Indian Temple: spirit possession practices at 244–255
speaking with the dead 232–235
spellbinding skalds 191–202
Spencer, Lawrence R. 287
The Spiral Dance: A Rebirth of the Religion of the Great Goddess (Starhawk) 312
spirit communication 241
spirit possession phenomena 4
spirit possession practices at South Indian Temple 244–255
"spiritual but not religious" (SBNR) 325–326, 330
spiritualism: Christian 235–237; as vernacular religion in Central Ohio 231–241
spiritual medium and soundscape 200–201
SRF yogi (Self-Realization Fellowship) 8
Srimad Rajchandra Mission Dharampur (SRCMD) 46n11
Srivastava, C. M. 10
stambhana (immobilizing) 10
Starhawk: *The Spiral Dance: A Rebirth of the Religion of the Great Goddess* 312
Stebbins, Genevieve 331–332; *Dynamic Breathing and Harmonic Gymnastics* 331
Stietencron, Heinrich von 32n16
Stine, Robert 193
Streeter, Carrie 333
Strieber, Whitley 282
Structure and Change in Indian Society 123n1
Stuart, George R. 295
Sufi festivals 13; in contemporary Morocco 145–159; in Morocco 148–158
Sufism 145–148, 150–152, 154, 155, 158, 159; in Morocco 145–148
sui generis theories of religion 3
Sukul, Kailashnath 90–91, 94, 109n8, 109n10
Sunni Egypt 64–74
Sunni Islam 64, 66–67
Sunni Moslems 74
supernatural: beings 83–84; entities 51, 68, 73–74; entities other than God 68–69; mechanical associations within 85
supernormal abilities and rituals 57
superstitions 11, 13, 53, 151–152
Swedenborg, Emanuel 232

Tamil Siddhars 160, 161, 166, 167, 172–174
Tamil vernacular: literature 160–161; religion 162–163, 167, 174; religious worlds 162; ritual practice 161; songs 174
Terhi Neem 93, 94, 98
Terlouw, Ruben 192
Thawabit of Sunni Islam 66–67
Thibdeau, John C. 13
Third Spiritual Summit Conference 39
Thomas, Gary 261
Thondup, Tulku 58
Tibetan Book of the Dead 52
Tice, Trevor 328
Tiwa Tribe 4
topographical knowledge 91
To Ride a Silver Broomstick: Next Generation Witchcraft (Ravenwolf) 312, 316
Traces of the Spirit 200, 203
Traditional African Religion 127, 139n3
traditional healer 13, 126, 127, 129, 138–140
transcendent features 3, 6
Transformed Heroes 123n1
"transgender homosexuality" 132–135
transgenders 126, 129, 132, 133, 135, 136, 138
transgressive expression 267–272
tree deities 105–108
tree marriage 104
tree temples 93
Triumph of the Moon (Hutton) 317
truth *(satya)* 4
Turlouw, Ruben 202
Turner, Victor 128
Two-Tiered Applied Ethics 35–36

Tyson, J. D. 210

uccatana (eradicating) 10
Uddisatantra 10
UFO folklore in United States 275–288
UFO influencers 277–281; post-project bluebook 281–284
Ullrey, Aaron Michael 8
United Methodist Church
United National Congress (UNC) 216
Unmatta Bhairavas 120–121
Upaniṣad 7

Valiente, Doreen 311
Varanasi, North India 89–90, 91, 92, 93, 94, 98, 100, 101, 102, 104, 105, 107, 108; Batuk (Little Boy) Bhairava in Kamācchā 120–121; Bhairava, Hanumān, and/or *bīr bābās* Folk 118–120; Bhairava in Deurā village 116–118; convergences and synergies 102–108; deified dead in Deurā village 116–118; folk registers of living Hinduism in 113–122; Hanumān in Deurā village 116–118; Krodhana, and Unmatta Bhairavas 120–121; as multi-layered city 114–115; vernacular/official registers of living Hinduism in 113–122
vasikarana (subjugating) 10
Vaudeville, Charlotte 106, 110n35
Veerayatan 37
Venkemans, Tine 12
vernacular Christianity 237
vernacular religion 242n1; mortuary ritual as 204–205; spirit communication and double valence of 241
"Vernacular Religion and the Search for Method in Religious Folklife" (Primiano) 12
vernacular ritual 201–202
vernacular tradition 20
vidvesana (dissent) 10
vijnaptipatra (invitation letters) 46n12
Violent Divine 257, 258
visibility and secrecy 129–130
visitor, individual travelling monks 39–40

Walsh Pasulka, Diana 14
Wardruna 13, 191, 192, 196, 197, 201
War of 1812 295
Way of the Shaman (Harner) 8
wellness culture: Delsarte gymnastics 330–333; difficulties of neoliberalism 335–337; folk 335–337; as folk religion in North America 325–337; mind and body in CorePower yoga 328–330; real religion 335–337; soul in SoulCycle and Peloton 333–335
Western Christianity 195
Western Esotericism 260, 262, 270, 273
Western Order of Jainism (Shah) 41
Western Orders 40–41
WhatsApp 45
Whelan, Melanie 334
White, Margaret 225
The White Goddess: A Historical Grammar of Poetic Myth (Graves) 310, 315–316
White Utopias (Lucia) 336
Wicca: A Guide for the Solitary Practitioner (Cunningham) 312, 314
Wiccan-Witchcraft traditions: Maiden, Mother, Crone 317–321; modern origins 309–313; overview 307–309; personal folk religion 313–315; transformation of Hekate 315–317
Wiccan-Witch literature 317
Wickerman and Blood on Satan's Claw 9
Wilentz, Sean 258–259
Williams, Eric 216
Willnus, Harry 279–280, 288n1
Witchcraft 11, 14, 69, 139, 193, 307–321
Witchcraft Today (Gardner) 308
The Witches' Goddess (Farrar) 316
The Witches Way (Farrar) 312
Woodlands Dark and Days Bewitched 9
World Religions 7, 10, 14, 15; projects 8; textbooks 8
World Vegetarian Congress 39
World War II 282
worship, through song and dance 70

The X-Files 276
Xingyi Wang 13

Yoder, Don 12, 19, 113, 122, 193, 245, 255, 327
yoga 10, 14, 40, 160, 166, 167, 170, 171, 174, 325, 328–333, 335, 337; balancing mind and body in CorePower 328–330; literature 160

zar 70, 71–73; appeasing the possessing spirits 70–73; as sacrilegious ritual 70–73
Zhancha divination 181–182
Zhanchajing 178–188; Ouyi and 182–186; practices according to 178–186; as text of divination 179–181
zikr/dhikr 70

Milton Keynes UK
Ingram Content Group UK Ltd.
UKHW031500071224
451979UK00015B/169

9 781032 190419